Only The
Strong
Survive

ONLY THE STRONG SURVIVE

THE ODYSSEY OF ALLEN IVERSON

LARRY PLATT

ReganBooks
An Imprint of HarperCollinsPublishers

Photographs on pages i, iii, vii, 1, 11, 23, 33, 49, 59, 73, 93, 123, 153, 173, 189, and 223 by Bill Cramer; pages 4, 88, 117, 136–37, 166, 180, 194–95, 206, 212, 219, 245, 248, and 258 by AP/Wide World Photos; and pages 16 and 70 courtesy of Sue Lambiotte.

A hardcover edition of this book was published in 2002 by ReganBooks, an imprint of Harper-Collins Publishers.

HarperCollins books may be purchased for educational, business, or sales promotional use. For information please write: Special Markets Department, HarperCollins Publishers Inc., 10 East 53rd Street, New York, NY 10022.

First paperback edition published 2003.

Designed by Brenden Hitt

The Library of Congress has cataloged the hardcover edition as follows:

Platt, Larry.
    Only the strong survive : the odyssey of Allen Iverson / Larry Platt.—1st ed.
        p. cm.
    ISBN 0-06-009773-6 (alk. paper)
    1. Iverson, Allen, 1975–. 2. Basketball players—United States—Biography. I. Title.

    GV884.I84 P53 2002
    796.323 / 092 B 21   2002031857

ISBN 0-06-009774-4 (pbk.)

04 05 06 07 WBC/RRD 10 9 8 7 6 5 4 3 2

For Bet (as in Black Entertainment Television), my true heart . . .

*And in memory of Alex, who changed my life . . . and Iverson mentor
Sue Lambiotte, a role model for teachers everywhere.*

Invisible Man/You got the whole word watching . . .
—Mos Def, "Hip-Hop"

I think in a combination of abstract visual patterns and muscular sensa-
tions; it is only later, when I wish to speak or write to another person,
that I translate these thoughts into words.
—Albert Einstein

CONTENTS

ACKNOWLEDGMENTS

This project grew out of conversations some three years ago with Ann and Allen Iverson about penning the Iverson family autobiography. This is not that book; instead, this is an originally reported, part bio, part meditation on the phenomenon that is Allen Iverson. But I am still deeply indebted to both Allen and Ann, for their tolerance of my questions over the years and their constant good cheer. Allen, in particular, has always been a straight shooter. I have tried to write about him with affection, but secure in my conviction that he'd have little respect for hagiography.

I am indebted to Dana Albarella and her posse at Regan Books, who were committed to this book from the start. David Black is, as always, not only an all-star agent, but a great friend.

David Teel of the Newport News *Daily Press,* a superb columnist, researched and shaped the Virginia sections of this book with great care and expertise. He interviewed countless sources, and his perspective on Allen and the times that spawned him was always dead-on. As a result of our close working relationship, I'm happy to say David has become a good friend as well.

Mark Kram and his generous editors at the *Philadelphia Daily News* provided me with an exclusive jailhouse interview with Allen's biological father, Allen Broughton. In addition, Mark was, as always, eager to share his uniquely thought-provoking take on Iverson.

Andrew Corsello may be the strangest genius I've ever met. His input on the manuscript was invaluable. He reminds me of Bubbachuck: a defiant, spiritual creative artist who is always "keepin' it real."

Corsello is a charter member of *my* posse. We call ourselves Cru Thin, 'cause we're a little light in the muscle department but have really high SAT scores. There's Scott MacDonald, whose creative thinking about Iverson's place in the culture at large runs through these pages. There's Ben Gay Wallace, whose insight into human nature, combined with his ignorance of all things athletic, made him a valuable manuscript reader.

Bob Huber is not only a good friend and trusted confidant, but a onetime annoying officemate as well. Rounding out the Cru: Ken Shropshire, Bob Baber, Joey Joe, Eric Reilly, Tex Cobb, Janet Ake, John Lucas, Iain Levison, and Vernon Maxwell. An all-star lineup of folks to watch big games with.

Over the last few years, I interviewed and/or picked the brains of close to one hundred sources for this book, and am indebted to each and every one. Space prevents me from listing them by name. You all know who you are and how much I appreciate your candor. In addition, special thanks to the Philadelphia 76ers, particularly the ever-professional PR department, headed by Karen Frascona and Chris Wallace.

There were countless writers whose stories about Allen Iverson I relied on for background material and who I now humbly salute: John Smallwood, Phil Jasner, Stephen A. Smith, Ashley McGeachy-Fox, Rick Reilly, Gary Smith, Thomas Boswell, and J. A. Adande, among others.

Also, Kevin Maguire and Suzann Vogel provided expert editorial assistance, and Rich Rys conducted some great last-minute interviews while I was pounding out pages.

Thanks to many magazine editors over the years, including: Eliot Kaplan, Ilena Silverman, Stephen Fried, Loren Feldman, Bill Shapiro, and Tim Whitaker.

Finally, a big shout-out to my wonderful parents, siblings, nieces, and nephew. And a special nod to Alex. I couldn't have written this book without his support and unflinching affection. He had me at "Meow."

introduction

TUPAC WITH A J

Bubbachuck was looking like a damned Ethiopian bodybuilder. That's what he likes to call himself when he's shirtless, the bones of his wispy upper body jutting out at sharp angles. Allen Iverson without a shirt is a striking sight; he does not have the physical presence one would expect from a man who regularly challenges NBA behemoths under the boards and in the lane, men a foot taller and in some cases nearly twice as heavy. He's listed at six feet, 165 pounds, but on this May 2001 morning, in the bowels of his team's practice facility, he appeared willowy thin. A buck-fifty and maybe five-eleven, tops—somebody who could easily be mistaken for a rambunctious ballboy, rather than a man who was about to be named the National Basketball Association's Most Valuable Player.

On this day that would name him, in his words, "the best in the world at what I do," Iverson knew how the accolade would be spun in the media. He was having none of it. He knew it would be presented as his redemption, even though he saw it as just another moment of vindication, another in a series of "I told you so" moments.

That is why his thoughts were strictly on those whom he never felt the need to prove anything to: the crew from back home. Iverson was raised on the rough streets of Newport News, Virginia, a small Southern city with a strong migratory connection to New York City. On those streets throughout the 1980s and early '90s, he'd brashly tell whoever would listen that he'd one day star in the NBA or NFL. Older guys, guys with rap sheets and shady connections, would shake their heads and laugh, but they'd look out for him, too—because they saw a prodigy in the making, someone they could help make it out.

Still bare-chested, Iverson eyed two outfits laid out before him. His business adviser, Que Gaskins, awaited his verdict. Gaskins had received a phone call the night before from Gary Moore, Iverson's personal assistant. Moore was the grade-school football coach who took in a twelve-year-old Bubbachuck—an amalgam of two uncles' nicknames—when things got crazy at home; Ann, Allen's single mother, all of fifteen years his senior, couldn't care for him. Now Moore couldn't make it back to Philly from Virginia in time for the press conference; could Que find Allen something to wear in front of the cameras?

"I just want him looking fresh and clean," Moore said.

"Well, we know he ain't wearing no suit," Gaskins said, prompting both men to laugh. Iverson's disdain for business suits was well known. "If he's going to go urban, it should be sophisticated urban."

So Gaskins laid out in front of Iverson a baby-blue velour Pelle Pelle sweatsuit and a black sleeveless Sean John ensemble. "These are phat," Iverson said, looking them over. "And I will wear them, but I ain't wearing 'em today."

Bending over and rummaging through his locker, Iverson extracted a black T-shirt recently given to him by one of his friends from back home. BAD NEWS HOOD CHECK, the T-shirt boldly read in front; a list of street corners adorned the back—the toughest spots in Newport News, the very corners where Iverson came up. There was Sixteenth Street, where the troubled Ridley Circle housing projects were located, just blocks from the Stuart Gardens Apartments, where Allen lived for a time. There was Jefferson Avenue, where the hustlers hawked their illicit wares a chest pass down from the Boys and Girls Club.

"I want all my niggas back home to see this," Iverson said, pulling the shirt on. If hip-hop culture is all about carving self-identity while maintaining your roots, then Iverson is all hip-hop culture; its defiance fuels his demeanor, both on court and off, and its music was the sound track of his turbulent upbringing, from the very first time he heard Kool Moe Dee and Biggie Smalls flow about their lives as though they'd been living his. Of the twenty-one tattoos that adorn his body, two pay homage to Newport News and four salute Cru Thik—his crew from back there, many of whom stay with him in Philadelphia during the basketball season.

When Iverson, wearing the Hood Check T-shirt, Timberlands, a scarf encircling his braided hair, and some $300,000 worth of ice dangling from his earlobes and around his neck, took the podium that day on May 15, 2001, it was much more than just another press conference to name a league's MVP. It was, in a sense, the end of an era, nothing short of a generational handoff. Suddenly gone were the days when a black athlete had to be deferential and nonthreatening in order to be loved. Iverson's team was winning and his name had just surpassed Anna Kournikova's as the most searched on the Internet, in or outside of sports. Of course, the talking heads would go on to paint a portrait of Iverson as a man who had undergone an epiphany. They'd give us a New and Improved Iverson: onetime bad boy morphed into heroic moral exemplar. But the press

Iverson after being named the NBA Rookie of the Year in May 1997. The NBA would refrain from publicizing the award because of Iverson's white skull cap.

accounts said more about those who wrote them than about Iverson. The new conventional wisdom revealed a hunger to squeeze Iverson into a safe, familiar narrative. Which is a pastime made particularly hard by Iverson, because as well as he plays, he just refuses to play along.

For Iverson is neither hero nor villain, and he knew it that day. Instead, he is what the artwork burned into his skin shows him to be, a product of hip-hop culture never before seen in the "crossover"-oriented world of sports. The sound bites of his MVP press conference would focus on Iverson making nice with his old-school coach, Larry Brown, with whom he had feuded in the past—and would again in the not-so-distant future. But a widely ignored part of his remarks that day spoke to the singularity of the event. Iverson looked to the back of the room, squinting, until his eyes settled upon his beaming, high-fiving friends—his once much-derided "posse." They were dressed like him: baggy-jeaned, tattooed. These are the guys who took care of his mama and baby sister when he was in jail, the guys who kept a vigil for him on the other side of the prison's fence for five months, even though, not wanting to be seen in his county jumpsuit, he refused to make eye contact with them.

But on this day of his vindication, Iverson searched them out and his gaze never wavered. There was Ra, his eyes, as always, visibly red-rimmed. There was Eric Jackson or, as Iverson called him, "E." There was Marlon Moore and there was Andre "Arnie" Steele, who was busted in 1998 behind the wheel of Iverson's Benz CL 600 V-12 after allegedly taking part in a drug deal, and who was convicted in 1990 of cocaine possession with intent to distribute.

"What makes me proudest is that I did this my way," Iverson said, still looking straight at his boys, echoing the refrain long crooned by a previous generation's entertainer who was seen by some to have similarly remained loyal to gangsta roots. "I never changed who I was."

Months later, Iverson came face-to-face with the dark side of his "keeping it real" ethic. How real, after all, is too real? On the eve of the 2001–2002 season, five months after being named MVP, four months after winning over fans with his hustle and determination against the mighty Los Angeles Lakers in the 2001 NBA Finals, and just two months after marrying his high-school sweetheart, Tawanna Turner, the mother of his two children, Iverson learned that his best friend, Ra, had been murdered in Newport News. Shot eight times. Killed after arguing with a guy over who could rap better.

"I don't want to die in no projects, man, laying in the grass, people walking by, and be bleeding to death," a crushed Iverson whispered to his former bodyguard Terry Royster when he called to tell him the news. They talked about a supposed friend of Ra's—and theirs—who goes by the name of Fiend. He was there and could probably have prevented the altercation from escalating—but didn't. Now Fiend was nowhere to be found. "It just don't seem real, you know what I'm saying?" And then he paused. "But it's also *too* real. I don't want nobody telling Tawanna and the kids I died like that, over something so stupid."

He donned a black elbow pad with Ra's name on it. From then on, he'd tap it before every foul shot. "Some people see too much too soon," Gary Moore had once said of Iverson, who witnessed his first murder at eight years old. In one summer alone, eight of his friends were felled by gunshot wounds. With Ra's death, Allen Iverson would once again take his pain and use it as fuel to excel on the basketball court, the one constant sanctuary of emotional escape he had found in his twenty-seven years on this earth.

Whether he is proclaiming to the media throng that he's "maintained who he is," privately agonizing over the cost of keeping things too real, or, most recently, staring down felony weapon charges, Allen Iverson has left an indelible cultural mark. More than any other athlete on the public stage, he is, by virtue of his groundbreaking game and his unwillingness to sanitize his ghettocentric style, at once a product and a shaper of his times.

Since 1993, Iverson has heard himself described as a thug and a drug dealer and an ex-con. His response? To simply *represent.* After years of hearing himself judged, he made of his body his own personal billboard and advertised his ethic on his very own skin. (Not surprisingly, Iverson had all but two of his tattoos etched onto his body only *after* he became a multimillion-dollar basketball star.) White men in suits—like the white men in suits who sent him to jail at seventeen—lectured him about what he'd have to do to "cross over," to garner mainstream acceptance as a modern-day "role model" sports star. Instead, he defied the sports punditocracy and NBA old guard with the tattoos and by catalyzing a youth culture trend as the first basketball star to braid his hair in cornrows, a style prevalent among black prison inmates.

The sportswriters and league elders alike were used to athletes, from Julius Erving to Michael Jordan, who subscribed to their middle-class "role model" mores; they were mystified by Iverson's in-your-face persona. It was a classic culture clash; they saw Iverson as a basketball player, when, in fact, he had already transcended his sport and become a hip-hop icon.

"In a sense, Allen Iverson is Tupac with a jumpshot," says cultural critic Michael Eric Dyson. "Like Tupac, he carries his history with him. Usually, America says to somebody, If you want to be successful, you gotta be blanched, you gotta be whitewashed. This is the United States of Amnesia—we want to distance ourselves from everything. Get over your blackness. Now here comes this basketball player who understands that the ghetto is a portable metaphor for how he has faced odds and won. Like Tupac, he says to America, 'It's not that I've transformed—*you* have changed your understanding of what is capable of coming out of a black body from the ghetto with writing all over it and cornrows, the very things that once signified the worst elements of blackness to you.'"

Indeed, cared for by drug dealers, abandoned by his biological father, raised by another man who was constantly in and out of prison for dealing crack cocaine, Iverson often seems to be living a rap lyric. When he first heard Biggie Smalls, it was as if the Notorious B.I.G. were speaking directly to him: "Either you slinging crack rock/Or you got a wicked jumpshot . . ." The previous generation of ballplayers, from Erving to Jordan, embodied the integrationist vision found in the politics of their day and were made over for the comfort of white America, even while Madison Avenue marketed the likes of Joe Namath and John McEnroe as rebels in the tradition of James Dean and Elvis. They had to make concessions Iverson would never consider. Erving, for instance, cut his trademark Afro in 1979 when he decided he wanted to be a businessman. Jordan, early in his career, spelled out his marketing strategy: "I smile a lot and I get along with everybody. People understand me as much as I want them to."

Now comes Iverson's story, containing the four elements that characterize the generation of black youth that came of age during the Reagan eighties: basketball, rap, dope dealing, and the ethic of "getting paid." He is known for basketball's crossover move, having done for dribbling what

Erving did for the dunk: turn it into a weapon of intimidation. But he has also garnered *cultural* crossover acceptance—without compromising. Like rap mogul Master P, who has gone from (reputed) drug dealer to music impresario to tryouts with the NBA's Charlotte Hornets and Toronto Raptors, Iverson embodies the New Crossover, where (seeming) street-level authenticity trumps Madison Avenue glitz. It's no accident, after all, that some 70 percent of hard-core rap CDs are bought by white kids in the suburbs, or that Iverson's sneaker and jersey sales at malls across America dwarf the numbers racked up by Kobe Bryant, dubbed "Karaoke Jordan" by USC cultural studies professor Dr. Todd Boyd.

As the baby boomers age, a vibrant, even dominant youth culture is up for grabs. Kids raised on MTV and hip-hop are eager to embrace sports stars who have what marketers call "edge," who reflect antiestablishment mores. "Madison Avenue has seen how powerful the urban consumer is," says Gaskins, Iverson's cornrowed, baggy-jeaned business adviser, who holds an MBA from the Kellogg School of Management. "They've seen [urban fashion company] FUBU [For Us, By Us] explode on the scene, they've seen Lauryn Hill maintain her identity while getting the cover of *Time* magazine. There's a new audience out there that craves authenticity and embraces characters like Allen, who won't let himself get pimped out."

At a time when P. Diddy is partying with Donald Trump and Martha Stewart in the Hamptons and the oft-obscene rapper Lil' Kim is doing Calvin Klein ads, Allen Iverson has similarly come to embody the New Crossover by suggesting a new way to think of the American Dream. It's no longer solely about "rags to riches." It's still about attainment, yes, but it's also about achievement born of a ballsy, antiestablishment style; in rap song after rap song, after all, none other than the Donald is celebrated as much for his renegade mind-set as for the fortune he's amassed.

And so we get Allen Iverson, holding a defiant press conference at the end of the 2001–2002 season in which he blasted the press and, by extension, his old-school coach, for publicly questioning his practice habits. The media compared it to a Mike Tyson–like public meltdown, yet people ate it up. Here was a sports star unafraid to speak his mind, or to turn the dynamic around on his interlocuters.

And then we get a series of felony and misdemeanor charges against Iverson in the summer of 2002, for allegedly threatening two men with a gun when he was in search of his wife late one night. His mug shot adorned newspaper front pages, Jay Leno made him a running gag, and the sports columnists called for Iverson to be traded, without citing even *one* on-court reason for such a move.

At the same time, far from the hand-wringing pundits, there were different perspectives. On the streets, people—usually black people—wore FREE IVERSON T-shirts. On Philadelphia playgrounds, kids and young adults of all ages wore Iverson number three jerseys. Not only that, countless wore long, protective sleeves on their left arms, from their biceps to just below their wrists. Iverson, of course, had played the entire season like that to protect a still-tender surgically repaired elbow. Yet, because he had, the sleeve had been adopted as an inner-city style statement. Yes, at all of twenty-seven years old, Allen Iverson had achieved rarified status: that of a true American antihero.

BAD
NEWZ

NEWPORT B

I grew up in Newport N
but we call it Newp
'cause a lot of bad shit h

It sounded like the house was about to collapse. The boom was so loud, it would send Butch Harper to the window, time and again, just to make sure. Yep, he'd chuckle to himself. *They're throwing that kid around again.*

Harper, an environmental engineer and substitute teacher in the Hampton, Virginia, school district, lived at 35 Jordan Drive, a tree-lined street of shoe-box one-story, two-bedroom homes in the Aberdeen section of Hampton, the neighboring town of Newport News. Next door, in a faded yellow house with a cramped backyard, lived a large, boisterous, rotating cast of Iversons. There was the matriarch, Mrs. Mitchell, and her eldest granddaughter, Ann, known as "Juicy." There was Ann's sister, Jessie, called "Li'l Bit," who ran track at nearby Bethel High, and there were the boys, Stevie and Greg, not to mention an ever-present cast of cousins and aunts and uncles and friends. They slept, thirteen of them, in the two bedrooms. "I smelled my share of stinky feet," Ann Iverson remembers today.

And there was Juicy's son, Bubbachuck, the kid who, at all of four and five years old, would be there, every time Harper looked out his window, day and night, playing football with the older boys. They wouldn't coddle him; far from it. Harper would watch this tiny kid—the football was almost as big as he was!—pivot and stutter-step and run, eluding his frustrated elders. He was always in motion—that is, until they caught him. Then they'd hit him, and they'd hit him so hard he'd go slamming into the back of the house; sometimes Harper swore he could feel the reverberations under his feet next door. But the kid would get up, time and again, shaking his head, not letting them see him stagger, and then he'd be right back out there, running and cutting and running some more.

Harper got some peace and quiet when the Iversons got booted from the comfort of Jordan Drive three years later. They settled at the Stuart Gardens Apartments in Newport News's east end. Stuart Gardens wasn't the projects per se—but it was close enough to the dicey cluster of government-provided housing that, over the years, its residents had come to see themselves as indistinguishable from those, say, in the troubled Ridley Circle Homes just blocks away.

The east end of Newport News was only a ten-minute drive from Aberdeen, but the differences were vast. When it came time for Allen to play in a rec league, Ann—no stranger to the perils of the street—didn't want her son walking from Stuart Gardens to the Boys and Girls Club or the Dorrie Miller Rec Center in downtown Newport News. So she called Harper, who was also commissioner of the Aberdeen Athletic Association. He waived the rule that forbade those living in Newport News from playing in Hampton leagues, and vice versa.

That's when the legend began to form, well below the surface of media attention. The Bubbachuck phenomenon was grassroots all the way. In barbershops and on street corners, from the take-out line at Wilkes Bar-B-Q on Victoria Boulevard to the makeshift pews at the Gospel Spreading Church of God in the shadow of the projects, people started talking about this eight-year-old who just couldn't be caught, let alone brought down.

Football came first. Gary Moore, who had been a collegiate baseball standout at Hampton University, coached him in Aberdeen and couldn't believe what he saw: a lethal combination of speed, quickness, fearlessness, and toughness. Just as he did on Jordan Drive, the kid would spring back up no matter the ferocity of the hit that had—finally!—taken him down.

But Ann wasn't satisfied. "You're going to basketball practice today," she told an eight-year-old Allen one day after school.

"Hell if I am," he snorted. "Basketball's soft. I'm a football player."

Ann stood in the doorway. "Well, you ain't coming in until you go to basketball," she said, arms crossed. Grudgingly, alternately sobbing and cursing his mother, Allen Iverson headed for the basketball courts for the first time in his life.

Once there, he was surprised to see all his buddies from football. He sat back and watched for an hour, picking things up. So that's a layup, he observed, when a player scored close to the basket. That's a jumpshot, he noted. When he got in his first game, knowing only one speed, he was a blur. After two possessions in which he literally did whatever he wanted, it dawned on him: I'm the best player here.

Allen's de facto father, Michael Freeman, known as "House Mouse" on the streets, would take a ten-year-old Bubbachuck to the courts at Anderson Park and knock him around, one-on-one. "Get yer ass up," the five-foot six-inch Freeman would growl every time Allen would hit the asphalt. Freeman was an aficionado of playground ball; his favorite team was Dr. J's high-flying Philadelphia 76ers, who had been changing the once-staid NBA. Along with such colorfully ghettocentric characters as World B. Free and Darryl "Chocolate Thunder" Dawkins (who, after a magazine writer made an oblique reference to his "Devastating Dunker" in the locker room, penned an eloquent letter to the editor: "Been looking at my dick, mother-fucker?") and, later, Andrew "The Boston Strangler" Toney, Erving was making the once-taboo one-on-one street game a fundamental staple of NBA play. That was the game that Allen was first introduced to, one born of creativity and freedom, where shots were celebrated for their degree of difficulty, regardless of whether the ball actually made it through the twine. From the earliest age, Allen Iverson was shown that basketball is art, not craft, that playing and self-expression go hand in hand.

Eventually, Allen started to run with the older guys in the early evening at Aberdeen Elementary School. Uncle Stevie and Greg were among them, as were a bunch of the older guys who would spend the next few years looking out for Bubbachuck, including Tony Clark, a mentor. Soon the legend extended to basketball. Mike Bailey, the basketball coach at Bethel High, had heard the stories about this Bubbachuck kid, this playground phenom, a skin-and-bones energy freak who would outrace all the older guys, despite the fact that he was *dribbling* while sprinting. Bailey had to see for himself. He walked into the gym at Jefferson Davis Middle School, where, it was rumored, Bubbachuck would be. He poked his head in and saw a kid in desperate need of Ritalin throw a behind-the-back pass out of bounds. He also saw that every eye in the gym was on this indefatigable child.

It would take some time—years, really—for the basketball establishment to take note of Iverson. For now, he was an underground phenomenon, a gift to a town in need of one. For a time in the 1980s, Newport News was flourishing. The Newport News Shipyard, at the height of the Reagan era's upsurge in defense spending, was the area's largest employer—some thirty-two thousand locals were on its books. When the 4-P.M.-to-midnight shift let out, the town would be ensnarled in a bumper-to-bumper traffic jam in the dead of night.

By the late eighties, though, the Cold War was over and the Shipyard was faltering. But even when the Shipyard boomed, other policies of the Reagan eighties started to have a deleterious effect. Throughout the country, an underclass began to develop; the gap between those doing well and those barely making it broadened. The top 10 percent prospered while the bottom 90 percent treaded water, at best, waiting for their promised windfall to "trickle down." Corporations, finding themselves competing in a newly global marketplace, began exporting low-skilled manufacturing jobs. Words like *downsizing* and *outsourcing* entered the national lexicon.

Iverson saw the adults around him bounce from odd job to odd job, or turn to hustling in the burgeoning underground economy. Those dealing crack cocaine seemed to be the only businessmen making it in the new economy. As the drug-dealing character of Nino Brown, played by Wesley Snipes, pointed out in 1991's *New Jack City,* "You got to rob to get rich in the Reagan era."

Ann, by turns, drove a forklift, was a typist at Langley Air Force Base, manned a cash register at a local grocery, and welded at the Shipyard, where she met Freeman, the man who raised Allen and fathered Allen's two sisters, Brandy in 1979 and Ieisha in 1990. Freeman had spent a good part of his adult life in and out of prison for dealing crack cocaine. As far as Allen was concerned, his stepfather had only been trying to put food on his family's table. Unlike the fictional Nino Brown, he wasn't chasing some new twist on the American Dream; he was just trying to stay afloat. Watching Ann, Freeman, and others in the neighborhood, Iverson began to get the message, even then: sports would be the only way out.

It's a message Ann had long accepted as the gospel truth. Many of our feel-good sports narratives portray the mother of the indigent athlete pushing education—sometimes even after the kid has made it, as when Isiah Thomas, later in life, completed his undergraduate degree at his mother's urging. But Ann Iverson didn't subscribe to the "you need something to fall back on" school of thought. No, her baby was born to make it. When folks started talking about her son as if his mere presence had been divinely granted, she didn't humbly object. No, Ann Iverson had long known that God had a plan for her and her baby.

Like her son, Ann Iverson doesn't just smile; she emits joy. First, her mouth, framed by liberal swipes of righteous ruby lipstick, begins to widen, revealing gleaming white teeth, and then the smile keeps expanding, wide and bigmouthed, until Ann Iverson is beaming the way her red Jaguar's headlights beam. But the smile predated the red Jag; it was there, in fact, on June 7, 1975, in the maternity ward of Hampton General Hospital, when her boy was handed to her; suddenly the pregnant lady who hadn't stopped talking and bitching and demanding more drugs to ease

Boo Williams's thirteen-and-under AAU team. Iverson, twelve (second row, second from the left), is the smallest but already best player.

the pain of childbirth, this mouth that ran a mile a minute and had nurses rolling their eyes, started to beam when she took in one specific sight: the length of her baby's arms, which dangled down to his kneecaps.

"He gonna be a ballplayer!" she cried.

She knew it then, just like she knew it when the whole clan landed on Jordan Drive in Hampton—you think that's coincidence, she'd say, that my baby lives on a street the same name as the guy who is The Man of the NBA?

Because she knew God had a plan for her, see. She'd inherited from her grandmother, Ethel Mitchell, a strong spiritual sense, and she just believed. In her view, Allen was her Baby Jesus; she even later claimed—in the hallowed pages of *Sports Illustrated,* no less—that he was immaculately conceived, which would make her the Virgin Mary.

Ann grew up in Hartford, Connecticut, a tomboy who climbed trees and kicked little boys' asses. Her mother was a waitress; her father was long gone. In the fifth grade, she met Allen Broughton. They started dating in seventh grade.

Like Ann, Broughton was a basketball player, a teammate of Rick Mahorn's. (Mahorn would later spend a year as her son's teammate in the NBA.) She and Broughton were in love, according to Broughton, who is currently serving time in Connecticut for assault after stabbing his girlfriend six times in 1998. It was Broughton she was talking to on the phone the night her mother, Ethel, was rushed to the hospital for an appendectomy. Doctors botched the operation and Ann's mother died on the table. The hospital paid the Iversons $3,818.18 to settle any future legal claims.

Ethel Mitchell committed to raising her grandchildren over her husband's objections. "I've already raised mine and I don't want to raise no more," he said.

"I guess you better be on your way, then," Mitchell told him. Without her husband, she moved her brood to the comparatively safer streets of Virginia, where she'd grown up. Before the move could take place, however, Ann decided to lose her virginity with Broughton on her fifteenth birthday, though she claims he never penetrated her. Not so, recalls Broughton. "We were in love and we wanted to make a baby and be together," he says. They were in the eighth grade and consumed by the tragedy of their impending separation. "I wanted her to have a part of me," says Broughton.

The possibility of divine intervention notwithstanding, Ann and Broughton certainly passed on basketball genes to their son. Ann played point guard in high school, rumbling the length of the court while five months pregnant. Broughton, five-six, was the playmaker on the men's team. He was lightning quick and tough—almost as tough as Ann.

Once the move took place, Ann and Broughton kept in touch for a time. He even visited once, buying baby clothes for Allen. "We were kids, man," Broughton recalls today. "Kids making a kid." Ann soon met Michael Freeman, and they had Allen's sister Brandy together. She had started a family with another man. Allen Broughton was out of the picture.

So this was the school skipper extraordinaire. She had heard a lot about him, but she hadn't been prepared for just how engaging he could be, or how talented. And she wasn't even thinking of his athletic skills.

Sue Lambiotte was a teacher and president of the Peninsula Literacy Council. Along with her husband, Butch, a lawyer, the Lambiottes were steeped in sports. All four kids had grown up playing. Clay Lambiotte, Sue's youngest, played in Boo Williams's Summer League with a thirteen-year-old Iverson, which is how Sue came to be on Williams's board of directors, which is how she first came across Bubbachuck.

Boo Williams is well known and widely respected in basketball circles. In 1982, Williams came back home to the Peninsula area after starring at St. Joseph's University in Philadelphia. He started a summer league with $400 in his pocket. Over the years, it has grown into one of the premier summer programs in the country, and Williams has earned accolades as one of the nation's great barnstorming Amateur Athletic Union coaches. AAU coaches often come under fire as the scourge of college sports; unregulated and operating in the shadows, they have been accused of steering their high-school ballplayers to sneaker companies and college coaches with whom they have forged under-the-table deals.

Williams, though, enjoys a stellar reputation compared to most. And he has coached some of the most talented basketball players in the country. Alonzo Mourning, J. R. Reid, Joe Smith, and Bryant Stith have all passed through his program. The thirteen-and-under team that went to a national tournament in Kansas with Sue Lambiotte as a chaperon was no exception. In addition to Iverson, Williams put on the floor Tony Rutland, who would star in high school with Iverson and go on to play with

Tim Duncan at Wake Forest; Aaron Brooks, now a quarterback with the New Orleans Saints; and Damon Bacote, who would go on to play hoops at the University of Alabama.

During that trip, Lambiotte was taken by the happy-go-lucky class clown that was Allen Iverson. In Kansas for a week, Lambiotte insisted on taking the team to local museums. There was no need for a tour guide, however, as Iverson—a talker, when he gets going, right out of the mold of his mother—kept his teammates in stitches with his own running commentary. When he wasn't cutting up on his teammates, he was breaking into dead-on impersonations of them or quickly drawing their caricatures on loose-leaf paper. Lambiotte was amazed at the frequency and depth of his artistic expression. He'd find the one distinguishing characteristic in his subject's makeup—later, in Shaquille O'Neal's case, it would be his slightly crossed eyes—and he'd exaggerate the detail to uproarious proportions.

During practice at the University of Kansas during that trip, the then–head coach of the Kansas Jayhawks walked into the gym. There he saw the shortest player on the court, chirping loudly and goofing off while his coach tried to capture his frantic, easily diverted attention. "Who's that little kid?" Larry Brown asked, not knowing that he'd just laid eyes on the player who would grow up to be the most important, and maddening, he'd ever coach.

This Bubbachuck was not what Lambiotte had expected. She had been warned about him. She knew how, already, he was well on his way to becoming one of the most truant students in the history of his school district. She had heard the stories of how, when he didn't show for a practice or tournament, Boo and his coaches would fan out across town, inevitably finding the kid on a dimly lit playground court, shooting around by himself—sometimes well past midnight.

Iverson's lack of reliability was one of the reasons Williams hadn't already brought him up to play on the main barnstorming team. In the spring of Iverson's eighth-grade year, Williams and his coaching staff debated whether to give the high-maintenance Iverson a chance. Coach Carroll Williams lobbied against Iverson. "We don't want to mess with this kid," he said. "He doesn't want to come to practice."

Coach Bill Tose was the lone dissenter. He'd heard that the kid was a problem and he'd listened to other coaches insist that Iverson was a great playground player who would never amount to anything. Basketball lore was full of such flameouts, guys who never realized their potential, either because of their inability to tame their improvisational styles to conform to team play or because they succumbed to bad grades, drugs, or crime. But when Tose had worked with Iverson one-on-one—when the kid showed, that is—Iverson had always been immensely coachable. In fact, he had always *helped* him coach, like that time when Tose got on Antwain Smith during a time-out for being passive; when Smith responded with a ferocious alley-oop dunk on the inbounds play, there was Iverson right up in his teammate's face—Tose didn't even know the kid had been listening in the huddle!—yelling encouragement: "That's what he's talking 'bout! That's what he's talking 'bout!" Besides, Tose argued, every thirteen- and fourteen-year-old deserves a tomorrow.

Williams, noting that Tose was often the softest touch among the group, opted to elevate Rutland instead, in part because his game—as an outside shooter—would mesh better with that of Michael Evans, an older kid out of Norfolk. Williams was convinced Evans would be the program's next superstar—following in the sneaker prints of Reid and Mourning. (Sure enough, as a senior at Norfolk's Granby High School, Evans would go on to be ranked as the nation's number two point guard behind Jason Kidd; because of injuries and academic neglect, his college career never panned out.)

But then Evans couldn't make a tournament in Memphis, so Iverson was picked to go in his place. During the fourteen-hour drive to Memphis, Williams started to regret it: he'd never heard someone talk for fourteen consecutive hours. Often, it was just Bubba bitching. One favorite complaint was the beat-up rental van: "Coach, why don't Alonzo buy you a damned real van, man?" he called out. "Tell you what, when I make it in the NBA, I'll get you a real van." Williams laughed at the kid's presumption. ("I'm still waiting on that van," he jokes today.)

He didn't regret having Iverson on the court, though. The team went on to capture second place, losing in the finals to the Arkansas Wings, led by future NBA star Corliss Williamson, a behemoth even then. Iverson wasn't cowed; he challenged Williamson at every turn. He earned all-tournament honors and the team took home the runner-up trophy. During the long van ride back home, he cracked everybody up by opening his window and flinging the trophy onto the side of the road. "We don't take no second place," Iverson said. "That's not what we came to do."

"But that still would've been a nice dust collector," Tose deadpanned.

Meantime, Iverson's life away from the court was still turbulent. The coaches had addresses for him, but were never quite sure where he was spending the night. They'd still conduct nighttime searches, trying to track him down. The family had been evicted from Stuart Gardens; for a time, he went to stay with Gary Moore while Ann and the two girls moved into a shelter.

Mike Bailey, the Bethel head coach, took Allen in for three weeks that summer between ninth and tenth grade to make sure Allen attended summer school. Bailey's wife, Janet, taught English at the high school, and had even taught Gary Moore during his Bethel days. Early on, Bailey made a deal with Iverson: you're going to come to study hall at my house, and we're going to stay on top of everything you need to do to stay eligible so you can go to college and make something of yourself for your family.

It wasn't easy. The first time he went to pick up Allen to come over, he showed up outside the locker room after football practice as they'd arranged. No sign of Allen. But then, pulling out of the Bethel parking lot, Bailey spied a 1981 black Toyoto Tercel. That was Michael Jackson's car, a sweatbox with no air-conditioning. Jackson, whom Iverson called "Thrilla," was a tailback on the football team and one of Iverson's closest friends. They bonded when, as twelve-year-olds, Jackson was the only kid who could beat Iverson in a footrace. Jackson, a stellar student, drove Iverson to and from school every day—doing his best to get Bubbachuck there on time. Now Bailey pulled up alongside Jackson.

"You seen 'Chuck?" he asked. "We're supposed to meet for study hall."

"Haven't seen him, Coach," Jackson replied, his eyes darting nervously. Bailey glanced into the backseat; in his peripheral vision, he saw a form crouched low on the floor behind the driver's seat. Bubba.

"Well, if you see him, tell him I'm not giving up," Bailey said. "Tell him I'll see him tomorrow." The next day, Bailey successfully corralled Iverson on the football field.

Bailey's commitment might have appeared self-serving to an outsider. His job, after all, was to win basketball games, and Iverson, for all the headaches he caused, could do that for him. But others attest that Bailey truly loved Iverson like a son. This was because, like Lambiotte, he saw some potential that had gone untapped. He'd had experience in dealing with inner-city black kids. The hardest thing to combat was their fatalism, the sense that they were doomed, that no one was there for them. He knew so many kids who lived for today, even if it meant they'd die tomorrow. Hearing Iverson talk about how he just had to make it to the NBA, how he wanted to use sports to help his family, Bailey sensed that, unlike so many of his generation, he lived for the next day. Lived for his family. Hell, he'd already promised Ann that, when he signed with an NBA team, he'd buy her that candy-red Jaguar she'd always wanted. The kid was fixated on the possible while others around him were succumbing to hopelessness.

So that summer, Bailey took him in for three weeks while Iverson took a history class he had failed. Bailey would wake him up at 5 A.M. and watch as Iverson ironed his T-shirt, trying to smooth over its holes. He'd fret when Friday came, because along with it came the call of the streets. Bailey would cruise Newport News on Sunday night, trying to find him. One missed class, after all, in such a truncated semester, resulted in a failing grade. One Sunday night, Bubba was nowhere to be found. A distraught Bailey headed home.

The next morning, Bailey checked the history class. There was Iverson. He'd scratched together enough pennies to afford a taxi from the streets of Newport News to the school at dawn. Another time, he called Bailey at 6 A.M.: "Coach, my ride didn't show. Can you pick me up?" After three weeks, he'd gotten a B.

But that's not what sticks most in Bailey's mind of this, his first summer of Bubbachuck. No, what Bailey remembers is what made him realize that, to reach Iverson, he'd have to "coach him with my heart." In their first sit-down together, when Bailey spelled out all that he'd be expecting of Iverson—the study halls, the promptness, the attitude—he wasn't even sure if Iverson was listening. Iverson was looking down or looking away, rarely making and holding eye contact. Bailey finished by asking, "Now, what do you expect from me?"

And this thirteen-year-old who had no recollection of meeting his father, whose de facto father was hustling on the streets when he wasn't doing time, who, almost every day, found himself among a hushed crowd jockeying around yellow police tape while cops crouched over yet another chalk outline, this thirteen-year-old raised his head and looked Mike Bailey squarely in the eyes. "Will you always be there for me, Coach?" he asked.

ONLY THE STRONG

this is a cross of daggers knit

reading ONLY THE STRONG SU

that's the one true thing i've learne

That was one crazy-ass summer," Allen Iverson would say, some ten years later, of the summer of 1992. It was the summer that the basketball establishment was stunned into taking note of the five-foot ten-inch prodigy from the forgotten streets of Newport News. It was the summer death seemed all around, everywhere Iverson turned. And it was the summer Iverson met many of those who would play meaningful roles in his life.

The Iversons had moved to 3710 Victoria Boulevard, to a one-story rectangle of a house two doors down from Wilkes Bar-B-Q; Ann did her best to get bills paid, but each month began with one certain uncertainty—which would be the first to be shut off, the electricity, phone, or gas? In the living room, there was a tattered couch and easy chair. The only other piece of furniture was a bookcase displaying Allen's 209 trophies and 62 plaques.

A burst pipe under the house resulted in an ever-present sewage stench and constant backups, forcing Allen and his sister Brandy to wear boots inside so as to sidestep the raw debris that often floated across the floor. Allen could tolerate it, but he couldn't stomach watching two-year-old Ieisha live in such conditions. From the first day Ieisha came home from the hospital, Allen was smitten, often rushing home from school to see this little sister who looked just like him, who had his big hands and feet. She also had his toughness, according to Ann, whose pregnancy with Ieisha was troubled. Born nine days late, Ieisha was admitted to Norfolk's King's Daughters Hospital, where doctors told Ann not to expect her baby to make it. From there, it was on to Georgetown University Hospital for treatment of, among other maladies, recurring seizures.

Allen hated to see Ieisha living in the decrepit house on Victoria Boulevard, the location of which made for an ironic incongruity; just a quarter mile away sat Darling Stadium, where thousands had cheered for Iverson the previous fall during Bethel football games.

Iverson played wide receiver as a freshman, when he was timed running a 4.7 forty-yard dash, the same speed posted by NFL superstar Jerry Rice in his rookie year. As a sophomore, Iverson moved to quarterback and also played safety and returned kicks. Without taking any time off between football and basketball seasons, he went on to average 27.1 points a game, leading Mike Bailey's team to a 15–8 record, the school's best in ten years. The test, for Bailey, was getting Iverson to peacefully coexist with the team's other star, Tony Rutland, who was also a sophomore. Bailey referred to them as "The Terrible Twos." When he'd take one out of a game, he'd take the other out, too, and sit between them on the bench, trying to foster chemistry, talking them through their inevitable spats that usually began with one or the other moaning, "Man, I was open!"

But now it was summer, AAU time. Bust-out time. By summer's end, basketball cognoscenti across the nation would be touting Iverson in the same reverential tones Newport News locals had been using for years. Boo Williams, who coached Alonzo Mourning in his most dominant summers, still shakes his head when he thinks of Iverson's summer of 1992. "I can't explain it, but it was the greatest display of basketball I've ever seen," Williams says. "Not even Alonzo ever had a summer like Bubba's."

Iverson had always been fast, but now he'd become a blur. Stealing the ball from him was out of the question; his low-to-the-ground dribble combined with his quickness and jumping ability to make him unstoppable. But perhaps the best explanation for his suddenly dominant play could be found in the tumult swirling around Iverson away from the hard courts. Life at Victoria Boulevard was a struggle; he'd stay on the playground till all hours, not out of some workmanlike desire to perfect his game, but because heading back home, where it was likely dark, cold, and smelly, was so daunting. "It ain't supposed to be like this," he told Bailey one night when he sought to crash over at the coach's house.

Other times, he'd head over to Gary Moore's, or to Tony Clark's place, book bag in tow. Clark was twenty, a mentor who kept at bay the street tricksters looking to gain instant notoriety by fucking with Bubbachuck. A former athlete and high-school dropout, Clark preached the wisdom of education to Iverson: "Don't end up like me—stay in school," he'd say. If Bubba came over without his books, Clark would send him right back home for them—no matter the time of day or night. That summer, Clark was murdered by his girlfriend. Stabbed in the neck. When he heard the news, a disbelieving Iverson raced to his mentor's place, where he saw a river of dark purple blood staining the street and sidewalk.

"I still ain't over that one," Iverson says matter-of-factly today.

Eight other acquaintances died that summer, all from gunshot wounds. It felt like a daily occurrence: Iverson would be on the playground, fooling around, when some kid would come running with an account of trouble. The whole neighborhood would turn out, it seemed, and Iverson would hang near the back of the throng—"scared as shit," he remembers today—catching glimpses here and there of the lifeless body of someone he'd regularly played ball with.

That summer found Iverson hanging with some new friends. One was Rasaan Langford, or "Ra," a good-natured court jester who, along with Eric "E" Jackson, turned Iverson on to rap. They'd hang out till all hours, freestyling. Iverson had been raised on Ann's music, R&B. Finally, here was something that described *his* life. He got hooked on the poetic stylings of Kool Moe Dee, and, later, would flip when Biggie Smalls seemed to perfectly capture both his own upbringing and his ambitions to make it big, as in Smalls's song "Juicy," which was dedicated to "All the teachers that told me I'd never amount to nothing": "We used to fuss when the landlord dissed us/No heat, wonder why Christmas missed us/Birthdays was the worst days/Now we sip champagne when we thirst-ay . . ." Biggie took all his boyz—known as the Junior Mafia—with him wherever he went; when he made it big, they made it big. Iverson decided early on that that was how it was going to be with Ra and "E" and some of the other guys, like Marlon Moore and Arnie Steele. Together, they called themselves, first, Dynasty Raiders and, later, Cru Thik. They made a pact: If Allen made it out through hoops, the others were along for the ride. If one of the others blew up as a rapper, Allen would be there, too.

To this day, Iverson considers Ra and "E" the two best rappers he's ever heard. That summer, taking a cue from them, he started writing his own raps, having finally found a creative form to rival that of basketball. But no other talent of his could approach what he was suddenly able to do on the basketball court, not drawing, rapping, or even playing football. No, in the summer of 1992, Iverson became something special in basketball, and this fact was not unrelated to all the turmoil around him. If he was, as those who witnessed him that summer attest, an artist on the court, he was using suffering to fuel his creativity, as so many artists had done before him.

"The basketball court was my one escape," he recalls today. "I mean, I'd go out there and it was the one place I could just do my thing and have no worries, forget about everything."

The coming-out party began at the state tournament in Richmond. Back then, only the state champion advanced to play in the nationals, so the stakes were high. In the title game, Rutland hit a game winner off a penetration and no-look assist from Iverson. Afterward, the team stopped at a barbecue joint in Richmond. Iverson was, as usual, a nonstop chatterbox. But, even for him, the braggadocio was reaching new levels.

In the parking lot, he approached coaches Williams, Bill Tose, and David Six. "I'm as good as Mike, you know," he said. "I can take Mike."

The coaches all looked at one another and snickered. "Maybe you can," Tose said. "But Mike Evans is pretty good. It'd be a good matchup."

"No, no, no," Iverson corrected him. "I can take *Mike*. Mike Jordan." At the time, Iverson had just painted Jordan's likeness on his bedroom door. When it came time to move, in fact, he was found trying to unhinge the door to take it with him.

In late July, Iverson put on a Jordan-like display at the AAU seventeen-and-under nationals at Wake Forest's Joel Coliseum. Most of his teammates, and most of those they were going against, were all heading into their senior seasons. Iverson was not only younger and shorter than everyone else, he was less experienced, too. His teammates were Rutland, Bacote, Joe Smith, Faisal Abraham (who would play at Marquette), and Tarik Turner (St. John's). They were going against the most-hyped players in the country, but it didn't matter. It became the Allen Iverson show.

Iverson averaged 25.5 points over eight games, with a high of 37. He made threes from NBA distances and dunked off alley-oops, rising above seven-footers. He scored 33 in a triple-overtime win over the Cleveland team, including all 7 of his team's points in the final overtime. He led his team with 24 in the semifinal win over the Arkansas Lakers. In the final, Iverson had 25 points, 6 rebounds, and 5 assists in an 82–78 win over the much-heralded Charlotte Sonics starring Jerry Stackhouse, Jeff Capel, and Jeff McInnis. He was named MVP of the fifty-seven-team event.

"I knew I was this good!" Iverson announced to his teammates, clutching his MVP award and the championship trophy all the way back to Newport News.

"You gotta understand," says Boo Williams. "Almost nobody knew who this rascal was. People were just stunned."

The success made Iverson's off-court demeanor easier to good-naturedly tolerate. "Socks, shoes, uniforms, playing time: ain't nothing right according to Bubba," Williams says, laughing. "He's a constant complainer. But he never cheated you with effort."

Coach Koz, a bear of a man with a growl of a voice, had a shirt-and-tie rule on game day. Dennis Kozlowski was not only Bethel High's football coach, he was also its athletic director, and his rule was sacrosanct: if you didn't wear a shirt and tie to school, you didn't play. On the day Allen Iverson's junior season was to begin, a security guard told Koz that his star quarterback was wearing a T-shirt.

Kozlowski was perplexed. Last spring, after Iverson had led the Bruins to a 10–1 record, the sophomore was a finalist for the annual Peninsula Sports Club and *Daily Press* Athlete of the Year award, announced at an annual banquet. Kozlowski had personally taken Iverson shopping for a shirt and tie back then—and that had been only five months earlier. What happened to the clothes he had bought him?

"One of my mother's boyfriends took 'em, Coach," Iverson replied.

"C'mon," Kozlowski said, taking his player shopping again. It wasn't the first time he'd had to go beyond what many coaches might do for a star player. The previous year, Iverson's sophomore season, Kozlowski got wind that Iverson wasn't eating regularly. He called him into his office and told him that he could get him placed on the school's Underprivileged Meals Program so he wouldn't have to pay for lunch.

Iverson's eyes widened, and with wounded pride in his voice, he protested, "I ain't underprivileged."

"Well, forget what it's called," Kozlowski said. "Would you do it if nobody knew you were doing it?"

Iverson grudgingly agreed that yes, if no one were to find out he was getting meals for free, he'd eat them. So Kozlowski approached Mrs. Johnson, a white woman who ran the cafeteria staff, which consisted of all black women. He explained the situation to her and she explained it to her staff; to them, Mrs. Johnson was helping out one of their own. All involved saw to it that Allen not only ate, but that it never cost him anything.

Shortly thereafter, Kozlowski received a call from a friend on the Newport News police force. Turns out, a drug task force had recent video footage of Allen buying narcotics. Kozlowski was stunned; Iverson had always been vociferously antidrugs. Plus, unlike so many other kids, he had always, as Coach Bailey observed, been aware of just how much he had at stake. The police, Kozlowski was assured, were not going to do anything with the tape—provided he straightened the kid out. He called Allen into his office, and after telling him their conversation would be just between them, confronted him with what he'd been told. Angry denials—"Coach, I don't do drugs!"—were followed by, finally, an embarrassed admission.

"Coach, I was running an errand for my mom," he said.

It was, the coach would later recall, the hardest heart-to-heart he'd ever had with a player. "Do you really want to help your mom?" Kozlowski asked him.

"More than anything," Iverson said.

"How do you think you're going to do that?"

"C'mon, man, you know," Iverson replied. "By going to the NBA or NFL."

Kozlowski took a deep breath, trying to make the moment as dramatic as possible. "But if you get caught with drugs, the dream ends," he said. "I know you love your mom, but, in the future, if she asks you to get anything for her, just send some of your friends. Don't go yourself." He made Allen promise to heed his advice.

By the time his junior season rolled around, Iverson's football team was on a roll and his local celebrity was approaching mythic proportions. A kid himself, he couldn't go to the Coliseum Mall, for example, without being mobbed by kids seeking his autograph. "It was crazy, man," remembers Jamil Blackmon, a street-smart hustler at Hampton University at the time; he promoted rap concerts on the weekends and always seemed to have wads of cash at his disposal. Ann, according to Blackmon, had been trying to convince him to become her family's benefactor. "Every time he touched a ball, whether at Aberdeen Elementary, Anderson Park, or Bethel, there was a crowd. He had people crowding around him in restaurants like he was Michael Jordan. Guys who are celebrities in the game now, I know they never experienced anything like what he went through when he was that age."

Blackmon befriended Iverson and started looking out for him. Often, Iverson would stay at Blackmon's apartment on Marcella Drive in Hampton. Just as Tony Clark had done, Blackmon would send him home if he arrived without his schoolbooks. Ann would open the door and laugh as Allen moped his way inside. "He sent your ass home again, huh?" she'd say. When Ann needed a bill paid, she'd often turn to Blackmon. "And the way Juicy was, it'd be like, 'This four-hundred-dollar phone bill is due in ten minutes, or they're cutting off my shit,'" Blackmon recalls. Meantime, Ann kept pitching Blackmon on taking her and her family under his wing; he kept promising to consider it. "Once my baby gets rich, you'll never want for nothing," she'd say. "You and me, we'll have mansions right next to each other."

Before any mansions could be purchased, though, there was a high-school football state championship to contend for. Iverson was having a dream season in what many considered to be his best sport. "As unbelievable as he is in basketball, he was more amazing in football," recalls Gary Moore, his first football coach.

As a sophomore, Iverson intercepted 13 passes and accounted for over 1,500 yards of total offense. Now, as a junior, he easily surpassed those numbers. He amassed 2,204 yards, ran for 21 touchdowns, passed for 14 more, and picked off 8 passes. But a litany of statistics doesn't do his game justice. As in basketball, he would do things on the gridiron that defied belief. Like the time his touchdown punt return was called back on account of a holding penalty against one of his teammates. Fielding the ball upon the rekick, Iverson found an even higher gear and repeated the touchdown run, using almost the exact same route. "It was like everyone else was playing football and he was playing PlayStation," recalls basketball coach Mike Bailey, who would cringe every time his star player got hit during a football game. "Everybody looked at each other and wondered, 'Did we just see a replay, or was that really live?' "

Kozlowski was a staunch believer in psychocybernetics. He'd preach the value of visualization long before such mental gymnastics were in vogue. He had Allen read the book *Psycho-Cybernetics,* by Maxwell Maltz, a plastic surgeon who maintained that, even after reconstructive nose surgery, many patients would still see their old nose when they looked in the mirror; such was the power of the brain's imagery. Kozlowski would tell Iverson to tie his shoe while continuing to carry on a conversation with him. Iverson would be speaking to him, looking up at him, while kneeling and tying his shoe. "See that," Kozlowski said. "See how you didn't have to look at yourself tying your shoe? See how you didn't even have to think about it? I want you to play like you just tied your shoelaces—automatically. The way you do that is by having an image in your mind of what you do before you do it."

"Allen took psychocybernetics to a new level," Kozlowski recalls. Today, Iverson doesn't like to talk about how he does what he does on the basketball court. "I just do it," he says. Partially, like any artist, he is wary of overanalyzing his gift. But it could also be that he's known since high school that the real explanation defies easy answers, that the answer is, at heart, both beneath and above the level of language, and connected, on some level, to his psyche. In other words, missed in all the hand-wringing about his lackadaisical practice habits in the NBA is the possibility that so much of his work is *cerebral*. Unlike, say, Jordan, who was a craftsman, someone who would take hundreds of jumpshots a day, Iverson imagines possibility and then acts it out.

"Let me tell you about Allen's workouts," says Terry Royster, his bodyguard from 1997 until early 2002. "All the time I've been with him, I never seen him lift a weight or stand there and shoot jumper after jumper. Instead, we'll be on our way to the game and he'll be quiet as hell. Finally, he'll say, 'You know how I usually cross my man over and take it into the lane and pull up? Well, tonight, I'm gonna cross him over and then take a step back and fade away. I'm gonna kill 'em with it all night long.' And damned if he don't do just that. See, that's his workout, when he's just sitting there, thinking. That's him working on his game."

Imagining himself doing great things had its desired effect his junior year of high school. Iverson was named Virginia's Football Player of the Year, and he led the Bruins to the state title game against E. C. Glass in Lynchburg. The day before the big game, Kozlowski took the squad to practice at Lynchburg's Heritage High School. It was a rainy, cold day, but Kozlowski wanted to run through some game situations one last time. When it came time to practice punt returns, Iverson took his place deep in the backfield, awaiting the kick. He fielded it, took two steps, and then, as the play was going on, simply stopped and stood there, motionless. Kozlowski whistled the play dead and approached his star.

"What are you doing?"

"Coach, we shouldn't be out here," Iverson said. "It's cold, the ground's wet."

Kozlowski was taken aback. "Allen, you're on a team—everybody else is practicing," he said. "Now let's do it again, get it right, and we can all go back to the hotel."

The next punt came to Iverson, and again, he caught it and stood still. Kozlowski blew his whistle—and his top. "That's it! You're out!" he yelled. "You're not playing tomorrow! Go stand over there!"

For the next hour, the team practiced in a drizzle while Iverson huddled under the awning of a shed. One of the assistant coaches approached him.

"Are you crazy? Don't you want to play tomorrow?" he asked.

"I don't care," Iverson said. "We shouldn't be out here. I'm *right*. And you all know I'm right."

Iverson may have been surprised by Kozlowski's hard-line response. After all, Iverson was still setting all sorts of truancy records in the school district, and yet he hadn't been sat down for a single football or basketball game. Indeed, one Bethel administrator at the time recalls an argument with Iverson over whether he'd missed sixty-nine *or* seventy-five days to date in that school year. (Many of his absences came because he was home caring for Ieisha.) Perhaps he figured that, if he hadn't been held accountable for skipping school all that time, no one would dare bench him on the eve of the championship game.

The next morning, led by Michael Jackson and Xavier Gunn, the seniors appealed to Kozlowski to reverse his decision. "We've come this far together and we want to play together tomorrow," Gunn said.

The players were unanimous. Kozlowski said he'd leave it up to them, but not before warning them: "We might be doing a disservice to Allen in the long run."

That day, Iverson intercepted two passes, passed for two touchdowns, and scored two more—including a breathtaking punt return in which not one defender could so much as touch him—and the Bruins won, 27–0. Many of the Bethel faithful had come down for the game. They were, just as at all the Bethel home games, a truly mixed crowd: black, white, young, old, united by this team and this special player. And they were jubilant, especially when Allen, interviewed on the sideline, was asked what was next. "We gonna get us one in basketball," he said, referring to the state championship. He knew that in three days—and after just one basketball practice—he would begin trying to make that prediction come true. He'd score 37 points to beat Kecoughtan High, where his new girlfriend, Tawanna Turner, was a student.

But, as he danced and hugged and smiled his mother's beaming smile on the sideline the day he won the state football title, he didn't know that the unity sparked by him and his team would be short-lived. An event loomed in the future that would set his hometown against itself, white versus black, young versus old. He had no way of knowing he was about to be at the center of his town's biggest racial maelstrom since the assassination of Martin Luther King Jr.

chapter 3

PRAYING HANDS

A set of hands between my grandma's initials—Ethel Selena Mitchell, who died when I was real young—and my mama's initials, Ethel Ann Iverson. They taught me to pray every day, 'cause when you send prayers up, lessons come down.

When the trouble came, there were those who thought it all had its roots in the simplest of things, nothing more than high-school rivalry run amok. It's impossible to tell, of course; no one will ever know precisely why it went down the way it did, any more than they will know *what* exactly happened the night that Allen Iverson's life, as well as his hometown's history, changed.

It is true that Bethel High School was a relative upstart, particularly in athletics. After all, the school had only been around since 1968, and it was only in the era of Iverson that its teams had begun dominating. Its cross-town arch rival, Hampton High, was the more established school. By virtue of its longevity, Hampton had graduated much of the town's power elite: countless judges, lawyers, and business owners. Bethel's backers were wary; Iverson was in the process of following up the state football title by leading the Bruins on a state basketball championship run. Would the town's powers-that-be take steps to guard against Hampton losing out on two more championships next year, when Iverson would be a senior?

Most objective onlookers viewed such fear as melodramatic. But those in the trenches of area high-school sports, guys like Coaches Kozlowski and Bailey, insisted that anything was possible. They knew firsthand the passion of this particular high-school sports rivalry. Add such incendiary emotions to the always combustible context of race relations and there was no telling what could happen.

Before the trouble, though, there were basketball games to be played. Early on, against Hampton, Coach Bailey (already known as a demonstrative sideline coach) was at his most animated. In fact, Iverson had once penned a caricature of Bailey on the sidelines, shirt all rumpled and untucked, hair unruly and unkempt. Here was that caricature come to life as Bailey constantly yelled instructions to his point guard. "Allen! Pass the ball ahead!" he called.

Iverson wheeled around at midcourt. "Coach! Stop telling me how to play all the time!" he yelled.

"I'll do just that," Bailey said, and he pulled Iverson from the game; in the ensuing huddle, Iverson muttered "fuck you" to his coach. He had 29 points at the time and Hampton led, 65–51. Bailey kept him on the bench through the third and fourth quarters and the final score was 101–67, Hampton. It was an uncharacteristic move on Bailey's part; he was not known to be stern when it came to Iverson. Walking off, Bailey approached his star. "Do you like me not coaching you?" he asked. "It's real easy when you're sitting on the end of the bench for me to not say much to you."

Iverson looked away, said nothing.

In the locker room, Iverson's teammate and close friend Xavier Gunn called a twenty-minute team meeting. "Allen, you're selfish," he said.

Iverson leaped to his feet. "How can I be selfish when I average ten assists a game?"

"Not the basketball part," Gunn replied. "You gotta be right all the time. When Coach Bailey said what he said to you tonight, when we say things to you sometimes, you always gotta be right."

No one raised his voice. Iverson stewed in silence, taking in the criticism from significantly lesser talents. In the next game, against Menchville, he decided he would prove a point: he wouldn't take a shot. He'd show Bailey and Gunn and everyone else just how unselfish he could be. Bethel found itself down 41–25 at halftime. Iverson had made some beautiful passes, but his teammates—never expecting, or wanting, to be taking *this* many shots—were befuddled by this apparent new strategy. Bailey knew he had to do something, so in front of the team, he decided to appeal to his star's most prominent and laudable quality: his competitiveness.

"Allen, if you honestly feel that not taking a shot is the best way to win a game, then by all means, pass the ball—I have no problem with that," Bailey said. "As long as your decision making is driven by what's going to make us win, we'll all be all right. We all have confidence in your judgment and competitiveness."

Iverson said nothing. As would often be the case, Bailey wasn't even sure he was getting through, so sporadic was Iverson's eye contact. But Bailey knew from experience that Iverson was a much better listener than he appeared to be. In the second half, Iverson started draining threes and penetrating at will. With him leading the way, Bethel scored 37 points in the eight-minute fourth quarter and won, 86–74. Iverson had 21 of his game-high 40 in the final quarter.

"That game was our turning point," Bailey recalls. "I think Allen saw that his teammates, and me, would both stand up to him *and* stand by him. And that's the key with him. It's why he's so loyal to those guys from back home. They've stood by him."

The Bruins won nineteen straight games after the Menchville win, but as Iverson would say, all was not "peaches and cream" from then on. In early February 1993, Bailey benched him again, after Allen missed a practice. Cleverly, the coach got Ann and Gary Moore on board with the punishment before telling Iverson of his fate. "I know you do what you do because you love him," Ann told Bailey.

Still, Iverson would not speak to his coach. The next game was before another overflow crowd. Before the game, a security guard interrupted Bailey's team meeting. Fans were going to have to use the locker-room bathrooms, Bailey was told—too many were crowding into the rest rooms upstairs. Bailey objected. "You don't like it, too bad," said the security guard.

Now Bailey and the guard were face-to-face, exchanging unpleasantries. Suddenly, squeezing between them was Iverson, staring the security guard down, wagging an index finger. "You don't talk to this man that way," he said calmly. Immediate silence ensued; both men backed off. He's not speaking to me, Bailey thought, incredulous, and now he's telling other people how *they're* supposed to act toward me?

Shortly after that win, Iverson was at a party at the Sheraton on Hampton University's campus. A twenty-two-year-old bouncer tossed a guy, who came back with an Uzi. After the shots, the assailant calmly walked back out. Iverson and two of his teammates were upstairs. They heard the shots and huddled together until it was safe to come down. When they did, they heard the victim laughing that one of the bullets had hit him in the ass. He died later that night.

Mike Bailey heard that his star player had been at the scene of a homicide. He had always known, given the type of people looking out for him—people who were doing good by him, but who didn't always do good themselves—that the kid was perpetually one ill-timed moment away from calamity. This was too close, he felt.

The next night, Bailey's players celebrated another win in the locker room, but Bailey quieted the party. "This is not a moment we should be celebrating," he said. "We should be reflecting. Because three members of our team were someplace last night that wasn't the best place to be. I'm not saying they were doing anything wrong, but we don't need to be doing these things. We need to reflect on what's at stake. Think about, what if it was you, shot at a party? Think about your loved ones, how they'd react. Reflect tonight on what's truly important. That's all I'm saying."

The players were silent as the meeting broke. Bailey stood in front of Iverson and both men wrapped their arms around each other and hugged. "I wanted to do this a week ago," Bailey said.

"Me, too," Iverson said.

"What stopped us?"

"Pride," Iverson said.

Bailey and his star walked out of the locker room together, and Bailey offered a piece of advice he'd forever regret. "You know what you need to do, Bubba? You need to do high-school things, like any other teenager would do," he said. "You know, go to the movies. Or get a bunch of guys together and go bowling, blow off some steam."

Hampton and Newport News, Virginia, commonly referred to as the Virginia Peninsula, changed sometime after midnight on Valentine's Day, 1993, when a brawl broke out at the Circle Lanes bowling alley. The fallout wasn't apparent right away. But over the course of the next year, as groups chose sides and sharpened their rhetoric, as the media onslaught began, it became clear that the character of a town was being inexorably tested. The Hampton and Newport News area, as part of the New South, had prided itself on its racial comity. Any quick scan of the stands during Bethel or Hampton sporting events showed this—showed blacks and whites, side by side, united in a common purpose.

But then came the bowling-alley incident, where how you perceived what happened determined who you were, just as who you were determined *how* you saw things. The divergence of opinion, almost without exception, broke down along racial lines.

Allen Iverson, Michael Simmons, Melvin Stephens Jr., and Samuel Wynn were among a group of black students bowling in lanes nine and ten and were, according to witness testimony, being boisterous. Twice, bowling-alley employee Brandon Smith, a student at Bethel, approached them to ask Simmons not to stand on the chairs. A little after midnight, Iverson, with a friend in tow, made his way toward the snack bar. Nearby was a group of white bowlers from the wealthy neighborhood of Poquoson. According to testimony from one of them, six-foot two-inch, two-hundred-pound Steve Forrest, Iverson approached them and, unpro-voked, said, "What's your problem? What are you looking at?"

Iverson and others maintain that Forrest, who had been convicted of felony cocaine possession in the past, called Iverson a "nigger" and "little boy." The two were soon squaring off, an arm's length away. According to Forrest, he told Iverson he didn't want any trouble, which is when, he tes-tified, Iverson's friend Michael Simmons came up and blindsided him with a punch to the back of the head. Iverson claims that Forrest broke their stare-down by swinging a chair and hitting him on the head, at which point someone, seeking to protect him, grabbed Iverson and ushered him outside. He didn't throw a chair or punch anybody, he maintained.

That's how it started. What followed was a dizzying, violent mess of a brawl that sent bowlers scurrying down lanes, seeking to hide behind the pins. Simmons was a wannabe filmmaker, a senior, and he'd been docu-menting the last semester of his high-school career. He had a video camera with him that night, which was on and which stayed on, capturing the jumpy, scrambled, confused mess of a rumble. There were people scream-ing and falling, chairs being hurled, and sounds of sobs and curses echoing through the air. Things quickly calmed down, but escalated again soon after. One witness said that Iverson reentered the bowling alley, or had never left, though others refute that claim. Brandon Smith would go on to identify Iverson as the assailant who hit a twenty-three-year-old white college student named Barbara Steele over the head with a chair; Steele, who was knocked unconscious, required six stitches around her left eye and later suffered amnesia. Smith would later testify that he tried to help Steele, but that Iverson knocked him over the head with a chair, shattering his glasses.

All in all, the melee might have taken two minutes. But when it was over, more than one witness told the *Daily Press,* the local newspaper, that the bowling alley looked like a "war zone." According to the *Press,* in the stunned silence after the violence, the only thing that could be heard was Michael Jackson's hopeful voice over the piped-in sound system: "It doesn't matter if you're black or white . . ."

Just hours after the brawl, Dennis Kozlowski's phone rang. A former student of his, a white alumnus of the Bethel track team, was on the other end of the line. He'd been knocked around in a bowling-alley brawl earlier, he said, and he wanted to give Kozlowski a heads-up. Iverson was the only recognizable face there, and the cops were going to blame the whole thing on him.

The next day, Ann Iverson got Simmons's amateur tape into the hands of Boo Williams and Mike Bailey. Before turning it over to the authorities, they watched the grainy footage some fifty times and were convinced Allen was nowhere to be found on the tape. Bailey instinctively knew why this was: Allen was being protected. The whole reason his friends came running in the first place was that they had Allen's back; it only made sense that one of them would, as Allen maintained, get him out of there. "If you understand that culture, the one who can make it, they're going to protect him," Bailey says. "I can't tell you how many times I'd be driving around some pretty iffy sections of Newport News looking for Allen in the middle of the night and I just couldn't believe where I was. I once said to Allen, 'What's going to happen to me when I go to these neighborhoods looking for you?' And he said, 'Nothing, Coach. They know you're with me.'"

Most observers of the video couldn't tell if Iverson was in it or not. It didn't incriminate, but neither did it exonerate him. Shortly after the brawl, the *Daily Press* reported that Iverson was under investigation, violating its own policy against publishing the names of juveniles accused of crimes. But what had happened at the bowling alley was hardly a well-guarded secret; the whole town was talking about it, so the paper was obliged to write about it. Kozlowski asked Iverson if he wanted to speak to his lawyer.

"Gary Moore's got someone for me," Iverson replied. "Gary's gonna handle it." Moore arranged for Iverson to be represented by seventy-three-year-old Herb Kelly, a lawyer of counsel to Hampton University, where Moore was employed, but someone who hadn't tried a case in court for over a decade. More ominous was the fact that Kelly wasn't considered politically connected to the Hampton establishment.

Many in the Iverson camp were concerned. Once the *Daily Press* got on the story—soon the national media would swarm in—it ceased to be about the facts. There were also politics to consider; the white victims were from Poquoson, a traditional bastion of wealth and power.

On February 16, just two days after the incident, the much-hyped basketball rematch between Bethel and Hampton took place in front of eight thousand fans at the Hampton Coliseum, the largest crowd to see a Peninsula District game in fifteen years. Bethel authorities and Iverson's loved ones were a wreck; Iverson seemed like the only person unaffected by the controversy surrounding him. He led his team to a 69–67 win over Hampton, ending the Crabbers' seventeen-game winning streak. He scored 23 points, and five days later was named to the *Parade* magazine high-school all-America team, with averages of 31.1 points, 11 rebounds, and 10 assists per game.

Just two days later, the newly minted all-American was placed under arrest. As would be the case throughout his life and career, Iverson would feed off the drama he found himself starring in. He would locate the calm eye at the storm's center and nestle in. Later, in the pros, he developed an almost comical knack for orchestrating blowups with his old school coach Larry Brown, creating a psychodrama with himself at its center— only to rise up out of the squabbling in epic fashion. It was a pattern reminiscent of another tortured artist who also happened to express himself in the field of sports, tennis great John McEnroe. Like Iverson, McEnroe was an artistically inclined "natural" with poor work habits who, in order to summon his genius, needed to raise the stakes to the point where his outbursts would create a "me versus the world" tension.

So it was that, just hours after he was arrested, booked, and released, all eyes were on seventeen-year-old Allen Iverson as he took to the floor for the Peninsula District Tournament semifinals against Ferguson High. In attendance that night was the singer/songwriter Bruce Hornsby, who lived in Williamsburg and fancied himself something of a basketball player.

He'd heard about this kid who'd been arrested earlier that day. And then he sat there, slack-jawed, watching this slight, speedy junior put aside all the distractions—his very future, at all of seventeen, was in peril!—en route to scoring more than half of his team's points. Iverson lit up Ferguson for 42 points in an 81–78 Bethel win.

Iverson could control his world on the basketball court, which is why it was always such a comfortable escape for him. Off the court was another matter. While Iverson took his team on a thrilling run toward the state championship, worries among Iverson loyalists escalated when Judge Louis Lerner disregarded the recommendation of the juvenile probation officer, Ernest Madison, and opted to charge Iverson and the others as adults. Iverson was seventeen at the time of the incident and had a clean record, save for a conviction the previous fall for reckless driving and driving without a license; he'd subsequently failed to meet with a juvenile probation officer five times. Moreover, the charge was particularly ominous sounding: maiming by mob. Ironically, maiming by mob was a seldom-used Virginia statute put on the books to prosecute Ku Klux Klan members, a way to hold individuals accountable for the havoc wreaked by the group.

A July trial date meant that for the rest of the basketball season, charges would hang over Iverson's head. Even though the state championship loomed, for Iverson and the entire community, the worst was just beginning.

The road to the state championship promised more roadblocks beyond the distraction of Iverson's legal travails. It also contained a six-foot nine-inch pothole named Joe Smith. Smith, a close friend of Iverson's, starred at Maury High, the team to beat statewide. He'd go on to star at the University of Maryland before becoming the first overall pick in the 1995 NBA draft. Briefly, in 1997, he and Iverson played together on the Philadelphia 76ers.

But for now, Smith was an obstacle. Bethel was a small team; no one topped six-two. But Bailey had a secret strategy that, when unveiled, led those who were watching to wonder if they were really seeing what they were seeing. At the right moment, he was going to have Iverson, at all of five feet eleven inches, guard Smith.

As expected, Smith was having his way with the Bethel defense. But he was a one-man team. Of the 50 points Maury ended the game with, 37 were Smith's, a career high. He had scored 35 of those with two and one-half minutes to go, when Bailey put Iverson on Smith. Some in the crowd started laughing as Iverson "bodied up" against Smith down low. Though he towered over Iverson, Smith was rail thin—more of a finesse than a power player. Amazingly, there was Iverson, pushing Smith out of the lane, keeping him from getting position down low. Smith's teammates looked for him a couple of times, but Iverson wasn't allowing Smith an angle to receive an entry pass. Smith's teammates would pump-fake the ball to him and then pass it elsewhere; someone else would end up taking the shot. So it was until the buzzer sounded; Iverson held Smith scoreless down the stretch, save a meaningless bucket at the buzzer, and Bethel eked out a 52–50 win, earning the school's first-ever trip to the Group AAA Tournament quarterfinals.

As Bethel's run continued, the line for tickets on game days would form four or five hours before tip-off. By the time of the state semifinal game against Woodbridge, all of the Peninsula had caught Bethel fever. But, in the first half, it looked like the dream was over. Woodbridge's Damion Keyes, at six-four and 250 pounds, was dominating inside. He was just too big and too strong for the undermanned Bethel defense. At halftime, Bethel was down 11 points, Keyes had scored 18, and Iverson had three fouls. Bailey and his players were at a loss as to how to counter the Woodbridge attack.

"Let's go to a matchup zone," one of the players called out.

"Uh, we've never played zone, let alone a matchup zone," Bailey pointed out.

There was silence. It was not, Mike Bailey would later concede, one of those great Knute Rockne–like moments. Finally, bewildered, he simply looked at his team and said, "Forget it. Let's just go play."

Once on the court, Iverson sidled up alongside his coach and put his arm around him. "I can guard him," he said, nodding toward Keyes.

"Are you crazy?" Bailey said. "You got three fouls, he weighs two-fifty and you're one-sixty. You're crazy!"

"Coach, I can guard him."

"I'm not wasting my best player," Bailey said. "Why don't these other guys have the heart you have? Why don't your teammates want to guard him?"

Grudgingly, Bailey let Iverson open up the second half checking Keyes. Again, it made for a comical sight as Iverson put his bony hip alongside Keyes's beefy one and tried to hold his ground. Even today, in the NBA, Iverson is a surprisingly proficient low-post defender, thanks to his singularly stubborn will—combined with his high-school experiences against the likes of Smith and Keyes. When he came into the NBA, Iverson's size was thought to be a major liability; bigger guards, the thinking went, would exploit him under the basket. It has never happened because Iverson has never let it. Against Keyes, as against NBA players later, he decided to use his strengths to minimize his disadvantages. And his strength, as usual, was his quickness.

As expected, Woodbridge began the second half by dumping the ball into Keyes on two consecutive trips down the floor. Both times, Iverson waited until the last possible instant and then darted out from behind his man to steal the ball and score two straight layups. It sparked a comeback that, in the fourth quarter, was imperiled when Iverson, having dunked after stealing another pass, turned an ankle. He was barely able to make it to the sideline, where the trainer worked on him while Bethel's hopes faded. But Bailey knew. He remembered that time, two years earlier, when Iverson saw every doctor in Hampton after spraining his ankle, in search of the one who would give him the go-ahead to return to the court. Sure enough, two plays later, he got up. "I'm ready, Coach."

With Bethel down three with twenty-six seconds left, Woodbridge double-teamed Iverson in the forecourt. He ran right at the double team, freezing one defender before blowing past the other and rising for a con-tested three-pointer. Overtime.

In the extra session, Iverson overpenetrated and was called for an offensive foul—his fifth and final foul. Having blown such a big lead, Woodbridge seemed demoralized, but who would pick up Iverson's slack? Bailey called on seldom-used sophomore Lovett Gaither, who scored 9 points in the overtime to seal the win.

On the sideline down the stretch, it was as though there were two coaches, Bailey and Iverson, who was part cheerleader, part assistant coach. In the NBA, Iverson has not been known as a vocal team leader, but in high school evidence of his leadership abounded. Prior to the start of his junior year, for instance, Bailey had decided to cut Kelly Rodgers. Rodgers was the team's strongest rebounder, but he frequently violated one of Bailey's few ironclad rules: he didn't play hard every single play. Bailey had had enough, until Iverson came to him.

"Coach, we need him," Iverson said.

"Allen," Bailey explained, "it's not fair to you or your teammates to play a guy who takes plays off."

"Let's do this, Coach," Iverson said. "Let him be my responsibility. I'll get him to play."

Bailey mulled it over, finally hammering out a deal with his star. "Okay," he said, "but your name is going to be Rodgers from now on. He screws up, and it's you who pays the price."

From that moment on, Bailey would watch while Iverson would take

Rodgers aside, during practice and games, always cajoling effort out of him. Bailey never again had a problem with Rodgers, who became an integral part of the Bethel team.

There was also Iverson's locker-room banter, nonstop teasing that drew the squad together. He nicknamed everyone on the team, including Tony Rutland—the Pippen to his Jordan—whose mother was Korean. Rutland was dubbed "Kong Fu." Melvin Stephens, who often suffered bloody injuries in practice, became "Lip Therapy."

Then there was Bobby, the special-education student who served as a manager for the team. Early in the season, Bobby approached Iverson. "Allen, I got a new play for you," Bobby said. Bailey, watching, knew that Iverson was already growing tired of how everybody was always telling him how to play. Just don't hurt this kid's feelings, Bailey thought, watching nervously.

"Turn around, I'll show you," Bobby said. Once Iverson turned, Bobby started scratching out a crazy array of directions on his back with both index fingers—for about thirty seconds. "That's it!" Bobby said.

Iverson spun around, eyes wide. He snapped his fingers. "That'll work, Coach!" he said, and Bobby beamed for the rest of the season, especially when Iverson and the others continued to call him Coach.

Fourteen weeks after winning the state football title and boldly predicting that a basketball one was to follow, Iverson delivered. The night before the big game, he rounded up his teammates and organized them into a late-night Monopoly tourney, during which he displayed his competitiveness.

The next day, he ran rampant on the court. Iverson and Rutland combined for 58 points (Iverson 28, Rutland 30), as the 27–3 Bruins beat John Marshall High at the University of Virginia's University Hall, 77–71. The go-ahead basket, fittingly, came when Iverson penetrated and dished to Rutland; ever since their turbulent "Terrible Twos," as Bailey used to call them, they'd not only come to mesh on the court, but to respect and admire each other off it. In fact, Rutland was playing overseas when Iverson, having just completed his fourth NBA season, heard that Rutland's father was in the hospital back home. One day, a Bethel administrator went to see Larry Rutland in the hospital. Poking her head into his room, she saw the NBA star sitting by his bedside, deep in conversation.

When the state championship was won, Iverson and Rutland embraced and the crowd started chanting "Iverson! Iverson! Iverson!" He shook his head no and pointed to his chest, leading them, letter by letter, on a new chant: "B-E-T-H-E-L!"

Next came the celebration, but not before Iverson had to borrow fourteen dollars from an assistant coach to help pay for twenty-eight dollars' worth of in-room movies he watched at the hotel during the team's stay at the University of Virginia. Then it was time for the championship ceremony back at Bethel, where the players wore tuxedos. The local TV stations all turned out.

"Iverson," an announcer asked, "is this your first experience in a tux?"

"First experience," Iverson replied, shy as ever when the TV lights were on him.

"How do you like it?"

"I don't like it," he said, breaking into a devilish half smile. "I don't like wearing my pants this far up."

With basketball over, there was little to do but wait for the summer trial date. In the spring, Bailey received a call from Bruce Hornsby, who hadn't been able to shake the image from his head of this basketball prodigy whose future was in jeopardy.

"How can I help?" Hornsby asked.

So it was that on one day in the spring of 1993, Allen Iverson was nowhere to be found—which concerned quite a few people in the 'hood. Jamil Blackmon remembers calling Ra and Arnie and E: "You guys seen 'Chuck?" he asked.

"We all thought he was with you," they said.

Instead, he was visiting Bruce Hornsby. Bailey picked him up and drove him to Colonial Williamsburg. Iverson's eyes widened when they had to pass through a set of wrought-iron gates, complete with a security check, to enter the Hornsby compound. "This is like living in a castle," Iverson said.

For Iverson, the visit was a chance to see the life of somebody who had made it. Hornsby, after all, had just won a Grammy and was well compensated for his musical talent. Seeing Hornsby, Bailey reasoned, could reignite in Allen his desire to overcome all the obstacles—both in his past and looming in his future—and achieve his dream. In addition, it was a chance to see how (though no one would ever call Bruce Hornsby a rapper) someone who had made it big had kept it real. After all, Hornsby still lived where he grew up and still hung out with many of the guys he'd gone to high school with.

For Hornsby, it was a chance to play one-on-one against the best basketball player he'd ever face, a certain future pro. He'd played high-school ball, the only white on a team of blacks, and he stayed in shape by playing hoops on the road. As a piano player, however, Hornsby had to guard against any injury to his hands. So he'd come up with what he called his "Piano Hands Rules." Each player would get one shot each time they got the ball, and any rebound would be an automatic change of possession.

At Hornsby's house, Iverson gawked at the Grammy and played "Chopsticks" on Hornsby's baby grand. Then they went to a local gym to play ball. Iverson would later joke about Hornsby's "funky" jump-shot, with his elbow sticking out at an odd angle. Still, the shot went in. Just before they started playing, a nervous Bailey reminded Iverson: "Don't hurt his hands."

Iverson played tentatively as a result and didn't like the Piano Hands Rules. He'd take one shot, and whether it was good or not, he had to automatically play defense. He couldn't get a rhythm going. Hornsby could, though—and he won. The two started a friendship that continues to this day. Hornsby not only kept in touch while Iverson was incarcerated, he was among many celebrities who surreptitiously helped foot the bill for the private-school completion of Iverson's high-school education when he got out.

When Bailey dropped Iverson off at home later that day, he leaned over to him. "Listen," he said melodramatically. "I'll never ever tell anybody this happened. Because the worst thing that can happen to an athlete is that people find out that somebody in a band beat you."

Later that night, Iverson approached the corner where Jamil Blackmon hung. "'Chuck, where you been?"

"I spent the day with Bruce Hornsby," he said matter-of-factly.

Blackmon scrunched up his face in puzzlement. "Bruce Hornsby and the muthafuckin' *Range*? *That* Bruce Hornsby?" he asked.

"Yeah."

Blackmon, ever the mentor, inched closer. "Listen, nigga, that's cool and all, but don't go advertising in the 'hood that you been hanging with Bruce Hornsby and the muthafuckin' Range, okay?"

As the trial approached, Iverson grew more and more fatalistic. It was as though he already knew this wasn't going to turn out all right. He cut a photo out of the newspaper of a black man in handcuffs being carted off to jail. He cut off the man's head and, in its place, simply wrote "Allen Iverson."

When Mike Bailey mentioned in passing something about playing in the summer league so they could repeat their victory in his senior year, Iverson looked down and paused. "Coach, I'm not going to play next year."

"Why not?"

"I just think I'd be better off going to another school," Iverson said, still looking down. "So that's what I'm gonna do. Go to a different school."

Bailey was stunned and, at first, a bit hurt. "Okay, Allen," he said. "I'd love to have you back, but we can play without you, if that's how you feel."

It wasn't until later that Bailey realized what his star was doing. Of course he wanted to play next year, and play for Bethel. He wasn't unhappy. He'd love nothing more than to make it back-to-back titles in both sports. No, what Allen Iverson was doing was preparing his coach for his absence. Somehow, the kid knew this trial would be a big deal. And that it wouldn't end well. Looming in the near future was not only the trial, but a widespread backlash against the sports star, the fury of which no one fully anticipated. Except, perhaps, Allen Iverson himself.

chapter | 4

THE SOLDIER

this is a soldier's head, because i feel like my life has been a war and i've been a soldier in it.

ost observers saw the bowling-alley incident not as a harbinger of social change or as a case study in the chasm between the races, but as little more than an unfortunate fight between a bunch of kids. The assumption was that, since these were kids without prior records and two of them—Iverson and Melvin Stephens—were juveniles, all they'd get would be a slap on the wrist.

But that didn't happen. The juveniles wouldn't be tried as juveniles. The charge would be a serious one—and all the more menacing for being so obscure. Clearly, the prosecutors were going to make an example out of the star athlete who might or might not have done the wrong thing, but who most certainly was in the wrong place at the wrong time.

Just days before his trial commenced in the courtroom of Judge Nelson Overton, Allen Iverson made a big mistake. He kicked ass on a basketball court. There was nothing new in that; only this time he was doing so in Indianapolis, where he was dominating Nike's All-American Basketball Festival. *USA Today* called him "the jewel" of the 125 college prospects on display during the five-day tournament, despite the charges he was facing. "Every school in the country wants him," Bob Gibbons, the tournament's player selection chairman, told the newspaper. "If he was John Dillinger, they'd take him."

Iverson's mistake came *after* his on-court domination, when he agreed to let Nike fly him back from the camp for the trial's Friday opening, and then fly him back to Indianapolis the next day for an all-star game. The move only buttressed the prosecutors' portrayal of Iverson as an arrogant, coddled athlete who was finally going to be held accountable. It was a perspective that may or may not have resonated with Overton, a white-skinned, gray-haired, no-nonsense Peninsula lifer who peered out at his packed courtroom over half–reading glasses perched on the bridge of his nose. To those in Iverson's corner, Overton was no impartial jurist. He was part of the Hampton establishment, having graduated from Hampton High and Virginia Military Institute.

Prosecutor Colleen Killilea delivered a blistering closing argument. "Mr. Iverson had two choices—either stay and participate, or get out," she said. "He stayed and participated, and became a member of the mob. He made the wrong choice... We don't care how good a basketball player Mr. Iverson is, or how well liked he is by his coach or Mr.

Williams. The fact is, he acted like a criminal that night." Killilea pointed out that two white women and a white man were injured during the fracas, in which she said black people "started hitting whatever white people got in their way." Then, in a reference to Nike's efforts on Iverson's behalf, she closed by playing on the company's famous credo. "Now," she told the judge, "it's our turn to 'just do it.'"

In his summation, Iverson's attorney, Herb Kelly, argued that prosecutors had misapplied the law in the charges against his client. Iverson couldn't be convicted, he argued, because no mob existed—at least not as the word is defined by law. Iverson and his friends were at Circle Lanes that night to bowl, not brawl. "There is no common purpose when people come running from everywhere because of the words *fight, fight, fight,*" Kelly said.

Nelson Overton wasn't having it. At 9:34 on the morning of July 12, 1993, he found Allen Iverson guilty of three felony counts of maiming by mob. (Iverson had opted for a bench, rather than jury, trial, but would later claim that Kelly never presented him with a choice.) When Overton pronounced his judgment, Iverson stood there, blank-faced, as the judge explained that the now convicted felon could remain in his mother's custody until sentencing in September. Iverson would be unable to leave home after 8 P.M. unless he was coming to or from work or school. His whole future was now up in the air. Would colleges continue to recruit? Would he be able to play his senior season at Bethel or, for that matter, anywhere?

Reaction to the verdict was tellingly split. Most local whites applauded; most blacks suspected something dirty was afoot. Still, at that point, the outrage was muted, confined to living rooms and barbershops on the Peninsula. Most continued to think—hope, really—that Overton would be lenient come sentencing time, even though state guidelines called for a punishment of eleven years and ten months for the three convictions.

Like Iverson, Michael Simmons and Samuel Wynn were convicted of felonies. Less than ten days after Iverson's conviction, the fourth defendant, Iverson's teammate Melvin Stephens, became the only one of the "Hampton Four" to go to trial before a jury. Stephens's first trial ended in a hung jury and his second one resulted in three misdemeanor convictions. According to the trial testimony, Stephens led the charge of those coming to Iverson's aid and threw a chair, even though he said himself that he didn't hear any racial slurs directed at Iverson. In short, though the testimony seemed to indicate that Stephens was more of an instigator than Iverson, the jury reduced the charges to misdemeanors. Later, Iverson would sue his lawyer for never discussing with him the merits of opting for a jury trial.

Daily Press columnist Jim Spencer had a different view. He argued that Stephens had benefited not because a jury brought perspective and common sense, but because his lawyer played the race card. In a July 21 column, Spencer, himself a white man, opened with an incendiary lead: "You honky punk, you redneck pig, you hillbilly cracker, you wimpy, fat, overprotected, rhythmless, short-striding, low-jumping, no-basketball-playing, small-handed, clumsy white boy. Are words like these enough to justify a riot?"

Spencer went on to claim that Stephens's trial produced "an outrageous defense for mob violence," going on to berate Stephens's lawyer, Jimmy Ellenson, for suggesting that "a white person calling a black person a nigger produces fighting words that justify whatever happens." Spencer wrote that "each time Ellenson talked about how the fight was justified by a racist comment, [black spectators] muttered agreement like a church congregation listening to a sermon. Too bad they didn't consider the flip side—how they would feel if a lawyer said it was okay for a gang of white folks to indiscriminately beat up blacks at a bowling alley because one of them referred to a white guy as a cracker."

The column struck a nerve. Soon Spencer would be seen in the black community as the voice of the white oppressor. No doubt Spencer did speak for many whites who saw fit to morally equate terms like "nigger" and "cracker," as though blacks and whites shared a common history. To blacks, nothing could compare with the violence implicit in the epithet "nigger"; for a white man to deny them that wound was seen as racist in and of itself. (Besides, none other than the Supreme Court of the United States had long ago established the precedent for "fighting words"— words that would lead an otherwise reasonable man to violence, making Spencer's argument more an attempt to stir emotions than enlighten.)

On September 8, the combustible case burst into flames upon Iverson's sentencing. Before Overton sentenced him, Iverson chose to address the court. He stood and, in a soft, hoarse, inflectionless voice, said, "I would like to apologize to my family and friends and the community if I caused them any embarrassment. And I think I've got my chance now to talk, so I did feel bad for what happened to the people that night at the bowling alley. I wouldn't want that to happen to anybody in that situation."

Simmons and Wynn declined to address the court. Their attorney, Buddy Fox, spoke for them and for many when he argued that the charges were too severe. "What's been lost in this entire matter is perspective," Fox said, pointing out that no guns or knives were used and that there was no evidence of any sort of drug use. Simmons was sentenced to five years and Wynn to three.

When Overton sentenced Iverson to five years—five per felony count, with ten years suspended—a chorus of gasps filled the air. While Iverson stood, stoic, staring straight ahead, and deputies moved to handcuff him and remove him from court, Ann sagged and sobbed behind her baby in the first row of the spectator section. Mike and Janet Bailey hung on to each other, each fearing the other's collapse. Boo Williams paced the court's corridor, venting, as Allen was led off to the Hampton city jail, the same place where, less than four years before, he'd visited his stepfather and gone home barefoot, having left Michael Freeman with his own pair of pristine sneakers. Just like that, he was gone, seemingly doomed to be another statistic in a country where more black men go to prison than to college.

In a courthouse stairwell, Gary Moore cornered a local newspaper reporter. "This is your fault!" he raged. "This is on you!"

Meantime, on the courthouse steps, the months of simmering racial animus detonated. In the weeks leading up to the sentencing, as outrage over Spencer's column combined with the frustration that, in an alleged race riot, only four young African-American men had been charged, a group had formed. Called SWIS, after the first letter of each defendant's last name, its two hundred members collected two thousand signatures on a petition asking Overton for leniency.

After the sentencing, the group's members ratcheted up the rhetoric and railed at Overton. "We're beginning to see Klansmen in robes of another color," said Joyce Hobson, an African-American teacher at Hampton High and one of SWIS's founders.

"I'm outraged," said Linda Mines. "Drug dealers get less than that.

Murderers get less than that. People with guns and knives get less than that."

"It's a high-tech lynching without a rope," fulminated Marilyn Strother.

Up until now, Mike Bailey had been prohibited from speaking publicly about the case by his school. On the courthouse steps, though, he made a terse, anguished statement to the media. "We didn't lose a tremendous high-school athlete today, we didn't lose a member of our student body," he said. "We lost a friend." Days later, Allen's girlfriend, Tawanna Turner, would make a special trip to Bethel High to tell the coach how much Allen appreciated his comments. "He knows you could have talked about losing a player and it meant a lot that you talked about losing him as a person," she said. "It meant a lot because it was from the heart."

Immediately following the sentencing, the media maelstrom began. Tom Brokaw, *Sports Illustrated*, *USA Today*, and the *Washington Post* all swept in, their cameras capturing the countless African-Americans wearing FREE IVERSON T-shirts and the JUSTICE FOR BUBBACHUCK graffiti that appeared, seemingly overnight. Benjamin Chavis, then executive director of the National Association for the Advancement of Colored People, and the Reverend Jesse Jackson both weighed in in support of SWIS.

SWIS printed up and distributed flyers calling for an economic boycott. Protesters were urged to write the word "injustice" in red marker on all dollar bills spent in Hampton. SWIS called for an immediate boycott of Circle Lanes and for an immediate cancellation of all subscriptions to the *Daily Press*. A petition seeking the recall of the commonwealth attorney began making the rounds. Most controversially, SWIS called on churches to come up with "Educational Alternatives for School Attendance," whereby students who, in protest, chose not to attend school would "learn about the historical struggle for freedom as experienced by Americans from the Pilgrims to the Haitians."

On Tuesday, September 14, a *Daily Press* editorial took on the protesters. "We believe Iverson's case was handled fairly and appropriately," the paper wrote. "Now, the legal system is under fire because it has provided Iverson a lesson in consequences . . . Incredibly, there is even some talk of pulling children out of school."

The same day, SWIS had scheduled a rally in support of Iverson at the Bethel African Methodist Episcopal Church, which had a seating capacity of four hundred. At the eleventh hour, the venue was changed to the larger Queen Street Baptist Church to handle the overflow crowd; despite sweltering heat, protesters turned out, filling the sanctuary and its balcony and milling about on the street outside. Joyce Hobson, the Hampton High teacher, told the crowd that she had received a reprimanding letter from her principal about her vocal support for the Hampton Four. "There is one thing that will squelch my voice—and that's a bullet," she defiantly announced, to roaring approval.

But the loudest cheers came when Paul Gillis, a regional NAACP representative, singled out columnist Jim Spencer, who stood alongside the church wall—one of the few white faces in attendance.

"I don't need Jim Spencer telling me what's wrong with black America," Gillis shouted. "I'm sick and tired of listening to white folks telling me what's wrong with my people." The crowd rose en masse, clapping and fist-pumping, cheering and pointing derisively at Spencer.

The same day, a group of black pastors held a press conference in support of SWIS. Calling the conviction and sentencing a "judicial lynching," the Reverend Marcellus Harris Jr. declared that "our community is determined and convinced we have a Rosa Parks–type vehicle here. And we're not going to give up this issue. Nothing short of justice will be satisfactory to us."

Whites were outraged at the parallel between Rosa Parks and Iverson. In fact, those who invoked the civil rights heroine didn't mean to morally equate Iverson with her; by talking about a Rosa Parks "vehicle"—someone they could *ride*—they were, perhaps ill-advisedly, invoking Parks in the context of a catalyst for change. But the two sides, the two races, were long past the point of hearing each other. "Rosa Parks didn't hurt anyone," the *Daily Press* editorialized. "Iverson is a troubled young man who hit a woman with a chair during a brawl. To compare the two is an insult to Rosa Parks."

As time passed, SWIS continued to protest. There were rallies in the streets, where protesters chanted "No Justice, No Peace!" and "Free the Hampton Four!"

The controversy showed no sign of abating. Few, if any, white people seemed to understand the depth of pain felt by area blacks. "It was the biggest travesty ever," Butch Harper, onetime neighbor of the Iverson brood, recalls today. "When that judge gave him five years, I'll tell you what, Joe Louis lost a fight, Martin Luther King Jr. got killed, Muhammad Ali was stripped of his championship. And Allen Iverson was going to jail."

And through it all, the by-now eighteen-year-old prodigy, who had come to symbolize so much to so many of his own people, was working in the kitchen at the Newport News City Farm, where he'd been transferred in the days following his sentencing. There, every night, he'd very consciously remind himself to keep the faith that, one day, his hoops dream would become reality.

The roughly 250 inmates at the Newport News City Farm, a minimum-security prison, worked on road crews or on the sprawling grounds of the facility. They could be seen tending to livestock or cutting grass, a white picket fence the only thing separating them from visitors. But the most famous of the City Farm inmates didn't make it out into the fields too often. Mostly, Allen Iverson drew kitchen detail, where he worked in the prison's bakery.

When he did get to go outside, he'd see them. His boys. There they'd be, on the other side of that fence, keeping their almost daily vigil. There was Ra and Arnie and Marlon and E, all the guys who, in his absence, were looking out for Ann and Ieisha and Brandy. When bills needed to get paid—those guys did it, no matter how they had to come up with the cash. Oftentimes, his teammates would be out there, too, trying to catch a glimpse, show their support. But he tried to keep his back to them and never made eye contact, not once. Oh, he wanted to; he wanted to break down, to show how much it meant to him, their presence and their tributes—he'd heard that his teammates were traveling to away games with his empty uniform. But he didn't want anyone to see him like this, caged.

There was no cell block at the City Farm. Iverson lived in a dorm with fifteen other kitchen workers. The younger guys in the prison population were the rowdy ones. They were the ones eager to test this new inmate, the star. But the older guys were guys like Michael Freeman, and they took the infamous inmate under their wing. Iverson was used to having older mentors on the streets: Gary Moore, Tony Clark, Jamil Blackmon, even Arnie Steele. At City Farm, the older guys walked with Iverson to the cafeteria through the part of the prison called "The Jungle." That's where the younger, harder guys were, the guys who'd call things out to him, who talked about taking him on. But it was just talk—he knew that from Michael Freeman, who had counseled him to avoid making eye contact with those who would try to rattle him, to always keep walking.

Throughout his time at City Farm, Iverson was a model prisoner. He was up at 5 A.M. and off to the kitchen, where he'd work with the bakers, making bread, biscuits, and pastries. Then he got two hours for recreation. There was an old, broken-down basketball rim and a deflated ball. "I'd worry about him playing basketball," recalls Billy Payne, the City Farm's warden at the time. "Those boys played rough." Eventually, Iverson started playing one-on-one with a former Iowa football player, in the dark after long days in the bakery.

But Iverson was depressed at first. He didn't comb or wash his hair, stopped ironing his clothes. And then Ann came to visit. All she had to do was say one thing: "Baby, it hurts me to see you like this. You gotta stay strong, for me," she pleaded, and he started taking care of himself, started reminding himself every night that he wouldn't give in or give up. People were depending on him.

On weekends, when she could get a ride or otherwise scrounge up money to make the twenty-minute trip by car or bus to the Farm, Ann would bring Brandy and Ieisha. Often, others on Allen's visitors list would also converge. Tawanna would always be there, as would the Baileys. When the weather was nice that fall, they'd all sit outside, Tawanna and Allen huddled together on a bench, holding hands. She was pretty, a light-skinned girl with delicate features who seemed shy and unassuming. But she was strong—"To this day, she's in charge," says Janet Bailey affectionately—and fiercely devoted to the boy who had taken her to his prom. "He was no Don Juan in high school," Mike Bailey recalls.

Now that her boyfriend was incarcerated, even she was experiencing some of the backlash fanning out across the region. Tawanna's own mother, according to Blackmon, gave her a hard time about standing by her man, arguing that he'd "never amount to nothing." Still, she was there, every visiting day. The Baileys heard the same kind of sentiments. One fellow teacher asked Mike Bailey, "Why are you doing so much for him? Don't you know he's just a ghetto kid?"

Another visitor around this time was Larry Woodward, a lawyer in the prestigious local firm of Shuttleworth, Rudolf and Giordano. Woody, as he was known, would be handling Allen's appeal. His firm's senior partner, Tom Shuttleworth, was politically connected. The walls of Shuttleworth's Virginia Beach office were filled with photos of him beside the likes of Colin Powell, former president George Bush, and democratic strategist James Carville. Together, he and Woodward began lobbying then Virginia governor Douglas Wilder—the first and only African-American governor in the nation—to grant their new client clemency. They were joined by Bruce Hornsby, who happened to be a longtime friend of Wilder's chief of staff.

Meantime, tutor Sue Lambiotte couldn't shake the idea of this promising youngster, with all his mental energy and artistic talent, languishing in prison. She hated to think that all those naysayers were right, like the one teacher who predicted, when Iverson was sixteen, that "he will never play a day of college ball." Her husband, Butch, was friendly with City Farm manager Billy Payne. Through Payne, they set up once-a-week tutoring sessions with Allen in a room smaller than her closet at home. They started out working on basic math and English skills.

An agreement was reached with the Richard Milburn High School, a private, alternative school for troubled students, to oversee Iverson's remaining high-school course work. Milburn was costly, however; among those chipping in to foot the bill for Iverson were Hornsby, Spike Lee (who had been sending Iverson books on Malcolm X while in jail), Bill Cosby, and Michael Jordan. Once the tuition was paid, Lambiotte and Iverson began working on math and sociology, the first of the six classes he needed to complete his senior year.

And then, in December, two things happened. Ann went on a pilgrimage to Georgetown's John Thompson, making a heartfelt plea on behalf of her son. And Woody came through. It was only fitting, after all the racial division, that the nation's only African-American governor was coming to Iverson's rescue.

FEAR

A screaming skull with a red lin

FEAR NO ONE. That's me, m

catch me looking like this

They were only four simple words, but they were said with so much conviction, so much raspy emotion, that they closed the sale. Ann Iverson looked directly at John Thompson and said, simply, "Please help my baby."

They were in Thompson's office on the campus of Georgetown University. Just outside the closed door sat Jamil Blackmon, Butch Harper, and Boo Williams, the catalyst for the meeting. Blackmon and Harper were nervous; Williams, given his long association with Thompson, was more confident that, after Ann and Thompson emerged and they all piled into their rented van to head back to Newport News, there'd be some celebrating going on.

As November had given way to December, Woody's reports of a possible clemency deal grew more and more optimistic. With the looming possibility of Iverson's release, Williams started shopping him to prominent basketball programs across the country.

There were not a lot of takers. All those coaches who had salivated over the eleventh-grade phenom were unwilling to consider offering a scholarship now that he was a convicted felon; the PR risk was too great. "It's too racial and too controversial," one well-known coach said. Williams quickly surmised that he needed to target coaches who had enough clout within their university to, in his words, "get the kid past their presidents." Two names came to Williams's mind: Georgetown's Thompson and Temple University's John Chaney, both champions, and taskmasters, of the disadvantaged black athlete.

Williams called Thompson first and found the baritone-voiced bear of a coach well schooled in the particulars of Iverson's case. Thompson, Williams thought, would be just what Iverson needed. Throughout his illustrious coaching career, Thompson had been a protector and loyal champion of his players, often deflecting scrutiny from the likes of Patrick Ewing and Alonzo Mourning by strategically steering controversy *his* way.

Williams had known Thompson for years, ever since their mutual friend Sonny Vaccaro had helped build Nike into the sneaker company of all sneaker companies back in the early eighties. Nike sponsored Williams's summer program, just as it did Thompson's team. In fact, Thompson sat on Nike's board of directors, and there were those who felt that the sneaker company was a silent partner in Mourning's Georgetown recruitment, given that it was the common denominator between Thompson, Williams, and Vaccaro (who happened to be in Hampton the weekend that Mourning ended the suspense and committed to Thompson).

Additionally, Williams knew Thompson was street-smart, a big plus when dealing with Iverson. Thompson had once confronted a drug dealer who had gotten a little too close to Mourning for his liking. He'd coached and, when he needed to, jettisoned his share of players with rap sheets, like 1984's Michael Graham, he of the menacing shaved head, long before it was in vogue. Thompson simply wouldn't be played. Which signaled to Williams that if Thompson had come under criticism in the past for seeming absurdly overprotective of his more renegade players, he was also quite capable, if need be, of kicking Iverson's behind with his size fifteens.

Thompson, for his part, told Williams he'd only consider taking on Iverson if Ann personally asked him to. So Ann made the call, and here she was, making her pitch, despite Allen's own misgivings about Thompson. At the time, Iverson's friend and high-school rival Joe Smith was starring at the University of Maryland; that's where Iverson wanted to be, with Joe, doing it Newport News–style in the acclaimed Atlantic Coast Conference. Thompson, six feet ten inches himself, onetime backup to Bill Russell, had produced Ewing, Mourning, and Dikembe Mutombo, and his current team featured Othella Harrington. He was a big man's coach, Iverson argued, and a control freak to boot. He ran a heavily choreographed offense and had never given a point guard the freedom to improvise—a skill that was at the heart of Iverson's game.

Beggars couldn't be choosers, Williams responded. Even though his program had had some down years of late, Thompson was one of the few coaches with enough power at his own university to get Iverson a scholarship. Besides, Williams pointed out, Thompson knew the game. Once he saw what Iverson was capable of, he'd be foolish not to let him run. And John Thompson was anything but foolish.

Thompson was intrigued by Iverson, who was probably the most talented guard he'd ever have the chance to coach. Just as significant, he was touched by Ann's plea. "I saw the love of a mother for her son," Thompson would later recall. They hugged; Ann beamed as she strode from Thompson's office, arm in arm with the behemoth coach. Thompson outlined for Williams and the others the game plan: if Iverson was released, he pledged to send his academic coordinator, Mary Fenlon, to the Peninsula in a few months to check on the progress being made with Sue

Lambiotte. If Fenlon reported back that Iverson could do college-level work and if he scored over 700 on the SATs, he'd become a Georgetown Hoya.

Just as Williams had predicted, the ride back home was a blast. Ann turned up the volume when Sister Sledge started sermonizing that "We Are Family," and Ann started shimmying right there in her seat, throwing in the occasional thanks heavenward between the bumps and grinds. She'd never lost the faith. And now she was surer than ever. God was still looking out for her and her baby.

O h, my goodness!"
    Ann Iverson's shriek could be heard from the sidewalk outside 3710 Victoria Boulevard when the car pulled up. She swung open her front door and there, just beyond the phalanx of TV cameras and newspaper reporters, was Woody and Tom Shuttleworth getting out of the car, and then, finally, Ann's smiling baby. There he was, free after three and a half months in jail, wearing a green-and-gold sweatshirt—the Bethel team colors.

It was Thursday, December 30, and Ann Iverson had gotten her Christmas present five days late, when Governor Doug Wilder ordered Iverson released. In what even a Wilder aide described as an "extraordinary" move, the governor had become convinced that Iverson had been treated unfairly. "While there is not sufficient evidence at the present time for me to grant the extraordinary relief inherent in a traditional pardon, there is sufficient doubt to merit that Allen Iverson be granted limited freedom and the opportunity to continue his education," Wilder said in a statement released by his office. A source in Wilder's office, the *Daily Press* reported, said that Iverson wrote a letter to Wilder in which he admitted wrongdoing and asked for a second chance. Wilder granted his wish, but attached conditions to the clemency. Iverson would have to complete his high-school studies, not play organized sports (the better to focus on academics), and abide by a curfew (10:30 on weeknights, midnight on weekends).

When she heard the news, SWIS's Joyce Hobson was in the car, fifteen minutes from home. "I screamed the whole way home," she breathlessly told the *Daily Press.* Like Hobson, an entire community breathed a sigh of relief. But another clenched a collective fist.

At the time he released Iverson, Doug Wilder was one of more than eight thousand African-American elected officials in local, state, and federal government throughout the United States. That number was up from fewer than three hundred twenty-five years earlier. In reality, much of that upsurge took place in the nine years after Jesse Jackson's first run for the presidency, in 1984. Another boost came following Jackson's subsequent run in 1988, when he garnered 7 million votes in the Democratic primary and gave birth to a generation of black officeholders.

Doug Wilder was part of that movement. But, as with any movement, it had its backlash, as could be seen in the aftermath of the Iverson clemency, when many whites cried foul. How predictable, they complained: a black governor bails out a black criminal. The *Daily Press* editorialized that "those who believe Iverson was treated appropriately by the criminal justice system—and that includes us—may wonder about the governor's motives." An accompanying news story suggested that Wilder, preparing to challenge Senator Chuck Robb in a statewide primary, was trying to "bolster his support in the black community." (At the time, most political observers believed Wilder needed to demonstrate an ability to cut into Robb's white support, so it was unclear how granting clemency to a convicted black celebrity could be politically beneficial.)

Sue Lambiotte found herself living in the midst of the backlash every day. Allen, now free, would begin his studies with her, six hours a day on Mondays and Thursdays and four on Tuesday, Wednesdays, and Fridays, at her Kumon Math and Reading Center. She opened the center in 1992, providing individualized instruction for students (often athletes) from kindergarten to college. Allen's work would technically be completed under the auspices of the Milburn School, but Lambiotte was in charge of the one-on-one instruction at her center, which was located, ironically, in well-to-do, lily-white Poquoson, where anti-Iverson sentiment reigned. More than once, working late, she'd receive threatening phone calls, with a voice telling her, "Your center isn't going to be there tomorrow," or calling her the most vile of names. She'd call her husband, Butch, and he'd come get her. But the next morning, she'd be back at the center, preparing for the moment when Bubba came striding in, invariably late, often with half-finished homework, but there nonetheless, ready to work.

K nowing when, in Sue Lambiotte's words, to "drop the hammer" is the toughest part of being a teacher. How forgiving of a student's failings ought you to be? Where is the line between discipline and granting opportunity? When does being a teacher morph into being a co-conspirator in a student's spree of irresponsibility?

Lambiotte, a tall, regal, patient woman with the singsong voice of a Southern belle, wrestled with all these questions during the frantic ten-month period, beginning in December 1993, that she worked with Allen Iverson. Actually, as she will tell you, "wrestled" is too weak a word; it was, she says, her central agony those months, when she'd lie awake at night and wonder whether she was doing the right thing for the student she had called Bubba ever since that trip to Kansas with Boo's team some seven years earlier. As a tutor to athletes, she'd heard the rap for years. Not only that they're coddled and irresponsible, but that they've been surrounded by an enabling crew of academics, tutors, teachers, principals, and universities who, bit by bit, sacrifice classroom standards because a kid can run or jump or shoot a ball. In the long run, no service was done to such students, she knew. Maybe if they were made to pay the price early, they'd become better citizens down the line.

From the start, Sue Lambiotte had a different definition of "success" for Allen Iverson than many of those surrounding the phenom. For them, succeeding meant the riches of the NBA. For her, it meant college. They would talk about his talent, and it was clear they were referencing his blinding speed and on-court moves. When Lambiotte discussed his talent, she was talking of his artistic flair or his critical-thinking skills, the way he'd vociferously argue a unique point of view when he became passionate about an issue. "What a tragedy it would be if this boy never got to college," she'd tell Butch.

But riling Iverson to passion—there was the rub. Iverson would come to the center, sit down to work, and his cell phone would ring. He'd answer and start chatting.

"Bubba!" Lambiotte would screech.

"Oh, yeah, sorry," he'd say, hanging up.

Other times, he'd sit there, impassive. "Bubba!" she'd prod him. "I know you're thinking something in there. Just say it!"

She searched for ways to reach him. She and Butch took him to a museum, but he lost interest halfway through. How to engage him? Bubba had told her once that he cut all those classes in high school because it was just so boring, the same routine, day after day. At the City Farm, he loved working in the kitchen—at least that was action, banging those pots and pans together. This was worse; forced to sit in a classroom each day felt more constricting than actually being in prison.

Lambiotte decided she had to tailor the curriculum to her student's particular quirks. She divided her lesson plan up into fifteen-minute units, so Allen's attention was never in danger of waning. They'd spend fifteen minutes working on, say, his paper on Malcolm X (three rewrites until he wove his own analysis throughout the biographical information), the next fifteen on a geometric proof, and, finally, fifteen on artwork—as a reward. When he was engaged, Lambiotte rarely had a better or more insightful student, as when, for sociology, he wrote a paper creating an entire civilization. In his dreamworld, it turns out, women did most of the work—the men occasionally hunted for food, but mostly they'd lovingly play with the children.

Still, there were mornings he would arrive at the center having completed only two of the previous night's five homework assignments. When she'd express her disappointment, he'd say, "But, Mrs. Lambiotte, look how much I *did* do!" To him, she realized, he was working harder at school than ever. Lambiotte begged Ann not to let Allen out of the house until he completed his homework each night, but it didn't often work out that way. One of his buddies would come around and off Bubba would go.

"Mrs. Lambiotte, I think I have trouble saying no to some of the guys," Allen would say. Lambiotte arranged for a teacher to work on SAT preparation with him, and in one exercise, Allen was called on to match human character traits to different animals. He scanned the list of animals and smiled. "I'm a beaver—the one who is always jumping around, tail flapping, here, there," he said. "I'm just like that. So's my mom, which is why we fight so much."

Despite such moments of self-awareness, Iverson was disengaged more often than not. At one point, Lambiotte had had enough. Bubba hadn't shown up again and she decided to quit. But, still, she had doubts. Was this the time to drop the hammer? She decided she needed to seek the advice of someone more experienced in dealing with disadvantaged black athletes. She called John Thompson and told him she was ready to throw in the towel.

"As you know, I'm a spokesman for the disadvantaged young black man," Thompson told her after hearing her frustrations. "And I believe that, for the group, special considerations ought to be made, like with the culturally biased SAT. But in individual cases, I'm all for holding kids to standards. If he's not dotting his *i*'s and crossing his *t*'s, and if you feel you've done all you can do, if your best judgment is to cut him loose, I support you in that."

Lambiotte had half expected to hear a plea on Allen's behalf from his prospective coach: how this may be the youngster's last chance, how he has had it pretty hard growing up. Allen, after all, may have represented Thompson's coaching future at the time. Instead, she got a high-minded dose of empathy from him, one educator to another. With Thompson feeling her pain, she decided to stick it out with Allen. Her son, Clay, laughed when she recounted her conversation with the coach and her subsequent decision not to resign. "Mom, you are so gullible," he said. "He played you like a violin!" To this day, Sue Lambiotte wonders if she was manipulated by the wily, street-smart coach. If so, she's thankful for it.

As Thompson promised, Georgetown academic adviser Mary Fenlon visited the center. Lambiotte laid out on a big conference table all of Allen's work, and Fenlon spent twenty minutes going over each assignment, showing no reaction. Finally, her eyes peered up over her Ben Franklin glasses and she uttered the phrase that Sue Lambiotte needed to hear. "I think we have a diamond in the rough here," Fenlon said.

Life at Victoria Boulevard was getting harder and harder. Michael Freeman was in and out of jail. When he was around, his drug dealing wasn't making ends meet. Allen once saw him collapse into a chair at the kitchen table after a hard day at the "office," his shoulders slumped as though life itself had left his body. He dropped his head into his hands and began sobbing.

One day Allen showed up late to study with Lambiotte. There was nothing new in that; on this day, though, he was also dressed better than usual, in pressed pants and a button-down shirt. He'd just come from the courthouse, where Freeman had had yet another hearing on drug charges. Freeman was heading back to jail, but, Allen told his teacher, they spoke before the man he called Dad was taken away.

"You're the man now," Freeman told him. "You've got to take care of your mother and sisters."

To Allen, it was a challenge to start earning some money. Lambiotte didn't have to ask how. They'd been over this territory before, she and

Allen. They were constantly arguing over Allen's view that, if you're making money for your family and the only way you can do it is by selling drugs, then that's what you do. It's a sacrifice he saw Michael Freeman make.

"Bubba," Lambiotte said. "What's wrong with working at McDonald's?"

"You can't raise no family working at McDonald's," he replied.

Still, Lambiotte echoed the advice Allen was hearing from all his friends—even the ones who dealt drugs. And it was advice, by all accounts, he followed. "Bubba," she said. "You looking for short-term money isn't a way to help your mother and sisters. The best thing you can do for them is to get this academic stuff done right, get to college, and build a future, for you and them."

Meantime, the sewer system under the house on Victoria Boulevard had structural flaws and the plumbing problems were worsening. The carpet had turned black and clumps of mold were sprouting up. The toxic smell gave everyone constant headaches. Finally, one day, Blackmon came over and couldn't bear the stench. Lifting his shirt to shield his nose, he took Juicy up on her longtime request. "Y'all can't live like this," he told the Iversons. "Come on and live with me."

So Ann, Allen, Brandy, and Ieisha squeezed into Blackmon's place in the Central Park apartment complex on Marcella Drive, where he had a three-bedroom with two roommates, Ellis and Scott. Sometimes, Ann would borrow one of their cars to run an errand and be gone for a matter of days. Allen's friends would come over and hang out: Arnie, Ra, Marlon, Gary Moore. "They'd sit around and talk ghetto shit," Blackmon recalls. "You know, bitches, weed, getting drunk. What else were they gonna talk about? Clinton's health-care plan?"

Iverson didn't go out much, because of the curfew and the fact that anywhere he went, there was likely to be some Iverson detractor looking to start something with him in order to scuttle his future, once and for all. He'd play pickup games at Bethel High after dinner; Coach Koz would usually be on the other team and Allen would blow by him like he wasn't even there. Often Tawanna would come by and they'd spend the night watching TV or catch an early movie. He saw *Pulp Fiction,* which catapulted onto his list of all-time great flicks, right up there with *Scarface* and *Dead Presidents.* The Samuel L. Jackson character was a particular favorite because here was the embodiment of cool. A *righteous* hit man, Bible in one hand, Glock in the other, doing what he had to do, administering his own brand of Justice.

It was in Blackmon's laundry room that Iverson started fretting about developing a basketball persona. He was hoping to make it to the legendary Rucker Park at 155th Street in Harlem sometime that summer. The best playground ballers in the country played there, street legends who, for one reason or another, hadn't made it in college or pro ball. They all had their own if-only stories, tales of how their talents got pulled off track, whether because of drugs, bad grades, or an inability to temper their wildly improvisational street games to the regimented style of organized basketball. Like other prodigies—Mike Tyson's encyclopedic knowledge of boxing history comes to mind—Allen was well versed in who was doing the craziest shit up in Harlem. They were showmen, guys with funny nicknames who would play to the crowd on sweltering summer nights, guys like "Half-Man, Half-Amazing," or "Skip to My Lou," a legendary ball handler.

"Man, I need a cool nickname," Iverson said while Blackmon folded laundry.

"Chuck, you're 'The Answer,'" Blackmon said. "'Cause you're the answer to all the NBA's woes."

"The Answer," Allen said, instantly brightening. "I like that."

Blackmon kept theorizing. "I mean, everybody's in love with Mike, everybody wants to be Mike," he said, referring to Jordan, who had left basketball to pursue a short-lived minor-league baseball career. "But Mike ain't around. So you're the answer, now."

As Blackmon talked, Iverson got more and more hyped, so much so that one of Blackmon's roommates gave him a lift over to the army-and-navy store in Yorktown, where he got his first tattoo—THE ANSWER—on his left biceps.

He didn't make it to the Rucker that summer. Instead, in early August, he orchestrated his own coming-out party. Georgetown was fielding a team in the Kenner Summer League, held at McDonough Gym on the university's campus. He was determined to play.

"Are you sure, Bubba?" Lambiotte asked. "It's been a year and a half since you've played organized ball. This summer league is comprised of college players and pros who are in shape. You may not have your legs to compete against them."

He smiled knowingly. "Mrs. Lambiotte, my team is going to win the championship."

Poor kid, Lambiotte thought. He's about to learn the hard way.

If word of Iverson's plan to play got out, Lambiotte and Boo Williams knew that the cozy gym confines would be packed and the media attention would be jarring. Allen didn't need that kind of pressure—especially when nobody knew how he was going to play. So they enlisted the help of a friend who had an old Dodge pickup, because no one would suspect that Allen Iverson was being driven around in a beat-up truck. And Lambiotte had friends in nearby Alexandria, so that's where Allen would spend the night.

On August 5, 1994, roughly 750 people were in the stands of the 2,400-seat gym. Iverson, playing with his future Georgetown teammate Jerome Williams, hit an early three-pointer. When the public-address announcer intoned, "Allen Iverson," a murmur swept the crowd. When, seconds later, Iverson stole a pass and outraced everyone down the court for a slam dunk, the murmur became bleacher-stomping applause. Throughout his career, Iverson had always thrived in dramatic moments of his own making; this was certainly one. He played the entire first half in one speed: overdrive. He scored 30 points in the half alone and added 10 more after halftime.

By the next night, word was out. Over three thousand people packed the gym. It was standing room only, but even those with obstructed views weren't disappointed. Just twenty-seven seconds into the game, Iverson threw down a windmill dunk. He hit his first seven shots, nailing back-to-back NBA three-pointers after his first dunk. On an inbounds play, he took off from just inside the foul line and caught an alley-oop pass high above the rim before slamming it down with a backboard-rattling jam. All eyes were on him, and he always seemed to be wherever the ball was, scoring 33 points, including 6 three-pointers.

The next night, he led his team onto the floor for the tournament championship. Outside, security guards turned fans away. Inside, some four thousand screaming fans, including his future NBA teammate Dikembe Mutombo, watched Iverson prove he was no fluke. He scored

To illustrate "propaganda" in social studies, an eighteen-year-old Iverson rendered how others were seeing him through portrayals in the media: the angel and the devil.

High school graduation day, 1994. In a class of one, Iverson was valedictorian.

26 points and his team won, 72–66. Just as he'd predicted to Sue Lambiotte, he led his team to the championship. "I think he's a great player," marveled Adonal Foyle, the opposing team's center who would go on to star at Colgate and later play for Golden State in the NBA.

As soon as the final buzzer went off, security swooped onto the court and hustled Iverson out a side exit. He wouldn't even get the chance to accept the championship trophy or his MVP award. Instead, he was rushed through the building's bowels, through a series of seemingly secret tunnels, and ushered outside, where the Dodge pickup waited. He was whisked away to avoid the media—Thompson prohibits his freshmen from giving interviews—and any would-be troublemakers. On the way back to Newport News, Lambiotte looked at him in wonder. How did he know? she asked herself. How did he know?

Even as she marveled at his athletic accomplishment, Lambiotte knew she couldn't let up on him. They were so close to completing his high-school studies. By the end of the summer, Iverson finished work on his last two courses: U.S. government and psychology. He'd taken the SAT and qualified to be eligible come the fall for his freshman year of basketball, and now he was about to seal the deal with a high-school diploma. Lambiotte had a cap and gown fitted for him and invited his family, friends, and the coordinator of the Wilburn School to her center for a graduation ceremony honoring the Class of '94, a class of one. The night before graduation, Lambiotte's son, Clay, said, "Have you thought about the fact that Allen is his class valedictorian?"

Lambiotte howled in laughter. Finally, revenge would be hers. After all the times he'd made her pull at her hair, tomorrow she'd spring on him, on the spot, that he was expected to make a valedictory speech.

When the time came, a shy but moved Allen Iverson spoke softly. "I just want everybody to know how much I appreciate what y'all did," he said, looking at Ann, his sisters, and his boys. "I know I didn't always make it easy, but I want all y'all to know how much this here means to me. And how I'm gonna make all y'all proud at Georgetown."

Seeing her pupil in his cap and gown, holding that piece of paper, Lambiotte finally felt relief. Now, she thought to herself, if he stumbles and breaks both ankles, at least he'll have exposure to good instruction and ideas; now I know his talent won't be wasted. Knowing Bubba was headed to Georgetown, Sue Lambiotte slept well that night.

chapter 6

THE BULLDOG

this was my second tattoo. i had the bulldog put on my arm when i decided to go to georgetown, where the mascot is a bulldog.

Among sports columnists, the *Washington Post*'s Thomas Boswell was an all-star. His pieces about the intricacies of baseball had already become legend by the time Allen Iverson was poised to debut as a collegiate basketball player. But baseball was not Boswell's only forte; he had also been a basketball lifer, having spent much of his career in shoe-box-size gyms just to check out the hype about *the* next phenom.

Boswell had seen can't-miss high-schoolers like Moses Malone, Alonzo Mourning, Ralph Sampson, and Patrick Ewing. He'd seen an eighth grader named Adrian Dantley who was already being targeted for the pros. He'd seen Lew Alcindor, a lanky scoring machine with unheard-of skills, well before he became a household name.

In early November of 1994, Boswell was sitting along press row at Georgetown's McDonough Auditorium prior to the Hoyas' exhibition game against the Fort Hood Tankers, an army-base squad of bruising, grown men. It was to be Allen Iverson's first appearance in a Georgetown uniform. When John Thompson's players took their places for the introductions, Boswell leaned over to then *Post* beat writer J. A. Adande. "Which one is Iverson?" he asked.

"The one on the end," Adande replied.

"You mean the little guy in the droopy shorts with the skinny legs?" Boswell asked.

"The first second he gets the ball, you'll know who he is."

Sure enough, on the first play, Boswell's jaw dropped. "My God," he said. "He's a blur."

Iverson soared and dazzled his way to 24 points in the first eight minutes. By halftime, he had 28 points and 4 assists in thirteen minutes. He hit jumpers, threw no-look passes, and drove to the basket, either making the shot or getting fouled. And he hit 16 of his 17 first-half free throws. He'd go on to total 36 points and 5 assists. "Now I have two memories on my first-impression top shelf," Boswell wrote the next day. "The man who became Kareem Abdul-Jabbar, and Allen Iverson. Ewing is third."

Late in the first half, Fort Hood center Brian Pitts, who stood six-eight and weighed 275 pounds, set a pick near midcourt on Iverson's blind side. Iverson ran full force into the behemoth, whose elbows had been up too high for Thompson's liking. Some in the crowd gasped; Iverson comically ricocheted off the ground, bouncing back up onto his feet. If he was shaken, he did a good job of shielding it, bursting into a big smile as Thompson came charging onto the court.

"Don't hurt my boy!" the coach screamed at Pitts, restrained by the refs. "You can't take him out like that!"

It was confirmation that Thompson knew just what he had in Iverson. And it was a foreshadowing of the lengths to which Thompson would go in order to give Iverson the sense that his coach was in his corner— unconditionally. The first time Thompson had met Iverson, they spoke about the bowling-alley incident. Thompson was characteristically blunt. "If you think I'm going to pass judgment on the judge and tell you how terrible the judicial system is, you're crazy," the coach said.

But, Thompson said, sitting in judgment of Iverson was the judge's job—not Thompson's. "I'm not blaming you," he said. "There's a difference between understanding how something can happen and condoning it. All of us have done something at sixteen or seventeen that we're glad we weren't caught doing."

It was straight talk that, in effect, said to Iverson: *When you screw up, I understand, because I've been there. But that doesn't mean I'm not going to demand better from you.*

Thompson's teams had long had a tough, rebellious image; Georgetown jerseys in the 1980s had become a staple of inner-city style. But Thompson was known as a disciplinarian. When Iverson showed up for college wearing an earring, Thompson told him to remove it. His players were prohibited from wearing big gold chains and from experimenting with wild hairstyles. They were required to dress in a suit and tie when traveling to and from games.

"A man that's in college that doesn't have a suit has no projection for his future," Thompson would later say, when asked about his dress-code rules. "Don't tell me the poverty story. You can go to Goodwill and get a suit. But you need to own a suit if you expect to run something, if you expect to own something, if you expect to administer something. That's my responsibility as a teacher."

Thompson taught by bellowing, but also through humor. Later, Iverson would regale others with stories of how the bulky coach, in attempting to prod his big men to move their feet on defense, might serve up an example of light-footedness by breaking into a jig or two-step, with a sly

"I know I look like a fool" smile on his lips. Then there was the way Thompson would feign anger before affectionately playing off Iverson's reputation. "Iverson, you little shit!" he'd bellow throughout the gym, silencing the team, before breaking into a smile and putting his arm around his point guard. "I've had some criminals in my time, but you take the cake." Iverson and his teammates would laugh at Thompson's ribbing.

On the court, as Boo Williams had predicted, Iverson had no reason to worry about Thompson restricting his style of play. Thompson told his prized recruit from day one that he was granting him unprecedented freedom. The ball would be in his hands and he would be off to the races. Thompson's great teams of the past had played a scrambling, pressing defense. Their offenses, however, tended to be plodding and dull and there were those who wondered if the times hadn't passed Thompson by. The previous year's team, after all, was a merely respectable 19–12. Thompson hadn't been to a Final Four since Ewing's time, in 1985. He had even been unable to take his team that far when Alonzo Mourning and Dikembe Mutombo played together on the same Hoyas team.

This year's team, Thompson said, would break from the past. "Georgetown will run this year for one reason: Allen Iverson," he said. Of course, the new style was, first and foremost, a basketball decision. But Thompson also took into account Iverson's needs psychologically. Here was someone who had already been denied his freedom. "Think about what's happened in that child's life," Thompson explained. "The last thing he needs is structure. He needs to be free as a bird. He needs to fly."

Almost half of the 1994–95 Hoyas were freshmen or transfers. Three starters returned from the previous year, including center Othella Harrington, who had scored a team-high 14.7 points and grabbed a team-high 8 rebounds per game. Also back were senior forward Don Reid, who would be Iverson's roommate and a steadying force, and senior guard George Butler, whom Thompson would kick off the team at midseason for academic reasons. Transfer six-foot nine-inch forward Jerome Williams was expected to contribute as well.

The season began with a daunting challenge. In the inaugural Martin Luther King Jr. Classic Tournament in Memphis, they faced the defending national champion Arkansas Razorbacks, led by Corliss Williamson— no stranger to Iverson, thanks to their AAU days. Come game time,

Thompson's new up-tempo style played right into the hands of Arkansas's experienced, athletic team. Iverson, who had scored 39 points in Georgetown's second exhibition game, was held to just 19 points on 5-for-18 shooting. He played out of control at times, committing eight turnovers. But he showed a dogged spirit, continuing to drive the ball to the basket, his moves often drawing gasps from the crowd. After the 97–79 drubbing, Nolan Richardson was a believer despite Iverson's mediocre statistics.

"I've never seen anything like that," the coach said. "I've seen three calf shows, nine horse ropings—I even saw Elvis once. But I've never seen a guard do what he can do with the basketball. I saw him go through traps of ours nobody's ever gone through. He's awesome. Wait till he starts playing. He's always on the attack. That boy's going to make that team so good it'll be unreal."

Richardson's words were prescient. The Hoyas started winning and Iverson's twisting, acrobatic shots started falling. In early December, he scored 30 points in a win over Providence College, becoming just the second player under Thompson to ever score 30 or more points in back-to-back games. The Hoyas were soon 7–1 and ranked twelfth in the nation, and Iverson was averaging 21.5 points per game.

But Iverson's scoring—and Thompson's toleration of his star's shooting—was having an adverse effect on Othella Harrington. In his career, the big man was nearly a 16-points-per-game scorer. So far, he was barely getting five shots a game and averaging just over a third of his career numbers. But the team was winning, in part because Iverson couldn't be stopped.

Meantime, media fascination with Iverson rose to new heights. As he did with all freshman, Thompson prohibited his star from giving interviews in his first semester at school. Come January, however, and owing to an overwhelming number of press inquiries, Thompson stood by Iverson's side one day at practice and allowed the player to answer basketball-only questions. Media outlets from all over the East Coast descended on the pair.

"I talked to Coach before I came here and he told me he was going to let me play my game, let me run up and down the court, and he's done that," Iverson said. "I don't feel like I'm playing like I want to right now, but I'm learning. A lot of times, I get caught up in the hype in a game, and I get out of control sometimes. That's the thing Coach tells me the most about, patience."

"Have you been impressed by Allen, Coach?" asked one writer.

Though Thompson looked at his questioner upon replying, the response seemed aimed at Iverson—as a coded reassurance that the coach had the player's best interests at heart. "If you've been in this business for a while, you're not here to be impressed with people," Thompson said. "You're here to attempt to help mold them and get them prepared for the next stage of their life. That's what education is about. Allen has done what I've asked him to do, and when he has not done it, we've sat down and talked about it, and that hasn't been frequently at all. He's been extremely easy to work with."

By late January, the Hoyas were ranked tenth in the nation with only two losses, to then number-one-ranked Arkansas and number-two-rated Connecticut. Iverson made his first trip to his future home, to face Villanova in Philadelphia's Spectrum. The Villanova Wildcats upset the Hoyas, 66–60, in large part because Iverson could only play ten minutes on a sprained ankle. But Thompson was more upset by the reception his star had gotten than by the score.

The Philadelphia crowd rode Iverson all night long. One sign called Georgetown CONVICT U. Another read: IVERSON: THE NEXT JORDAN, only JORDAN was crossed out and O.J. written above it. "I will not continue to play under these circumstances," Thompson told Villanova officials. "I am not letting that child play in that atmosphere."

Security guards confiscated the signs, though the catcalling continued, which was nothing new—it was just louder in Philly. In Pittsburgh, a singsong "jailbird" chant started when Iverson was on the line; when he sank a free throw, quieting his taunters, he looked right at the student section and smiled.

Though the Hoyas dropped the game to Villanova, Harrington broke out of his doldrums, scoring 21 points and grabbing 11 rebounds. Of course, his inspired play—largely in the injured Iverson's absence—fueled doubts about Iverson's game that would linger for some time in the pros as well. Yes, he was a great scorer, the thinking went. But will he ever slow down long enough to accommodate a teammate? Could others flourish alongside him? Or, in the interest of his creative pursuits, were others stifled?

Off the court, Iverson took to college life, though his past was never far away. In fact, the day before leaving for Georgetown, he visited

Freeman in the Hampton city jail, where his stepfather was once again incarcerated. "I'm going to leave after two years and go pro and take care of you," Iverson promised.

At school, in the dorm room he shared with Don Reid, Iverson plastered the walls with clippings chronicling his high-school championships and with photos of Method Man, Redman, and the rest of the Wu-Tang Clan. Wu-Tang was, after all, an inspiration. Here were guys who had hung out back in the day all making it—together. Iverson was, in his mind, authoring the same kind of script for Cru Thik. At the dawn of the school year, however, the future of Cru Thik seemed imperiled when "E" was arrested and charged with maiming in a shooting death that occurred during the summer when a stray bullet killed a Newport News woman. A shaken Iverson went off to Georgetown worried for his friend. He'd finally gotten *his* freedom—and now "E" was going to have to go away? Early in Iverson's first semester, though, the charges against "E" were dropped after witnesses refused to testify against him.

From then on, "E" joined Arnie, Ra, and some of the others who always seemed to be down in Washington. On weekends, Blackmon would come to town. Once or twice, Michael Jackson—Thrilla—visited.

"You need anything?" Iverson would ask Jackson, who was attending Hampton University.

"Man, you're a college student just like I'm a college student—how you gonna take care of me?" Jackson would say.

Iverson had access to an apartment in Bethesda, Maryland. It belonged to some friends of David Falk, Thompson's agent. The Cru Thik members would often stay in Bethesda and mess around in the apartment's recording studio. Meantime, tension developed among those around Iverson. Blackmon started referring to himself as "Mr. Cellophane," because he felt he was being looked right through. When Arnie was around, 'Chuck wouldn't give Blackmon the time of day. Still, Blackmon hired a tutor for Iverson (someone who Blackmon now claims wrote papers for Iverson). As Iverson quickly emerged as the most exciting college basketball player in the country, the jockeying for position around him intensified.

It's an old story, really. The late sportswriter Mark Kram, who covered Muhammad Ali in his prime, saw it in the sixties, the way those around Ali fought for his ear and his approval and his attention. "You always had to read the body language of the entourage to figure out who was up and who was down on a particular day," Kram once recalled. "They competed against one another."

Midway through his freshman year, Iverson became a father when Tawanna gave birth to Tiaura. Tawanna was back in Hampton, living with her mother, taking care of the baby. Allen would visit when he could, often showing up outside Michael Jackson's window at two in the morning after an evening at home with Tawanna and the baby. He'd throw rocks at Jackson's window until his friend would come downstairs and they'd sit on a curb and talk into the wee hours.

Around the same time Tiaura was born, Iverson had contact with his biological father for the first time since he was an infant. When Iverson had been arrested at seventeen, Allen Broughton saw his son, all grown now, on TV, handcuffed and being led off to jail. He tracked Ann down through NBC, which had aired the story he'd seen. The TV station passed his number along to Woody, who gave it to Ann. She called her ex-boyfriend, who asked if there was anything he could do. No, she told him, the lawyers were handling it. But the two kept in touch, and when Allen went off to Georgetown, Broughton said he wanted to have a relationship with his son.

"You can't go to him like he's a kid," she warned. "He been through a lot. So when you talk to him, talk to him correctly. Be straight up." She gave Broughton her son's phone number in the dorm.

All told, the two men had about ten phone conversations; the stilted tone of the first call never really abated. "How are you doing?" Broughton asked.

"Fine."

"Are you upset with me about the past?" Broughton asked.

"My ma told me it was hard back then."

"I wish I could have been there for you."

"It's no problem."

Broughton had read the interviews about how Allen called Michael Freeman Daddy. That didn't bother him so much as the parts where Allen credited Freeman for teaching him basketball. Well, he may have taught Allen to play ball, but, Broughton thought, everything Allen did on the court came from my genes. After all, Allen Broughton had played ball all his life and everybody who grew up with him did double takes when they saw Iverson play, so similar was Iverson's style to Broughton's.

Iverson was always polite, but terse and resistant to Broughton's plans. Broughton targeted a series of dates to visit Georgetown, see a game, and meet his son, but Allen demurred every time. "I'm really busy," he said.

Broughton was still hoping to visit his son late in Allen's sophomore season when his girlfriend of ten years, Chrystal Owens, broke up with him. He told her she would not live to see her thirty-first birthday in four days. Two days later, while she was ironing her work uniform, Broughton, drunk, stabbed her six times, twice in the arm and four times in the stomach. He'd await trial for two years before being sentenced to nine years in prison in 1998. From jail, he has tried to send letters to Ann and to Allen, tried to convince them he's not after anything other than a relationship with his famous son, but to no avail. He hasn't heard from either of them since.

In mid-February, the Hoyas had another shot at the now number-one-ranked team in the country, Ray Allen's Connecticut Huskies. Georgetown was ahead by 8 points with nine minutes to go when Connecticut unveiled a pressing, trapping defense designed to discombobulate Iverson. Georgetown turned the ball over four times in five possessions, blew its lead, and lost the game, 91–85. Iverson notched 29 points, 8 rebounds, and 9 assists, along with a move that would go on his permanent highlight reel, a no-look hook shot while in traffic that kissed the glass and went in.

Despite the fact that Harrington and Iverson were still unable to have good games at the same time, Thompson was as tolerant as ever of his prodigy after the loss. "He's a child who gives you a bucket of milk and then kicks it all over you," Thompson said, smiling. The problem was that Iverson and Harrington played at vastly different speeds. Unlike Iverson, Harrington worked best in a patient, slow-down offense, with support players willing to work the ball inside to him. Often, by the time he'd set up underneath the basket, Iverson would already have launched a shot. "[Allen's] just starting to realize that fast is good, but not always fast," Thompson said. Shortly thereafter, in an upset over Syracuse, Iverson and Harrington played well together for the first time. Harrington had a season-high 27 points and Iverson scored 21, on 9-of-18 shooting—the first time he'd hit at least half his shots in six weeks. Iverson, shooting just below 40 percent on the season, wasn't a bad shooter. He just took too many wild shots, yet they were taken with Thompson's approval. The coach was not about to inhibit his star.

The Hoyas finished the regular season 18–8 and Iverson, who averaged 19.8 points per game in eighteen conference games and set a league record with 64 steals, was named Big East Rookie of the Year and Defensive Player of the Year. In his dorm, he received a phone call offering congratulations: "You may be beating up on those college boys, but what are you going to do about this forty-year-old piano player?" Bruce Hornsby asked.

In the NCAA Tournament, Thompson's team went to Tallahassee, Florida, to face Xavier in the Southeast Regional first round. The relationship between Thompson and Iverson had ebbed and flowed; Iverson had never received such tough love. Thompson often singled him out in front of the team, though usually using humor, not rage, to ride his star.

On the eve of the game against Xavier, though, the relationship between player and coach entered a new phase. Iverson was summoned to Coach's hotel room for a one-on-one meeting. Usually Coach didn't ask to see you mano-a-mano if you weren't in the doghouse. But Thompson had something else in mind.

"I want to let you know something I haven't told you all year," Thompson told his nervous star. "That I'm very proud of you. Regardless of what happens, I wanted to let you know that. I'm going to get on you and curse you out, but I'm proud of how you've handled yourself and the pressure you've withstood." Iverson stood in stunned silence for a moment, before shakily extending his hand.

"I think the kids are more comfortable with me when I'm fussing and yelling at them," Thompson said later, laughing as he recalled the moment. "He was probably thinking, 'What the hell's wrong with Coach? He's being nice to me today.'"

The Hoyas beat Xavier and advanced to the Sweet Sixteen round, where they ran up against Dean Smith's University of North Carolina Tar Heels. Led by Jerry Stackhouse and Rasheed Wallace, the Tar Heels were the favored team. The game was played in Birmingham, Alabama—not exactly Iverson country. But by game's end, Iverson would have the crowd on his side.

In the first half, it looked like the kid was all hype. He was nervous and sloppy; in one ten-second sequence, he badly missed three out-of-control shots in a row. He misfired on all six of his first-half attempts and Georgetown was down by as many as 16.

In the second half, though, Iverson battled back. Against Dean Smith's legendary defense, he cut loose for 21 points in fourteen minutes, bringing the Hoyas to within 4 points. Carolina withstood the furious charge, however, to win, 74–64. When Thompson took Iverson out, the crowd gave him a rousing ovation. These were not solely Georgetown fans; they were basketball fans, and they were cheering not only the eye-popping second-half performance they'd just seen (24 points, 8 rebounds), but also a stellar freshman season (20 points per game) and, perhaps, a year-long display of grace under pressure in the face of taunting crowds.

"Watch 'em next year, they ought to be something," Smith said after the game. "[Iverson] has his own solo fast break. Then he scores. He can really break a defense down."

It had been a draining season. And the off-season promised to be just as tumultuous. First, a three-judge panel of the Virginia Court of Appeals announced it was reversing Iverson's 1993 maiming-by-mob conviction and expunging his record. "Although the evidence would have been sufficient to prove individual assaultive conduct, it was insufficient to prove beyond a reasonable doubt that Iverson acted as part of a mob," the court wrote. "Iverson's confrontation with [accuser Steve] Forrest was an incident that may have precipitated a brawl, but was separate from any mob activity. No evidence proved that Iverson was a member of any mob that later formed."

When Thompson got the word, he placed two phone calls. The first was to Georgetown University president Reverend Leo O'Donovan. O'Donovan had withstood a lot of media criticism when he signed off on Iverson's enrollment. Thompson thanked him for "giving this young man an opportunity." Then he called Ann. "This is not a time to gloat," he told her. "This is a time to be happy. The important thing is for him to move on, put this behind him and do something successful with his life."

In August, Iverson went overseas for the first time in his life to compete in the World University Games. University of Illinois coach Lon Kruger took a team to Japan stockpiled with big names. Player of the Year candidate Tim Duncan of Wake Forest and Charles O'Bannon of the NCAA champion UCLA Bruins were on the team, as were Iverson's Big East rivals Kerry Kittles from Villanova and Ray Allen from UConn. The relationship between Allen and Iverson would go on to become cordial over the years, but it was anything but on this trip. Inside a hotel room, Iverson playfully threw some candy at Allen. Allen reacted too seriously for Iverson's liking: "You better stop or I'm gonna fuck you up," he said.

The battle of words escalated. Iverson ended up decking Allen right there, bloodying his teammate's nose. On the court, Iverson was just as combative, often dominating. He scored 21 points on 10-of-15 shooting to lead the U.S. team to a 105–81 quarterfinal win over Lithuania. In the gold medal game, he led all scorers with 26 points in a 141–81 rout over Japan.

By the time his sophomore year rolled around, Iverson knew his game had holes—and what he had to work on. As a freshman, he had shot a mere 39 percent from the floor and committed a turnover for every assist. "I have to be more patient," he acknowledged to friends and teammates. And he'd have to add some nuance to his game instead of just relying on overdrive all the time. Little did he know that the precise tweak his game needed would be provided by a walk-on teammate.

During warm-ups, Spike Lee stalked the Madison Square Garden floor, shooting footage through a camcorder. First he was focused on the shortest guy warming up on Georgetown's side. Then he zoomed in on the shortest guy at the other end of the floor. Lee's cinematic machinations were the first sign this would be a special night.

It was to be a much-hyped "heavyweight" battle in which both combatants weighed less than 170 pounds. It was the semifinals of the preseason National Invitational Tournament in late November 1995, and Iverson's 3–0 Georgetown Hoyas were facing the 2–0 Georgia Tech Yellow Jackets, led by freshman point-guard sensation Stephon Marbury. Marbury had been a high-school phenom on Coney Island. He'd even had a book written about him already, which chronicled his high-school hoops dream.

Less than three minutes into the game, Marbury had committed three turnovers. Though he used an assortment of spin moves and fakes to get by Iverson at times, Iverson was clearly the more experienced player. He scored 15 first-half points and 23 for the game, with 6 assists and 5 steals. Marbury ended up missing 10 of his 14 shots en route to 13 points, 8 assists, and 7 steals. The difference for Iverson was his new backcourt mate, freshman Victor Page, who scored 25 points.

After the game, Iverson talked about how he'd been working on improving his shot selection and patience. And he heaped praise on the player he would consider a rival for years to come. "He forced it a couple of times," Iverson said of Marbury. "That's just Stephon's heart. He has a big heart. He tries to do things for his teammates just like I did last year. I think it's incredible, his heart. He's a freshman, coming in with all of this notoriety, and he's backing it up."

The Hoyas would lose the NIT championship game to Arizona, despite 40 points from a battered and weary Iverson. Then the easy, early part of Georgetown's schedule kicked in, pushover games against lesser opponents. Wins over Rutgers and Duquesne followed. In a blowout win over St. Francis, Iverson soared over a six-ten forward to grab Page's missed foul shot as the ball caromed off the rim and, in one fierce motion, slam-dunked. A moment later, when he dove out-of-bounds for a loose ball, the hometown crowd gave him a standing ovation.

After beating DePaul to go 12–1, Georgetown became the nation's sixth-ranked team. This was largely due to the growth in Iverson's game. As awe-inspiring as he had been his freshman year, this season's version seemed far more developed. Through thirteen games, he was averaging 23 points, 6 assists, 4 rebounds, and 4 steals per game. Most impressive, his shooting had climbed to 53 percent. Thompson heaped the praise on. "We've never had anybody who's given more effort," the coach said. "In that respect, he reminds me of Ewing. Allen has gotten twenty stitches in his face this season diving for a loose ball—in practice."

Later, in the pros, Iverson wouldn't enjoy a reputation as a dedicated practice player. But at Georgetown, he often stayed after practice to play one-on-one against walk-on guard Dean Berry. Berry had known Iverson since the eighth grade, having played against him in AAU tournaments. Now, Iverson was clearly the better player, but one who, in Berry's estimation, got by on pure talent alone. He was so quick he never had to develop moves in order to get to the basket. He could just get there, period. But that would not be the case forever; as the level of competition rose, so, too, did the challenge to invent ways to succeed.

Berry, with his limited skills, had spent years developing his game. A cerebral player, he started studying tapes in the seventh grade of great ball handlers. Over and over again, he'd watch Tim Hardaway's crossover dribble, commonly referred to as the "UTEP Two-Step." (Hardaway, now starring for the NBA's Golden State Warriors, had gone to UTEP.) He watched Isiah Thomas's unique version of the same move. He saw John Stockton remove all the bells and whistles and confound opposing guards with it.

No matter the permutation, the crossover defied basic ball-handling tenets. Since biddy basketball, kids were taught to use the body as a shield between the ball and the defender when dribbling; this way, if a defender tried to steal the ball, he'd have to commit a foul. The crossover, on the other hand, put the ball directly in front of the defender; the ball handler, alternating the dribble between his left and right hands, would coax the defensive player into leaning one way and then change direction and dribble the other way—right in front of him. It was a risky move because the ball was exposed throughout.

Berry adopted facets of every crossover he studied. He mimicked the way Hardaway's crossover dribble barely came up off the floor, the way Hardaway stayed low to the ground. If a defender wanted to swipe the ball away, he couldn't reach it. From Thomas, Berry borrowed the quick cut. The crossover dribble needed to be fast and hard, because it accelerated the ball handler around the crossed-up, shaken defender.

The reason Iverson kept playing Berry after practice was that he couldn't stop Berry's crossover—even when he knew it was coming. He'd tell himself not to go for the fake, and he knew he was quicker than his teammate—the twelfth man on the team!—but then Berry would drop a cross on him and the next thing you knew, the walk-on was around him.

"Man," Iverson finally said, "you gotta show me that shit."

From then on, Berry taught his superstar teammate his favorite move. Iverson's deft feel for fakes combined with his natural speed soon made the move the most lethal Berry had ever seen. Iverson started adding his own in-your-face touches to it. He'd establish a rhythm to set up his man. First, he'd dribble in on the defender, the ball right out there in front of him, almost between the two men, tempting. He'd slowly move it from his left to right hand, real low, almost daring the defender to take a swipe. The defender, mildly hypnotized, would sync himself to Iverson's rhythm—lock himself into it. Then Iverson would raise up and take a high, shoulder-length dribble with his right hand; if the defender started to raise up out of his defensive crouch, too, Iverson would have him. In a flash, he'd take one hard, low dribble from right to left directly in front of his startled man; the high-to-low movement, combined with Iverson's preternatural burst of speed, had him around the defender and en route to the basket before recovery was possible.

Soon something started happening whenever Iverson crossed his man over. The crowd started buzzing and screaming and high-fiving, a reaction that, until now, had been reserved for the slam dunk. Fans started coming to games to see Iverson "break ankles" the way a previous generation of fans came to games hoping to see Michael Jordan soar through the air.

In late February, the Hoyas raised their record to 22–5 with an 81–60 upset over number three Connecticut and Ray Allen, whom many were touting as the collegiate player of the year. Iverson came out before the tip and motioned for the home crowd to get on its feet and make some noise. He scored 26 points and had 8 steals. Early in the second half, he dunked over Connecticut's Rudy Johnson; sitting courtside, NBA scouts Jerry West and Kevin McHale shook their heads, as though there were a chance their eyes had gotten it wrong.

By now, though still only a sophomore, Iverson had emerged as a team leader. He not only excited the hometown crowd, he got in his larger teammates' faces as well. And he led by example in practice—something he'd be criticized for not doing as a pro. At the end of every practice, Thompson had his team run length-of-the-floor sprints. At every practice he attended at Georgetown, Iverson never took a single sprint off, winning each one.

"I saw his leadership in our first game that year," remembers Berry. "It was against Colgate in the Preseason NIT. Early in the second half, he tried to dunk on Adonal Foyle and it was an ugly collision. He dislocated his shoulder and busted his nose. We didn't need him for the rest of this game, but he'd never hide behind an injury. He came back out. We knew it wasn't because the game was that important. We could handle Colgate. It was important for him to be there for his teammates."

Iverson's commitment in practice had everything to do with his rela-

In two seasons as a Georgetown Hoya, Iverson quickly became the most exciting college basketball player in the nation.

tionship with Thompson, Berry and others attest. "He was like the obedient son," Berry, now a Florida businessman, says today. "They were like father and son. Allen was never late for practice, because that would be disrespectful to Coach. I'm not saying they didn't have blowups. But Coach would never go to the media with that stuff; he'd come directly to us. Things never got out of the gym and that meant everything to Allen."

Thompson also tended to be indulgent of Iverson's class-clown tendencies, as opposed to coaches in Iverson's future, like Larry Brown, who would see his wisecracking as proof that the player wasn't taking the game "seriously." Thompson, on the other hand, seemed to derive great joy from Iverson's pen-and-paper caricatures of him with a giant stomach and even bigger head. Similarly, Iverson's teammates were amused when Iverson would sneak up behind a sleeping player on a plane and lean down, his mouth just behind the slumbering teammate's ear. He'd start doing his impression of a buzzing fly until his victim, half-asleep, started swiping at the air around his head.

In the regular season finale, Iverson scored 37 points to lead Georgetown over Villanova. The Georgetown students, much to Thompson's chagrin, pleaded with Iverson to remain in school after this season by chanting, "Two more years! Two more years!" Thompson had never had a player leave early for the NBA, and he doubted Iverson would. Still, he grew angry anytime the subject was raised.

During the game, television announcer Billy Packer called Iverson a "tough monkey." Eighteen minutes after the remark, Packer apologized for saying it, but stressed that "it had absolutely nothing to do with race." Both Iverson and Thompson said after the game that they were not offended by the remark. Jesse Jackson called for the network to take action against Packer, who responded by saying, "I only apologized [during the game] to those people who have those sensibilities . . . I'm not apologizing for what I said, because what I said has no implications in my mind whatsoever to do with Allen Iverson's race. Al Capone was a tough monkey. Mike Ditka was a tough monkey. I don't think of Allen Iverson as a black player. I think of Allen Iverson as a player."

As would happen often throughout his career, Iverson was front and center in a morality play that went beyond the basketball world. The *Washington Post*'s Courtland Milloy excoriated Packer's version of his own color blindness. "The sportscaster would have us believe that he is immune to what ails the rest of America," wrote Milloy. "Where police see black, where the courts see black, where the media see black, Packer sees . . . well, tough monkeys. His response reflects the arrogance and denial that are the cornerstones of racist thinking in America today."

Meantime, as the Big East Tournament got under way, Thompson sought to put an end to the rumors of Iverson's early departure from Georgetown. The constant media speculation about his plans, Thompson felt, amounted to attempts to "solicit" him to leave school. "Allen's not going anywhere unless I tell him it's time to go," the coach said. "Tomorrow, I may tell him it's time to go. If Allen Iverson leaves, it will be because I told him to go. Quote me on that."

In the Big East championship game, the Hoyas led UConn by 11 with five minutes to go. Iverson was in foul trouble and Ray Allen had missed fourteen shots in a row. Until the crushing game winner, that is—a bank shot that bounced around the rim and finally fell through the hoop with 13.6 seconds to play. Neither Iverson nor Allen played particularly well. But Allen redeemed his subpar performance with the clutch shot.

Iverson was devastated. In the locker room after the game, Thompson went to console his star. When Iverson looked up at him, the coach could see the tears welling up. Thompson realized it was the first time he'd seen Iverson cry—remarkable, really, given Iverson's past. "I don't know as a child if I would have been able to handle what he's handled," Thompson would later say.

Iverson spent that night and many others replaying in his own head the final sequence of events, including his own fallaway jumper at the buzzer that missed. It was hardly a consolation when Iverson, with averages of 24.7 points, 5 assists, 4 rebounds, and 3.5 steals per game, was named to the Associated Press all-American first team days later.

When the NCAA Tournament began, the 26–7 Hoyas were seeded second in the East Regional. Their first two games would be played in Richmond, Virginia, just an hour from Newport News. There was Ann, arriving at halftime, sitting courtside in her Georgetown number three jersey, holding a sign reading PLAY BALL, BABY! and MOMMY LOVES YOU!

Also in the stands was now former governor Douglas Wilder, who came specifically to see the player to whom he'd given a second chance. When Ann saw Wilder, she gasped and ran toward him. Wilder looked up, squinted at the signs in her hands and at the jersey (IVERSON'S MOM, it read), and before he could speak, she'd enveloped him in a bear hug.

During the tournament, Thompson continued trying to protect Iverson. When a reporter asked the player to talk about the "second chance" he'd received after the bowling-alley incident, Thompson stepped in. "No, he can't speak about that," he said. "He came to play basketball. He's a child. Have some sensitivity toward him. Do you want me to ask you about your personal life, your family, your children, your wife?"

The Hoyas beat Mississippi Valley State, New Mexico, and Texas Tech, even though Iverson was suddenly in a shooting slump. Finally it came down to an East Regional championship showdown between Georgetown and the University of Massachusetts. UMass manhandled Iverson and wore him down. After scoring 17 points in the first half, he hit only one of ten shots in the second. As usual, there was a highlight. After crossing over defensive specialist Carmelo Travieso, six-foot eleven-inch shot blocker Marcus Camby stood between Iverson and the basket. Iverson threw down a two-handed slam over Camby that seemed to stun the defensive player. But UMass outlasted the Hoyas, 86–62, ending Iverson's sophomore season. And, maybe, his collegiate career.

Would he stay or would he go? That was the question the moment the Hoyas were ousted from the NCAA Tournament. The conventional wisdom was that he should stay in school. The *Washington Post*'s Mike Wilbon wrote, "Don't do it . . . If you're going to hit 16 of 50 shots (32 percent) and register a total of six assists and seven turnovers in the two games against Texas Tech and UMass, then how are you ready to play point guard in the NBA? Don't believe the hype, Allen."

NBA director of scouting Marty Blake pronounced Iverson "not ready." In the years to follow, countless underclassmen would declare themselves eligible for the NBA draft. But in May of 1996, it was still a rarity.

While the debate raged, few knew that Iverson's decision had been made long ago. He'd even been driving a $130,000 S600 Mercedes-Benz since early April, courtesy of an auto dealer who was a Georgetown booster. The arrangement was not permitted under NCAA rules; had Iverson intended to remain eligible, he no doubt would have refused the car. But the truth was that Iverson had always planned to come out after two years, just as he had pledged to Michael Freeman that day in the Hampton city jail before he left for his freshman year.

Iverson's decision had been made, but others loomed. After the Massachusetts game, for instance, Iverson was consoled by Spike Lee, who was wearing an Iverson jersey. Lee had offered to be his agent; Thompson had offered the services of David Falk. Iverson soon sought the opinion of Freeman, who felt one couldn't go wrong aligning oneself with the man who made Jordan.

So it was on May 1 that Iverson, Ann Iverson, Thompson, and Falk sat at a podium to announce that Allen Iverson was heading for the NBA. "My family needs me right now," Iverson said in a voice hoarse with emotion. His four-year-old sister, Ieisha, he explained, still suffered from seizures and needed medical attention. His one-year-old daughter, Tiaura, needed financial support. "I didn't like the things going on back in Hampton with my mom and my sisters' living situation."

"I'm really grateful to Coach Thompson and his staff," said Ann Iverson. "They made my little boy a man."

Despite the doubters, Thompson expressed no reservations about Iverson's impact at the next level. After all, as good as his freshman year had been, he had improved dramatically as a sophomore. His scoring went from 20.4 to 25 points per game, his shooting accuracy from 39 to 48 percent, his three-point shooting from 23 to 37 percent. He had reined in his racehorse pace to accommodate teammates like Harrington. Every time he had set his mind to doing something on a basketball court, it had gotten done. No, Thompson had no worries about Iverson's ability to flourish in the NBA.

But there were other concerns. Iverson would be leaving the safe cocoon of Thompson's team. Thompson knew firsthand of the emotional challenges facing professional athletes. John Thompson wasn't concerned about the two hours a day when Allen Iverson would be expressing himself on a basketball court. "I'm worried as hell about the other twenty-two hours," he said.

chapter | 7

CRU THIK

cru thik is the name of my crew, the guys I grew up with.
that's also what we've called our rap group. I got CRU THIK
in four places because that's who I represent.

T hat is one crazy white dude," Allen Iverson said, staring at the TV screen. He was hanging at Uncle Stevie's place and they were watching the NBA draft lottery on TV. A thin white guy with close-cropped hair and a goatee was jumping up and down as a panel of NBA suits looked on in astonishment. The guy even hugged David Stern, the staid and venerated league commissioner. His energy seemed to leap off the screen and into Uncle Stevie's living room.

It was Allen Iverson's—and most of the nation's—first glimpse of Pat Croce, the new president and part owner of the Philadelphia 76ers. Prior to the live airing of the lottery, Croce and the other draft team representatives had been warned against making any public displays of enthusiasm during the telecast. But Croce—like Iverson, actually—was not a man whose self-expression would be easily squelched. Croce catapulted from his seat when his team won the lottery, and thus the rights to Iverson, and started high-fiving and hugging the stunned conservative older men whom he had just beaten out. Just days later, Commissioner Stern would affectionately call Croce "stark raving mad." Maybe so. But back in Uncle Stevie's living room, Iverson had looked at his new boss letting it all hang out and realized he was witnessing something genuine.

The ensuing marriage between Allen Iverson and the Philadelphia 76ers was, at least in the minds of Iverson and Croce, the union's two protagonists, nothing short of a cosmic convergence. Throughout Iverson's adolescence, the 76ers had been Michael Freeman's team and Allen had been raised on tales of the one-on-one exploits of Dr. J, World B. Free, and Andrew Toney. His grandmother had always told him that everything happens for a reason, and just as he stayed true to the aphorism when he was in jail, now he was convinced that a bigger plan for him was in motion. After all, Freeman was incarcerated as Allen finished his sophomore, and final, year of college and declared himself eligible for the NBA. It was as though, to Iverson, the Sixers picking him first overall redeemed all the sacrifices Freeman had made for him—including the sacrificing of his own freedom, time and again. That's why, in interview after interview leading up to draft night, Allen proclaimed his desire to be a Sixer. And that's why Philadelphia would be the only team he would visit and work out for prior to the draft.

Besides, it had to be more than just coincidence that the 76ers, long a league doormat, were setting out to turn things around, just as he'd turned things around in his own life. They had a new arena, new management, and—perhaps most important of all—new ownership.

The public face of that ownership was the ebullient, charismatic Croce, whose ascent in Philadelphia was well known. At forty-one, he was the town's preeminent rags-to-riches story. A street kid from a white, working-class part of Philly, Croce spent his adolescence partying and raising hell in local taprooms. Like Iverson, he was tattooed, sporting a colorful pirate ship on his left forearm. Like Iverson, he cultivated an outer toughness that in part compensated for a thin, wiry build. A black belt in karate, he had been tossed from his first college for hospitalizing his dorm's resident adviser.

As the eighties dawned, Croce went back to school to study athletic training and physical therapy and was among the first to anticipate the nation's oncoming fitness craze—or, rather, its consequences. People, he realized, were going to start hurting themselves. He became trainer to the Philadelphia business elite. In the basement of a ritzy Main Line mansion, he taught karate to a college kid named Jay Snider. Snider's father, Ed, owned the local hockey team, the Philadelphia Flyers.

In that house, he first heard the word "entrepreneur" and realized that that was what he wanted to be. "He was just always around, watching and asking questions," Ed Snider recalls. "The kid had a lot of moxie. You had to like him instantaneously."

The senior Snider began dispatching Croce to soothe the body aches of his friends and colleagues, among them Chuck Barris, host and creator of TV's *The Gong Show.* Soon Croce became the Flyers' and Sixers' strength-and-conditioning coach; in the process, he created a high profile for himself as trainer to stars like Mike Schmidt, Julius Erving, and Charles Barkley. He began hosting a high-energy radio show during which he'd hang up on callers if they didn't begin by shouting his by-now-famous tag line: "I feel great!"

To many, Croce was little more than an amusingly hyper media personality. Behind the scenes, though, he began building an empire. He opened a string of fitness centers, offering the average Joe the same type of intense workouts and rehabs that made pros like Barkley hurl in front of a crowded, gawking gym. Along the way, T-shirts starting appearing: I SURVIVED PAT CROCE. He even transformed members of the media into something approximating good condition (for them), virtually ensuring that nary a negative word would be written or spoken about him.

In 1993, Croce sold his forty fitness centers for $40 million to a company that then merged with rehab giant NovaCare, and he began setting his sights on the next big thing. Wouldn't it be cool, he thought, to embark on a different type of rehab project? By the 1995–96 season, the once-proud Philadelphia 76ers franchise was floundering. Under head coach and general manager John Lucas, they'd won only eighteen games that season. Croce began pestering then owner Harold Katz about selling. Later, Katz would say he only sold because "Pat Croce called me fifty times, until I said yes."

In April of 1996, Croce catalyzed a deal that established Ed Snider, Comcast Corporation (owned by Ralph Roberts and his son Brian), and himself as partners. Croce became president of the Sixers with 10 percent ownership of the team and 2.5 percent of the overall $500 million deal. (Snider became chairman of the newly formed Comcast-Spectacor, under the aegis of which Comcast's new sports-and-entertainment acquisitions would be run: the Sixers, the Flyers, the then-named brand-new Corestates Center arena and its predecessor, the Corestates Spectrum.) The boisterous, backslapping Croce would report to the reserved Snider, who had a reputation for cutthroat business practices. At the press conference to announce the deal, Croce took to the podium and erupted in an ear-piercing Tarzan yell before shouting "I feel great!"

Croce immediately embarked upon his reclamation project. Soon Philadelphians were treated to a local commercial for Sixers season tickets in which Croce, perched perilously atop the new arena, shouted his motto into the heavens. His first substantive move was to hire a general manager who could oversee the remaking of the basketball team and who would not squander the precious first pick in the draft, as past Sixers regimes had done. Along with a Snider lieutenant, Croce interviewed a host of candidates before settling on Brad Greenberg, a forty-two-year-old coaching and player personnel veteran. For eight years, Greenberg had been director of player personnel for the Portland Trail Blazers, responsible for the talent evaluations that went into forming a roster that made it to the NBA Finals just three years earlier.

Croce, a detail freak, was impressed by Greenberg's preparation for their interview. Unlike many of the other candidates, Greenberg came equipped with preliminary scouting reports of the top players and he didn't hedge when asked whom he'd pick with the number one choice. Iverson, he said, had "ridiculous skills" and possessed what he called the "wow factor." "He's the kind of player that makes you say 'wow!' and look at whoever's next to you and say, 'Did I really just see that?' " he remarked. He'd still do his due diligence on other players, Greenberg said, and he'd be open to the possibility that, in a workout, one of them might blow him away and change his mind, but if forced to choose now, he'd pick the player who would be the toughest to guard at the NBA level. That would be Iverson.

So it was that, during the weeks leading up to the NBA draft, Greenberg and Croce arranged for their first meeting with Iverson. Croce got to the lobby of the Embassy Suites hotel near the Philadelphia airport before Greenberg and took a look around. He didn't see a basketball player waiting for him, as had been the plan. He inquired at the front desk and the clerk nodded to the lobby's far corner, where a baby-faced kid sat in big, baggy sweats with headphones on, slumped down, head thrown back, eyes closed, mouth open.

"*That's* Allen Iverson?" Croce said, before making his way over and shaking the ballplayer awake. "Allen Iverson? I'm Pat Croce!" he said, loudly, jarring the kid.

They moved to a small table, where they were soon met by Greenberg. Iverson quickly got the sense that Croce wasn't just another suit by the way he refused to tiptoe around issues surrounding Iverson's troubled past. "I've got to know about that bowling-alley scene," Croce told him. " 'Cause that's the baggage you carry around with you, that's what everyone's going to throw in your face."

Iverson volunteered his version of events, how he'd been called "nigger" and then was rushed out of the bowling alley when all hell broke loose. Croce sat still for a moment, before inching forward in his chair.

"You mean to tell me," he said, "that a guy called you a nigger and you didn't hit him?"

"That's right."

Croce paused. "Well, then you're a fuckin' punk."

Iverson flinched and lurched forward in his chair, chest puffed out. "I'm tellin' you, man—I couldn't," he said, in a forceful tone, making solid eye contact. "I ain't stupid, man."

Looking back, Croce would target the moment as the real beginning of their relationship. He'd challenged the kid, sending the message that there'd be no bullshit between them. And the kid responded in kind, by looking him in the eye.

Greenberg brought up the subjects of drugs, his mother, and his friends. "I respect my mom, I love my mom," Iverson said. "I've heard rumors all my life about my mom and drugs and it hurts me. She says she doesn't do them and I believe her." Of his friends, Iverson said, "I liked to hang around older guys 'cause guys my age were doing some bad things—worse things than the older guys I hung around with." He mentioned Arnie Steele and Marlon Moore as two of the guys who would come with him to Philly. He reassured Croce and Greenberg that if he did something stupid or wrong, it wouldn't be because of his friends. "If I fuck up, it's going to be because I fucked up," Iverson said. "Not because some guy told me to fuck up."

Greenberg worked Iverson out that afternoon and saw nothing to dissuade him that this was his guy. But Greenberg's work was just beginning. He brought in other potential picks as well. He and Croce had dinner with Stephon Marbury; during his workout, he paused for a moment to throw up—before resuming play. They also hosted Marcus Camby, Iverson's collegiate rival Ray Allen, and the most intriguing draftee, eighteen-year-old local high-schooler Kobe Bryant. None, Greenberg thought, came off as real as Iverson did.

Bryant had starred at nearby Lower Merion High School; just a year earlier, he had been invited to a Sixers practice by then coach John Lucas and spanked the Sixers' go-to man, Jerry Stackhouse, in a game of one-on-one. Bryant was a phenomenal talent, but Greenberg knew the Sixers needed a star right away. Already, Greenberg could tell that Bryant possessed a star's ego from the way the teen strolled through the Sixers' workout facility—indoors—wearing expensive shades all the while.

Compared with Iverson, Marbury seemed overly polished, schooled by his agent to talk in sportspeak clichés. The conventional wisdom was that Marbury was a purer point guard than Iverson, someone who, like point guards of old, would sacrifice his own scoring for the good of his team. Iverson, the thinking went, was not that sort of player. Indeed, come draft night, when Marbury was selected by Minnesota with the number four pick, he drew a distinction between himself and Iverson: "Iverson is a scorer in a point guard's body," he said. "I make other players better."

Greenberg sensed it was a more complicated issue. In their conversations, Marbury kept referring to his prospective team as "my team," as though he were interviewing for the position of owner. Iverson, on the other hand, talked about how he'd do whatever it took to win, including whatever it took to make his teammates better. (Ironically, after a few years in the league, Marbury's reputation would come full circle, and especially after his trade to Phoenix for Jason Kidd in 2001, Greenberg's view of him as a me-first type of point guard would become widely shared.)

Meantime, Greenberg continued looking into Iverson's background. He interviewed John Thompson, who told him Iverson didn't like school, was not a thug, had some "'hood friends," but was "coachable, football-tough, and liked by his teammates."

University of Illinois's Lon Kruger, who coached Iverson in the World University Games, called him the "most talented point guard I've ever seen" and dubbed him "high maintenance." The one time he pulled him from a game, Iverson retreated into himself for a day. "His instincts are to pout a little," Kruger said. "He's as competitive in a good way as anyone I've ever seen. He could struggle in dealing with his teammates if they aren't competitive enough."

A private eye hired by the Sixers reported back that Iverson's home life had been erratic, that he frequently came to school dressed in dirty clothes, and that "sources and interviews reveal that Iverson's mother and her associates have been involved with drugs at Iverson's place of residence."

The Sixers also subjected Iverson to a battery of psychological tests. The psychologist's report found that Kruger was on the right track when he called him "high maintenance." Terming Iverson a "restless type of personality . . . who continues to harbor a great deal of anger and frustration," the psychologist diagnosed that, under prolonged stress, he "can often revert to being sullen, defiant, and feeling misunderstood. . . . He's a loyal guy, wants to belong," wrote the psychologist. "He needs direction and guidance, but needs an arm around him also. Fully confident on the court, [but] off the court is a mistrusting place. He has blind spots to his behavior that aren't good . . . more a case of not knowing the appropriate behaviors than being disrespectful of others." The psychologist recommended that, in dealing with Iverson, authority always had to be carefully balanced with sensitivity, and that he could use a "positive locker-room role model."

Just days before the draft, Greenberg was close to making his final decision. Iverson just had too much talent to pass on. He and Sixers assistant coach Maurice Cheeks, a legendary point guard, talked often about Iverson's "freakish skills," as Greenberg put it. In the NBA, when a player dribbles by his man, the next move is almost always to either shoot or pass—defensive players are so quick to react, there's always a second defender lurking nearby to come to the aid of his beaten teammate. But Iverson was the exception to the rule; he'd go by his man, and then the next, and then the next. He'd find a way not only to get to the basket, but to score—or "finish" in basketball parlance—often over the outstretched arms of seven-footers. "He's got a Ph.D. in little-man tactics to score," Greenberg told Cheeks. Together, they'd marvel at Iverson's technique in changing directions while dribbling, how he'd push off his outside leg to make the sharpest, quickest of cuts. Or how he'd subtly raise up while dribbling in on his man, elongating his posture, a hesitation move that a defender would invariably mimic—allowing for that split-second opening for Iverson to blow on by. "Maybe it's a football thing," Greenberg theorized, "the way he can fake a guy out to avoid being tackled, and now he applies the same change of direction and change-of-pace moves on the basketball court."

There was no question, then, as to talent. But Greenberg wanted to see one more thing. He'd just hired his head coach, Johnny Davis, who had been an assistant in Portland. Before settling on Iverson, he wanted to confirm Thompson's view that he would be coachable. He called David Falk and told him the Sixers were prepared to make Iverson the number one pick, provided Falk got his client to come to Philly for one last workout. This time, it would be done surreptitiously—there'd be no press conference. "I want to see him go all out," Greenberg said. "If I see what I hope to see from him, he'll be our pick."

Falk was ecstatic; he was working on a $50 million endorsement deal for Iverson with Reebok that had a higher chance of coming to fruition if Iverson was the top pick, especially in a major market like Philadelphia. The next day, Iverson met Davis, and Greenberg told him he wanted to see "all game shots—no tippy-toe shots." It was a test of his character, not his game. The coach and general manager wanted to see how he would respond to their wanting more from him. Would he give them more? How bad did he want to be the number one pick? They weren't disappointed. One thing Iverson always possessed was a seeming reservoir of energy; he spent the workout in constant motion.

That night, Cheeks and Greenberg took the twenty-one-year-old to dinner at the Italian restaurant inside the Korman Suites hotel, just a few blocks from Cheeks's center-city Philadelphia apartment. In stark contrast to his seemingly sullen, monosyllabic interview style, Iverson exhibited a Croce-like level of enthusiasm as he soaked up Cheeks's wisdom about the NBA game.

"Who is your favorite point guard?" Cheeks asked him.

"Oh, Gary Payton," Iverson replied.

"Why?"

"Because he's tough," Iverson said. "And when a guy scores on him, he comes right back on him."

Cheeks, renowned for his selfless play during a career of setting up scorers like Julius Erving and Moses Malone, smiled. "Is that what you do when a guy scores on you?"

Iverson smiled, bragging now. "Yeah, I go right back at him."

Cheeks paused. "Well, as a point guard, if a guy goes at you and scores, do you think it's always the best thing for your team for you to go right back at him?"

Now Iverson, suddenly unsure of his position, looked back and forth between Greenberg and Cheeks. Cheeks filled in the silence. "All I'm saying is, there are four other guys with you. If you get caught up in your own private game with your man, what about your guys?"

Iverson smiled. "So who do you like?" he asked, part question, part challenge.

"John Stockton," Cheeks replied without hesitation.

"John Stockton?" Iverson asked, his face scrunching up in surprise. Stockton could play, no doubt, but there damn sure wasn't anybody on the playgrounds emulating the game of the player with the shortest shorts in the league.

"Yeah, John Stockton," Cheeks said. "You want to talk about tough? He never misses a game. And he's been the best screener on Utah's team for years. That boy can play. He knows the game."

Watching the exchange, seeing Iverson's eagerness to soak up knowledge, Greenberg made up his mind. That night, he reviewed all his scouting reports and interview notes one final time. There was Kruger, talking about Iverson's "extra gears." And Duke coach Mike Krzyzewski saying Iverson "has the heart of a lion." He penned his final player evaluation report, which would be shown to Croce and Ed Snider before the Sixers made their decision. "There aren't many players in professional basketball that are this competitive," Greenberg wrote. "Similar to Jordan in that respect. He doesn't have Jordan's discipline nor the fundamentals that Jordan had when he left college. If he could develop in those areas then he could approach being a Jordan type in a six-foot package. I can't predict that for him because the environment Allen experienced prior to entering the pros suffers by comparison to Jordan. However, the mere fact that I bring up Jordan in some sort of comparison tells a lot about his talent level."

Later, in retrospect, the choice of Iverson would seem to have been a no-brainer. But at the time, there was considerable risk, owing to what Croce called Iverson's "baggage"—the controversial past, the dysfunctional upbringing, the shady friends. But this was the NBA, where you rolled the dice on talent.

Draft night was at New Jersey's Meadowlands. When David Stern leaned into a microphone and intoned that "with the first pick of the 1996 draft, the Philadelphia 76ers select Allen Iverson, Georgetown University," the Iverson clan burst into a paroxysm of celebration. There was Arnie, Marlon, and Ra surrounding their fellow member of Cru Thik—who was wearing a suit. When once asked what he had been thinking on the night he was drafted into the NBA in 1984, Charles Barkley replied: "I thought, 'I ain't poor no more.'" Now the same thought likely occurred not only to Iverson, who would soon sign a three-year, $9 million contract, but also to a whole contingent of Iverson supporters. They were with him, as he liked to say, "from day one," and they were with him on draft night, whooping and hollering as the evening wore on. And right in the middle of the celebratory tumult was Ann, who, moments after her baby was selected, shocked NBA front-office personnel by loudly proclaiming, "We are going to par-tay tonight! I am getting *fucked* up tonight!"

The Allen Iverson era had dawned.

The NBA in 1996 was at a cultural crossroads. Michael Jordan had not only remade the league, he'd redefined tried-and-true sports marketing notions. Before Jordan, stars of individual sports such as John McEnroe had led the way in endorsement income. But Jordan's impact went beyond the bottom line. He debuted in the 1980s and immediately altered pop-culture style trends, ushering in the shaved-head look, hoop earrings, and sleek, tapered suits; it all added up to a level of seemingly color-blind crossover acceptance at a time, not coincidentally, when *The Cosby Show* was the number-one-rated sitcom in both white and black living rooms.

Throughout the first half of the nineties, the search was on for the next Jordan, for an icon-in-waiting who would advance Jordan's athletic, business, and cultural legacies. Every year, it seemed, a new candidate would be anointed Jordan's "Air Apparent." There was the upper-middle-class Grant Hill, by way of Duke University. There was Anfernee "Penny" Hardaway, a Nike endorser. There was Harold Minor—nicknamed "Baby Jordan" for his leaping ability. (There was only one problem: he couldn't quite play.) And there was Iverson's new teammate on the 76ers, Jerry Stackhouse, who came into the league with an above-the-rim game, a University of North Carolina pedigree, and a big marketing push from Nike competitor Fila.

All had, like countless others, signed on to the popular Gatorade-marketed mantra at the time. They all were trying to be "Like Mike." All, that is, except this new kid, the upstart Iverson, who didn't seem interested in repackaging himself in order to garner white, suburban acceptance. Shortly after Iverson's entry into the league, it became clear that he represented an epochal moment, the dawn of a new era for the black athlete. Something more in-your-face, more consciously authentic than the Jordan model, an image that owed more to hip-hop than to Motown.

Before Iverson even played his first NBA game, proof of his groundbreaking impact surfaced. Prior to Iverson's first pro training camp, Falk, the visionary who altered the landscape of professional sports by matching Nike with Jordan, worked out a ten-year, $50 million endorsement deal for Iverson with Nike competitor Reebok. Iverson chose Reebok in part for their canny approach to what would be his signature shoe. Called "The Question"—a play on Iverson's nickname—the $100 shoe would hit stores by January. In his second year, the company would change the product's name to "The Answer."

Cleverly, Falk encouraged Reebok not to market Iverson as though he were Jordan. Iverson himself insisted on marketing imagery that, instead of transforming and mythologizing him, merely reflected the way he saw himself. For a profile in *The New York Times Magazine,* Falk allowed writer Lynn Hirschberg to sit in on a strategizing session with Team Reebok:

"We're here to talk about who Allen is," Falk begins. "The single most important thing is to manage his image. It gets so diffuse. Every company wants to be Fellini and control the guy's image. It cannibalizes the guy's appeal and it confuses the audience."

Everyone agrees, and Iverson sits quietly, listening. "How do you feel about that?" Falk asks Iverson. He thinks a minute. "I would be more into it," he replies slowly, "if I could be myself." . . . *"Would you say speed and innovation work for you?" Falk asks Iverson. There is a long silence. "I would say creativity," Iverson says, finally. Everyone nods.*

From Reebok's perspective, the alliance with Iverson gave the company a leg up in the race to win over an emerging demographic, the hip-hop kids. The athletic shoe market was a $7 billion industry and 40 percent of it belonged to mighty Nike. Reebok, though number two, had fallen on hard times, its market share slipping a full percentage point to 20 in the year prior to Iverson's signing. In the months following Iverson's deal, however, investor confidence in the company's future rose. Reebok stock climbed from $26 per share to $38. Iverson was seen as the key to turning Reebok into a hip, cutting-edge brand.

Reebok's executive charged with managing the Iverson line would be Henry "Que" Gaskins, a thirty-one-year-old Washington, D.C., native who had been a buyer for Saks Fifth Avenue after getting a master's in business administration from the Kellogg Graduate School of Management at Northwestern University. Gaskins, a black man who dressed in stylishly baggy clothes and would soon wear his hair in cornrows, moved to the Philly area to manage the Iverson account. Some saw his role as that of glorified baby-sitter; indeed, he admitted, there was some of that.

But Gaskins had seen firsthand some of the missteps his company had taken in the marketing of its other star endorser, Shaquille O'Neal. Shaq was a huge name, yet his shoes weren't selling. Indeed, Gaskins knew that the shoes of big men rarely sold as well as those of smaller, quicker players. Children idolize athletes who remind them of the way they see themselves in their dreams: nimble, rising, untouchable. Jordan, in the mind's eye, invariably floats; Shaq, as great as he is, remains earthbound, a stone leviathan. It is difficult to even picture him in motion.

Iverson would be just the opposite. It would be impossible to imagine him at rest. Shaq, moreover, under the business tutelage of his then agent Leonard Armato, was starring in kids movies and his image was even reproduced on Saturday-morning cartoons. Gaskins knew that a new urban youth culture was emerging, a demo with money to burn. Just as they were spending it on rappers such as Tupac Shakur and Biggie Smalls, so, too, would they flock to a ballplayer who represented antiestablishment mores. Being dubbed the anti-Jordan in the sports pages surely posed a risk, but it was a risk that only applied to that insular world. In the culture at large, there was a market for someone like Iverson.

Gaskins made his case time and again to his superiors at the lily-white multinational corporation, and to Iverson himself, who didn't seem too charged up by strategic talk of his "positioning." The athlete's sole demand was that the company not try to change him, and he got no disagreement on that front from Gaskins.

This was new territory in professional sports, so naturally the 76ers had concerns. "We knew Reebok wasn't doing one of those corporate marketing plans with Allen," recalls 76ers general manager Brad Greenberg. "It was going to be more of a hip-hop theme, geared to younger kids and urban kids. Reebok endorsed his being this sort of anticorporate guy. I understood that, but in some ways it was a bit contrary to the direction we hoped he'd go. There were posters of him with his jeans down to his ass, without his shirt on, flexing his skinny muscles. But they had a plan and Que was a bright guy, so it wasn't really an issue."

As training camp approached, word reached Greenberg that Iverson's street credibility—which Gaskins was so enthused about—might be more risky than anyone had thought. Greenberg learned that gunshots had been fired at Iverson's Mercedes-Benz outside a party back in Hampton. Iverson was inside the party at the time, but two of his friends, Michael Powell and Alex Rhoden, were in the car. Powell, a closer friend to Arnie Steele than to Iverson, had two felony convictions on his record, cocaine possession in 1990 and possession of a weapon by a felon in 1992. Powell and Rhoden were unhurt in the incident, but Greenberg sat Iverson down the moment Iverson arrived for training camp.

"If they can shoot at your car, that might be a message," Greenberg said; Iverson assured him the incident was just one of those wrong-place, wrong-time things. After receiving assurances that neither he nor his friends were involved in anything that could warrant such violent message sending, Greenberg felt relieved. Enough of the off-court stuff; it was time to concentrate on basketball.

Well, almost. The Sixers played a couple of exhibition games against the Knicks at the Nassau Coliseum on Long Island. Iverson's friends took rooms at the same hotel as the team, and, over three days, they ran up thousands of dollars in room service and phone charges. "How long can these guys stay on the phone? How much room service can they eat?" Greenberg wondered when he was shown the bill, which he paid, deducting the amount from Iverson's next paycheck.

Just prior to tip-off of the first preseason game, Greenberg noticed that the only people not standing for the national anthem were Iverson's friends. It wasn't that they were trying to make a political statement. As his team psychologist had predicted about Iverson—and now Greenberg realized the same applied to his friends—they were sometimes oblivious to commonly accepted standards of appropriate behavior. It led to the first of many conversations with Iverson, during which Sixers officials from Croce to Greenberg to Coach Davis tried to get him to see that his friends' conduct reflected upon how people viewed him. "It ain't up to me to tell them how to act," Iverson would say whenever he was approached with news that one of his friends had, say, left a car in a handicapped parking spot or gotten in the face of an arena usher. Getting Iverson to come around on this point might be more of a battle than getting him to dominate on the court. As his rookie season dawned, all the distractions notwithstanding, there was no quarreling with Allen Iverson on the court.

Two hours before the Answer's NBA debut, Pat Croce stood in the concourse of his brand-new building, playing host. As fans rushed in, the new owner would extend his hand for shaking or raise his arm for high fives. Much has been written about the surliness of the Philadelphia fan, but this scene would consistently repeat itself over the next five years. As if his feel-great gregariousness were contagious, Croce would be swarmed by well-wishers dressed in Sixers garb—and, more often than not, in Iverson number three replica jerseys.

On this night, the crowd parted around Croce when, as if to classic funk background music, Ann Iverson approached. Croce had yet to meet the mother of his new franchise player, but he'd heard from his staff that she was, in his words, "a trip." ("Honey," she'd later say, "I ain't no trip. I'm a damn *journey*.") Now here she came, parting the crowd as though she were starring in her own movie, wearing a big fur coat, jeans, an Iverson jersey that read IVERSON'S MOM on its back, and, of course, her trademark ruby-red lipstick.

"Mr. Pat! Mr. Pat!" she called, not walking so much as sashaying toward him. "You gotta come see my new Jag-Wire! You gotta see the Jag-Wire my baby bought me!"

Before Croce could respond, she was upon him, bear-hugging. Croce, a hugger himself, instantly sensed he'd found someone who could match his frenetic zest for life, who shared his legendary penchant for celebrating the moment. She took his hand and led him past the turnstiles and the onrushing crowd to the entrance, where ticket holders were still streaming in; there, parked right outside, in the middle of the crowd and fifty yards from the nearest parking lot, was a shiny red Jaguar. Just as he'd promised so many years ago, Ann Iverson's baby had gotten her that candy-red Jag.

"Ann!" Croce said, laughing. "You can't leave that there!"

"Mr. Pat, I need to ask you something," she said, somber now. "You think you can give my baby an advance on his paycheck? My baby don't got nothing in his refrigerator."

"No wonder!" Croce said, throwing his arm around the bubbling ball of energy before him while nodding at her new ride. "There's where the money went!"

Ann laughed, and threw her arm around her new friend. "You gotta make sure my baby eats, Mr. Pat," she said. "He got nothing in his refrigerator. I'm counting on you now."

Meantime, down on the basketball floor, the team that warmed up was an immensely talented one that nonetheless had aficionados doubting whether it could actually win. First-year coach Johnny Davis had his challenges. In addition to the well-hyped rookie Iverson, he had shooting guard Stackhouse, who had led all rookies the year before in scoring (over 19 per game), but whose game had some surprising holes, given his North Carolina roots. A tremendous athlete, he wasn't a consistent shooter, he often seemed disinterested on defense, and he had a tough time dribbling the ball, as evidenced by his league-leading total of turnovers the previous season. Stackhouse needed the ball; how would he mesh with Iverson, who likewise was accustomed to being "The Man" with the ball in his hands?

One forward spot belonged to Clarence Weatherspoon, a solid, if uninspiring, small forward capable of putting up respectable numbers. Mercurial veteran Derrick Coleman was the power forward as well as the big question mark. NBA observers had long agreed that Coleman was one of the league's most talented players. He could shoot, rebound, pass, and possessed a stellar basketball IQ. His career to date, however, had been a disappointment. He hadn't consistently led his teams to winning records. The conventional wisdom: he had an attitude problem. While with his previous team, the New Jersey Nets, he'd been portrayed as a ho-hum player skating by on talent. In New Jersey, he'd once feigned enthusiasm in an interview by declaring "whoop-dee-damn-do," and at the start of one season, he even offered to write a check then and there in the amount of a season's worth of fines for violating the team's dress code.

Most coaches tolerated Coleman because, when healthy, he was a legitimate 20-point, 10-rebound producer. But on the eve of this season, he sent a disturbing signal when he rejected Davis's offer to be a team captain. Croce, given his holistic-health-care roots, worried: Sure, Coleman could put up good numbers, but what kind of influence would he be on Iverson, who, the team psychologist had said, was in need of positive veteran teammates?

In front of a sellout crowd of more than twenty thousand fans, including John Thompson, Ann, and thirty Iverson loyalists from back home in Virginia, Iverson's first game foreshadowed much of the coming season. There were breathtaking plays that seemed to portend endless possibilities, followed by playground-style turnovers. In the second quarter, Iverson took a Coleman outlet pass, raced the length of the floor, and lofted an alley-oop to Stackhouse, who threw down a reverse slam to thunderous applause. Minutes later, Iverson and Stackhouse broke out on a two-on-one against Milwaukee's Johnny Newman; where most point guards would set up their shooting mate, Iverson instead faked the pass and took off, soaring for a dunk that inspired Philadelphia's TV color commentator Steve Mix to exclaim, "Oh! Oh, my!"

At other times, Iverson would bring the ball up court and look to Coleman in the post; if he was covered, Iverson would fake out his man and launch a long jumper—none of his teammates having so much as touched the ball.

But that's not what the crowd was buzzing about. Who *was* this hustling blur of a little man—this kid—who seemed to be scoring at will? Iverson would end up hitting 12 of 19 shots for 30 points, while dishing out 6 assists. But his inexperience showed when, with his team nursing a 98–96 lead with just over three minutes to play, he committed a foolish foul away from the basket, giving the Bucks two free throws. Compounding the error, he pursued referee Mike Mathis, who was known for his oversensitivity, asking over and over, "What'd I do? What'd I do?" It wasn't what he said so much as how he said it: demonstrative, in-your-face. Mathis, certain he was being "shown up" by a rookie, blew the whistle and called a technical foul; Milwaukee would never trail again. To make matters worse, Iverson's collegiate nemesis, Ray Allen, also a rookie, nailed a three-pointer to seal the win.

After the game, a jostling media pack surrounded Iverson at his locker. He was upbeat about the NBA game and characteristically confident. "There are no zones, no junk defenses," he said. "In the NBA, it's just you and your man. I feel I can score on anybody."

Watching the media swarm around his new teammate, Sixers big man Scott Williams, who had played on the championship Bulls team with Michael Jordan, recognized that something special was in the making. He'd spent many nights earlier in his career watching Jordan in wide-eyed wonder, but there was something just as awe inspiring going on here. "He's got a Ford motor up his butt," Williams marveled while looking at his point guard.

The next game, Williams's former team awaited. In retrospect, Iverson would claim that his rookie season changed irrevocably after he first squared off against Michael Jordan.

There was a lot of love on that other bench. That's what winning could do, Allen Iverson knew. He was watching his opponents celebrate the hoisting of yet another championship banner to the rafters of Chicago Stadium prior to the start of his second NBA game. Iverson had heard all about how Scottie Pippen and Dennis Rodman didn't talk to each other; he'd heard the tales of how demanding and insensitive Jordan could be as a teammate. But, staring over at the mighty Chicago Bulls, winners of a record seventy-two games the season before en route to another NBA title, he saw that winning cured all ills. On a losing team, personality issues were "dissension." On a winning one, they were constructive friction.

The game wasn't close. Jordan scored an effortless 27; the Bulls won, 115–86. It was over quickly. Iverson was nervous at first and committed all five of his turnovers in the decisive first half; his passes bounced off teammates' hands and his shots clanked off the rim. He'd end up scoring only 15 points on 4-of-13 shooting.

Still, even when the outcome was no longer in doubt, Iverson played at only one speed: blinding. Even on the receiving end of a blowout, he chirped away at the superior opposition, his mouth moving almost as fast as his feet. Once garbage time came, Jordan and Bulls guard Ron Harper retired to the bench, laughing at the arrogant newcomer.

Afterward, the battle extended to the postgame interviews. None other than Dennis Rodman fumed about the rookie's irreverent on-court behavior. "I don't like too many of these young players, but I like him the least," Rodman said. "You've got to respect the game and the players you're playing against. He doesn't respect people. He thinks he's God. He thinks the court is his street, his playground, and he can do anything he wants and say anything he wants."

"He just has to learn to be quiet," Harper said, making sure to praise Iverson for his play, if not his style. "I thought I could play defense. Now I don't know."

During the game, both Rodman and Pippen razzed Iverson about taking too many of his team's shots. A previous generation of black athlete would have been schooled in turning the other cheek. But Iverson, who came of age in a generation that saw such Jackie Robinson–like restraint as tantamount to selling out, responded with a blistering comeback: "I don't care what Scottie Pippen says," he said. "Scottie Pippen doesn't know what goes on in my family, so it doesn't mean anything to me. Rodman, I don't pay him no mind. His whole game is about trying to throw you off."

His comments wouldn't have sparked any controversy whatsoever had it not been for Jordan's simultaneous remarks in the home-team locker room. According to Jordan, he tried to console Iverson on the court when Rodman and Pippen were picking on him. "At one point, I mentioned to Iverson, he was going to have to respect us," Jordan said. "If you don't respect anyone else in this league you have to respect us. He said he doesn't have to respect anybody."

And so the media had its story—one that would dominate the league for months to come. Allen Iverson had dissed Michael Jordan. For those who knew Iverson, it was absurd to think that he didn't respect Jordan; this was a kid, after all, who had once painted Jordan's portrait on his bedroom door and tried to take the door with him when it came time to move. Iverson tried time and again to explain that he was simply speaking of matters *on the court* when he said he didn't have to respect Jordan. He'd seen too many players fear Jordan on the court, and he knew Jordan thrived on intimidating the opposition. To Iverson, his statement was an announcement of his own competitive fires, something that should have been applauded, not jeered. David Falk, agent to both men, elaborated: "Allen idolizes Michael, and because he's aware that he idolizes him, he doesn't want his respect for Michael to interfere with his ability to compete against him."

Nonetheless, for purposes of the soap-opera-like daily sports narrative, Iverson was the perfect bad-boy foil to Jordan's good guy. The story line was set: Sinner versus Saint. Over the next few months, Iverson would find himself branded as the preeminent symbol of a generation of athletes seen as too selfish, too spoiled, too cocky for their own good. Iverson saw the maelstrom for what it was, the natural by-product of a generational hand-off. He said as much after the game against the Bulls, when he reacted to the suddenly swirling controversy by saying, "I think the younger guys want to show that we belong up there. We want to make our mark, too."

Indeed, the names were different and the times had changed, but like so many media plots, the story felt vaguely familiar. In the seventies, a seemingly ghetto fabulous character named Dr. J came into the league wearing an Afro and big gold chains and displaying a high-flying playground style. The old guard looked on in disdain. None other than legendary Celtic coach Red Auerbach remarked that "Julius Erving is a nice kid, but he's not a great player." Similarly, in the eighties, Jordan showed up for his first all-star game not in an Armani suit and Kenneth Cole shoes, but in baggy jeans and a backward baseball cap. Back then, he was the irreverent, arrogant newcomer who needed to be taught a lesson; veteran players, led by Isiah Thomas, even froze him out—refusing to pass him the ball—during the 1985 all-star game.

Even as Jordan grew, he wasn't always deserving of the automatic halo the sports press bestowed. As Sam Smith spelled out in his book *The Jordan Rules,* Jordan was the kind of superstar who reduced teammates to tears, blew off team meetings to play golf, took it upon himself to cancel practices, and checked his statistics with the official scorer during games.

One NBA coach said that when Bulls coach Phil Jackson closed practice to the media, it was so no one would find out just how often Jordan didn't bother showing up. So while Iverson was portrayed as somehow antithetical to Jordan, the truth was that, in both their strengths and flaws, in their competitiveness, egocentrism, and brilliance, Jordan and Iverson were more alike than different.

Early in his career, Jordan heard some of the same criticisms Iverson was now facing, though they were never voiced quite so vituperatively. Jordan's first three seasons were losing ones; experts compared him to established stars like Earvin "Magic" Johnson and Larry Bird and wondered if, like them, he'd ever make his teammates better. But thanks to his ingratiating crossover style, the criticism never reached the crescendo of condemnation Iverson encountered in his rookie year.

Despite the distraction of more media attention than he'd anticipated, Iverson led the Sixers to their best start in years. They finished November with seven wins and eight losses, not bad for a team that had won all of eighteen games the entire previous season. Iverson led the team and was among the league leaders in scoring (21.8 points), assists (6.4), and steals (2.67). But he also led the league in turnovers, committing 5.3 per game.

Part of the high turnover rate was attributable to unprecedented attention from the referees. With the crossover, Iverson had done for the dribble what Dr. J did for the dunk—turn it into a fan-friendly spectacle and a weapon of on-court intimidation. In his first game against the Knicks at Madison Square Garden, for instance, he scored 35 points as not one but *two* opposing point guards fouled out trying to stop him. Charlie Ward committed six fouls in twenty-nine minutes, and his backup, journeyman Scott Brooks, fouled out in all of fifteen minutes. On one play, Iverson dribbled the ball from side to side in front of Brooks, teasing him, before faking one way, luring Brooks into a reaction. Iverson was off in the opposite direction once Brooks merely flinched; the defender stumbled and fell, the crowd gasped, and Iverson scored.

At this point, Iverson was clearly the impetus behind a league memo that called for a crackdown not only on Iverson's type of long, droopy shorts, but also on his style of dribbling. In truth, his crossover dribble did flirt with being a carry; the word went forth that the refs would be calling palming more often. Iverson's high hesitation dribble on the crossover was suddenly being called illegal, sometimes two or three times a game.

The Sixers weren't a deep team, and injuries started to mount. The team went into a tailspin. Coleman fractured his pinkie finger and was out for weeks; while recovering, he fell badly out of shape. Backup players Don McLean and Lucious Harris likewise went down. Meantime, on the court, the turnovers mounted. League-wide, Iverson and Stackhouse were number one and number two, respectively, in giveaways. They were also, potentially, the most explosive backcourt in the league. But Iverson and Stackhouse were both learning on the job, in front of a particularly demanding fan base that saw their raw talents and couldn't figure out why it was taking so long for them to put it all together. But they were the youngest backcourt in the league; had both stayed in school, Stackhouse would have been only a senior and Iverson a junior.

Complicating the problem was that both came with their own loyal amen corners, entourages composed of friends and family who saw it as their role to let their guy know that *he*—and not that other dude—was really the Sixers' go-to man. Columnist Peter Vecsey reported that, outside the team's practice facility, Iverson's three-man posse "got into an impromptu rumble" with Stackhouse's. In his trademark acerbic style, Vecsey wrote that the respective entourages had been "forced to mill around together outside [the facility] and casually mull over whose homeboy deserves more money, minutes, magazine clips (as in shots, I think) and pub . . . Naturally, it was time to choose up sides, three-on-three. Call your own felony. Suddenly fists and feet were flying and landing everywhere."

Coach Johnny Davis was in danger of losing his team. They'd not only lost seventeen of eighteen, but Coleman had blown off some practices, and Iverson was increasingly tardy at team meetings and practices—just as Croce had feared. And now, in a sign of just how much the NBA was changing, Croce and Greenberg had to deal with a possible altercation that didn't involve their players, but their players' *friends.*

Both Iverson and Stackhouse denied the report, and the Sixers soon said that Vecsey apologized for the column. (Today Vecsey says—rather implausibly—that he doesn't recall whether his report was accurate or not: "Do you remember everything you wrote six years ago?" he said in 2002.) By the time the new year rolled around, whether their friends got into it was beside the point. Stackhouse and Iverson came to blows during a practice—not an unheard-of occurrence among teammates. Ostensibly, the scrap was over Iverson's failure to pass Stackhouse the ball.

But their problems weren't personal. A temporary flare-up of tempers notwithstanding, Iverson and Stackhouse liked each other and even hung out together. Later in the season, when the team visited Charlotte, Stackhouse's mother would prepare an artery-hardening home-cooked meal for her son's backcourt mate.

Instead, the Sixers' chemistry ills could be traced to a confluence of factors. There was the youth and inexperience of Iverson and Stackhouse, plus the ego-distorting refrain each heard from his respective cheering section. Plus, both men had grown up poor and black; at least one former NBA star says that, often, the call to put your team before your own interests can run afoul of a lifetime of learned every-man-for-himself survival skills. "Only people who have something can afford to be unselfish, unless you're a saint," writes former NBA star Chet Walker in his memoir, *Long Time Coming*. "In the ghetto, you often must take what you can before someone takes it away."

Then there were the lessons prodigies like Iverson and Stackhouse learned from the league itself. It doesn't take long for players to get the message that individual statistics like shots and minutes played are to be fought for. Even relative newcomers like Iverson and Stackhouse heard the stories about the players who followed their coach's advice and concentrated just on passing, defense, and setting screens; the same player, come contract time, would be denied a raise or altogether cut loose because, the general manager would say, "you only averaged six points a game." It is a cutthroat league and players like Iverson and Stackhouse— whose outsized egos were exactly what had gotten them to the highest level of their profession in the first place—were tacitly encouraged to get theirs, to look out for number one. It's why Bulls coach Phil Jackson was fond of saying that the hardest thing to do in coaching is to get players to "sacrifice the me for the we."

The Sixers limped into the all-star break with a desultory 12–34 record. Iverson traveled to Cleveland to play in the all-star rookie game. It had been a trying first half of his rookie season. Little did he know it would only get worse, and soon. He was about to walk into a media buzz saw.

The 1996–97 season marked the fiftieth year of the NBA, and in keeping with David Stern's flair for marketing the league brand, the all-star game would honor the fifty greatest players in league history. There, assembled on one floor, would be Wilt Chamberlain, Bill Russell, Kareem Abdul-Jabbar, Michael Jordan, Magic Johnson, Larry Bird, Oscar Robertson, Jerry West—and forty-two other legends.

However, it would be a player who wasn't even in the all-star game—let alone among the fifty greats—who would steal the headlines. On some level, given that every generation tends to wring its hands over the next (think of the onetime hippie baby boomers who today deride their hip-hop offspring), the ensuing media squall ought to have been predictable. Here you had the greats of yesteryear, convened for the first and only time. And here came the sudden symbol of the new NBA—*their* NBA. And he was dressed to make a statement.

Iverson had decided to go to Cleveland for his rookie game appearance sporting a new style: cornrows. (In his case, the onetime look was really more like mini-cornrows, because his Afro hadn't yet grown out enough.) Black male rappers like Snoop Dogg were wearing their hair in braids, and the style was catching on—though not among professional athletes, where the Jordan-inspired shaved head still predominated. Athletes' agents, still wedded to the crossover model of marketing, wouldn't countenance cornrows, which were seen as too in-your-face, too black. Iverson may not have known specifics about the style's Afrocentric roots—cornrows were worn during ceremonies in the time of the Third Dynasty Egyptian ruler Akhethoptep—but he knew it was not the traditional way African-Americans sought to assimilate.

So when Iverson arrived in Cleveland with his hair braided, it was a shock to the NBA's old guard—every member of which just happened to also be in town. The *New York Times* reported that it didn't go over well with the veterans: "Rookies making fashion statements do not often sit well with veteran players, who privately mocked [Iverson's] new hairdo behind his back."

The older players let the rookie have it, and the media was all too happy to play courier in a war of words between the generations. "Allen Iverson plays the game like a runaway train," said Hall of Famer Elvin Hayes. "The bottom line is what your team does, and his team is not doing anything."

"The mugging and the trash-talking of today was not part of the game when I played," agreed old-timer Jerry Lucas. "In some ways, we're going in the wrong direction."

Without singling out Iverson, Magic Johnson expressed concern for—and maybe some financial envy of—the new generation. "They are not making the kind of money they are making because of what they have done," he said. "They are making it because of what we did."

"Somehow, blackness became equated with how thuggish you look and how tough you act," said Isiah Thomas. "When we were growing up, it was okay to wear a suit and tie and to respect people."

The most vocal critic of Iverson and the hip-hoppers was, ironically, Charles Barkley, who, just seven years earlier, had declared himself "a nineties nigga." (Indeed, one columnist referred to Barkley during all-star weekend as "the conscience of the game"; within the next year, said conscience would hurl a heckler through a plate-glass barroom window.) "Iverson has to understand that Michael Jordan and I had shoes before he had his shoes," Barkley said. "He's not the greatest, just the latest . . . Allen Iverson doesn't know anything. Grant Hill listened to us and took the criticism."

Suddenly the always-controversial Barkley had morphed into Paul Lynde from *Bye Bye Birdie*—gnashing his teeth over "these kids today." Why was Barkley so fired up? "Because we, the veterans, have an obligation to be caretakers," he said.

Rather than taking care of the game, the concerned players turned the fans against one player. When a mini-cornrowed Iverson took to the Gund Arena floor for the rookie game, the Cleveland fans serenaded him with thunderous boos. As always, rather than give in under the weight of fan disapproval, Iverson used it as fuel. He'd always believed that his heart was more important than his skills, that the emotion of his game *was* a talent. He came out with something to prove, scoring 19 points, dishing out 9 assists, and leading the East to a 96–91 win. Fellow rookie Kobe Bryant led all scorers with 31 points, but it was Iverson who was named MVP—an announcement that prompted yet more booing, even as Iverson made his way over to legendary coach Red Auerbach, who had coached Iverson's college coach on the Celtics years ago and who today directed the West squad. "It's a pleasure to meet Coach Thompson's coach," Iverson said, extending his hand.

Afterward, in the media room, Iverson said he was stunned by the reception he'd received. "Maybe people felt Kobe should have won the MVP," he theorized after the game. "I've never had people boo me for playing hard."

While being questioned by the media, Iverson clutched his two-piece MVP trophy, a glass star atop a marble base. "Here, hold this," he said,

In 1997 Iverson was one of the first players in the NBA to wear his hair in cornrows.

handing the trophy to Sixers PR man Bill Bonsiewicz, who promptly juggled and dropped it, shattering the top piece.

"Bill, my ma is going to kill you," Iverson deadpanned, before breaking out in laughter.

As if on cue, Ann Iverson came barging into the interview room, calling out, "Where's my baby?"

"Ma," Iverson called, "Bill broke your trophy!"

Iverson was still laughing at his team's PR man when Bonsiewicz introduced the star to his parents, who lived nearby. The next night, the Sixers played the Cavaliers on the very same floor. Iverson, still carrying a grudge against the Cleveland fans, lit up the home team, but the Sixers lost. Afterward, on the team plane back to Philly, Bonsiewicz sat near the back, frozen in trepidation, as Iverson got up from his first-class seat and made his way down the aisle, looking pissed. "Bill," Iverson whispered, taking the seat next to him, looking down. "You've got a great family. Don't ever take that for granted." He kept his voice low, Bonsiewicz would later realize, because he was guarding his tough-guy image. And it made sense to Bonsiewicz that someone who had already been on the receiving end of such judgment and denunciation would erect a self-protective wall of machismo. Iverson said what he had to say. Without looking the PR man in the eye, he brought his headphones up to his ears from around his neck and loped off, back up the aisle, lost in his internal world.

As Iverson's rookie season continued, so did the media pile-on. Mike Wise of the *New York Times* wrote that "Iverson has gone from being hailed as an emerging young player to being an emerging young pain in the neck, a 20-year-old who appears to be somewhat out of control on the court, and perhaps off it."

An Associated Press piece called him "a punk. A trash-talker. A ball hog. A brash kid who even dissed Michael Jordan early this season." Sportswriter Lisa Olson opined that Iverson "is impertinent and cocky and thinks legends like Larry Bird and Magic Johnson are just characters in a Sega video basketball game. Because he believes the game of hoops didn't really, truly begin until he arrived."

Come April, Iverson went on a historic scoring tear. If he didn't win Rookie of the Year honors, it would be because voters took off-court issues into consideration. He scored 40 or more points in an NBA record five straight games, beating Wilt Chamberlain's thirty-seven-year-old record. The Sixers lost all five, which had aficionados throughout the league saying their "I told you so's." The kid could score, they'd say, but he can't win.

Still, it was an amazing streak—something Jordan had never done, not even in his first three seasons when *his* team was losing. Iverson burned Atlanta for 40, Cleveland for 50, and Milwaukee for 44. At home against the Bulls, he would serve notice that, like it or not, a changing of *the* guard was in the offing. He scored 44, but it was just one of those baskets that will forever be remembered. It was the culmination of his long-ago prophecy, when a scrawny runt of a kid in Newport News proclaimed, "I can take Mike."

This time, he really did take Mike. Just in front of the Bulls bench, Clarence Weatherspoon had the ball on the wing, with Jordan on him. He handed it off to Iverson and Phil Jackson barked out, "Michael! Get up on him!"

Jordan jumped up above Weatherspoon's screen as Iverson dribbled the ball slowly to and fro before him. The crowd buzzed: this is what they paid to see, a one-on-one showdown between the two most creative players in the game. It all happened so quickly. "I wanted to see if he'd bite on a little cross," Iverson would later say, explaining the first part of the move, a mini-crossover to the left. Jordan did, in fact, bite, and Iverson hesitated for a split second, letting Jordan set his feet again. Jordan may have regained his balance, but Iverson knew he had him, because Jordan would be expecting the same tempo as the mini-cross. Iverson started to go left again, in almost an instant replay of the move Jordan had just recovered from; same pace, same cadence. Only this time, thinking that this was *the* move, Jordan lurched that way, to his right, and it was all over. Iverson switched gears and crossed to his right while Jordan, struggling to react, stumbled. Leaving Jordan in his dust, Iverson raised up at the right elbow and drained an open jumper.

The roar from the Philadelphia crowd was more deafening than anything anyone had ever heard before—louder than the cheers that ever greeted Dr. J's soaring flight patterns or Charles Barkley's length-of-the-floor rumbles. In the owner's box, Pat Croce leaped to his feet, arms raised, screaming, and felt fans grabbing at his shirt from behind; turns out, in his gleeful abandon, he was dangerously close to falling out of the box. "It felt like a moment that really meant something," Croce would later say. "That we were there to witness this passing of the NBA torch. Michael wasn't ready to give it up, so Bubba just took it from him!"

Still, there were nonbelievers. The Sixers finished the season winning just twenty-two games, only four more than the year before Iverson's arrival. Croce had had a rough rookie year as an NBA owner, once donning a goalie mask to face a handful of impatient season-ticket holders. He saw a lack of team discipline that he knew he never would have tolerated in his former life, when he was running the fitness and rehab facilities. Players wouldn't practice, or they'd show up late. He had signed off on the hiring of a rookie coach to direct a high-maintenance rookie, and it was, in retrospect, a recipe for disaster. We should have hired a veteran, experienced coach, he realized. The day after the season ended, Croce announced the firing of Davis and—to the surprise of some—Greenberg. Croce's senior partner Ed Snider thought Greenberg, who had hit a home run drafting Iverson but who struck out in hiring Davis, could be retained; Croce wanted a fresh start. In a rare move from a sports-team owner—or from anyone in public life, for that matter—Croce took full responsibility for the disappointing season, apologized to the fans, and vowed to not screw up again.

The season ended on at least one positive note, however. Buzz had it that Iverson was about to be named Rookie of the Year, though there were still some vocal detractors. Barkley, calling Iverson "me, myself, and Iverson," announced that Vancouver's Shareef Abdur-Rahim should be named Rookie of the Year. "Iverson is the playground Rookie of the Year," Barkley said. Kevin McHale, Minnesota's director of basketball operations, lobbied for his player, Marbury, saying that rewarding Iverson for his me-first play "tells young kids to come into the league and just put up numbers and you will get rewarded." (Of course, Marbury had the luxury of playing with superstar-in-waiting Kevin Garnett; Iverson had been given the green light by Davis because Davis had more confidence in a forced Iverson shot than in an open jumper by almost anybody else on his team.)

McHale's fears were realized when the Sixers got word from the league that Iverson was its Rookie of the Year on a Wednesday, six days before the award would be announced. Once the season had ended, though, Iverson had headed back to Virginia. Croce had a pager number for him, but the pages were unreturned on Thursday, Friday, and through the weekend. He didn't know if Iverson knew he'd won the award, let alone whether he'd be attending the press conference to announce it. At seven on Monday morning, the day before the press conference, Croce dispatched Bonsiewicz on a plane to Norfolk, Virginia, giving his employee a toothbrush and a scrap of paper with some phone numbers that *might* still be good for Iverson's relatives. "This'll be fun," the ever-upbeat Croce told his skeptical employee. "Operation Find AI."

Thanks to the boxing ties of Sixers vice president Dave Coskey, Croce had arranged for Bonsiewicz to be met at the airport by Peter Joiner, boxer Pernell Whitaker's bodyguard. Joiner, known as PJ, sported a sparkling gold tooth and drove a black Mercedes. For the next hour, while an amused PJ looked on, the six-foot-four and white Bonsiewicz, wearing a suit, knocked on doors, holding out his card. One door led to another, led to another. At one house, eight cars were parked in the driveway. Sounded like a party was going on. "He just left," someone said, before slamming the door.

Bonsiewicz called Croce. "Pat, it's crazy here," he said. "We're never going to find him."

Just then, Bonsiewicz's call waiting beeped.

"Bill! You down here?" Iverson said. "People are calling me from all over the place, telling me some white dude named Bill is looking for me!"

Bonsiewicz explained he was there to bring Allen back for his press conference, which riled up the Rookie of the Year. "You think I can't get to my own damned press conference?" he said.

"You don't even know when it is, do you?" Bonsiewicz challenged him. "One o'clock!"

"Wrong—it's noon!"

"Well, they can't start the damned thing without me!"

Finally, Iverson agreed to fly back to Philly in the morning with his mother and Bonsiewicz, who asked Iverson to recommend a hotel. "Go to the Days Inn, tell 'em you're Bill," Iverson said.

"I'm Bill," Bonsiewicz said upon arrival, "and I—"

"Bubba called." The clerk cut him off. "You're all set."

Relieved, Bonsiewicz got to bed early. But his phone rang at 4 A.M. It was Iverson's friend Arnie. "Be downstairs in half an hour," he told the groggy PR man. "We've got to find A.I."

Arnie picked up Bonsiewicz and they went over to Ann's house. At some point in the night, turns out, Ann and Allen got separated. Here it was, five in the morning and there were people strewn throughout the house, some watching the big-screen TV, some cooking breakfast. Like her son, Ann required little or no sleep at night; her "normal" regimen was to stay out all night and sleep till four or five in the afternoon. ("The

Iversons are like vampires: they come out after midnight, drinking Cristal," once quipped a member of the Sixers team.) Bonsiewicz got the feeling that no one in the house had slept a wink all night as he listened to Ann make phone calls, trying to track down her son.

Finally, a little after 6 A.M., Ann screamed, "I got him!" and they were all bustling out the front door, into the limo Ann had rented. They stopped at the Omni Hotel, where Bubbachuck stood, smiling, until he saw Bonsiewicz, and then he put on a face of mock anger. "I can't believe you thought I'd miss my own damned press conference, man," he said.

Once they landed in Philly, Bonsiewicz told Iverson breakfast was waiting at the arena. "I'm going home to change, man," Iverson said. Bonsiewicz's heart dropped; after all this, he couldn't go back to the office without him, could he? He called Croce to ask what he should do. "What are you worried about?" Croce said. "I trust Bubba. He'll be here."

A couple of hours later, the press was silent—maybe even a bit frightened—when Iverson walked in, followed by a procession of his stone-faced boys. All of them, including Allen, wore white Reebok warm-up jackets and white skullcaps pulled tightly over their heads. In fact, in the months to come, the league wouldn't publicize photos of Iverson receiving his award because of the skullcap. ("It looks like something people wear in prison," NBA deputy commissioner Russ Granik would tell Croce. "It's made by Reebok!" Croce would say, putting a few in the mail to him.)

But none of that mattered to Ann Iverson. Her son was about to be named the best of his class, and she waltzed in, beaming, and took her place at the podium, for Allen was giving this award to his ma.

Croce presented the trophy. "Now the world knows what we in Philadelphia have known," he said. "That Allen Iverson is one of the most exciting, most dynamic, most fearless players in the NBA."

Iverson talked humbly about how much he owed to his mother, and then he was gone, off to enjoy the summer months. He'd just decided to turn down his friend Spike Lee's offer to audition for, and most likely star in, a basketball flick Lee would be directing, *He Got Game*. Rebuffed by Iverson, Lee would ultimately give the role to Ray Allen.

Iverson's reason for turning down the movie?

"Man, this is my first summer with money," he told Lee. "I ain't working. Me and my crew, we gonna enjoy having money."

this is chinese for "respect." i feel that w
deserves a lot of respect—being from there, s
there, and staying true to everybod

Throughout his short life, Allen Iverson has often balanced dueling worlds. Sports in America, after all, is the province of middle-class values, a world where media, coaches, and even parents place higher standards of behavior upon athletes than they do on any other type of entertainer. Unlike rappers, actors, or even sports broadcasters, athletes are "role models."

Iverson is, by necessity, in that world, but not of it. He intuited early on that almost anytime a sports role model took center stage, the result was a thinly veiled commercial script; role models existed to sell kids sneakers and junk food.

The anti-Jordan would not play that game. He'd hawk the Reeboks, of course, but not if it meant—as he made clear to the company in their first meeting—he couldn't be who he was, someone who hailed from a parallel world. He was from the streets, where adopting the safe, middle-class mores foisted upon so many young black athletes could get one killed or—worse, perhaps, given his fatalism—disrespected.

No, Iverson would walk that fine line, keeping one foot in the rarefied air of the NBA, at the pinnacle of America's commodity culture, and the other in the asphalt streets that produced him. It wasn't a conscious decision so much as an implicit declaration of who he was.

Perhaps no twenty-four-hour period spoke more eloquently of Iverson's delicate balancing act than that which began on May 1, 1997, when he accepted the Rookie of the Year award. During that ceremony, even while his hip-hop garb so turned off the NBA's powers-that-be, Iverson seemed—weirdly enough—an exemplar of family values.

"Now it's her award," Iverson said, giving the trophy to Ann. "Without her, none of this would have happened. She gave me the heart that I have. She made me believe since I was young that I could do anything that I wanted to do. I dedicate the award to my mom."

Nor did he stop there. Iverson extended his tribute to other women in his life. "There was a space in my heart [all season] filled by my little sisters," he said of Brandy and Ieisha. "All of the different things I did on the court were for my sisters back home, watching on TV."

Less than twenty-four hours later, however, he was in a less wholesome setting, front and center in a scenario that wouldn't quite have middle-class fans dabbing at their eyes. Wearing a stylish gray suit and a collarless black shirt, Iverson raised his right hand and swore to tell the whole truth and nothing but, before taking the stand to testify for Michael Freeman, who was, for the fourth time in his life, facing felony charges.

On April 5, 1996, the man known as House Mouse on the streets of Newport News had been arrested and charged with possession with intent to distribute cocaine. Again. Freeman had been released from jail four months prior and was living at 704 Delaware Avenue, with his three brothers, their mother, and their uncle. When the house was raided by police, Freeman and his brothers were in the kitchen, with scales and sandwich baggies on the table in front of them. He had over a thousand dollars in cash in his front pocket, along with a plastic bag containing three grams of cocaine.

Freeman would testify that it was his brothers, not him, doing the dealing, that his brother Wayne had given him a folded-up stack of bills to hold. Wayne, for his part, told the same story on the stand. Both men testified that, unbeknownst to Michael, there was a bag of coke in the center of the wad of cash. Freeman's probation officer testified that Freeman had previously sought permission to move from the residence, because his brothers were dealing drugs. Permission was denied. And his brothers kept on dealing. "I ain't nobody to them," Freeman explained.

The defense—Iverson's lawyers Tom Shuttleworth and Larry Woodward—argued that Michael Freeman wouldn't have had to sell drugs in April of 1996 because he was fully aware that, in a matter of months, he would never have to make money illegally again. "I wrote him when I was in school and told him, you know, everything that I had planned on doing," Iverson testified. "Um, I asked him for advice on what agent I should get and things like that, but I just let him know that I was going to leave . . . and I told him that I was going to take care of him and take him with me to Philly or to wherever I went."

Iverson testified that, after his last season at Georgetown had ended, many of these conversations about their future took place when he visited Freeman at the Delaware Avenue house, where Freeman was confined by electronic monitoring as per the conditions of his parole.

"This is how Iverson lived his life as he was finishing up his career at Georgetown," wrote Iverson's former critic, the *Daily Press*'s Jim Spencer. "He was in and out of a Hampton crack house several times."

Shortly after Freeman was found guilty, Iverson slipped out a court-room side door.

As Allen Iverson evaded the phalanx of reporters outside the Hampton Circuit Court, Pat Croce was also trying to fly below the media's radar.

Unlike so many team owners, Croce didn't present himself as an expert when it came to the *Xs* and *Os* of his sport. No, he was a manager of people who lived his life in accordance with a never-ending supply of bumper-sticker-like aphorisms, such as "You can delegate authority, but you can't delegate responsibility." It was this thinking that caused him to apologize to Philadelphia after his rookie season of ownership, when he fired Davis and, over the objections of his senior partner, Ed Snider, general manager Brad Greenberg.

But that bold move had left him more vulnerable than ever. "I can't play, coach, or select talent—yet I'm the team now," he bemoaned to friends and colleagues. "I've got no one."

If he was going down, he figured, he'd go down trusting his gut. And his gut told him that he needed a marquee name, someone to rejuvenate the basketball side of his organization's operations. He'd liked Johnny Davis personally, but quickly recognized that the current generation of players had little respect for coaches who, in the players' parlance, had no "juice"—whose reputation didn't precede them.

He needed someone whose résumé would capture Iverson's imagination. First, he began stalking the youthful and energetic University of Kentucky coach, Rick Pitino. As Pitino led his team on a march to the NCAA Tournament championship, Croce had lavish gifts awaiting the coach in every hotel room along the way. The two had lunch in Kentucky; another of Croce's axioms is to "listen between the lines," and his ears perked up when he heard Pitino wax less than enthusiastic about Iverson's one-on-one style and Coleman's dour on-court demeanor. He asked the coach point-blank: "If you come back to the NBA"—Pitino had coached the Knicks earlier in his career—"would it be in Philadelphia?" Pitino gave it some thought before deciding that, if he returned to the NBA, he'd rather coach in Boston, where he had roots. (That's where he ended up, signing a lucrative ten-year deal as president and coach.)

Croce decided to think even bigger. Phil Jackson, leading the Bulls to yet another title, was in the last year of his deal. His contract allowed teams not in the play-offs to speak to him about their coaching vacancies. When Croce got him on the phone, the two spoke for ninety minutes. Unlike Pitino, Jackson loved the talent level of the 76ers. He believed they just needed a catalyst to turn themselves into a team. As Jackson went on, using terms like "empowerment" and "responsibility," Croce thought he'd found a kindred spirit, someone in line with his own careful tough-love approach to Iverson's tender psyche. With the Bulls, Jackson had gotten Jordan to buy into his system; Croce knew how much Iverson wanted to win—it was all he talked about—and that Jackson's championship rings, combined with Jordan's endorsement of the coach's unconventional, Zen-inspired techniques, would earn Iverson's loyalty. "There would be instant respect," Croce said.

But there was a catch. Jackson was only going to leave the Bulls if management—with whom he had often feuded—broke up the team and jettisoned Jordan, who was looking for a big payday. If owner Jerry Reinsdorf signed Jordan, Jackson would re-sign, too. But none of this could be resolved until after the Bulls' championship run in late June. Croce kept calling Jackson during the NBA Finals to see if anything had changed. No, Jackson told him. He was still in limbo. (Ultimately, Reinsdorf would sign Jordan to a $30 million contract for one year and bring Jackson back, as well.)

If Croce rolled the dice and waited, he could be out of luck. Indiana Pacers coach Larry Brown was rumored to be thinking of resigning, and five other teams were in the market for a head coach; Brown had a reputation for rejuvenating NBA teams. He was also known for his wanderlust and for being high maintenance.

"Good luck," Pacers owner Herb Simon said sardonically, when Croce called for Brown's agent's phone number.

"Good luck," echoed Pacers general manager Donnie Walsh.

When Croce finally got Brown on the phone, he heard moaning and groaning in the background. "Coach, are you at a gym?" he asked.

"No," Brown replied. "I'm in a hospital delivery room. My wife is giving birth."

Brown sounded remarkably, even strangely, calm. "Well, enjoy the moment," Croce said. "But tell me—is it a boy or girl?"

"It's a girl," Brown said.

Within minutes, Croce was on the phone to his favorite florist, telling her he wanted Mrs. Brown's delivery room to "look like a Mafia funeral parlor." Sixty-two pounds of flowers were soon on their way, and Brown was soon inked to a five-year, $20 million contract.

When Croce called Iverson on his cell phone to tell him the news, his star was underwhelmed. He'd played against Brown's Pacers, but knew little of the coach's background. He knew Brown had been a point guard himself—a long, long time ago—and that he'd never coached a team to an NBA title. And he knew through the NBA grapevine that Brown's team had rebelled against him during the season just past.

From Brown's point of view, he recognized the talent of Iverson and Stackhouse, but felt they "played like strangers." Privately, he wasn't looking forward to coaching Iverson. "I wanted nothing to do with him," he would later recall.

At first blush, no two men could be more different. Brown was a fifty-six-year-old Jewish man, raised on Long Island, who had spent a lifetime suppressing emotions behind a blank stare and a monotone that made Al Gore seem charismatic. He considered himself, first and foremost, a teacher; indeed, with his emphasis on the game's fundamentals, he seemed to have stepped right off the screen from the movie *Hoosiers;* he'd often fantasized about giving up the pro game to coach at the high-school level. He deemed his curriculum as nothing short of his sport's Holy Grail. He spoke of "playing the right way," and his pedigree showed he had the lineage to back up his basketball fundamentalism. He had played for the legendary Dean Smith at the University of North Carolina, who played for Hank Iba at Kansas, who played for none other than Dr. James Naismith, the inventor of the game.

When they heard Brown invoke his "playing the right way" mantra, the Pacers, particularly the talented young hip-hopper Jalen Rose, came to see it as the inflexible preachings of an old-school coach. He said "right way"; they *heard* "my way." But Brown viewed himself as the trustee of sacred basketball truths passed down from the game's fathers.

In Brown's view of the game, team trumps all. At North Carolina, bench players under Smith were required to stand and applaud when a teammate came out of the game. Similarly, when Brown watched video footage of his team or others, he'd often rewind the tape to focus on those who weren't even playing, trying to see who on the bench appeared supportive of his teammates.

On the court, Brown's style was to emphasize defense and rebounding; if a team helped one another when defending, he reasoned, they were more likely to share the ball on offense. He disdained many of the game's modern manifestations. He hated the three-point shot because it rewarded bad shot selection. The purpose of Dr. Naismith's game, after all, was to take the highest-possible percentage shot. The three-pointer was a low-percentage shot, yet the NBA now provided incentive to take it. Consequently, he was one of the last holdouts against the three-point specialist. Jackson had brilliantly paired Jordan with a series of long-range bombers who could hardly be called all-around players. Guys like John Paxson, Steve Kerr, B. J. Armstrong, and Craig Hodges might have been defensive liabilities, but they were deadeye shooters, particularly when set up by a constantly double- or triple-teamed Jordan. Brown wasn't having it; if you couldn't play defense for him, you didn't play.

Brown's practices consisted of the same high-school-type drills, day after day. Ad nauseam, his players practiced basic "L" cuts and the most minute nuances that go into the setting of picks. Other coaches tried to keep their players engaged by mixing up their regimen; some, like Jackson, spent almost as much time coaxing commitment out of their players' psyches as they did drawing up plays. Brown, however, was a throwback. "I coach execution, not effort," he said.

No one had ever doubted Brown's basketball acumen, but he was not known as a stable bet. He'd had eight head-coaching jobs in twenty-four years, once even quitting as coach of the New Jersey Nets on the eve of the play-offs. He was often referred to as a basketball nomad, someone who, despite outward appearances, made emotional decisions. He fell in and out of love with his jobs, with women (his marriage to the twenty-eight-year-old Shelly Brown was his third), and with players. As coach of the Denver Nuggets, he traded Bobby Jones to Philadelphia for George McGinnis; after McGinnis's first practice, he tried to rescind the deal.

On the surface, it appeared that Brown and the anti-Jordan would have little in common. There was Iverson, so focused on maintaining his identity, on taking his posse with him on this strange trip of a life. And there was Brown, who picked up stakes time and again, who not only had no posse, but who seemed to reinvent himself at every stop. In time, both men would reveal their similarities to each other; both had spent their lives fatherless, alternately in pursuit of, and recoiling from, male authority figures, and both shared a highly sensitive artistic temperament, quick to wound, slow to forgive. All this would become clear, in time. But shortly after Brown was named Iverson's coach, Tim Roye, the radio voice of the Golden State Warriors, put it best: "My money is on December," he said. "That's when *Sports Illustrated* will run the piece on Larry and Allen, feuding, under the headline CITY OF BROTHERLY LOVE?"

Que Gaskins knew from day one that Allen Iverson had the love and adulation of those who were, like the ballplayer, from the streets. After all, Iverson had burst onto the national scene bearing unmatched street credibility, the first African-American sports star to step onto our playing fields *from* jail—where he'd been unjustly incarcerated, to boot. Kids could relate to him, to his size, his style, his toughness, his loyalties; when the media chastised him for his choice of friends, they recognized it for what it was: The media don't want him to be around people like us, they thought. From Harlem to North Philly, Newport News to Watts, it was as though they recognized Iverson from their very own block.

Gaskins understood all that. But how to explain this? How to explain the packed, screaming, gyrating crowd on five levels of a mall in Chile, all jockeying for a glimpse of the American ballplayer? Iverson, eyes wide, looked at Gaskins. "This shit's crazy, man," he said.

It was summer, and they were on a three-week Reebok promotional tour of South America. Ann Iverson and Gaskins's wife, Cindy, along with representatives of the NBA, Reebok, and David Falk's office, were all part of the entourage. Whether in Chile, Brazil, or Santo Domingo, Iverson-mania reigned.

"Man, I got crazy love like this all around the world?" a stunned Iverson asked Gaskins.

At one point, when a crowd inside a mall pushed up dangerously close, the group made an about-face and started running away; Cindy Gaskins stumbled, and laughing, Iverson and Que rushed back toward the storming crowd to help her. They barely avoided being trampled.

"That's when Allen's mind opened to what an international presence he was," Gaskins recalls today. It also led Gaskins to be the first to identify Iverson's potentially unique crossover appeal. He realized that Iverson could be a prime example of what he liked to call "fusion marketing." Fusionism, according to Gaskins, was the science of connecting brands and consumers globally. It was shortsighted, he argued, to think of the Iverson brand consumer as an inner-city African-American back in the States. The cheering crowds throughout South America proved to Gaskins that Iverson's attitude, style, and way of playing—his whole persona—appealed across traditional lines of geography and demography. "The essence to Fusionism is summed up in a quote from the book *The Social Life of Information:* 'The way forward is paradoxically not to look ahead but to look around,'" Gaskins would later write. "Fusionism is way more than just skin color. It's about attitude. It's about a liberated mind-set. It's about the elimination of cultural boundaries and stereotypes."

Though others accompanied them on the tour, Gaskins and Iverson bonded on their journey. Gaskins would speak breathlessly of his spiritually based marketing theories. Iverson, more grounded in street-level realities, would affectionately kid him about being "the dumbest smart person I know." Other times, they'd watch videotapes of Eddie Murphy movies, Murphy being one of Iverson's favorite comedic actors. Gaskins not only sat through some thirty viewings of *Trading Places,* he was also entertained by Iverson's dead-on impressions of Murphy in the lead role.

From the beginning of their relationship, Gaskins saw himself as much more than a corporate watchdog for Iverson. Others in the industry snickered that he was a baby-sitter, but Gaskins viewed himself as a role model. He quickly saw that Iverson learns by experience, not by being lectured to. So he felt his best course of action was to conduct himself in a way Iverson could respect—and hopefully emulate. While Iverson's friends initially looked warily at this corporate interloper, Gaskins steadfastly resisted telling Reebok anything of their star endorser's doings beyond what headquarters absolutely needed to know. He saw the various and difficult demands placed upon the young star by those around him and insisted on pulling his own weight.

Most important, he took Iverson into his new home, just outside nearby Wilmington, Delaware. Iverson had already seen that Gaskins brought his stunning wife, Cindy, and their two young children wherever he went. Others seeking Iverson's acceptance tended to boast of how "hard" they were, of how many hardships they'd had to overcome; though Gaskins hailed from the tough inner-city streets of southeast Washington, D.C., he was determined to set an example of what the future could be. The first time Iverson came over, he looked at Gaskins and spoke in a hoarse, heartfelt voice. "You know how lucky you are, man?" Iverson said, looking around the comfortable suburban home. "I really respect the way you show love for your family."

Neither Iverson nor Gaskins cut their hair during their eye-opening trip. Despite the backlash engendered by his hairstyle statement during all-star weekend, Iverson was not cowed. "I'm gonna let my shit grow out and start the season with cornrows," he said.

"Man," Gaskins said. "You do that, and they gonna eat you alive."

"Whatchu mean, 'eat me alive'?" Iverson said.

"I'm telling you, you don't want to do this," Gaskins said.

"Whatchu mean? *You* can't do it 'cause you work at Reebok."

"Reebok don't care about stuff like that."

"Yeah, right."

Now Gaskins felt challenged. His mother, who ran a highly praised tutoring program for neighborhood kids back in D.C., had always told him that there are many different images of success—and that it was up to him to create his own image. Along with Allen, he could make a statement: Success, and traditional values, can come in different looking packages. "Tell you what," he said, smiling as he imagined the reaction his plan would get back in the corporate world. "You grow your hair, I'll grow mine."

They shook on it, and it was settled. Iverson would follow up on his all-star weekend buzz and be the first athlete to buck the NBA's style status quo. He and his mentor would braid away.

B ubba, you're killing us."

That was the first thing Pat Croce said to Allen Iverson as the two men broke from their hug. It was déjà vu all over again. Here was Iverson, in a suit, in a conference room in the Hampton County Courthouse, facing charges.

In early August, the news broke that Iverson had run afoul of the law once again. His 1996 Mercedes was pulled over on Interstate 64 in Virginia at 1:30 in the morning, doing ninety-three miles per hour in a sixty-five-mile-per-hour zone. Iverson was in the passenger seat; thirty-two-year-old Maduro Earl Hill was driving, and Damon Darnell Stewart, twenty-five, was in the backseat.

The state trooper smelled marijuana as he approached the driver's-side window. Iverson leaned over from the passenger seat. "Officer," he said, "I got a gun in the car."

The .45-caliber Glock was on the floor in front of Iverson's seat. The officer, Michael Pierce, considered it concealed; Iverson balked. "It's right out in plain view," he argued. (In Virginia, it was illegal to carry a *concealed* gun, even if it was registered.)

Iverson was released on $2,000 bail; now, in a deal Woody reached with prosecutors, he would plead no contest to a concealed-weapons charge in exchange for avoiding prosecution on a misdemeanor marijuana-possession charge. The sentence would be three years' probation. But first he ducked into the court's anteroom and Croce's outstretched arms.

"You know I love you, Bubba, but you're killing us," Croce said. Like Gaskins, Croce knew firsthand that patronizing lectures don't work with Iverson. Instead, he began talking about his own life and his own hard lessons. He reminded Iverson of some of the buddies he'd introduced him to at the arena, the guys from his rambunctious youth who now came to watch the games with him from the owner's box. They were no-nonsense tough guys with names like Meat and T-Bone who rode Harleys and had lived lives. "They're *my* posse, Bubba," Croce said. "Only there were times I couldn't hang around with one or two of them, because they wouldn't stop powdering their noses. They'd bring me down. When they got their shit together, I welcomed them back."

But that's just the thing, Iverson explained—these guys weren't even his friends. He hardly knew them. He had just written some lyrics at a party, and as was his custom when inspiration hit, he was rapping aloud in front of anyone and everyone, a group of relative strangers. Someone said they had access to a recording studio in Richmond. Next thing you know, he was giving up the keys to his Benz to someone who knew the way. "I can't believe I did something so stupid," Iverson said now, looking at Croce, but speaking so softly he just may have been addressing himself.

As would often be the case, he'd provided his critics with ammunition; the widespread rookie-year bashing of his friends resumed. The irony was, of course, that had Gary Moore or Ra or Arnie or Marlon been around, they'd have never let him drive off with perfect strangers. But the pundits weighed in. "The 'hood and the arena don't always mix," wrote *Philadelphia Inquirer* columnist Tim Dwyer. "Iverson may be suffering from a case of blind loyalty to the 'hood."

Michael Wilbon's tone in the *Washington Post* was mimicked in papers and on broadcasts throughout the country. "There's no sense in preaching to Allen Iverson anymore, because all the indications are he ain't listening," he wrote. "Entourages didn't do a lot for rappers Tupac Shakur and Biggie Smalls, did they?"

Iverson's old friend Jim Spencer went so far as to suggest that new coach Larry Brown ought to "bench Iverson . . . until he found some more savory friends."

For his part, Iverson continued the pattern. He used the off-court controversy for fuel the next time he hit the hardwood. He didn't have to wait long. The day after his plea bargain, he was en route back to Philly, determined to wow his fans at a charity game.

The Baker League was an institution in Philadelphia, as was its longtime organizer, Sonny Hill. Hill was a widely respected community leader who had spent years using basketball leagues to mentor area youth; one of Croce's first moves as president of the 76ers was to make Hill his "executive adviser." During games, Croce would greet fans at one entrance while Hill glad-handed at the other. Now Hill had arranged for a group of 76ers to play in an exhibition against the traveling team Mel Rhome, which featured a number of ex–NBA players, including Rick Mahorn, who had gone to high school with Ann Iverson.

All day long, rumors were rampant that Iverson would show for Sonny's game. Hints were made on Power 99, Philly's hip-hop station, and on WIP, the all-sports talker. But Iverson had already gained a reputation as a no-show. He'd recently blown off an advertised appearance with Stackhouse to model their team's new uniforms for the crowd at an area mall. Come game time at Temple University's McGonigle Hall in North Philadelphia, two thousand fans awaited the possibility of the Answer's arrival and the buzz was palpable: Would he or wouldn't he show?

Croce, in jeans and a polo shirt, stood at one baseline, near Hill. Larry Brown sat in the stands, impassive as ever. Then, at 7:27, three minutes before tip-off, a roar went up from the entrance opposite where Croce stood. The cheers carried across the arena as Iverson, with his flair for the dramatic, came bounding onto the court. He hugged Stackhouse and then lingered in an embrace with Hill, who, as was his wont, whispered sagacious words in Iverson's ear. "I knew I'd be around people that love me," Iverson would say later, when asked why he'd showed.

But first he got busy on the court. In front of his new coach, he scored 47 points, dished out 7 assists, and swiped 2 steals. He was quicker, more determined, feistier than anyone else on the court. He fed off the close, intimate crowd, often slapping hands with kids sitting courtside. He was all emotion, smiling widely when he'd come frustratingly close to a steal, cursing when a touch foul was whistled against him. The crowd, likewise, oohed and aahed at his every move. All, that is, but Brown, who sat there, stoic.

Inbounding the ball a couple of times, Iverson was literally a matter of feet from Brown. Their eyes, however, wouldn't meet. It was as though both men were studiously avoiding each other.

With a little over a minute to go, and the game safely put away, Iverson ran off the court—as swiftly as he'd charged onto it. In the locker room, he briefly answered reporters' questions while putting on some $300,000 in jewelry and donning a Washington Redskins jersey. Then he was out the door, hustled into the passenger seat of a black Mercedes, while legions of kids gave chase down a rain-slick city street. Inside the arena, Larry Brown sat in the stands, exchanging pleasantries with Croce and Hill. He and his star had been in the same room for two hours, often just a matter of feet apart from one another. And neither man had thought, or could bring himself, to so much as say hello.

When the elevator opened in the lobby of Atlanta's Swiss Hotel, a cluster of young black men strode into the room. Terry Royster sized them up. None seemed tall enough to be an NBA stud. No, this couldn't be Allen Iverson and his boys.

Royster didn't follow basketball. He'd never heard of Iverson, but in the days leading up to this tryout assignment, scores of friends had filled him in on this character, who was, he was given to understand, not only the best thing since Jordan, but also the toughest, hardest dude in sports. Iverson's latest brush with the law convinced the star, and those around

Under the boards, Iverson likes to say, he is the "littlest man with the biggest heart."

him, of the need for a bodyguard. Who knows? Had there been someone being paid to watch his back that night in early August, maybe Iverson would never have embarked on his ill-fated trip to Richmond.

Royster had been handling security for a spate of South Beach clubs in Miami when, at David Falk's instruction, the bodyguard for Alonzo Mourning had contacted him. At six feet four inches and with a black belt in jujitsu, the thirty-seven-year-old Royster had protected the likes of Janet Jackson and Lionel Ritchie. Now he was in the lobby of an Atlanta hotel, home base for a wild weekend of parties starring everyone who was anyone in the hip-hop underworld. He was waiting for this Iverson character to show up.

"You my bodyguard?" the shortest of the group to come off the elevator said to him. Could this be him? This little guy? Royster started laughing; having heard how hard Iverson was, he was expecting a cross between Mike Tyson and Suge Knight. They shook hands while Iverson's boys—Ra, Arnie, Marlon, "E," Gold—looked him up and down. Another interloper.

First, Royster accompanied Cru Thik to a music-industry party and basketball game between Puff Daddy's Bad Boy Entertainment and Jumaine DuPri's Atlanta-based So So Def Records. Iverson refereed and hit it off with the best baller there—Mase, of Bad Boy. Mason Betha had played high-school ball at Manhattan Center High School, where he had scored over 30 points against Stephon Marbury in a play-off game. His high-school teammates included Richie Parker—a phenom whose career had been curtailed because of sexual-abuse charges—Cameron Giles, and Tim Gittens. Giles is now better known as the rapper Cam'ron and Gittens as "Headache," the New York City playground legend. (Fans at Rucker Park would throw Tylenol onto the court when Headache played.) Other well-known rappers showed they could play as well, including Busta Rhymes and Jadakiss, who would later star with Iverson in a Reebok commercial.

That night, Puffy threw a party at Echo's in Atlanta. Iverson found a spot atop the railing by the bar, and he settled back to watch the crowd while drinking Rémy Martin. So far, Royster had seen nothing to warrant Iverson's hard-bitten street reputation. In fact, the bodyguard was struck by just how laid-back the star was. At clubs, such would often be the case;

Iverson would get a drink and hang, surrounded by his boys. He'd neither socialize nor dance. If he weren't a star, he would hardly be noticed.

On this night, Royster detected the makings of a fight from clear across the room. In a matter of seconds, the rumble started to approach Cru Thik. Chairs were being tossed through the air; Royster reached up and grabbed Iverson from off the landing—the Rémy Martin spilled all over Iverson's white shirt—and started knocking people out of the way in a mad dash for the exit. Once outside, Iverson was livid. "Look what you done to my shirt!" he shouted. "Now I'm gonna smell like Rémy Martin all night!"

The rest of the night, Iverson wouldn't speak to Royster. Instead, he'd address his friends with asides meant for Royster's ears. "Can y'all believe what this nigga did to my shirt?" he'd say, over and over again.

"Dude," Royster finally said, "I kinda almost saved your life. Forget the shirt already."

No such luck. When he first saw Royster the next day, Iverson said, "Try not to spill anything on my shirt today." The talk of the weekend was the predicament Stephon Marbury found himself in. He was afraid to leave his hotel room—something Iverson couldn't quite comprehend. Turns out, Marbury had hit on the girlfriend of a notorious drug dealer. The dealer had already twice slapped Marbury in public, once at a club and once in the hotel lobby. Puff Daddy tried to settle matters by suggesting that Marbury and the dealer go at it for real, mano-a-mano.

"That's some bullshit right there," Iverson protested to his friends after Puffy's proposed settlement. Iverson recalled Puffy's treatment of Marbury a year earlier, when Iverson and Marbury had joined many of the Bad Boys' players for a night of partying just after they'd been drafted into the NBA. Marbury had some of his friends from Coney Island with him; when he poured them some champagne that Puffy was paying for, Puffy turned on the young star. "You pay for that?" he yelled. "You lucky I'm letting *you* drink my Cristal, let alone your punk-ass friends!"

"That was wrong," Iverson recalled now. "We were just drafted, we didn't have no money, and we were celebrating. So Steph pours a glass for his man. And this nigga, who was showing us off like we his little toys, just flipped on him."

Iverson asked Royster to see if he could help Marbury. Royster approached the dealer, whose defiant tone immediately softened when Royster mentioned that he was working for Allen Iverson. "I didn't know he was a friend of Mr. Iverson's," the dealer said, backing off. Royster could barely contain his laughter; even though Iverson had been nothing but cold toward him, he could see that the player was, in his words, "as sweet as apple pie." But because of his past in jail, not to mention his hip-hop look, Iverson's street reputation was right up there with gangbangers you didn't want to mess with.

Maybe it was Royster's rescue of Marbury. Or maybe it was Royster's good-natured reaction when Ra—the most gregarious of those in Cru Thik—started teasing the bodyguard for wearing slacks and shoes. "Look at them Sears pants!" Ra cracked. "Look at that shirt. He dress like a preacher!" Iverson, who still hadn't had a meaningful conversation with Royster, nonetheless signed off on the idea that he needed a permanent bodyguard. Royster would be moving to Philly to be by Iverson's side when his second professional season began.

The psychodrama that would grip Philadelphia, and much of professional basketball, for the next five years—the saga of Allen and Larry—got off to an inauspicious start. The Sixers opened the 1997–98 season at home against the Milwaukee Bucks sporting new uniforms; Croce, knowing of Iverson's artistic interests, had sought input from him in their design. But tonight Iverson wasn't wearing his uniform. He was serving his one-game suspension for the August arrest.

In his absence, it was widely anticipated that Stackhouse would shoulder the scoring burden for the home team. But Stackhouse would only play twenty minutes, hitting just one of five shots for 5 points. This after leading the team in scoring during the preseason, at 17 points per game, not to mention leading all second-year players the previous season (20.7 points per game). Larry Brown was Stackhouse's third coach in three years, and after the game, the player was visibly frustrated.

"Man, Coach keeps saying not to think about scoring," he said, taking one last look at the hang of his olive-green Donna Karan suit before leaving the locker room. "That's hard to do when you're a scorer. That's my game. My preseason numbers were misleading. Look at the Boston game. Sure, I got thirty-three points, but even that was only on eight shots. The rest were free throws."

Just a few doors away, Brown was facing the media. He didn't single out Stackhouse for criticism, but there was little doubt whom he was speaking of when he said, "There are one or two guys in that locker room who aren't buying into what we're trying to do. They say the right things, but if you're not going to guard somebody, you're not going to play for me." In the first half, Stackhouse had gotten lit up by the Bucks' Ray Allen.

Given Stackhouse's North Carolina pedigree, few expected him to be such an early tenant in Brown's doghouse. But Stackhouse didn't come into the league with Dean Smith's wholehearted endorsement. He had had the temerity to complain about his playing time during his freshman year at North Carolina, and though Smith loved his athleticism, he was never fully convinced that Stackhouse was his kind of "team-first" player. Perhaps that explains why, during training camp, Brown stripped Stackhouse of his team captaincy in favor of newcomer Jimmy Jackson, who played a similar go-to-the-hole style.

From his perspective, Stackhouse was playing with a backcourt mate who detracted from his game. Because Iverson wasn't a pure point guard focused on setting him up for high-percentage scoring chances, Stackhouse maintained, his own shooting suffered. In basketball jargon, he was having to create all his own shots. "Allen is really a shooting guard," he said. "He's not interested in being a distributor."

Iverson came back for game two of the young season, but it didn't matter. In fact, the Sixers lost their first five games. After losses, once the media cleared away from their lockers, Stackhouse and Iverson would sit together, commiserating. Neither had ever lost so regularly before. "It's going to get better," Stackhouse would tell his backcourt mate.

"It's got to," Iverson said. "Can't get no worse."

When Seattle visited Philadelphia, an incident during the game's waning moments signaled the changing times confronting the NBA. A fan charged onto the court toward SuperSonics star Gary Payton. Rather than turning the other cheek, Payton "kept it real": the two jawed at each other, faces pressed together, while security rushed the court. When asked later why he didn't just walk away, Payton responded, "Hey, I'm from the 'hood in Oakland. If he pulled a gun, I'd knock him out."

A new cultural moment was upon the league. It consisted of a generation of players, who, like the music they were raised on, were more in-your-face than ever before. The Sixers lost to the Sonics, 112–105. After the game, Brown didn't talk specifically of what Payton's demeanor might portend for the league. But he was fuming about his team's me-firstism, and he saw it as not unrelated to the new attitude embodied by the likes of Payton and Iverson. He spoke sarcastically of the hip-hop lexicon used by today's player—how, if you're "the man," you refer to yourself as "a baller"—and he blasted his own team to the hometown press. "We're not a team," he said, in that tight monotone that masked bubbling emotions. "As soon as things go bad, we start playing like a bunch of strangers. We look like a summer league all-star game on MTV . . . We don't play like a team. A team does little things. They get on the floor for loose balls, they block out, make an extra pass, set a screen."

Two days later, the tension of their winless start began getting to the Sixers. At practice in Houston, Stackhouse and Iverson sat next to each other on the sideline. Iverson rose to make his way to the Gatorade and Stackhouse called out, "Get me one, too."

"Do I look like Mr. Fuckin' Belvedere?" responded Iverson, walking away with his cup. Stackhouse just shook his head.

That night, however, the two were finally in sync on the court—even if it was only for one game. Against Charles Barkley's Houston Rockets, Iverson dominated. He scored 26 points and dished out 15 assists, many to Stackhouse, who hit 8 of his 13 shots. Astonishingly, the point guard who had led the NBA in turnovers as a rookie didn't commit a single giveaway the whole game. The Sixers won for the first time under Brown.

Privately, though, the Sixers knew they'd have to trade Stackhouse. Salaries were exploding throughout the league; the collective-bargaining agreement would be up at the close of the current season and contentious negotiations loomed. Owners wanted to institute a hard salary cap that would give them cost certainty. The panic reached new heights when Kevin Garnett re-signed with the Minnesota Timberwolves in a record six-year, $126 million deal. ("Call me when you're serious," Garnett had told his team when rejecting its first offer of $117 million.) There were indications that Stackhouse, who was in the final season of his three-year deal, would be seeking somewhere in the neighborhood of $70 million. More important, the new axiom in the NBA was that, to win, you needed two players who required double-teaming. It was still unclear whether Stackhouse would consistently draw two defenders.

In the meantime, Brown went public with praise for Stackhouse in an effort to boost the player's trade value. "Stackhouse has really worked on his medium-range jumper," he said. "Except for Michael Jordan, the midrange game is a lost art. I'm just happy Stack is working on that."

Still, the team was struggling, as were its two stars. The jettisoning of Stackhouse would, in effect, signal the handing off of the team to Iverson, a risky proposition. Few teams in league history, if any, had ever been built around a barely six-foot player. And was Iverson ready to be an NBA go-to man?

It was a question raised by Sixers officials after a loss in New York in mid-December. Iverson had just two assists in the game. Worse, he hooked up with Mase afterward, and the two, accompanied by members of Cru Thik and Bad Boy, spent the night in New York clubs. Iverson missed practice the next day at the New York Athletic Club; the *Philadelphia Daily News* reported that it was his third missed practice of the young season.

Pat Croce flew to Boston—the site of the Sixers' next game—in order to confront his star player. He was in a rage. He was angry and disappointed in Iverson, of course. But he was also frustrated by his coach's penchant for nonconfrontation. If Allen was missing practices, it was because he felt he *could.*

The trip to Boston turned out to be cathartic for Croce, as he had time to ponder how to reach his star. In his previous life as a physical therapist, he'd considered his talent spiritual, not technical. Anyone could learn how to administer ultrasound; Croce believed his gift was to get inside his patients' heads, to begin the healing process by showing them he cared about them. Allen, he realized, doesn't know what he doesn't know. When he blows off a practice, he doesn't mean to let me down, or Coach down, or Que down. He's just tired and hungover and—like any kid—he's going to sleep it off. Yes, the more he thought about it, the more Croce realized that he needed Allen to know how angry he was, but also how much he cared for him. He knew from therapy, as he'd later explain, that "when someone feels that someone believes in them, there's no telling what can be accomplished."

In Boston, Croce stormed into the locker room. Unlike the last time he came to Iverson's side during a turbulent time, there was no hug. Croce took Iverson into the vacant Bruins locker room and began by cursing and yelling at the player. He got up close, invading Iverson's treasured space. Peering into his eyes, Croce asked, "Do you believe I care about you?"

"Yeah," Iverson said softly, taken aback.

"DO YOU BELIEVE I CARE ABOUT YOU?" Croce shouted, the two men jaw to jaw. At first blush, it might have appeared that Croce was pulling a drill-sergeant power trip on his young charge. But then he explained himself: "C'mon," he prodded, still shouting. "I need your mind to hear your mouth say it! DO YOU BELIEVE I CARE ABOUT YOU?"

"Yes," Iverson responded, more forcefully.

"LOUDER, BUBBA!"

"YES!"

"You gotta know, Bubba, if I'm pissed like this, there's a reason," Croce said. "It's because I want you to get better. Because I care about you."

Outside the door, a handful of Sixers players milled about, a little confused and a little amused by the shouting coming from within. From Iverson's perspective, that Croce took him aside, one-on-one, made all the difference in the world. It reminded him of his relationship with his college coach; whenever John Thompson had a problem with Iverson, he'd express himself directly. "And I can take that like a man," Iverson explained. It was an approach that stood in stark contrast to the way Brown had been treating him. In fairness to Brown, coaches for ages had used the media as a conduit to get messages across to players. But Iverson was particularly sensitive to the specter of male-authority-figure betrayal; he seethed when he saw quotes in the newspaper from his coach about his play or punctuality—the substance of which Brown hadn't always communicated to him, man-to-man.

Despite the tension between Iverson and Brown, the Sixers announced a blockbuster trade in mid-December, with the team's record at 6–16. Stackhouse and center Eric Montross were shipped off to Detroit for six-foot ten-inch shot-blocking big man Theo Ratliff and six-foot five-inch guard Aaron McKie, a Philadelphia native who had starred at Temple University.

The Sixers still struggled, but Iverson began to flourish in Stackhouse's absence. In early January, he led the team over the mighty Bulls, scoring

31 points. A week before outdueling Jordan, he was named the NBA's Player of the Week. At the same time, Brown made a little-noticed move that would prove critical to the team's long-term success. He sent a second-round draft pick to Seattle for backup point guard Eric Snow, who rarely logged minutes for the Sonics because he had the misfortune of playing the same position as Gary Payton.

By the time the all-star break rolled around, Iverson was averaging over 20 points and nearly 7 assists per game. He didn't make the East's all-star squad, however, a snub that he vowed to use as motivation during the season's second half.

Allen Iverson inherited his mother's body clock. Like her, he requires little to no sleep. Also like Ann, he is naturally peripatetic. Off the court as well as on, he is meant to be in motion. So it ought to have been no surprise that he became a staple in Philadelphia's hip-hop scene, regularly appearing at clubs in the wee hours.

Not that he lived ostentatiously. Typically, Iverson's nights began at TGI Friday's on City Line Avenue, the same spot where Charles Barkley had reigned years before when he was Philadelphia's resident basketball superstar. (In fact, it was at Friday's where Barkley met his wife, Maureen.) Until the local sports-talk radio station started reporting it, Iverson would park his Bentley in one of the restaurant's handicapped spots and he and his friends would hang out, eating fried foods and drinking until near midnight. Then it was off to either some strip clubs—Studio 37 and Prince's Black Experience were among the obscure favorites—or the clubs on Philly's Delaware Avenue.

One night, Iverson and his friends, accompanied by Sixers forward Tim Thomas, headed for a CD release party for the rapper Kurupt at Gothum Night Club. In the house was alleged Philly mobster "Skinny" Joey Merlino and Luke Campbell of the pioneering rap group 2 Live Crew. Upon entering, Royster exchanged words with the bouncer. "It's never a good sign when a bouncer has an ego," he told Iverson, once Cru Thik was searched and admitted entry.

As the night wore on, the crowd grew wilder. Campbell had come accompanied by some exotic dancers, who, at his urging, peeled off their formfitting dresses and began simulating oral sex for the crowd. Shortly thereafter, the gunshots started.

Seemingly en masse, the crowd rushed for the exit. But there were people outside shooting back *into* the club. The first wave of those seeking escape made an about-face and tried rushing back in; now people were getting trampled. The shooters made their way into the club; two feet in front of Iverson, a man was hit thirteen times in his chest.

"Trust me and follow!" Royster yelled, maneuvering his way through the screaming crowd. Along with a handful of others, they found their way to a side exit and crawled under a fence. They ran for the parking lot; except the shooting was now coming back outside; the only sound filling the night air was the *ping, ping* of bullets ricocheting off cars. While Iverson sprinted, a stranger appeared alongside him, stride for stride.

"Allen, I want you to hear this tape, man!" the man said, huffing and puffing to keep pace. "When you open your record label, call me! My name is on the tape!"

Iverson didn't break stride, but he did break out in laughter. Bullets were whizzing by—and this guy was trying to sell himself! Just then, a car came speeding down the street, shooting. Everyone dove for cover, with Royster on top of Iverson, who couldn't stop laughing. "This is something out of a movie, man! This is fun," he said.

Finally, safe in the car, Iverson couldn't stop laughing about their action-adventure sequence. "Y'all see me? Dive and roll, man, dive and roll!"

When Royster picked Iverson up for practice the next day at Iverson's home in Conshohocken, a suburb of Philly, the star was, as ever, mum. Getting in the passenger seat, he teased Royster about the Tupac song "All Eyez on Me" that was playing—as always. "This nigga knows one rap song and he's always got it playing, trying to impress me," Iverson would say to his friends while Royster laughed at the ribbing. "I think he adjusts it when he's in the driveway so when I get in, I think he's cool 'cause he's listening to a rap song."

As always, they stopped at a Wawa convenience store and Royster bought Iverson a copy of the *Daily News.* Iverson took his headphones off as he read the news account of the previous night's shooting. No mention of him, which was good. Nor did it capture anywhere near how many people had been wounded. Iverson had seen bodies being thrown into cars that barely slowed down before peeling away. Though he'd been laughing the night before, it was laughter born of adrenaline and crisis.

"Man, that shit was crazy last night," he said, folding up the paper. "We are not going back to that place." (According to press reports, a patron who had been thrown out of the club shot and killed the bouncer and wounded two bystanders.)

Unlike his rookie year, when a rotating cast of Cru Thik members resided with him in the Conshohocken house, Iverson's home life was becoming more settled. At Ann's urging, the friends no longer crashed at the house every night. Instead, Iverson rented a floor at the nearby Holiday Inn, where some of the wilder parties went down. That's where Ra, Arnie, Jamil Blackmon, and the rest stayed; often, after one or the other would ring up in excess of $15,000 in room service and phone charges, the account would come due. Iverson would pay up and identify one room—say, Arnie's—as the one that could order room service. So the whole crew would crowd into Arnie's spot, gorging, until that room's bill got big enough to be called to Allen's attention.

Meantime, at the house, Aunt Jessie—Li'l Bit—came to cook for her nephew. Tawanna and Tiaura would visit every so often from Virginia. When Ann was around, there was no missing her. The first time Royster met her, he wondered if she ever stopped talking long enough to catch her breath. "You the bodyguard supposed to be watching my baby?" she said. "You better watch my baby's ass!" Without missing a beat, she was on to a totally different subject, Royster's presence no doubt having reminded her of David Falk: "And where is that bald-headed muthafucka that's supposed to be getting me all my money every month?" she vented. "How come I never see his muthafuckin' ass around here?"

Iverson was providing for his mother, her boyfriend George Jackson (known as Jack), Allen's two sisters, Jessie and her three kids, uncles Stevie and Greg and their families, not to mention all his friends—and their kids, including their babies' mothers. Each month, Falk's office would cut checks to an extended, and rotating, list. At Christmastime, Iverson took about twenty of his friends and relatives to the Coliseum Mall back in Hampton for an unprecedented shopping spree. Guys bought computers and big-screen TVs for their parents, grandparents, and significant others; Royster estimates that Iverson spent close to six figures in one day.

For a guy with a reputation for being irresponsible, Royster thought, he's the most responsible person I've ever seen. It seemed like he willingly shouldered the burden of lifting up an entire community. And yet Royster never heard Iverson complain. Once, together, they counted the number of people Iverson supported. It came to twenty-nine. "You know what?" Iverson said. "You and me are the only two people I know who've got jobs."

"That's fucked up," Royster said.

"Yeah, but think how fucked up they'd all be if it wasn't for me," Iverson responded.

The Sixers were out of the play-off hunt early in the second half of the 1997–98 season, but the season's drama was far from over. The question hanging over the team was, would Iverson re-sign during the coming summer, or would he enter his third NBA season next fall as a potential free agent the following spring?

Iverson was still wounded from what he saw as Brown's hypocrisy—Brown would use words like "family" to describe his team, and then, from Iverson's perspective, he'd take their family business public during postgame press conferences, pointing fingers that ought to be pointed in the locker room. "I'll remember everything this summer," Iverson said. "I really will think about all the things that have been said about me this year."

As so often would be the case, Brown and Iverson were talking past each other. Brown bemoaned Iverson's oversensitivity; why, he wondered, couldn't Iverson realize the difference between *criticism* and *coaching*? Iverson's complaint wasn't with the substance of what Brown had to say; it was *who* he was saying it to. When he publicly questioned Iverson's shot selection, or—a common complaint—the fact that the point guard would often take a shot before one of his teammates had touched the ball, Brown seemed to be an accomplice in what Iverson considered the cartoonish media portrayal of him as selfish and disinterested in winning.

Indeed, as Brad Greenberg had predicted before drafting Iverson, he was the most competitive basketball player this side of the almighty Jordan. Jordan's competitive fires were played up in the media as the stuff of legend; how they'd fueled his gambling jones, how he'd force his teammates to play cards until he was ahead. Those around Iverson saw the same qualities, only it was hardly ever chronicled. They saw Iverson tire of losing at pool, of seeing his name with a zero next to it on his basement scoreboard, and *will* himself into being the best pool player among his friends. They saw him, tipsy after a night of clubbing, challenge others—strangers and friends alike—to 2 A.M. dashes down deserted city streets, cell phones and pagers flying off his body, determined to prove no one could take him in a footrace, even if he'd been drinking, even if he was wearing Timberlands.

"He's just not going to be in the losing column," Royster recalls today. "I don't care what it is. Once, in Norfolk, we played two-on-two touch football on a whim. He said, 'I'll take T, and I betcha we score every time.' He tells me, 'Just run this pattern and the ball will be there every time.' And, I mean, it was—a touchdown, every time. He'd take a three-step drop and throw that thing seventy yards, and it was there, every single time. And it didn't have to be basketball or football. We once played seventy-five games of checkers in his basement, until I couldn't beat him."

The Sixers started making moves that appeared designed to heighten the chance that Iverson would remain with the team. First, they traded Clarence Weatherspoon, Jimmy Jackson, and elder statesman Terry Cummings to the Golden State Warriors for Iverson's old friend from back home, Joe Smith. Smith, the top pick in 1995, had, so far, been a disappointment as a pro. The acquisition of Smith made the Sixers the only team in the league to have three players who had once been top picks in the NBA draft: Iverson, Smith, and Derrick Coleman. Yet with all that talent, Brown hadn't yet molded his roster into a team.

Coleman, in particular, presented a dilemma. Incongruously, Brown loved him. Though Brown was known as a coach who valued practice, Coleman didn't practice often; when he did, he could be lackluster. But he had a tremendous basketball IQ and would talk basketball for hours with Brown. From Croce's perspective, however, championships are built on intangibles as much as physical talent. It didn't bode well that, when Croce rounded up every player for a trip to Philadelphia's Children's Hospital to lift the spirits of ill kids, Coleman was the only player to decline. "I don't do hospitals," he said.

Well, it's *his* soul, Croce thought, storming off. But the more he mulled it over, the more convinced he became that, in his view, a soulless player would be an impediment to winning—and a bad influence on Iverson. Coleman's contract could be bought out for $5.5 million at season's end. Until now, Croce had kept silent on matters pertaining to basketball, deferring, as was his management style, to an expert like Brown. But now he made it known: he didn't want Coleman back. He told Brown it would be his call, but that there would have to be unanimity among the basketball staff: head scout Tony DiLeo and vice president of basketball operations Billy King, Brown's onetime assistant at Indiana, would have to sign on to bringing Coleman back as well.

Meantime, Brown experimented on the court with an idea that would ultimately alter Iverson's career and the Sixers' fortunes. His team was losing to Dallas by 14 with less than six minutes to go when, seemingly on a whim, Brown paired Eric Snow at the point with Iverson at shooting guard. Iverson, relieved of the stress attached to running the team and thereby spared Brown's carping, scored 12 points, including a clutch three-pointer with 5.5 seconds left, to lead the Sixers to a 91–90 comeback win. For the remainder of the season, Brown continued the experiment, finding fifteen minutes or so per game for Iverson as a two-guard.

Iverson didn't see much in the distinction between point and shooting guards. To him, his game was his game. "I'm not a point guard or a two-guard," he said. "I'm a creator." And in the modern NBA, the lines blurred. Old-time, classic "distributor" point guards like Mo Cheeks were becoming a thing of the past. Now Michael Jordan or Scottie Pippen brought the ball up for the Bulls—was either of them the "point guard"? Hardly. They were good ball handlers who could start the offense.

Iverson may have thought Brown was unnecessarily wedded to an antiquated model, but Brown was looking for a way to get Iverson's teammates some touches. (Phil Jackson had accomplished the same goal in Chicago by running the "triangle offense," a much-lauded system of cuts and passes, at least until a game was on the line; that's when Michael took over.) In Brown's estimation, the Sixers would never become a true team until other players felt the ball in their hands more often. He also started to realize that Iverson's teammates needed to be of a special breed; that is, they had to be willing to put their own egos aside, to forfeit their own scoring, in order to play with someone who would take so many shots.

Late in the season, *Sports Illustrated* published a story on Iverson that reverberated from the Sixers' locker room to a Connecticut prison. In Connecticut, where Iverson's biological father, Allen Broughton, had taped photos of his son to his cell's walls, a guard came to see him. "You don't have anything to worry about when you get out," said the guard.

"Your son said in *Sports Illustrated* that he's gonna take care of you when you get out."

Broughton's heart leaped. Then he read the article. Iverson said, when asked about his jailed father, "Soon as he gets out, I got him. I got him forever. Whatever he needs." There was only one problem: he was speaking of Michael Freeman, the man he considers his father. Broughton, heartbroken, still claiming he wanted nothing from his son but a renewed relationship, resigned himself to the fact that he'd never get what he wanted from his famous progeny.

While Broughton agonized over one line in the *SI* piece, Iverson was incensed by a quote from another would-be father figure who often disappointed him: Brown. "To Brown the problem is modern NBA superstardom, which too often prevents a player from getting to know his teammates, prevents him from *trusting* them," wrote Rick Reilly. "When you bolt every game with a phalanx of high school buddies, bodyguards and Reebok chaperones, any teammate who is trying to bond with you has to follow along in his own car. 'The company Allen's with is Reebok, not really us,' Brown says."

Iverson read the line over and over. He'd known that Brown hadn't been warm to Gaskins, had actually kept him from the locker room on occasion. But did his coach really think he was more loyal to Reebok than to his own team? How could his own coach help the media—which had been against him since high school—assassinate his character that way?

The season ended with the Sixers posting a 31–51 record. Though it was the team's best record since the 1991–92 season, more questions plagued the organization than answers. As they headed into a perilous off-season labor dispute, the jury was still out on whether Larry Brown and Allen Iverson could peacefully coexist.

中
心

l OLD
My
gOWN

Nonno
Douce

chapter 9

LOYALTY

this is chinese for "loyalty." because i'd rather
be loyal to the people that were loyal to me.

The summer of 1998 became the off-season that wouldn't end when, thanks to contentious collective bargaining negotiations, NBA owners locked out the players. The upcoming season was in jeopardy.

Commissioner Stern succinctly summarized the issue facing his league: "Revenues are rising, profitability is declining, and ticket prices are going up." The main point of contention centered on the players' share of league revenues, defined as "basketball-related income." According to the league, the players were now getting over 57 percent of that income, and some thirteen teams were losing money. But the players, led by Iverson's agent, Falk, and Jordan (who was keeping mum about his retirement plans, the better to maintain his leverage in the labor talks), weren't buying it. They argued that the owners had been crying poor despite the windfall from a whopping $2.64 billion TV contract with NBC and TNT. (Barkley even chided Stern about the commissioner's $9 million annual salary: "Have *you* ever heard the words 'salary cap'?") But the owners could afford to play hardball and institute a lockout because the TV money was guaranteed—whether there was a season or not.

The issue really came down to defining league revenues. Deputy Commissioner Russ Granik maintained that "basketball-related income . . . now basically includes the kitchen sink." Not quite. It didn't include the bulk of money generated by luxury seating or arena signage, for example. Comcast, the company that owns Iverson's Sixers *and* the arena they play in, assigned revenue generated by naming rights, premium seating, signage, concessions, and parking to their building—thereby protecting that money from being shared with the players. Moreover, Jordan argued that the owners were seeking givebacks from the players as relief from their own bad salary decisions. The owners had all made fortunes as capitalists, yet here they were, fighting for a salary cap, an artificial restriction on their laborers' earnings. In a way, Jordan cemented his place as the nation's premier working-class capitalist by arguing for a free market.

The negotiations were likely to directly impact Iverson. Given the precedent of the Garnett megadeal, he'd be looking at a long-term contract in excess of $100 million. But it was precisely those kind of numbers the owners were seeking to bring in line. Despite his personal stake in the issue, Iverson didn't get involved in the labor dispute. Later, he'd regret his disinterest. But the summer of 1998 found him once again basking in his off time, even if it had no end in sight.

In July, Iverson got ready to host the first Allen Iverson Summer Celebrity Classic, a weekend of activities in Hampton organized by Gary Moore to benefit the local Boys and Girls Clubs that Iverson used to attend. The decision to do something for area kids emerged from a pact he had made many years before with Gary Moore, his grade-school football coach and mentor, to remain committed to kids who grew up just as he had. "I just want these little kids, who aren't fortunate enough to have resources other kids have, to know they have someplace safe to go, you know what I'm saying?" Iverson explained.

But his good intentions were also colored by his characteristic defiance. After all that had happened to him in his hometown, there was a part of Iverson that wanted to stick it to those who had doubted him—by doing good. "I was incarcerated for something I didn't do," he said. "I could have easily been bitter and stayed out of Hampton and never done anything for the community. But I didn't. I was the bigger man in that situation . . . For what y'all did to me, I'm coming right back to the same place and I'm going to raise money for the Boys and Girls Clubs. I'm going to do something for these kids and this community, whether you like it or not."

Iverson's charity event was overshadowed by the news on the eve of the weekend that Arnie Steele and Mike Powell had been arrested in Norfolk driving Iverson's $138,000 Mercedes-Benz and charged with dealing cocaine. Iverson was not involved in the arrest, nor was he brought in for questioning. But his car was impounded and subject to Virginia drug-forfeiture laws. The Benz was history. More pressing, the arrests led to more headlines about the crowd Iverson ran with—at the precise moment when he was seeking to do something good back home. "He was pissed at Arnie at first," recalls Royster, who was with Iverson when he heard about the arrest. "But that quickly turned to being concerned for him and just wanting to make sure the guys were all right."

As the summer stretched to fall, there appeared no end in sight to the labor impasse. Iverson used the extended time to pursue another passion, rap music. Mase had blown up into a full-fledged superstar; his CD *Harlem World* had topped the charts the year before. He invited Iverson to Atlanta, where he was recording. In the studio, Iverson penned some lyrics and got behind the mike.

Iverson had always modeled his rapping style after that of "E" and Ra, the two best rappers he'd known. "E" especially had a distinct flow; he didn't rhythmically sync his voice to the beat so much as speak in a natural cadence that floated above it.

Now, as Iverson started rapping, Mase cut him short. "No, no," he said. "You gotta say it without it sounding like you just wrote it."

Mase encouraged Iverson to feel the beat. They pulled an all-nighter, taking time for only one break, during which they played hoops and hit a couple of strip clubs, before returning to the studio. They eventually emerged with Iverson contributing two verses on a single called "Pay Per View": "Yo, this is the Answer/It's a dirty, dirty, dirty dance/If we don't get the money we want, we're locked out/That's why I run with them Harlem World niggas / Everybody I'm running with is the highest paid in what we do/That's why this shit is Pay Per View . . ." Later, he raps: "A.I., Betha in Miami/G's in our pockets/Pullin' out on these bitches like Tubbs and Crockett . . ."

As the night wore on, Mase grew more and more outspoken about his own hoops game vis-à-vis Iverson's. Around two in the morning, Iverson had had enough of Mase's trash-talking. "Man, you keep running your mouth, I'll play you one-on-one for ten grand," he said, issuing his standard offer, a challenge so outlandish its mere mention served as an act of intimidation. "We'll play to twenty, I'll give you nineteen and the ball five times in a row. Then I'm gonna score twenty unanswered."

They went to Run and Shoot, an all-night inner-city gym. As promised, Iverson stopped Mase five times in a row. Then, with a crowd forming, he hit 19 in a row, even though Mase was trying to foul him on every shot. With the score tied at 19, Mase started to fret. Iverson missed a jumper; Mase, knowing the momentum was clearly against him, got the rebound and—without taking the ball back—put it back up for a layup. Then he started jumping around, hands in the air, as though he'd won. "Hell if I was about to pay him," Iverson would later recall.

Still, it didn't stop Mase from spending the rest of the night boasting about how he'd beaten the Answer. From Run and Shoot, they went to Atlanta's The Gold Club, a spot that would later make headlines for providing ballplayers (including Patrick Ewing and Iverson's future teammate Dikembe Mutombo) with sexual favors. There they were ushered into a private part of the club. Women were sent in. The bouncers at the door assured them that they wouldn't have to worry about anybody coming in and that they could do whatever they wanted. Royster didn't like the vibe. " 'Chuck, something's wrong here," he said. "I don't like the way they're force-feeding us. There could be cameras in here or something."

Iverson didn't necessarily share Royster's suspicions, but he didn't like the executive-type feel of the place. "Let's just go to one of our down-and-dirty spots," Royster suggested.

"That's what I'm talking 'bout," Mase agreed.

Once they got to a more downscale club, Mase regaled the crowd with chatter about his hardcourt "conquest." When Iverson took a sip of his Texas Tea, Mase boasted, "That's right—drown your sorrows!" When Iverson got a lap dance, Mase yelled to the girl to "ask him who beat his ass!"

"Yeah," Mase called out while Iverson laughed at his friend's playing the fool. "I just come from shutting Allen Iverson's lights out."

Then it was back to laying down tracks. Later, Iverson would speak about how much he learned from Mase in the studio. But he also realized something else. Rapping was fun, but basketball was his life. He yearned to get back on the court.

The lockout ended on January 7, 1999, leaving roughly three weeks for abbreviated training camps before the commencement of a fifty-game regular season in early February. The union agreed to a limit on the earnings of individual players. As a result, the new collective-bargaining agreement would cost Iverson more than $30 million. There was no doubt that as a franchise player he would get the maximum salary for a player beginning his third year. David Falk called the Sixers' Billy King and consummated the deal in about ten minutes, King would later tell Iverson. It was for six years and $71 million.

"I'm not greedy," Iverson said, when questioned about the effect the new agreement had on him. "I don't have to make twenty million dollars a year to play basketball, to do something I really love."

Unlike almost all other sports superstars dotting the public landscape, Iverson singled out his team owner as one of the main reasons he wanted to sign the deal and stay in Philly long-term. One day, shortly after the season opened, he sat in front of his locker wearing baggy jeans, Timberlands, and an Enyce sweatsuit, and he made it clear where his loyalties lay. From day one, he said, Pat Croce had kept it real with him. "He didn't shoot me no curves," Iverson said. "He didn't come in and kiss my ass or try and show me that he wasn't going to kiss my ass. He just ain't phony. Coach Brown is my coach, and I respect him for what he's taught me. But for whatever reason, Pat knows how to handle himself."

In the off-season, the Sixers had become Iverson's team. The other big names were gone. Coleman's contract, in keeping with Croce's wishes, had been bought out. Joe Smith was similarly jettisoned. Instead, the team signed shot blocker Theo Ratliff to a long-term deal and brought in free-agent center Matt Geiger, who had been a serviceable backup in Charlotte. Geiger was seven-one, with a reputation for toughness and soft shooting skills. With his shaved head, goatee, "Carpe Diem" tattoo, and avant-garde fashion sense, he added color to Brown's suddenly egoless locker room. Geiger, Ratliff, Tim Thomas, and Carolina alum George Lynch held down the frontcourt spots, and Eric Snow, Aaron McKie, and first-round draft choice Larry Hughes—the national freshman of the year at the University of St. Louis—complemented Iverson in the backcourt.

This is the team that got off to a 4–1 start, despite Iverson's early-season shooting woes. In one early-season win, Iverson hit on only 4 of his 17 shots. Afterward, McKie, who had become closer to him than anyone else on the team, noticed how upset Iverson was by his subpar shooting. "Would you rather have forty points and a loss or fifteen points and a win?" McKie asked him. "You choose. That'll show what type of player you are."

Beginning with Stackhouse, Brown had cleaned house of big-name offensive talents in favor of those willing to do defensive-oriented grunt work. Since his arrival in Philly, he had relentlessly preached defense; now his sermons finally began to pay off. Even when his team followed up its 4–1 start with four straight losses, he remained upbeat. "This is the proudest I've been in a long, long time," he said after a 76–69 loss to Atlanta. "It was as good a defensive period as we've played."

It was just one example of Brown's penchant for seemingly counterintuitive coaching. There was value, he'd learned, in being tough and critical when your charges were riding high, and in being soothing and understanding when times were tough. During a horrendous losing spell while coaching the University of Kansas in 1988, Brown had entered his team's locker room and was met by a squad expecting a Bobby Knight–type tirade. Instead, he told them he'd "never been prouder" of them, that he felt things were on the upswing thanks to their effort and unselfishness. It became a self-fulfilling prophecy, as Kansas went on to win the national title.

Brown's comments, combined with his early-season decision to move Iverson to shooting guard and play Eric Snow at the point for over thirty minutes a game, were panning out. Freed of the responsibility of running the team on every play, Iverson found new ways to distribute and create. Thanks to the intricate screens Brown devised, he often found himself with the ball in his hands only after all of his teammates had touched it. He was named the NBA Player of the Month for February, averaging 28.5 points, 6 assists, 5.8 rebounds, and 2.31 steals.

On March 11, the Sixers' record stood at 11–8, their best start since the 1990–91 season. But Brown—ever counterintuitive—was suddenly not happy. He pulled Iverson from an 85–70 win over Charlotte after Iverson launched a series of ill-advised shots while there was still plenty of time on the twenty-four-second clock. Iverson, for his part, never had much use for twenty-four-second clocks. He played on feel, not by design—a tendency that, given his preternatural self-confidence, led him to disregard such matters as the shot clock or his teammates' "touches." Brown, with his constant scribbling of intricate plays, didn't coach feel; despite his own emotional nature, he was the ultimate rationalist as a coach.

As Brown and Iverson struggled over issues like shot selection, the stakes were raised on the morning of March 12, when Royster called in Iverson's absence from practice. Tawanna, now living with Allen (along with their two kids), had recently suffered a miscarriage. The message was that she was sick and Allen had to stay at home and help with Deuce (Allen II), two, and Tiaura, five.

Brown was livid and complained publicly that he hadn't heard from Iverson himself—only "his guy," Royster—and stated that Iverson's unexcused absence was "not the first time." When Brown addressed the local media horde after the missed practice, there was no doubt whom he was speaking of, even though he didn't mention Iverson by name. "You've got to be a team in every sense of the word," he said. "That means you respect your teammates. You show them respect by how you act, how you practice, how you play . . . We have a lot of people who have good character and care, but that's not enough. You need all your people to do that."

Iverson wasn't happy about Brown's public airing, and he was even more upset by the comments of unnamed teammates in the *Philadelphia Inquirer,* one of whom said, "We simply can't have that. If he doesn't have a legitimate excuse, he's got to pay the price. Any one of us would have to. The same should apply to him."

Of course, as Jordan had proved in Chicago, rules tended to be different for superstars. Such was the case even before Jordan. In Philadelphia some thirty years before, after Wilt Chamberlain missed a game-day shoot-around, he told his complaining coach: "I'm coming to the arena once. You can have your choice: I'll come to shoot-around or the game." Come game time, he was in the lineup.

Iverson, in addition to feeling betrayed by his coach and teammates, was puzzled over just what the rules were. In the past, he'd had Royster phone in his absences and no one had said anything. As Croce had long feared, Brown's reluctance to confront his players face-to-face was now reaping consequences.

The truth was that few in the Sixers organization believed Iverson's excuse. They knew that Mase had been in town the night before and that the two had gone out clubbing till the wee hours. Their night started at Friday's, where they hung until closing. Then it was on to Club Risque, where Iverson kept knocking down Texas Teas. Then they ended up at the after-hours Palmer Social Club. Mase had been trying to turn in early all night; he was in the process of being saved and would soon give up his lucrative recording career to become a preacher. It was Iverson who kept dragging his friend to the next spot. "C'mon, you're in my town now," he'd say. (Many in hip-hop were skeptical of Mase's later conversion; Iverson, however, believed it. It had to be real, he said, because Mase wouldn't "go to no titty bars no more.")

Of course, both things could be true: Iverson could have been out all night *and* Tawanna could have been under the weather. That's basically what Iverson said when confronted by the media over whether he'd been out on the town with Mase. If ever there was a moment that best symbolized his anti-Jordan status, this was it, as Iverson stood before the TV cameras and defended his right to party all night with a rap star. "I guess people felt one of my friends was in town, I was hanging out all night," he said. "Well, I hang out all night anyway, if I want to. But I still come in here and give these people the same thing I always give them."

During the controversy, Iverson scoured both the *Daily News* and the *Inquirer* for critical public comments from Croce. He found none. "He kept it in the family," Iverson said. "He'll rip me man-to-man, but he won't go to the paper and try to tear me down, because he already knows they're not for me, they're against me. That's okay. People been against me my whole life. So it would shock me for Pat to talk about me like that."

Meantime, the Sixers traded Tim Thomas to Milwaukee for power forward Tyrone Hill, who would become a critical player for the team. The next night, the New Jersey Nets came to town, having just completed a blockbuster trade to acquire Stephon Marbury from Minnesota. Marbury didn't play on this night because he hadn't taken the mandatory posttrade physical yet. Nonetheless, when Iverson came out for the pregame warm-up, he was surprised to see David Falk sitting courtside with Nets owner Lewis Katz. Falk had recently taken on Marbury as a client and was said to have been the driving force behind the trade. Iverson said hello to Falk before the game, but he had not been pleased when he heard that his agent would also be representing his rival, nor was he happy that on this night, Falk was sitting with the opposing team's owner in *his* house.

Some had thought Brown would suspend Iverson for missing the practice. Instead, Iverson not only played, he started and scored 28 points—again flourishing at the center of a storm. Ratliff was dominant, with 23 points, 11 rebounds, and 7 blocks. The Sixers fought back from 13 down to win in overtime. As always, a win seemed to bury the controversy.

But Falk's appearance at the game—seemingly to support someone else—was the final straw for Iverson. Saying he "felt like the prey," Iverson severed ties with the agent some were calling the most powerful man in sports. The issues had been building up. Despite the fact that his new contract took all of ten minutes to hammer out, Falk charged Iverson his standard 4 percent. From Iverson's standpoint, since it was such an easy deal, he should have charged an hourly rate, as Ray Allen's lawyer had done. Moreover, there had been a recent news story about Iverson defaulting on his car payments to Mercedes-Benz. In his view, Falk's office was responsible for that. Then there was Ann, who said Falk's office had made travel plans for her; when she got to the airport, there were no tickets awaiting her.

Finally, the jettisoning of Falk signified far more than an agent-client dispute. Falk was a paradigmatic figure, a man who had taken a simple surname, "Jordan," and turned it into a cultural touchstone. Thanks to Falk, the Jordan name not only meant something to America (many things, actually), it *provoked* an emotional response. Jordan was—particularly to his white crossover audience—a soothing figure. He was a beautiful and beautifully athletic black man who, unlike so many other beautiful and beautifully athletic black men, was not "angry."

The Jordan crossover, as engineered by Falk, succeeded because white Americans got to participate fully in what was "Jordan" without ever having their race guilt triggered. Jordan's white fans didn't think of him as black the way Ali's white fans thought of *him* as black; Jordan didn't construct his public persona out of his blackness. As a result, the world's most dangerous man on the hardwood was utterly unthreatening as a symbol; he "transcended" race, which is to say that in his planed, smiling face, white Americans (unconsciously) sought and found permission to *forget* about race—both his and theirs. Thus the Jordan appeal, while giving the impression of having "overcome" race—of having "solved" the race problem—merely sidestepped the issue altogether. For creating this phenomenon, Falk was, unquestionably, a genius.

Unfortunately, he was also a one-trick pony. Which meant, almost by definition, that a Falk-Iverson relationship could only come to a sorry end. Was there ever a man more ill-suited than Iverson to become a soothing crossover figure—someone who could willfully and skillfully obviate his race by giving white America permission to forget it? There was not. Nevertheless, Falk tried to do with Iverson what he'd done with Jordan, to subject Iverson to the old crossover model of marketing. He constantly counseled Iverson against the tattoos and cornrows and baggy jeans, arguing that such style choices didn't attract corporate interest. That's why Falk had been able to get Iverson only one major endorsement deal, Reebok for $50 million. But as Que Gaskins was always pointing out, there was an emerging youth culture Iverson could tap into. Gaskins noted that DMX had the number one CD in the country—and those were suburban white boys buying those raps. And there was Lauryn Hill, braids and all, on the cover of *Time* magazine.

Falk was the ultimate handler, and Iverson wouldn't be handled. As he'd later say, he fired Falk in part because "I wanted to be in charge of my own shit." Iverson was aware that, in music, the crossover era had given us artists who were the product but who had little or no control. Stevie Wonder and Al Green didn't own their own master recordings, for example. It was hip-hoppers like Puff Daddy, Dr. Dre, and Master P who made themselves the product *and* the entrepreneurs behind it.

It was a distinction pressed upon Iverson by Earvin "Magic" Johnson, whose counsel he sought before getting rid of Falk. Johnson was managing Mase's career, and he spoke to Iverson while Mase was with him during a taping of the NBA TV show *Inside Stuff*. Iverson saw that Jordan, under Falk's tutelage, had made his money the old-fashioned way: by selling himself as a pitchman. Johnson, however, was building an empire by growing businesses in minority communities, employing people where they live. There were his string of Magic Johnson movie theaters and his groundbreaking partnerships with Starbucks and TGI Friday's, Iverson's favorite hangout. When Iverson sought Johnson's advice, the basketball legend didn't mention Falk but didn't hide his disdain for agents, either. "Too many guys forget the agents work for us, not the other way around," Johnson said. "The problem young athletes have is they let their agents and managers speak for them."

It was rumored that Johnson was getting into the agent game, though as a part owner of the Lakers, he was prohibited from doing so in any explicit way. But Johnnie Cochran had made public his plans to become a sports agent, and Iverson had already talked to Puff Daddy about his interest in steering Iverson's career. And Master P's No Limit Sports was signing up athletes as well.

But Iverson took Johnson's message to heart and decided it would be unwise to have anyone other than his lawyers, Shuttleworth and Woodward, look out for him. Aligning himself with Magic, Johnnie Cochran, Puffy, or Master P might make for a cool story, but at the end of the day, he didn't trust that putting his career in the hands of someone who was arguably a bigger star than himself would work to his benefit. Besides, though he wanted to learn about this business stuff and become a businessman like Magic, he didn't want to be distracted from ball. His team was finally winning, and as he observed to Gaskins one day, all this business stuff takes care of itself if you're winning.

"Winning means everything," he said.

Y'all got any new questions for me?" Iverson said, surrounded by the daily journalistic pack on the court at St. Joseph's University, just after Sixers practice. The questions, as he knew full well, weren't new. But they were fired at him anyway, and he answered, as usual, in a deep monotone behind droopy eyelids.

It made for a telling scene, one that played out in professional-sports-team locker rooms across the country. A young black athlete accosted by a sweating, jostling pack of overwhelmingly white, middle-aged sportswriters and broadcasters. The clichéd questions would come, the athlete would answer in like-minded clichés, and the whole interaction would smack of the impersonal. Both sides seemed unaware of their roles in a generational, racial, and cultural divide. The men—and they were mostly men—who presented Iverson to the world were alienated from him in at least two significant ways: they couldn't relate to his upbringing—eight friends killed in one summer!—nor could they grasp the riches in which he now basked.

Add to that schism Iverson's history with the media, how, at the tender age of seventeen, he felt turned on by the press of his hometown, *judged* by them, and his current bored, disinterested media mask became understandable. That history even explains the markings on his skin. It wasn't until his rookie year, when he didn't recognize himself in all the breathless coverage of him as a "thug" with a "posse," that he decided to use his body as though it were his own personal billboard. He would advertise who he was on his very own skin, because if he couldn't control how he was portrayed or perceived, he knew he could control his own body. It's the one thing he'd always been able to control, the one thing that had gotten him where he was today. And so he started going down to South Street in Philly, to a place called Body Graphics; he liked to say he got addicted to the needle, but he really got hooked on expressing himself, on the notion that he could carve into his own skin announcements of who he was. You want to know who I am, he'd say, "Just read my body."

Yet few in the media did. So used to judging athletes based on how athletes treat media, the writers and pundits and talking heads instead focused on the dour outward demeanor, and invariably contrasted it to the ingratiating gregariousness of Jordan. Ironically, it was their portrayal of Iverson that so captivated a wide audience of young people; seeming disinterest, combined with stunning achievement, has always been the province of cool. But those who knew Iverson say the somber postpractice demeanor was more a defense mechanism. They saw the chattering class clown, the cutup who, when Sixers traveling secretary Allen Lumpkin teased him one afternoon, scribbled out an uproarious caricature of Lumpkin on the locker-room chalkboard, complete with an exaggerated big belly.

That's what Croce saw one night after another home win. The Sixers owner and his wife, Diane, stopped by the family room, where the players' wives, girlfriends, and children were waiting. When five-year-old Tiaura Iverson saw Croce, she burst into a wide smile. "Uncle Pat Croce!" she yelled. But her attention was soon diverted when her father appeared, looking not much more than a kid himself, loping down the hallway, the personification of cool. Tiaura ran to him and the tough-guy pose melted; Iverson scooped her up and there he was, laughing and tickling his daughter under her chin. "How can that be a bad guy?" Croce said to his wife. "You can't be a thug with that smile!"

It was a smile that Iverson displayed on the court, but rarely showed the press. On this day, however, after the dispersal of the media pack with their predictable questions ("What do you have to do in tomorrow night's game?" "What were you thinking when you hit that shot?"), Iverson's eyes widened as though he'd just seen a sliver of an opening in the lane. His mouth expanded into the grin that so captivated Croce. He was asked about his kids.

"Deuce had a stomach flu," he said, explaining a recent *excused* practice. Iverson stayed home to help Tawanna nurse him back to health. "Now, Tiaura, all she wants to do is go to Chuck E. Cheese all the damn time. There be a whole lotta noise in my house. All these kids do is run around and tear up the house. Man, Tiaura, I don't even have to say nothing to her, I just give her a look and she knows: 'I better calm my ass down.'"

After games, Iverson seemed to take refuge from the press pack in his kids. Indeed, as more and more scrutiny rained down upon him, he had

Twirling daughter Tiaura in the air in July 2002.

turned increasingly to children, his and others. Kids don't heckle or boo or judge, after all, and his face would light up—as Croce noted—any time he'd wade into a crowd of them. Onetime boy-wonder soprano Bejun Mehta wrote in his essay *A Process of Prodigy* that his "childhood relationship" to his own voice had been "taken over by the opinions and expectations of the adult world"; like Mehta, Iverson was learning that the purity of his gift had been compromised by the chattering negativism of adults. But then he'd step onto the court and all the blather from the pundits and reporters and nervous coaches would fade away. He'd hear the kids. And he'd perform for them.

Even during the heyday of the rivalry, it was never like this. Back in the day, when Magic and Kareem would lead the Lakers into the old Spectrum, where Doc and Moses and Andrew Toney lay in wait, there had never been twenty-thousand-plus maniacal fans drowning out the PA announcer. Especially for a regular-season game.

Shaq and Kobe and all-star Glen Rice led the Lakers into Philly in late March to face the league's leading scorer, Iverson. Two days earlier, Sixers newcomer Tyrone Hill was surprised to hear Iverson on the team plane bemoaning an ensuing off day. "I wish we could play the Lakers right now," he'd said.

"Relax," the veteran Hill had said. "The game will come soon enough."

Come game time, there was a play-off-like buzz in the air. It was a triumphant return home for Bryant, whose parents were in the stands. He'd become a star in his own right, despite ongoing chemistry problems with Shaq, who dubbed Bryant "Showboat" and who felt the young star cared more about stardom than winning.

The Lakers had championship aspirations under coach Kurt Rambis. But the team was in some disarray: Dennis Rodman, whom they'd picked up as a free agent to bolster their rebounding, had bolted for an unspecified leave of absence. Something about trouble in his marriage to actress Carmen Electra. Still, with Shaq, Bryant, and the deadly outside eye of Rice, the Lakers were considered to be among the league's elite.

The game began as a showdown between Bryant and Iverson. Iverson missed 6 of his first 10 shots, while Bryant hit 4 of his first 7. But their one-on-one game within the game didn't bode well for the Lakers. His teammates stood around while Bryant time and again dribbled twenty feet away from the basket, before pulling up for jumpshots. At the other end, Iverson ran Bryant through screen after screen off the ball and was getting his shots in the flow of the Sixers' offense; Geiger or newcomer Hill would pop out to the top of the foul line and find Iverson open behind a double or triple screen. In the second quarter, he started to hit the open shots. And once Iverson's outside game was cooking, there was no stopping him. Bryant had to fight through the screens to get on him before another jumper could be launched; that meant Iverson could use the decoy of his sizzling outside shot to blow by Bryant and get to the hoop, where he'd draw Shaq to him and either loft a high, feathery scoop shot over the behemoth or lay the ball off to either Geiger (who would finish with 8 points, 8 rebounds) or Hill (11 and 10).

When McKie stripped Rice at midcourt and slammed home a fast-break dunk with 2:33 left and the Sixers ahead by double figures, Rambis called a time-out and the arena erupted in deafening cheers. Iverson chest-thumped McKie and skipped to the baseline adjacent to his team's bench, cupping his left hand to his left ear and looking pleadingly at the crowd, *his* crowd. The roar dutifully grew louder.

It was becoming something of a habit at key moments, this singular interplay between Iverson and the crowd. Other players at similar junctures during a game mugged for the TV cameras on the baseline; their celebration was about *them.* Iverson always peered over the cameras and appealed to the fans, suggesting, in effect, that every die-hard sports fan's fantasy is true, that he or she *is* integral to the game. Unlike Bryant, a cool craftsman who had brought former Sixers strength-and-conditioning coach Joe Carbone out to Los Angeles to work him out *after* grueling practices, Iverson's game was all inspiration. And his playing to the crowd was a tacit acknowledgment of a symbiosis between him and his fans.

Coming out of the final time-out, Iverson snuck a peek at the scoreboard and saw that he had 41 points. Uh-oh, he thought. I hope this isn't going to backfire on me. Ever since his rookie season, when he'd scored 40 or more points in five straight losing games, he'd been aware of his team's record when he scored 40 or more points. It now stood at 0–7. When the final buzzer sounded, and he'd led his team to a 15-point win with 41 points, 10 assists, 5 rebounds—one more than Shaq—and 2 steals, Iverson shouted heavenward, "Get that monkey off my back!"

The Sixers soon went to Miami, where they stunned Pat Riley's Heat,

88–84, behind Iverson and Geiger, who had become the team's second-leading scorer at 13 points per game. But, this being Larry and Allen's Sixers, the good times couldn't last too long. In the Lakers game, Iverson had suffered a bruised right quadriceps on a drive to the basket that ended up as a collision between his thigh and the solid steel of Shaq. When the Cleveland Cavaliers came to visit the Sixers, Iverson felt he was at 75 percent. He could play, but long periods of inactivity caused his body to stiffen up.

Against the Cavaliers, the Sixers came out sluggish. When Iverson missed badly on a three-pointer to close out the first quarter, Brown pulled him. Iverson mumbled his displeasure, but took a seat on the bench. With nine minutes, fifty-seven seconds remaining in the half, Brown called for Iverson to reenter the game. Iverson got up and, walking past his coach, was heard to say, "About fuckin' time."

Brown immediately called him back to the bench, where he sat, grim-faced. During time-outs, he only joined the team's huddle at the urging of teammates Geiger and Rick Mahorn, whom Brown had added to the roster to be a stabilizing force on Iverson. Iverson talked of getting dressed and going home, but his teammates persuaded him to stay.

He never reentered the game. Afterward, he told his coaches he wouldn't play again until he was 100 percent; some wondered if his sudden switch—before the game, he'd said he'd never take himself out of the lineup because "my team needs me"—was really motivated by a petulant urge to stick it to Brown. For his part, Brown kicked Royster out of the locker room after the game and exhibited uncommon testiness when questioned by Comcast SportsNet's Michael Barkann during Brown's postgame press conference.

"I'm not going to comment," Brown said tersely. "He said he was hurt, so he didn't play."

Barkann tried to follow up. "There's no need to follow up," Brown snapped. "I made the answer, all right?"

Barkann tried again. "Hey, hey, I'm the coach, all right?" Brown fumed. "I have the right to play a guy and not play a guy, all right . . . Hold it! Hold it! I ask a guy to go into the game, they go in the game. I ask them to go out, they go out. That's the way I coach."

Clearly, the rift between Brown and Iverson was wider than ever. Rather than seeing Iverson's disrespect for him as an utterance in the heat of battle, born of his star's desire to play, Brown saw it as a challenge to his authority. And given that it wasn't the first time that Iverson—among the league leaders in minutes played—had cursed at his coach about playing time in front of the team, who could blame him?

The coach and player would emerge from a twenty-minute meeting within the coming days, and they'd make nice for the cameras. "If y'all think that Larry Brown and myself are not going to have any altercations, I mean, that's just crazy," Iverson said.

In the aftermath of the controversy, none other than Charles Barkley weighed in with some incendiary comments about Iverson in *Sports Illustrated.* "I can't stand that guy," Barkley said. "He has a responsibility to cut the crap and not have some drama with the coach every week. He's showing no respect to anyone, least of all the game."

In true hip-hop form—you dis me, I dis you—Iverson responded by going nuclear. "He's nobody, man," he fulminated. "Why am I on his mind so much? Why is he thinking about me? What has he done to criticize somebody like that? He hasn't done anything but throw [somebody] through windows, spit on little kids. You can't say that about me. You can talk about my game all you want, but I've never spit on a kid. I can't understand why he tries to dog me out like that. I can't stand him, either. How many times has he been to the Finals? One time. Tell him to think about that. Think about that before you start criticizing."

Despite all the media attention and controversy—or, maybe, given both Iverson's and Brown's lifetime embrace of tumult, because of it—the Sixers were in the thick of the play-off hunt. The regular season ended with a thrilling home win over Detroit. The Pistons led, 93–89, with twenty seconds left when the Pistons' Stackhouse blew a kiss good-bye to the sellout Philly crowd that had heckled him all night. Snow, who had come into his own by now as a point guard, scored on a drive to the hoop. Then McKie stripped Stackhouse at midcourt—much to the fans' delight—and Iverson found himself with the ball on the baseline, some fifteen feet from the basket, as the clock wound down. Running at him was six-foot eleven-inch Christian Laettner. A seldom-talked-about facet of Iverson's game, overshadowed by his leaping and quickness, is his sense of spatial dimensions; when he challenges giants, he has a knack for knowing just how much of a looping arc to use in the shot. So it was here, with Laettner rushing him, arms outstretched. The jumper seemed to go straight up, a rainbow. It fell through the net, forcing overtime and a deafening chant of "MVP! MVP! MVP!" from the crowd.

When the five-minute overtime period ended with a win, the Sixers were the play-offs' sixth seed with a 28–22 record. A jubilant Iverson spontaneously grabbed the courtside microphone from the hands of the arena's public-address announcer.

"We need the kind of enthusiasm you guys showed now all through the play-offs," he barked. "We're gonna play hard because we owe this to you!"

Philadelphia was starved for a winner, but not just any kind of winner. Some winners of the city's past, though celebrated, failed to capture the imagination of the gritty, working-class town. Much had been made of the Philadelphia fans over the years, how they'd booed Santa Claus and came down hard—harder than any other city would—on superstars ranging from Dick Allen and Wilt Chamberlain to Mike Schmidt and Randall Cunningham.

It was all true. Traumatized by years of disappointment, the Philadelphia fans were well schooled in self-protection, wary of falling in love again. But once they fell, they fell hard. The dawning of the 1999 NBA play-offs marked the beginning of a tempestuous love affair.

It made sense that the fans would be smitten by this team, for like the town itself, it embodied grit and hustle. Philadelphia had long been a sucker for hustle, for guys like Pete Rose, Larry Bowa, and hockey's Bobby Clarke—lesser talents who overcame odds by virtue of work ethic and competitive fire. More than any other recent superstar in Philadelphia history, Iverson was beloved because, like the overachievers, he didn't come with any glitz. He excelled through heart, hustle, *and* talent.

Similarly, this Sixers team, having allowed opponents just 87.6 points per game, won thanks to a scrambling, frenetic defense and a marked selflessness. Gone were the days when Iverson's teammates would complain about his league-leading number of shots and minutes played, or the fact that, at 41 percent, he had the lowest shooting percentage of any NBA-leading scorer (26.8 points per game) since 1958. It was part of Brown's master plan to surround Iverson with players who, as he put it, "allow Allen to be Allen." Now that the team was winning, Brown was not only tolerant, but encouraging, of Allen being Allen.

The play-offs opened with the Sixers splitting the first two games in Orlando against Chuck Daly's Magic. In preparation for the series return to Philly, Pat Croce stoked the fires of the local faithful by shaving his head—and offering to shave fans' domes before game three. At game time, a sea of bald heads led the roar when the *Rocky* theme blared out and, on the arena-vision, an animated Rocky decked a reeling Mickey Mouse time and again with a left hook.

Sitting courtside was Philadelphia native Will Smith, the actor and rapper. "This is almost like a concert," he told the *Daily News.* "Allen Iverson is basketball's rock star."

And the star didn't disappoint. He scored 33 points and set a play-off record with 10 steals. As impressive as the points were, the steals spoke to the hustle he and the Sixers had come to embody. The only time the ear-numbing cheers for Iverson were surpassed was when, after a call, Daly grabbed the ball while complaining to the ref; ready to inbound, Geiger reached over and ripped the ball from the Magic coach. The Magic were done. The Sixers romped in game four to move on to the next round. Julius Erving, now a vice president with the Magic, was quoted criticizing Iverson—calling him, ironically, "playground"—but not even Erving's old-school lamentations could dull the moment for Iverson.

Next up for the Sixers was Brown's old team, the Pacers, led by Reggie Miller. The Pacers' experience showed against the Sixers, who fell in four straight. As game four ended, along with his season, Iverson took solace in the affectionate applause from the home crowd. His third NBA season was complete. And he was finally a winner.

chapter 10

THE PANTHER

this used to be a grim reaper holding a basketball, but i
had it changed to a panther after my friends teased me and
told me it looked like a damned flying monkey.

The secret was out. Allen Iverson had been a novelty act during the Sixers' eight-game play-off run the previous spring. After all, until the play-offs, the Sixers hadn't played a single nationally televised game on NBC all season long. Most basketball fans across the country had long been exposed to the *idea* of Iverson before seeing his game; they'd either first heard of him when he was a playground legend in jail, or when he was running amok in John Thompson's once tightly controlled system, or when, these last few years, he was presented as a cornrowed, bejeweled, tattooed threat to all that was Jordan. But all that would soon change. As the 1999–2000 season loomed, it was announced that his team would play eleven times on NBC. Moreover, just before training camp, he would make his national television-interview debut.

"I can curse, right, this is cable?" he asked upon first sitting down with Chris Rock, taping a segment for the comedian's HBO show before a live studio audience.

The eight-minute conversation could have served as a snapshot of the new NBA. Rock's audience ate up Iverson's laid-back candor, his mix of shyness and bravado. Rock joked about Iverson's friends—"I seen them in the green room, and *I* was scared," Rock said—before asking if Iverson hung with any white people. The guest paused, then smiled sheepishly. "Yeah. I mean, my lawyers."

The crowd roared. Rock then proceeded to list the hoops stars who were branching out into movies and rap CDs, before turning to his guest. "So, how you gonna embarrass yourself?" he asked.

Iverson laughed. "I don't look at it like that, man," he said. "I look at it like, the sky's the limit."

Walking off, Iverson was met with thunderous applause. For him, it was confirmation of all that Gaskins, among others, had been saying all along: that while he might be seen as a threat in the retro, corporate world of the NBA, there was a sizable audience out there who would identify with and embrace him for who he really was and what he represented.

Inside the world of the NBA, meanwhile, he continued to encounter difficulty. The Sixers got off to a desultory 0–3 start, all road games, with Allen shooting a paltry 33 percent from the floor. In the home opener, however, he busted out by scoring 37 points in a win over Seattle. In the next game, Iverson scorched the Magic for 46 en route to a 110–105 victory.

Afterward, Iverson found himself once again in the headlines for issues that had nothing to do with his game. Brown, it turns out, had consulted with McKie, Snow, and George Lynch and instituted a team dress policy. Brown was known throughout the league for his impeccably tailored suits. Now his players would have to wear suits or sport coats on road trips. Iverson wasn't having it. "If they take my money, so be it," he said nonchalantly. "I'm going to wear what I want to wear."

The season had just started and already Brown and Iverson were talking past each other. Brown, for his part, had come to appreciate fine clothes years before. Though he had grown up wearing his cousin's hand-me-downs, the cousin happened to be a stylish dresser, so Brown always had neatly fitted blazers and suits. At the University of North Carolina, he played his freshman year for legendary coach Frank McGuire, one of the sport's most debonair of dressers. "Coach McGuire could walk into a room with a thousand people and he'd be the only one you'd notice," Brown recalls today. McGuire used to tell Brown, "It's unfortunate, but people get a feeling for who you are by the way you present yourself."

When Dean Smith took over, there was no drop-off in the emphasis on style. After graduation, Brown was an assistant coach. "We had to wear a tie and jacket every day," he says. "There might be a prospect who showed up that day with his family and Coach Smith wanted them to understand what we were about."

For Brown, the fact that his team would be on national TV so much this season *meant* something. It was time to make an impression. For Iverson, all this talk about wearing suits meant that people—white, middle-aged people—were trying to change him. It wasn't that how he dressed was unimportant to him; on the contrary, his style choices had always been very consciously thought out. The image he projected was how he expressed himself; for someone to dictate how he dressed was, to him, tantamount to being denied the right to speak. To Iverson, the low-hanging jeans, the Timberlands, and the billowy, untucked designer shirts spoke of, and to, the generation that spawned him. He'd seen the photos of Larry Brown back in his ABA days, with the hilariously wide bell-bottoms and paisley shirts. Brown had once been of his time, too.

Ultimately, the dress code was never enforced, especially after Brown said he didn't care what his players wore "as long as they're neat and clean." That settled it; Iverson always dressed "neat and clean," even if he dressed differently from Brown. But the episode left Iverson feeling sour. Why couldn't people let him be himself?

Even the NBA seemed determined to change him. When the holiday issue of the league's *Hoop* magazine came out with him on its cover, Iverson was aghast to see that league officials had airbrushed off his tattoos and diamond earring. He was outraged. "It's like a slap in the face," he said. "Don't put me on your damned magazine if you don't want me as I am. Those tattoos are part of me, they mean something to me. What gives them the right to change me?"

The NBA apologized. Croce, who sports a couple of tattoos himself, thought that, once again, Iverson had prodded the system into having an open mind. "Maybe now people will realize that tattoos are not a threat to the game or the world as we know it," he said.

In December, Iverson broke his shooting hand's thumb against the San Antonio Spurs and was sidelined for three weeks. (The injury happened early in the game; he not only played with the break, he finished with 35 points.) Meantime, trade rumors circulated around Larry Hughes. Hughes was talented, but Brown was having a hard time finding him minutes now that Iverson was playing almost exclusively at the shooting-guard position—Hughes's natural spot. Plus, Hughes was moping about his diminished playing time—a no-no in Brown's universe. Concern over one's own minutes meant that individual issues were being placed before the team.

While Iverson was sidelined, the Houston Rockets came to town for Barkley's final visit to Philadelphia. He'd announced that this would be his last year in the NBA, even though he remained a good—though not great—player. Still fuming over Barkley's public criticisms of him the last few years, Iverson called in sick, saying he had the flu. That, in and of itself, wouldn't have merited headlines. But when he was spotted eating at TGI Friday's during the game, his no-show was taken as a huge dis of the onetime Sixer great.

Iverson soon returned to play. In his absence, the team had gone 6–4. After his return, they went 2–2, with Iverson connecting on just 38.8 percent of his shots. But then, as Christmas approached, he lit up Toronto for 37, and it looked like the rest of the season would be clear sailing. But this was the Larry and Allen psychodrama. All would cease to be harmonious on one Saturday night in Detroit.

At 11 P.M. on the Saturday before Christmas, Pat Croce's phone rang. It was his brother, John, the Sixers strength-and-conditioning coach. The team had just lost at Detroit and there was something about John's voice that prompted in Croce a sudden, sinking feeling.

"I'm on the bus with the team, Pat," John said. "Coach told me to call you. He wants Allen traded, Pat—now. He wants him traded now."

In the first half, the starters were sluggish and uninspired. They fell behind Detroit by 23 points. At halftime, Brown told the team, "If we don't start off showing some emotion, I'm going to play the second group." After four minutes of the second half, Brown pulled his starters: Iverson, Snow, Hill, Lynch, and Ratliff. Snow, Ratliff, and Iverson, who had 19 points at the time, did not return. The reserves whittled the Pistons' lead down to 7 before the Sixers lost, 104–91.

After the game, with Brown standing maybe ten feet away, Iverson waited until the media surrounded him—and then he vented, demanding a trade. "For some reason, my style doesn't fit this team anymore," he fulminated. "Something needs to happen. Something's got to give. If I'm hurting this team, I need to get out of here. I don't like what is going on. When I get back to Philly, I'll let that be known. I've never been done like that ever in my career."

The next day, Croce tracked down both coach and player. Neither had calmed down. During the afternoon, Iverson was at Dave & Buster's, a family restaurant and arcade, for Tiaura's birthday party. He went into the men's room to talk to Croce on his cell phone. "How can I be so disrespected?" Iverson shouted. "I'm a starter. I'm the only fucking all-star in the league who has to put up with this shit. I done everything for this fucking team and this is what I get?"

When Croce got Brown on the phone, the volume was turned down, but the hurt was palpable. "I'm not coaching him ever again," Brown said. "Get rid of him."

Croce told Brown what he'd told Iverson. "I hear you, it's not right for both of you," he said. "So, okay, we'll make it right. We'll have a meeting tomorrow morning."

Iverson agreed. Brown, however, refused. "I'm not coming," he said. "I'm not coaching him again."

For the first and only time as president of the Philadelphia 76ers,

Croce pulled rank on his highly sensitive coach. "I'm the boss," he said. "And you *will* be at that meeting."

Croce went to bed that night thinking that his franchise was blowing up. He needed both men; one without the other did him no good. After a fitful night, he decided to go for broke. If he got both men in the same room—and there was no guarantee Brown would show—he would mediate by instigation. He would pick at every grudge both men had zealously guarded and nurtured the past three years. He would orchestrate one of two endings: a catharsis or a mushroom cloud.

The next day, the Sixers were to host the Pistons in the second of a home-and-away series. Croce arrived early to the game-day shoot-around at the practice facility. Croce, Brown, Billy King, and assistant coach Randy Ayers were chatting in the conference room, just off the basketball floor. The door flew open and Iverson came storming in, the veins in his neck bulging. "I am fucking fed up with this shit!" he yelled, pacing.

"How about if we talk about this after shoot-around?" Croce said.

Iverson stopped and looked at him as if Croce had just been dropped onto the planet. "I ain't practicing, man."

They'd talk about it now, then. Brown and Iverson sat down across from each other, both leaning back with their arms folded over their chests. Croce had hoped to set the meeting's agenda, but Iverson wasn't done venting. He started ranting about all the past slights Brown had inflicted upon him, about how he was the only star in the league never to be consulted on personnel moves, about how Brown talks about family and then runs his mouth off in the media about family business. As Iverson ranted, he grew more and more incensed and stood up over Brown, shouting down at him, his fingers jabbing at the air. Finally, he paused.

"Are you through?" Brown asked calmly.

"Do I ask you if you're through when you're talking to me?" Iverson shot back, taking his seat.

Croce began as he'd planned to do earlier, by stating the crux of the problem: "Each of you perceives the other one as disrespecting you," he said. "Coach, I don't know if you realize it, but Allen's never been pulled from a game. To him, pulling him like that was an act of public disrespect. But, Allen, Larry feels you disrespect him when you come off the court and you 'motherfuck' him all the time. You say it right to his face in front of the fans and the team. When he's just trying to win the game."

There was a pause. Croce wasn't about to let silence fill the air—because who knows what crazy thoughts either man could bring to the surface? "You know, you both might as well just stand up and look in the mirror— both of you!" he said. "Because the reason we're in this situation right now is because you're both so similar. Not dissimilar. Similar. Headstrong and sensitive and talented and set in your ways. Take a good look at each other."

Another pause.

"There's a communication gap here," Croce continued. "Coach, Allen has told me this. He thinks you treat him like those white guards did when he was in prison—'sit over there, nigger, and don't move.'"

Brown had no visible reaction, but inside, he was stunned. Neither Croce nor Iverson knew it, but Brown had grown up idolizing Jackie Robinson, and not just for his athletic ability. Robinson stood for the triumph of merit, fairness, and racial parity. Brown had grown up a true liberal, someone who basked in his own color blindness. He often spoke movingly about how "our league" provides opportunity to young black men like his own Billy King, whom he had long mentored. Brown never imagined that anyone might interpret the way he communicated as somehow racially insensitive. But then he thought about it, how so many kids just like Allen had had little or no experience with a white authority figure. "Why *would* they have any trust?" Brown would later say, giving voice to the thoughts he entertained that day. "Because a lot of times in their life, no white person has ever shown them any respect at all."

Croce stuck to his plan: every time a sore seemed ready to heal, he'd rip the scab right off. "And, Allen," he said, "I don't think Coach likes you."

Now Brown had to speak.

"It's not about liking," he said. "It's about being a part of a team." Brown went on to reiterate his team-first philosophy, how, in his view, the minute one individual gets preferential treatment, a team becomes a loose collection of individuals. It wasn't about Allen and Larry, in his view; it was about Allen and a team. Brown came from a certain tradition, he explained; from coaches like Henry Iba, Frank McGuire, and Dean Smith he learned that if you were part of a team, you respected your teammates by showing up and being on time.

Nothing between him and Allen, Brown said, had ever been personal. And then he spoke from the heart, about his personal relationship with Allen. He talked about how, no matter the issues separating them, any-

May 2001: The MVP and his coach, Larry Brown.

time Allen walked out of the locker room and saw Brown's wife and kids, he'd always, in Brown's words, "treat them positively." Not everybody does that, the coach noted. He'd had players whose wives, if their husbands weren't playing, would have nothing to do with him or his family. On a personal level, Brown said, he knew what Allen was about—because he'd seen the player interact with his kids. Maybe Croce was right, maybe what divided them was their similarities, not their differences.

"Allen is a lot like me," Brown would later reflect. "Sometimes things happen right away and you react and don't have time to think about it. And when we do have time to think about it, we realize things could have been handled a different way."

Now it was Iverson's turn to unburden himself. By now, both men were leaning forward, engaging each other—calmly. Just as Croce's comment about race had touched Brown somewhere deep, so was Iverson moved to let his defenses down after hearing Brown.

"There are times when I'm listening to you and I can tell you're looking at me, thinking I ain't listening," Iverson said. "That's just the look on my face. My face is just my face. But I'm hearing you. You think I'm like, 'Man, get outta my face,' but I'm really right there with you." And then Iverson said the thing that would cement his relationship with his coach for a long time to come. "All I've wanted," he said, "is to have a relationship with my coach like Magic had with Pat Riley and Michael had with Phil Jackson. That's all I've ever wanted."

Croce erupted. "That is an arrow into the heart—dipped in honey!" he exclaimed, and—for the first time on a very tense morning—laughter filled the air.

More talk ensued. Billy King spoke of his relationship with his college coach, Mike Krzyzewski, about how, now, he looked back on things his coach said and did and realized that the coach only got on him so much because he cared so much. If a coach isn't pushing you, King said, it means he doesn't care about you.

Finally, Croce said, "Let's shake hands and get back to winning games." Iverson got up and walked around the table to shake his coach's hand.

Afterward, Iverson would say the meeting began as an "alley fight" and became "the most real talk we've ever had." Brown felt good as well, save for the fact that he had to be in the room in the first place. That afternoon, Croce received a call from his coach at home. "How dare you take sides." Brown said.

"Coach, it was a great meeting," Croce said. "I didn't take sides. I mediated." He apologized to Brown if Brown felt he'd been unfair. "No one ever teaches you how to handle these situations," he said.

As they had done so many times before, Brown and Iverson followed up on their turmoil with a pressure-packed on-court triumph. It was as though each man, on some level, created their soap operas in order to script a dramatic ending.

On this night against the Pistons, Iverson was everywhere. He scored 32 points to take the game into overtime. With time in the extra session ticking down, the Pistons held a 121–120 lead. Iverson drew the defense to him and found Snow wide open on the right baseline. Snow's jumper left his hand as the buzzer sounded; it swished through the net, the fans went wild, and Iverson leaped into Snow's arms while Brown ran from the sideline to embrace both of them. In the ultimate homage to Brown, Iverson had played a consummate team game, trusting an open teammate with the game's outcome on the line. Returning the respect, a smiling Larry Brown entered his postgame conference and said, "After all the junk, I would have liked to see Allen make the last shot."

It wasn't official yet, but it was in the air. Iverson knew it. Despite his being the league's scoring champ, the leading vote getter among Eastern guards for the all-star game and a first-team all-NBA player the year before, rumor had it he would not be named to the U.S. Men's Olympic Basketball team for the games in Sydney, Australia.

If the rumor was true, odds were that the Bucks' Ray Allen would fill the last available roster spot. Unfortunately for Ray, his team's schedule brought him to Philadelphia to face Iverson and the Sixers on the eve of the announcement that he'd beaten Iverson out for the spot.

It is said that, after he was cut from his high-school basketball team, Michael Jordan became expert at turning perceived slights into motivation. It was as though, from then on, every opponent, in Jordan's mind, wore the face of that high-school coach who so misjudged him. He always needed someone to stick it to. So it was with Iverson. Often, that foil would be Brown; he'd take to the court determined to show his nagging, doubting coach what a warrior he was. But just as often, it could be anything, something seemingly innocuous that Iverson seized on and used as fuel. It was a personality trait common among kids from ghetto upbringings who managed to succeed, who come from a hardscrabble world where nothing good ever just "happens," but must instead be fought for. Seen this way, to Iverson, excellence could only be achieved by way of conflict, by proving someone wrong. The subtext, of course, was race; in "showing them," a ghetto-born overachiever not only shows up whoever conveyed today's real or imagined insult, but everyone who ever doubted him.

Few close to Iverson doubt that when he lit up Ray Allen's Bucks for 45 points in early January, he wanted to show the Olympic committee—which included the 76ers' newly appointed general manager, Billy King—what a mistake they'd made. It wasn't just that Iverson scored at will. He also scored big baskets, late in a close game, to win it.

In the days that followed, the official Olympic announcement was made and the media crowded around Iverson's locker, asking why he thought he hadn't made the team. And why someone like Ray Allen—who had been chosen to do public-service announcements for the Thurgood Marshall Fund—did make it. "I knew I wasn't going to be on that team," Iverson said. "With the question you're asking, you want me to tell you the reason you already know, and I'm not going to do that. Everybody knows. It's no big deal."

Someone asked, would it bother him if his past were held against him? "People are going to do that," he said. "It's not right, but it's something I kind of understand, that people would kind of be scared. After the things I've been through, I can't blame people if they say, 'Maybe he's not the right guy,' but when they talk about basketball, I'm the right guy. Simple as that."

Not surprisingly, Iverson went on a tear after the snub. He scored a career-high 50 points on 40 shots in a win over the Sacramento Kings and their exciting point guard, Jason Williams. (The hype surrounding Williams, a white player with streetball flair, was indicative of just how thirsty the NBA was for a Great White Hope; the fact was, Williams, especially compared with the likes of Iverson, wasn't quite the genuine article—clichéd comparisons to "Pistol" Pete Maravich notwithstanding.)

At the all-star break, the Sixers were 27–23, and Iverson made his all-star debut in San Francisco. That weekend, he gave Arnie Steele $80,000 to throw an all-star bash in his name. Then he went out and totaled 26 points and 9 assists, and would have been named the game's MVP had the East prevailed.

In February, the Sixers finally dealt Larry Hughes, getting Toni Kukoc from the Bulls in return. Finally, it appeared Iverson would be paired with another legitimate scoring threat, someone defenses would have to double-team. At the press conference to announce Kukoc's arrival, Iverson showed up, all smiles.

But with twenty-two games left in the season, all smiles dissipated. With a record of 34–26, the Sixers were to play at division-leading Miami, whom they trailed in the standings by two and a half games. Croce, who has a vacation home in Florida, came to the game with his bags packed. He'd fly back with the team. When he entered the locker room, he was met by a pale, irritated Brown.

"Go talk to your kid," Brown said, motioning toward the trainer's room.

"What's the matter?" Croce asked.

"Just go talk to him."

Croce looked to King for help. "Allen missed shoot-around this morning," King said.

Here we go again, Croce thought. Iverson had been out late in the Miami clubs the night before. He had a headache in the morning and called Sixers trainer Len Currier to say he'd be staying in his room. By now, Croce was realizing that one of Brown's coaching tenets was to keep his distance from negative confrontations. So he confronted Iverson. "Bubba, you can't do this," Croce said to him. "I'm going to discipline you." Iverson was suspended for the game; Croce hurriedly got Ann on the phone so she'd hear the news first from him. "Ann, what can I say?" he said. "Bubba fucked up."

Just as back in high school, when Mike Bailey made sure to get Ann on board when he punished Allen, Ann was fully supportive. "I know you care about my baby, Pat," she said.

Of course, Iverson was unrepentant. "You think I'm going to come to Miami and not go out? I go out if I want to," he told reporters that night. "But don't question my heart. Don't question my health. I don't think this was fair at all."

Late in the season, Brown's contract was extended. He would now be the coach for the next five years, at roughly $6 million per year. Iverson, ever brittle but always resilient, played the last weeks of the season with a broken big toe on his left foot, but it didn't stop him from scoring 28.4

points per game, second in the league. The Sixers won fifteen of their final twenty-two games to finish 49–33. They'd face Charlotte—and Derrick Coleman—in the first round of the play-offs.

It was a locker room full of dropped jaws.

"I can't even begin to figure out where it comes from," said Aaron McKie, shaking his head slowly.

Dressing in front of a nearby locker, Matt Geiger offered his own theory. "It comes from God, that's where," he said.

They were talking about the performance just turned in by their superstar teammate in game one of the play-off series at Charlotte. The Hornets had come into the game as the hottest team in the league, winners of fourteen of their last sixteen games. But then they ran into Iverson. On this night, he scored 40 of his team's 92 points, hitting 13 of 25 shots. The basket, he would claim, "looked like an ocean" all night long.

The evening could be summed up in one stunning sequence. In the third quarter, Iverson stole the ball and raced up the court. It's a cardinal rule in basketball that you don't leave your feet with the ball without knowing precisely what you're going to do. It's a rule Iverson routinely ignores. For that is precisely when his creative inspirations hit, when he commits to a course of action while all is still possibility. On this play, he darted full speed into the lane with Charlotte's David Wesley squarely in front of him, and elevated while looking back, over his left shoulder, for a trailing teammate to pass to; Wesley, reading Iverson's eyes, lurched that way. But there was no one there; seeing no one, Iverson seemed to lengthen his stay in the air while completely turning, a floating, soaring, 360-degree spin, followed by an eight-foot bank shot on his way down, the ball released just before his feet regained contact with the floor. Those in the arena were confused; it happened so quickly—that couldn't have been legal, right? Instant replays showed that, indeed, it was. It was a move that couldn't be planned, let alone explained.

"It comes from within him," Tyrone Hill opined after the game.

For his part, Iverson had no answers for his zone-like performance, although in front of his locker after the game, he may have inadvertently provided one. While his teammates were jubilant, he was venting about comments Billy King had made in that morning's Charlotte newspaper. King had been asked if the marriage between Iverson and the Sixers could last, and he responded, "I want to think it can. But I think a lot of soul-searching has to take place by everyone."

Iverson had read the comments earlier and had been stewing all day. "If I can hear my general manager say that he doesn't know if the marriage is going to work in the paper to some reporter, it's time to stop feeling that way," he said. "I don't feel like they treat me like a franchise player. I'm treated nowhere near like a franchise player. I'm treated like the twelfth guy on the bench."

What had so wounded Iverson? On the face of it, King's comments were hardly incendiary. (King would nonetheless apologize.) Some saw Iverson's reaction as yet more evidence of a hair-trigger oversensitivity; others claimed he was astutely reading between the lines, sensing that the brass of his team—despite all the lovey-dovey bromides coming out of the December dustup—just might give up on him this off-season. Both views were onto something. Iverson, so skittish by now about trusting male authority figures, may have had reason to suspect Brown's motives where he was concerned, but he most certainly was also inventing a slight, which related to a third possibility. Was it possible that he was looking to invent hard feelings on the morning of the game in order to do what he did on the court?

As the series unfolded, Coleman played solidly, but didn't haunt his old team. In fact, Philadelphia sports-radio personality Angelo Cataldi riled up Philly fans before game three by having hundreds of doughnuts delivered to the hotel room of the power forward, whose weight had long fluctuated. The Sixers would go on to eliminate the Hornets in four games, despite the fact that Snow and Iverson were both nursing ankle injuries. With Snow out and Iverson hobbled by a chipped bone in his left ankle, McKie and Geiger stepped up, though Iverson admonished the hometown fans for having turned on the oft-injured Geiger recently by booing him. "That doesn't help a guy's confidence," he'd said.

Next up for the Sixers was a rematch with the Indiana Pacers. Though the Pacers were the higher seed, they were virtually the same team that had eliminated Philadelphia the year before. This year, the Sixers' youth would be buttressed by the experience gained from last year's play-offs. Besides, the Sixers were out for revenge.

Nonetheless, the Pacers won the first two in Indiana and then stunned Philly with a 97–89 win on the Sixers' home court. The Pacers' Jalen Rose, who had butted heads with Brown when he was in Indiana, was unstoppable. No team had ever come back from a three-games-to-none play-off deficit before.

After game three, the Pacers had written AND NOW . . . THEY SLEEP, R.I.P. on the chalkboard inside the visiting team's locker room. Iverson vowed that the series wasn't over, and the Sixers won games four and five, setting up a pivotal game six in Philly.

The day before the game, local sports-talk radio personality Rhea Hughes checked her usual bevy of E-mail messages from the Philadelphia less-than-faithful. One was from a retired math teacher who called himself a "Philadelphia sports hater for years." She was about to hit the delete button when the writer began questioning Iverson's intelligence, and just how he had gotten into Georgetown. Something about the E-mail's harsh tone made Hughes keep reading. Then the writer named Iverson's daughter. Then, in the most chilling language Hughes says she's ever read, he threatened to take Tiaura from Iverson, chop her up, and return her to the star in a box.

Hughes forwarded the E-mail to Sixers vice president Dave Coskey, who immediately contacted the police and the FBI. (An arrest would later be made.) Iverson was used to stalkers, even to threats. There was, for instance, the woman who had moved to Philadelphia from Los Angeles because she thought she had become his girlfriend after he'd politely said hello to her in a restaurant. But this was something different. Earlier in the season, discussing his "Fear No One" tattoo, Iverson had said that the only thing he feared was "something happening to my family, to my kids." So it was no surprise when he showed up late for game six, wearing green fatigues. He was in the bunker, embattled.

Iverson and his team played their hearts out, but lost game six, 106–90. Late in the game, he came to the bench, draped a towel over his head, and broke down, crying. His mother raced to the bench and embraced him from behind. When the final buzzer sounded, Ann accompanied her baby into the trainer's room. It had been a draining, emotional season, yet much of the melodrama would have been worth it had he led his team past Indiana. Now it had been topped off with the threats against his daughter. And his team had lost. Again. It all just spilled out. Iverson sat on a training table, his face nestled in the crook of his mother's neck, and he sobbed while Ann held him and soothingly rubbed his back. Her comforting presence might have suggested things would get better. And they would.

But first they'd get worse.

Only The
Strong
Survive
THE ANSWER!

chapter | 11

THE ANSWER

This was my first tattoo, when I was nineteen. I went straight to the tattoo parlor from the park to get THE ANSWER the day the guys gave me the nickname.

Almost as soon as the season ended, Larry Brown went on the offensive. Iverson had gone back to Virginia, taking a room at the Radisson Hotel in Hampton when he wasn't crashing at Uncle Stevie's house or pulling all-nighters in a recording studio with Cru Thik, where he was putting the finishing touches on a hard-core rap CD to be distributed by Universal Records.

Meantime, Brown surprised many by drafting tiny point guard Craig "Speedy" Claxton in the first round of the NBA draft, saying, "Maybe Allen's got to learn to share some time with other people." The comment was aired nationally, as were a series of other thinly veiled threats. Fed up with being asked about his relationship with Iverson—and still smarting over Croce's insistence that he sit down, face-to-face, with a player over whom he was supposed to wield authority—Brown said, "I don't know what any of you would do if you had an employee who didn't come to work or who always showed up late for work."

The groundwork for a trade was being laid. Throughout the league, rumors abounded. One had Iverson going to Detroit for Grant Hill. Another had him shipped off to the Los Angeles Clippers for Lamar Odom. Neither was a real possibility, but Iverson didn't know that. Knowing that the Clippers had long been a doormat organization, he dreaded a return to the losing days of his first two seasons.

"If they trade me, they'll be sorry," he vowed to Ann's boyfriend Jack. "I'm gonna average fifty points a game against them. I'm gonna average thirty-five points against everybody."

As the trade talk swirled, Iverson hosted his third annual Summer Celebrity Classic in Hampton. This time, it was a star-studded weekend, capped by a Saturday-night softball game before a throng of over five thousand fans. Croce attended, even while his coach was blasting his star player in the press. The day before the weekend, an even bigger story brewed. Dean Smith had called Croce, asking for permission to talk to his protégé, Brown, about the head-coaching position at the University of North Carolina. Croce granted the request. "If his heart isn't into staying here," he told Billy King, "I don't want him." Suddenly it looked like Brown was readying to pull another nomadic move and the Allen and Larry saga would meet an anticlimactic end.

Croce couldn't reach Brown by phone for days while Smith was talking to him. Meantime, Croce started running names past Billy King and Sonny Hill as possible replacements. He wanted to know if Isiah Thomas or Julius Erving might be interested—and how good they'd be as head coaches.

Privately, Iverson hoped Brown would take the college job and that John Thompson would become his pro coach. (Croce had also floated Thompson's name, but after his experience with Johnny Davis, he was reluctant to hire anyone who hadn't coached in the pros.) But when Croce arrived for the charity weekend, there was no talk of Brown's coaching status. Instead, Croce hung out in Iverson's suite as a stylist braided Iverson's hair. Then the owner and player made their way to the softball field, where they met up with Magic Johnson, whom Iverson had again called for career advice during the NBA Finals. The three men met for an hour in the trailer that would serve as a locker room for the evening's softball game.

Those around Iverson had long maintained that their man's close relationship with Croce ensured that Iverson would last longer than Brown in Philadelphia. "This is your team, not Larry Brown's," Iverson's friends would tell him. Now that Brown had a new, long-term deal, however (initiated by Croce's senior partner, Ed Snider, who was becoming more active in Sixers business now that the team was winning), the balance of power had shifted. The organization was committed to Brown—that is, if he stayed in the organization. (Within a matter of days, Brown rebuffed his alma mater, in part because his wife and their two young children were happy in suburban Philadelphia and uninterested in another move.)

Croce didn't want to trade Iverson, but his management style was to defer basketball decisions to those he'd empowered in that area. So, as he did with the jettisoning of Coleman, he'd told Brown, King, and director of player personnel Tony DiLeo his preference—"I'd like to take another shot, one more year with this group"—but gave them the freedom to make a deal, provided they were unanimous in their belief that they'd be getting equal value for Iverson.

"I can't defend you when you're tardy and you don't do what the coach says," Croce said now, in front of Johnson, explaining that he would be unable to veto a trade if one were made. "We go back, Bubba. We came in together as rookies. And I've told Billy and Larry what I'm telling you, that I don't want you traded. But I can't stand in the way of a trade because you're not doing what you're supposed to do, like coming to practices and doing off-season training." Iverson sat there, looking down. By now, Croce knew that, even when he wasn't making eye contact, Iverson was listening. But Johnson leaned in closer.

"You see this man here?" Johnson said, pointing to Croce. "It means something that he's here. Not too many guys have relationships with their owners like I've had with Jerry Buss. But you can have that, Allen, 'cause this guy's here. But you've got to make it work.

"People love you, Allen," Johnson continued. "Wait till you see the crowd tonight. My son is eighteen, and he's in love with you. He's all Mr. Tough now, see, and he's got that 'A.I.' attitude. He can come to Lakers games with me and sit courtside, but if you're on the dish, he's staying home to watch A.I. You've got the younger generation sewed up, and you don't even realize it. You just gotta stop making things hard for yourself. The kids are going to love you regardless, but the dads like me might have to say, 'You can't follow Allen because of the choices he makes.' I always loved practice, man. I came early and was the last to leave. If you're the best player, that's the job. It's not enough to just be the best player. You've got to set the example, too."

Johnson was simply reiterating messages from countless authority figures—from Brown to Cheeks to Rick Mahorn to Croce—but Croce sensed this was different. Since it was coming from Johnson, with all those championship rings, Iverson might take the advice as information—and not as a threat. Now Johnson burst into the wide smile that had made him millions in endorsements. "I know what a pain in the ass coaches can be," he said. "Don't forget, I played for Pat Riley. He was much tougher than Larry Brown. But I loved it. And I loved him, because that's how he cared about me."

Iverson looked up. "I don't hate Larry Brown," he said. "People think I hate him. I don't hate him. He didn't do anything to my kids or my mom. People think I'm gonna go back to Philly and be spiteful, but I'm not about that. I'm going to go back there and this is all gonna be about business."

If he got back to Philly, that is. Shortly after his weekend in Virginia, Croce learned that a trade had indeed been made. It was a blockbuster deal between the Sixers, Lakers, Pistons, and Hornets. Iverson and Geiger would go to Detroit and the Sixers would get all-star guard Eddie Jones from Charlotte, Glen Rice from Los Angeles, and Iverson's collegiate teammate Jerome Williams from Detroit. From Brown's perspective, Jones was a defensive upgrade, and the combination of Jones and Rice would compensate for Iverson's scoring.

As a lifelong Philadelphian, Croce knew the trade made no sense from a business perspective. He knew that Iverson was more popular than Wilt Chamberlain, Julius Erving, or Charles Barkley had ever been. Moreover, in the last year, he'd watched Phil Jackson lead the Lakers to an NBA title in his first season in L.A. He saw Jackson earn his salary—roughly in line with what Croce was paying Brown—by using his communication skills to bridge the chemistry gaps between Shaq and Kobe Bryant. Jackson was paid to solve a problem, not to throw up his hands and start fresh. "But I don't know if Larry's capable of solving this problem," Croce wondered to friends.

Faced with no other choice, he called Iverson. "It breaks my heart," he said, "but it looks like you're about to be traded, Bubba." He expected to hear either resignation or anger in Iverson's voice. Instead, he got breathless passion as Iverson pleaded for one more chance. "I just turned twenty-five, Pat," Iverson said. "If you're going to fuckin' trade me, trade me for someone who's better and who will help the team. But if you're trading me because of little things like coming late, missing a shootaround, I can change all that. I want to come back and be a captain, I'm gonna get married, I'm gonna start doing the right things." Croce loved what he was hearing, but he feared it was too little, too late.

And then Matt Geiger, with, ironically, an assist from David Falk, saved Iverson and, ultimately, the Philadelphia franchise. When Geiger signed as a free agent with Philadelphia, his agent, Falk, had negotiated for a 15 percent "kicker" to be paid by any team acquiring Geiger in a trade. Now Detroit would only go through with the deal if Geiger waived their obligation to pay him the onetime fee. Geiger refused. The trade was scuttled.

Still, it was unclear whether Iverson could really start anew. In late August, Magic Johnson appeared on *The Tonight Show with Jay Leno* to promote *his* upcoming charity basketball game, which, he announced, would feature Allen Iverson. Come game time, however, there was no sign of Iverson.

Johnson knew firsthand what the no-show was about: Iverson's posse. He knew his mentoring of Iverson was seen as a threat by those already in

With teammate Matt Geiger, who, upon first seeing
Iverson's "What Would Jesus Do?" bracelet, quipped,
"You should add, 'Not This.'"

the young star's ear. "Those guys around him should have made him come to my game, but it was the other way, for sure," Johnson said. "I've told Allen, you can't reach a certain level if you have guys who haven't been there. None of those guys have ever been to this level. I get guys asking me all the time how to get to this level. Allen has asked. And I've told him, number one, I don't deal with the posse. When you come meet with me, *you come meet with me.* When we do something, it's gotta be you and I and somebody who's going to execute this thing, but not all these other guys. See, I had to pass a test. Businessmen I've done deals with couldn't believe I was on time to meetings, that I didn't bring a hundred guys with me, that I wasn't wearing all the jewelry. I was in a suit and tie, I was up early, and I knew my numbers."

Shortly after Iverson's no-show, Johnson bumped into Iverson at a Mary J. Blige concert. "Man, don't stop calling me," Iverson said sheepishly. "Don't be mad at me."

"Look," Johnson said. "You got a get-out-of-jail-free card from me now. But the next time, that's gonna be it for me."

Meantime, perhaps the makeover Iverson promised Croce had begun. In September, he purchased a $2.4 million mansion on the Main Line, just minutes from where Croce, Snider, and Brown all lived. It came with five bedrooms, six baths, three fireplaces, and $25,000 in yearly taxes. He rented his previous home—and ultimately sold it—to Geiger, for $834,000. He and Tawanna began planning a wedding. He met with Brown and asked to be a team captain, a request Brown granted. And he finished up the rap CD. It was, he felt, like taking a page out of Magic's playbook; rather than constantly handing out money to his friends, he'd empower them with record deals, as they'd long fantasized. When a promotional single from the CD was released on the eve of training camp, though, it hardly appeared that Allen Iverson was changing anything.

We're about to shock the world," Ra said, smiling. He was dressed in a wifebeater top and baggy jeans, standing by the recording studio's pool table, chatting with Dan DeLuca, music writer from the *Philadelphia Inquirer.* In the other room, Iverson was putting the finishing touches on a cut entitled "Virginia Ain't for Lovers."

DeLuca's ears perked up at the lyrics. "Bitch niggas take cover/Virginia ain't for lovers," and "This ain't for kids with action figures/This is for the hardcore niggas." Great line, DeLuca thought. Over the next five hours in the studio, he grew convinced that Iverson's rapping would be much better than Shaq's goofy rhymes or Kobe's lame attempt. (*Vibe* magazine would later give Iverson's CD a respectable three stars.) Throughout the evening, Ra and "E" and others took turns with Iverson on the mike. As Coronas were drained and pizzas devoured, Iverson and his boys kept coming back to Ra's point: This was *their* time. This was what they'd been waiting for all their lives. The world might see them as nothing more than a bunch of hangers-on and sycophants, but the CD would show them to be equals in this artistic endeavor.

Days later, DeLuca received a copy of "40 Bars," the CD's promotional single, from the record company. Only it was the uncensored version. He heard Iverson rap, "Man enough to pull a gun, be man enough to use it" and "Come to me with faggot tendencies, you be sleeping where the maggots be" and "Get money, kill and fuck bitches/I'm hitting' anything and planning on using my riches."

DeLuca called Croce and read him the lyrics over the phone. "That doesn't sound too positive to me," Pat Croce was quoted as saying in DeLuca's story. "This is going to be a problem."

Training camp was about to start, and now this. The Philadelphia chapter of the Gay and Lesbian Task Force denounced Iverson's lyrics, as did civil-rights activist C. Dolores Tucker, who, along with Bill Bennett, had taken on Time Warner over the gangsta raps of Suge Knight's Death Row label.

When training camp at Penn State University opened, there Iverson stood, cornered by a press pack bewildered by the rhymes he had written. Iverson stood among them, defiant and defensive, refusing to discuss his CD, saying that, with the exception of the rap-specific press, no one in the media "understands hip-hop because y'all don't want to understand hip-hop."

For one of the few times in their relationship, Iverson felt Croce had spoken out of turn. Together they found a conference room away from the media throng and Iverson made his displeasure known. "If you got something to say to me, you can just talk to me," he said. "I gotta read in the paper that you think I'm doing something that isn't positive?"

"You're right," Croce said. "I apologize. I shouldn't have talked to the press before I spoke to you."

Iverson, naively, was taken aback by the controversy. When he heard that gay groups were outraged by his use of the word "faggot"—which he and many hip-hoppers used as a synonym for "weak" without regard to sexuality—he was upset to think he'd offended people. "I have a gay cousin," he said. "I'd never want to insult him." He couldn't understand what all the fuss was about. "I'm just talking smack, rapping," he said. "It's an art form. Bruce Willis don't do the things he do in a movie, right? It's just a movie."

Among those who didn't quite get the distinction was league commissioner David Stern, who summoned Iverson to New York. Theo Ratliff, the team's player rep, accompanied his teammate, and later regaled the Sixers with his version of the meeting's highlight. Stern, known for a ferocious temper, at one point yelled, "If you go through with this, I'm going to kill you!"

"See, I don't think you *really* gonna kill me," Iverson coolly replied. "You just talking smack, like I did on wax."

Once again, Iverson found himself a combatant in a cultural and generational clash. On one side were his overwhelmingly white and middle-class interlocutors, who reacted to his rhymes literally, at face value. On the other side of the divide were a generation of young hip-hoppers with their own set of mores.

Iverson issued a written apology and met with the offended groups. After all her public posturing, Tucker was a no-show; Jerry Mondesire, head of the Philadelphia NAACP, not only attended, but praised Iverson for squarely facing the issue—and then asked for his autograph. Meantime, Iverson's old friend Spike Lee was in Philadelphia, promoting his new film, *Bamboozled.* On local TV news, Iverson saw Lee criticize him; Lee went so far as to call Iverson's type of hard-core rapping "the new minstrelsy." Iverson vowed never to speak to Lee again, not because Lee had criticized him, but because he had done so publicly. In Iverson's view, Lee had aided and abetted a media eager to bring him down.

From Iverson's perspective, his naysayers simply didn't understand his art form. Chuck D, pioneer rapper of the group Public Enemy, once said that hip-hop was the "CNN of the ghetto"; it used literary technique to tell gritty, sometimes offensive stories that were, above all else, a real depiction of inner-city street life. That's what Iverson thought he was doing, as evidenced by his CD's original title, *Non-Fiction.* (It was later changed to *Misunderstood;* still later, he decided against releasing the CD, because the controversy took all the fun out of it for him.)

As Iverson well knew, nearly 70 percent of rap records are bought by suburban white kids, in large part because hip-hop offers a safe and authentic travelogue to another culture. Those consumers were aware of the multiple fictions rappers used to tell stories. They knew, for instance, that Eminem was an artist who had created the character Slim Shady, a rap protagonist who mouthed offensive lyrics for dramatic effect, like countless characters in popular movies. Similarly, there was Iverson's alter ego, Jewelz, who presented a snapshot of street life that brought down this torrent of judgment upon the basketball star.

Iverson saw himself as an entertainer; The Answer was his basketball character. Jewelz was his rap alter ego, who chronicled underworld violence—which is not necessarily the same thing as endorsing it. (In fact, the CD's cover read: "Allen Iverson *as* Jewelz.") When Iverson reacted defensively to the media horde, it was because he felt they were there to judge him, and that the controversy was being fueled by a deep-seated animus toward young black men who wear the hip-hop "uniform." After all, he pointed out to Gaskins and others, where was the outrage when the Lakers' Rick Fox played a murderer on the violent HBO series *Oz?*

Plenty of pundits weighed in, arguing that this latest controversy proved that Iverson's pledge to rededicate himself to the game was nothing but lip service, words he'd had to utter to avoid being traded. But Larry Brown sensed something else. While the national news crews descended upon training camp, Iverson not only avoided the media swarm—he took solace in the cocoon of his team. He got to every practice early, he practiced hard, and he hung with his teammates at night.

One day during training camp, Iverson's high-school coach Mike Bailey visited. He was now coaching nearby, in Williamsport, Pennsylvania. That night, Iverson agreed to follow Mike and Janet Bailey to Mike's sister's house, twelve miles outside State College. Allen and Gary Moore, plus Tawanna and the kids, drove behind the Baileys, deep into the woods. "I want a house like this," Iverson said, getting out of the car and taking his first glimpse of Bailey's sister's secluded farmhouse. "You got to be lost in order to get here."

They stayed and visited for two hours. Moore, who had spent a good part of the previous four seasons shuttling between Virginia and Philly, was now committed to spending the season by Iverson's side, as his personal manager. Some around Iverson were suspicious of Moore's motives when it came to Iverson. At times, even Iverson pointedly joked about Moore's stewardship of the Crossover Foundation charity: "You better give some of that money to the kids, Mo," he'd say. But Gary Moore had been there for him in Newport News, had clothed him and fed him when no one else could. Now that Moore, who was in his forties, had committed to being by Iverson's side, the Baileys were convinced he would be a steadying influence.

As the evening wore on, Iverson, as always, gravitated toward the children in the room, sitting cross-legged on the floor and playing with his kids and Bailey's young nieces and nephews. At one point, Iverson reminisced over old high-school exploits, even telling Bailey he was still mad that Bailey hadn't intervened when Coach Koz tried to punish him one time by making him do a hundred push-ups in front of the crowd during a timeout of a JV basketball game.

As Iverson and Moore were about to leave, Iverson turned serious. "How long have y'all been married?" he asked the Baileys.

"All our lives," joked Janet Bailey.

He looked at his former coach. "You think I can make the long haul?" he asked.

"You mean the championship?"

"Nah, man. You think I can get married and stay married?"

The Baileys smiled while Tawanna shyly blushed. "I have no doubt," the coach said.

The 76ers team that opened the 2000–2001 season was Larry Brown's kind of team. Up front, Ratliff was a shot-blocking intimidator, and Hill and Lynch egolessly did the little things that account for winning: setting screens, rebounding, defending. In the backcourt, Snow was a steadying floor general, intent on feeding the ball to Iverson. On the bench, McKie was fast becoming a clutch outside shooter and defensive stalwart. Geiger—though oft-injured now and the focus of the boobirds—was a big body able to defend legitimate centers. Kukoc was still a question mark; he seemed uninspired defensively and tended to defer to Iverson on offense, rarely asserting himself.

On the eve of the regular season, Brown signed veteran shooting guard Vernon Maxwell. "Mad Max," as he was known, had a troubled NBA past, but there was no doubt he could play. He had been a starter on Houston's championship teams in the midnineties and none other than Jordan had once described him as among the league's toughest defenders. At thirty-four, his career was winding down, but Brown thought he could add depth to the bench. Iverson was ecstatic to see Maxwell in a Sixers uniform. "Don't tell me they brought this crazy nigga in here!" he shouted, upon seeing Maxwell at practice for the first time.

The year before, Seattle's Gary Payton had lobbied his team to sign Maxwell, saying, "We need some ghetto in here"; the two, both combustible personalities, ended up feuding, however (Maxwell threw an iron plate at Payton in the locker room, striking and injuring their teammate Horace Grant), and Maxwell was traded. Now Iverson quickly struck up a friendship with this most unlikely of role models.

Once the regular season opened, the Sixers followed up their focused and disciplined training camp by storming out to a league-best 10–0 start. Even though Iverson once again started off shooting poorly from the field, the team was winning Brown's way—by playing hard-nosed, scrambling defense. In fact, Iverson, perhaps seeing how much Maxwell liked to practice, seemed newly dedicated. On defense, especially, he was making great strides. Brown couldn't stop praising his best player.

"He's all about playing the right way," the coach said of Iverson. "His defense is one hundred percent better, his turnovers are down, he's getting rid of the ball sooner and enjoying it more. I hear a couple of jerks in the stands yelling for him to shoot. But the one thing I had always hoped, once he won the scoring title and made the all-star game, was that he'd start to realize all of that is great, but the bottom line is about winning. You can't convince a player until he buys into the program. His overall game is the best since I've been here."

When Eric Snow went down for nearly three months in early December with a stress fracture to his ankle, the love fest didn't miss a beat. McKie stepped into the starting lineup and put up better numbers than Snow had. The Sixers remained one of the hottest teams in the league. Because the team was so workmanlike, it captured a wide fan base.

Inevitably, the first bump in the road hit, and it was much more than a pothole. It was a crater, and it jarred everybody aboard.

With a first-place record of 17–5, the Sixers lost to the Dallas Mavericks at home, 112–94. Dallas forward Dirk Nowitzki was unstoppable, scoring 37 points. In the locker room afterward, Brown, in keeping with his counterintuitive instinct to be tougher on a team when it's doing well, was harshly critical. Iverson spoke up for the team, criticizing Brown for not adjusting during the game to provide George Lynch with some defensive help in trying to contain Nowitzki.

The next morning, in a team breakfast meeting in Chicago, the rhetoric escalated. Iverson, apparently with the green light from his teammates, told the coach in front of the squad that his constant carping was wearing thin. "We got the best record in the league and you treat us like we're in last place," he said. Moreover, guys were afraid to speak up about it, for fear that Brown would cut their minutes. Iverson told Brown that he was "whining all the time like a little bitch."

Brown was horrified. He coached that night in a stupor, barely communicating with his team during a win over the lowly Bulls. The next day, the Sunday before Christmas, Pat Croce awoke and commented to his wife, Diane, "Can you believe it was a year ago today that everything blew up between Allen and Larry in Detroit? Now we're in first place. What a difference a year makes."

Not exactly. When Croce returned from church early that afternoon, Diane had a message for him. "Billy King called," she said. "It's urgent."

What could be so urgent—we're 18–6, Croce thought. Then he got King on the phone. "Pat, there was a blowup before the Chicago game," King said. "Coach is offended and taking time off to reflect and he's thinking of quitting."

"No!" Croce exclaimed.

"I think he just needs some time off," King said.

Croce called Brown at home. Shelly Brown answered and told Croce her husband couldn't come to the phone: "He's too upset." The next day, she called in her husband's absence from practice, saying he was still "too emotional."

It was unheard of in professional sports: an AWOL coach. When the players showed up for practice on Monday, Croce addressed them. "Coach is at home, reflecting on his relationship with you," he said. "He just doesn't want to have a negative relationship with you, like he had with Reggie Miller and the Pacers at the end. He doesn't want to let you down."

There was silence. Then, according to one player who was there, Iverson spoke up, angrily. "This punk is quitting on us, then," he spat out. "Well, fuck him."

"Allen, it's not just you, it's his relationship with the team," Croce said. " He's emotional right now. The best way you can show support for him is to practice hard."

When Iverson had spoken up against Brown in Chicago, it marked the first time that it was Iverson *and* the team versus Brown. In previous controversies, Brown had always allied with the likes of Snow and McKie in trying to bring Iverson around to their shared vision of what constituted a team. But now this. It was all too similar to what had gone down in Indiana. During Brown's fourth and last season there, he'd lost that team. This was now his fourth year with the Sixers.

"Larry's a great builder, but not a finisher," said one NBA head coach of Brown's strange sabbatical. "He builds teams up, and then when they're ready to kill his ass, he leaves."

That's what had happened in Indiana. "Those were guys who were really important in my life," Brown recalls about his last year with the Pacers. "I didn't treat them the way I should have. The word was out: I was too demanding, I never let up on them." His riding of the Pacers was so bad, in fact, that when Brown first returned to Indiana as head coach of the 76ers, even some of his mild-mannered former players, like Rik Smits, took snarling, trash-talking delight in beating their old coach.

It's a fine line, Brown maintained. He had always felt an obligation to teach, even if his teachings might grate. Then, too, he was aware of his less-than-tolerant nature. "I can't coach assholes," he says. "I know that about myself."

When coaching Kansas in the 1980s, Brown had been the subject of an academic study that gauged his positive-to-negative reinforcement ratio. He was pleased to find he was an overwhelmingly positive coach. "The problem is that players don't hear when you're positive," he says. "They have selective hearing."

In Indiana, one of those refusing to listen was a young, prodigiously talented hip-hop player. After Brown left, that player, Jalen Rose, became a star, blossoming under Brown's replacement, the laid-back Larry Bird. Brown knew how much Rose loved to play and he wished that more players cared so deeply for the game. But the six-eight Rose wanted to be a point guard, seeing himself as the next Magic Johnson, and Brown saw him as a small forward. Brown held firm, and Rose retreated into himself. "I'm still disappointed I couldn't reach Jalen," Brown says even now. Once Rose was lost, the rest of the team followed and Brown became convinced Indiana needed a new coach.

Could it all be happening again? Was Larry Brown about to flame out in his fourth year in Philadelphia? Doug Moe, one of Brown's closest friends in the coaching fraternity, once quipped that Brown "is only happy when he's unhappy." Brown took exception to the remark—"Doug's the one with the ulcer, not me"—but if he bolted now, with a first-place team, his coaching epitaph would be forever sealed: *Great basketball mind, victim of his own tortured genius.* For the story of Brown's life was a story of abruptly severed relationships. There was the succession of jobs, the father who died when Larry was seven, the three marriages, the long and mysterious estrangement from his brother Herb—a recently repaired split that had developed because both coaches (Larry then with Denver, Herb with Detroit) coveted Marques Johnson in the 1977 NBA draft. (Neither got him.)

After missing two practices, Brown finally spoke to Croce. "Coach, you can't quit now," Croce said. "You finally have the players you want. We're in first place!" Then came calls from McKie, Lynch, and Snow, urging his return. The Brown who came back, these and other players would later attest, was a kinder and gentler one. Larry Brown had obsessed over the way his tenure had ended in Indiana and he was determined to do one thing when he returned. "I didn't want what happened in Indiana to happen again," he said.

By early January, it had become clear that the change in Brown involved a subtle alteration in tone; he hadn't compromised on matters of coaching principle. His team would still play like a well-schooled college squad. At a time when most NBA offenses lacked imagination—how often did they dump the ball into a big man down low, wait for the double-team, then kick it out for a three-point bomb?—Brown's team led the league in classic backdoor cuts and give-and-go's.

Nor did he deviate from his usual practice regimen. During one practice, he whistled a play dead to reprimand Kukoc for the way he was setting a pick, one of the game's most fundamental acts. "It's not that complicated," Brown chided. "Set the screen *even* to the ball, and then roll." Kukoc had been setting the screen perhaps fifteen inches from where Brown wanted. "Those fifteen inches," McKie would later explain, "could be the difference between an open shot and a blocked shot."

But according to players like Geiger, with whom Brown had a long heart-to-heart once the coach returned, Brown seemed more aware of the effects his words could have. On January 9, the Sixers visited New Jersey to face the Nets and Marbury, Iverson's longtime rival. During pregame warm-ups, a fan let Iverson have it, calling him a "gunner" who cared only about himself and his scoring average. Iverson turned on the fan and bellowed: "Man, I already won a scoring title. I'm going for that ring now!"

Just a few feet away, Brown almost let himself smile. He had more reason to smile during the game, when Iverson took only 14 shots but played a flawless floor game en route to another win. The next day, Brown called his star into his office at the practice facility. "There are a lot of things I've been proud of you for, things that you've done, what you've become," he said. "But that might have been one of the most satisfying games I've ever coached last night, because I know that playing against Marbury is big for you, and you just played to win."

As the all-star game approached, it became commonplace to hear Brown laud Iverson not just for his guts and hustle and talent, but also for how he kept his teammates involved—giving them touches—and how he was finding his scoring chances out of the natural flow of the offense. Similarly, Iverson could be heard praising his coach. "He's got a tough job," he said. "He's always drawing up and calling the right plays. He's got to make tough substitutions, 'cause we got twelve guys who want to play. And he's got to keep me happy."

For his part, Croce had given up trying to figure out both men. "They're both geniuses," he said. "And genius is something I can't relate to."

Brown smiled when he heard what Croce had said. "I don't know about being geniuses," he said. "But Allen and I both have loose wires."

The good feelings showed on the court, where the Sixers were 13–3 in January. Iverson averaged 34.6 points, 4.6 assists, and 2.67 steals a game and was named NBA Player of the Month. The only downer came in the last game before the all-star break, when Ratliff, who was to join Iverson as an all-star starter, suffered a stress fracture to his right wrist. He'd be out at least six weeks and maybe much longer.

Brown coached Iverson in the all-star game, for which Iverson won

Forcing teammate Dikembe Mutombo to double over in laughter on the bench.

MVP honors. He scored 25 points, including 10 of his team's final 16, and elicited a string of oohs and aahs from the Washington, D.C., packed house every time he crossed someone over or skied for an alley-oop. Manning the middle for Iverson's squad was Atlanta's Dikembe Mutombo. Against the best players in the world, Mutombo grabbed a game-high 21 rebounds. Because of Mutombo's dominating presence, Brown was able to "go small"—play shorter, quicker guys like Marbury and Iverson together. The East won; afterward, when David Stern presented Iverson with the NBA trophy, the star searched the crowd. "Where my coach at? Where my coach at?" he called. "I couldn't have done this without Coach Brown."

The Sixers won five straight after the all-star break, giving them an NBA-best record of 41–14. On the morning of the league's trading deadline, Brown did something he'd never done before, something few coaches would ever do. Before practice, he pulled aside his three team leaders: Iverson, McKie, and Snow. "This is just between us," he began, "but I want to tell you what we're thinking of doing, and I want your input."

Brown proceeded to spell out the details of a possible trade that would send Ratliff and Kukoc to Atlanta for Mutombo. With the best record in the league, some could argue Brown was aiming to fix what wasn't broken. But with Ratliff injured and his future unknown, and Geiger often out of the lineup with chronic knee problems, the center position looked like a gaping hole. Besides, if his team did make it to the NBA Finals, Mutombo would give them a presence in the middle to at least match up against Shaq and the Lakers or the twin towers of Tim Duncan and David Robinson in San Antonio. As Brown outlined the deal to his players, he withheld one key fact. He didn't tell them he was giving them veto power. If just one of them strenuously objected to the deal, he planned to nix the trade.

McKie was the first to respond. "Coach," he said, "you know I'm going to be loyal to the guys who got us in this position. But that's personal, that's not about basketball."

"I wouldn't expect anything else but loyalty from any of you," Brown said. He looked at Iverson, mindful of Iverson's longtime complaint that he was seldom consulted on personnel moves.

"Coach, I love Theo," Iverson said. "But if you think this is going to make us better, I guess you gotta go for it."

"Well, you never know, Allen," Brown replied. "But I keep coming back to the fact that we don't have Theo now, and who knows when we get him back and how he'll be when we do?"

Snow, Ratliff's best friend on the team, looked up. Brown knew that his reaction would be key. "If we don't have Theo, Coach, and we don't know when we're getting him back," Snow said, sighing, "I can't stand in the way of this."

That night, the deal for Mutombo was made. Iverson was ecstatic to play with a legitimate all-star center for the first time in his pro career—a fellow Georgetown product, no less. Sitting in front of his locker before Mutombo's debut, McKie thought back to Brown's pretrade consultation with the players. "It meant a lot that Coach came to us, that he involved us in the decision," he said. "In the past, it was more like Coach might just as well have gone up to a club box seat and yelled down orders *at* us."

It was a bold move on Brown's part. Seldom does a league-leading team make a blockbuster deal. But Mutombo was a seven-foot one-inch, 280-pound shot blocker who was a three-time NBA Defensive Player of the Year and who was currently leading the league in rebounding at 14 per game.

But the adjustment to Mutombo's plodding style didn't come easily. At the time of the trade, there were only twenty-eight games left in the season. Iverson wouldn't play in nine of those because of the injuries to his hip, tailbone, and elbow that had been plaguing him all season. The Sixers would close out the season with a mere 15–13 record after acquiring Mutombo. Still, the Sixers ended the season with the best record in the East, 56–26, and Iverson had had his best season as a pro. He scored 31.1 points per game, good enough for his second scoring title and making him the first player since Jordan to average over 30 points per game for a season. He was favored to win the MVP award. In fact, shortly after the close of the regular season, the Sixers swept the postseason awards, when McKie was named Sixth Man of the Year, Mutombo Defensive Player of the Year, and Brown Coach of the Year.

Now all that remained was a lengthy play-off run. And the first team that stood in their way was—who else?—the Indiana Pacers.

Under first-year head coach Isiah Thomas, the Pacers were rebuilding after having advanced to the NBA Finals the year before. They had barely qualified for the eighth and final play-off spot. Still, Brown knew that any team with Reggie Miller and Jalen Rose presented challenges.

The play-offs are different, and the Pacers veterans had been there before. Iverson had had his way against the Pacers during the regular season, but Thomas designed a defense to frustrate the all-star guard for game one.

Before a boisterous, packed crowd in Philadelphia, the Sixers built an 18-point third-quarter lead. But Iverson was stymied by Thomas's swarming, double-teaming defense. Every time he touched the ball, guard Travis Best would be joined by either forward/center Jermaine O'Neal or Miller or Rose, and they'd play Iverson two on one. Iverson couldn't get a rhythm going. He'd either force the issue or find the open man—who would, more often than not, miss. In the second half, the Sixers' other starters shot a paltry 3 for 14, with the usually deadeye McKie hitting just 3 of 10.

Iverson scored a mere 16 points. With 2.9 seconds to go, Miller—who had connected on only 4 of 20 shots—eluded Iverson behind a screen and George Lynch failed to leave his man and switch out on one of the great clutch shooters in NBA history. Miller drained a game-winning three, stunning the crowd into silence. "Our asses got tight," Iverson succinctly said after the game.

The Sixers had worked all season long for home-court advantage, and they'd given it back on the first night of the play-offs. The next morning, Iverson was the first to arrive at the Sixers' practice facility. Before practice, he and Brown went over the tape of game one. Thomas had said after the game that the purpose of the aggressive double team was to turn Iverson from an instinctive player into a thinking player. Brown countered by drawing up a series of offensive sets designed to get Iverson free off the ball. He'd be tougher to double-team if he was running off screens without the ball. When he did have it, Brown told him to trust his teammates.

In game two, the Pacers again threw swarming double teams Iverson's way, but the outcome this time was strikingly different. Iverson didn't waste time dribbling, as he often did, to set up his man. He came off screens and made moves the moment the ball touched his hands. In the third quarter alone, he scored 19 points, using a vast repertoire of moves to keep the defense honest. On one play, he jolted Miller with a crossover and sensed forward Austin Croshere coming over to help; in midair he faked a pass to Croshere's man, freezing the defender. At the last possible instant, he arced a floater over O'Neal and through the hoop. He also hit from outside, which enabled him to start driving to the basket. He made 15 of his 27 shots, scored 45 points, and trusted his teammates, as evidenced by his 9 assists. The Sixers won, 116–98.

Afterward, Iverson couldn't stop talking about his coach. "I learned a lot more about Larry Brown as a coach," he said. "It's unbelievable how he prepared us for this game. Coach put in so many things to help me, so many different plays where they couldn't double-team me like they wanted to."

The Sixers won game three behind Iverson's 32 points and 6 assists, while McKie added 22. In game four, Iverson went for 33 points and the Sixers closed out the series, three games to one. As they were walking off, Miller embraced Iverson. "You've got to make your team believe they can win," the veteran told Iverson. "We've put you through enough wars. This is your first step." Iverson was jubilant, recalling how, just a year earlier, the Pacers' dismissal of his team had caused him to break down, sobbing.

Next up came Vince Carter's Toronto Raptors, a series that would pit two of the game's rising stars against each other. NBC billed it as "The Answer versus Vinsanity." Once again, the Sixers made things hard for themselves, dropping game one at home. Iverson and Carter canceled each other out, with Iverson scoring 36 and Carter 35. The difference was Toronto's outside shooting specialist Dell Curry, who totaled 20 points.

The pressure was on for game two. It was a seesaw battle; the longer the game stayed close, the more pressure it put on the Sixers. Yet it seemed as though, on this night, Iverson would not let his teammates' asses get tight again. In the fourth quarter, he was unstoppable, seeming to will high, arcing shots into the basket while opposing players frantically clutched at him. He made an astounding 21 of 39 shots, for a franchise play-off record 54 points. Amazingly, he scored all of his team's last 19 points—in a 97–92 win. Afterward, when asked where such a clutch performance came from, Iverson provided a telling two-word response: "Poverty. Life." After the press conference, with his kids tugging at his legs, he walked to his car in the center of a large entourage that included Ann and Jack. "If you lose this game, the series is basically over," someone said to him. "Surely you felt that pressure?"

Iverson stopped and look puzzled. "Pressure?" he said. "After all the shit I've seen in my life, you think I'm gonna feel pressure from a muthafuckin' *basketball* game?"

The series against the Raptors was epic. Carter scored 50 points to lead Toronto to victory in game three, before Iverson's 30 helped the Sixers eke out a game-four win on the road. With the series tied at two games apiece, Iverson was named the league's MVP the day before game five in Philadelphia.

During the ceremony, Croce had a beaming Iverson sit on his coach's lap for a photo op that appeared in papers across the country. In his off-the-cuff speech, Iverson, in addition to paying homage to his boys in the back of the room, singled out his teammate Aaron McKie as an influence. "I told Blue [McKie] that it was going to be important for me to become a professional, like he is day in and day out," he said.

When Brown spoke, the Larry and Allen narrative had come full circle. "I'm so proud of what Allen has done," he said. "Maybe I didn't give it enough thought or time to understand what this kid is about, and that's the neatest thing about my improved relationship with him. He doesn't always do it the way I would expect or sometimes like. But I know where his heart is. This kid has great character."

Before game five, Iverson was presented with his MVP trophy. And then he decimated the Raptors with 50 points for another Sixers win. When Toronto held serve at home, a pivotal game seven loomed in Philly.

The morning of the game, Carter was in North Carolina, taking part in his college graduation ceremony. He took a private jet back to Philly by game time; the media had a field day with "should he" or "shouldn't he" debates. Meantime, Iverson was ailing. The long season, and the brutal beatings he'd been taking, were adding up. Early in game seven, Iverson collided with Toronto enforcer Charles Oakley, further aggravating his chronically bruised tailbone. He was hobbled; his outside shot was front-rimming, a sign that the usual lift wasn't coming from his legs. So he did the next best thing: he reined in his offensive impulses and concentrated instead on setting up his teammates. It was like he was a point guard again, only wiser and more careful with the ball. McKie led the team with 22 points, but Iverson, who scored 21, tallied a career-high 16 assists. When Carter missed a long jumper at the buzzer, the Sixers had won, 88–87. Iverson went running, arms raised, to the opposite baseline, where he flung himself into his mother's arms while fans stormed the court.

Things didn't get any easier, though. Ray Allen's Milwaukee Bucks came to town next. In game one, Iverson torched George Karl's team for

Iverson's Tarzan yell after scoring 54 points, including his team's final 19, in a 2001 play-off win over Toronto.

34 points and the Sixers finally won an opener at home. In game two, however, the Bucks evened the series behind Ray Allen's 38.

Iverson, still hobbled by the tailbone, opted to sit out game three. He and Gary Moore watched the undermanned Sixers take on the Bucks from Iverson's hotel room at the Pfister Hotel while Iverson tried to rest. The Sixers fought valiantly, but lost by six. When they got back to the hotel, Iverson was in the lobby, grinning proudly, applauding his teammates as they got off their bus.

Game four found Iverson not only playing but seeming to gain strength in the second half. At one point, Ray Allen elbowed him in the mouth. Iverson played on, knowing that if the refs saw that he was bleeding, he'd have to leave the game. So he kept letting his mouth fill with blood before swallowing—this while scoring 11 of his team's final 13 points in a 89–83 victory.

Snow, playing with a stress fracture in each ankle, scored 18 points, including the game winner in game five. The Sixers dropped game six to the Bucks in Milwaukee, despite a furious comeback attempt led by Iverson, in which he scored 26 of his 46 points in the fourth quarter.

Once again, it was win or go home as the Sixers hosted the Bucks in game seven of the Eastern Conference Finals. Before the game, Iverson limped slowly around the Sixers' locker room, looking brittle and sore. When asked how he was feeling, he shrugged. "Like shit," he said. "But I won't feel a thing once I'm out there."

Forty-four points, 7 assists, 6 rebounds, and 2 steals later, Iverson was hugging Brown and Croce at midcourt while he and his teammates donned "Eastern Conference Champion" T-shirts and caps. There was Mutombo, who had totaled 23 points, 19 rebounds, and 7 blocks in game seven, bending down to embrace Iverson. And there was Ann, as always, right near her baby, looking on with pride while confetti littered the court. Her son was going to Los Angeles to kick Goliath's ass.

The Los Angeles Lakers had not lost a basketball game in sixty-seven days, ever since, appropriately enough, April Fools' Day. Since then, Shaq, Kobe, and Phil Jackson had decimated the best teams in the Western Conference. They swept Scottie Pippen and the Portland Trailblazers, Chris Webber and the upstart Sacramento Kings, and—most stunningly—they rolled right through Tim Duncan and the San Antonio Spurs. Eleven games, eleven wins. They didn't just beat these teams; they demoralized them. As

Bryant was fond of saying, they "ripped the hearts" out of their opponents.

There wasn't a pundit alive picking the Sixers to win the series. Most weren't picking Philly even to win a game.

Though he rarely played the media game, Iverson liked to read virtually everything written about him. Now he was national story number one, given that the various story-line permutations of Shaq, Kobe, and Phil had all been exhausted long ago. Iverson was new and different. He was showing up to press conferences wearing a 'do rag covered in dollar-sign insignias, dressed in trendy hip-hop clothes, with Deuce bouncing or, depending on the time, asleep on one knee.

But Iverson didn't like all of what he was reading. Other sports stars might have bought into the cliché-ridden sportswriter hype about how, suddenly, he'd "grown up" this season. To Iverson, it was much too simplistic a take. Yes, he'd matured—the same way any young man grows between the time he's twenty and twenty-six, which he'd turn the day after game one. In the press conference the day before the big game, a questioner, anticipating a wholesome, feel-good response, prompted him: "It must be nice, the way the public has seemed to embrace you?"

Iverson licked his lips. "I don't care," he said, without a trace of rancor in his voice. "All I care about is what my family feels about me, my friends, my teammates . . . [There is] nothing easy about being Allen Iverson where everybody is looking at your every move, criticizing you for just saying a curse word when you get mad. Making you feel like you're some type of villain, the smallest man on the court but the biggest villain in life."

The Lakers should have been taking note: Iverson was fine-tuning his "me against the world" outlook. In fact, Tupac Shakur's song by that very name was one Iverson could often be heard humming to himself. Come game time, he played as though the world were indeed aligned against him. When he saw fans in the stands holding brooms, meant to signify "sweep," he took note. He'd use that. When the crowd booed him, he smiled. He'd use that. When the refs blew a call, he clapped his hands together and looked skyward. Just another obstacle. He'd use that.

In the game's first twenty-nine minutes, Iverson scored 38 points. He hit jumpers, he hit fastbreak layups, he challenged O'Neal, despite being more than a foot shorter and half the giant's weight. The Sixers forced overtime, where Iverson rose to the occasion again. Trailed doggedly by speedy Laker sub Tyronn Lue, Iverson hit a three from deep in the corner with 1:19 left; Lue, having lunged at him, lay at Iverson's feet while the ball sailed through the air. Once it dropped through the twine, Iverson made an emphatic show of stomping over the prone, disbelieving form of Lue—as if to say, *There. Take that.*

Then came a jumper from the corner, for a 4-point lead with forty-eight seconds left. Then came a runner by Snow to seal the overtime win.

On the way to the locker room, Iverson shouted, "Put the brooms away!" He told his team, "We didn't do nothing yet. We got a long way to go." The Sixers announced that McKie had suffered a chip fracture in his right ankle. But he'd continue to play, as Snow had been playing through twin ankle fractures, as Iverson had been playing with his deep tailbone bruise and an elbow in desperate need of surgery. "We've got heart," Iverson said after his 18-for-41, 48-point performance. "We're going to play with that first, play with the talent second."

Jackson, who had coached Jordan for so long, couldn't quite believe what he'd just seen. "Here's a young guy that's as slight or small as almost anybody we've had in this league, and he's not only able to get off shots but lead the league in scoring," he said. "How he does it, I'm still in a quandary about."

The next day was Iverson's twenty-sixth birthday. He wanted to hang in the hotel room with his friends, but there was business to be done. *GQ* magazine had set up a photo shoot for its October cover. Reebok was scrambling to produce a national TV commercial to capitalize on Iverson's stunning national popularity—and to counter Kobe Bryant's marketing blitz for Adidas.

It seemed like a Bryant ad was airing during every time-out on NBC. Yet it was the unpackaged Iverson who was capturing the attention of America. His sneakers were outselling all others; in the week ending June 3, retailers took in roughly $1 million in Iverson jersey sales alone, far outdistancing all other athletes. Sales of Sixers-related team merchandise dwarfed that of the Lakers and Knicks. How critical was Iverson to Reebok's bottom line? Just three years prior, the multinational corporation announced massive layoffs and didn't renew O'Neal's $3-million-per-year endorsement deal. Now Reebok announced that Iverson had boosted their sales by 20 percent during the first half of the year. Thanks to Iverson, said Reebok CEO Paul Fireman, his company posted second-quarter earnings of $14 million, or twenty-four cents a share, up from $10 million and nineteen cents a year earlier.

Part of Iverson's appeal seemed to be that he didn't give a shit about any of the aforementioned facts. Across the country—these Finals would be the highest rated since Jordan had retired—fans were taken by Iverson's single-minded passion for the game. So it should have come as no surprise to *GQ* or Reebok that, on his birthday, he just didn't feel like doing anything. No prior commitments. Just wanted to hang. "Man, I give Reebok a commercial every time I step out on the muthafuckin' court," Iverson said.

Needless to say, this made for a stark contrast to Bryant, who very consciously signed on to the Jordan crossover marketing model. Bryant's name seemed to be attached to every product with an advertising budget: Adidas, McDonald's, Spalding, Coke. Bryant's father, Joe, had played for the 76ers in the seventies, and then professionally in Italy, where Kobe lived until he was fourteen. While there, Kobe's grandparents would send him videotapes of *The Cosby Show* and of Michael Jordan's games and press conferences. He'd study Jordan's moves with his father, using the VCR's freeze-frame to analyze and break down his idol's game. From Jordan's public statements, Bryant learned how to conduct himself in a non-threatening, if seemingly prepackaged, way.

They were a study in contrasts, Iverson and Bryant. Bryant was classically trained; Iverson was a freestyling rapper. Bryant took 1,500 jump-shots a day; his teammates had once resented the competitive zeal with which he attacked practice. Iverson's game was less about the repetitive training of his muscle memory than it was about being open to spontaneous bursts of creativity. And practice? Much to Brown's chagrin, Iverson would duck out of it to gulp down a handful of Taco Bell burritos, or he'd lie on his belly and exaggeratedly grunt while his teammates—suckers!—did push-ups all around him.

But they had many things in common, these two stars: their indomitable spirits once a game got under way, their utter fearlessness, their shared addiction to competition that, as with Jordan, could seem borderline unhealthy. All of these qualities were on display at the close of game two, after the Sixers had nearly opened up a commanding two-games-to-none lead. The Sixers were down just three with two minutes to go when Jackson had to call a time-out to settle down his team. "One shot is not going to bury them," he told the Lakers, who shakily held on for the win. Just before the final buzzer, there was Iverson, excitedly clapping his hands and smiling, jawing at Bryant, who gave it right back. Neither man would comment on the exchange, but one Sixer overheard Iverson chirping, "Y'all better respect us now! We heading to our house now!"

And a rocking house it was. Philadelphia had caught Sixers fever, in a way that felt unparalleled in the city's history. They'd had winning teams before, but none so beloved. Partly, the chord struck between this team and its city had much to do with the scrappy style of these wounded Sixers—a much-talked-about *Daily News* cover photo even had McKie, Snow, and Iverson doctored up in Revolutionary War garb under the headline THE SPIRIT OF THE 76ERS. And then there was Croce, a local working-class hero, who saw to it, somehow, that practically every car within the city's limits sported a Sixers pennant and who climbed to the top of the 374-foot Walt Whitman Bridge to hang a banner reading GO SIXERS, BEAT L.A. (He wanted to rappel into the water from the top of the bridge, but was told he needed permission from the police.)

But mostly the bond between city and team had to do with Iverson. Had there ever been a player more aptly placed? Philadelphia, after all, was a city of resentments, nestled as it was in the shadows of New York and Washington, D.C., a city that made a folk hero of pitcher Tug McGraw because, in a packed stadium during the city's 1980 World Series parade, he'd inexplicably told New York to "stick it"—even though his team had just beaten Kansas City, not one of the Big Apple's franchises. Who better, then, to carry McGraw's legacy than Iverson, someone who not only resented, but turned resentment into triumph, time and again? He was a cornrowed, tattooed, real-life Rocky; when an L.A. journalist asked before game three, a bit hopeful, if Iverson was "feeling fatigue yet," he snorted. "Fatigue is army clothes," he said.

Game three was another nail-biter, with Iverson pumping in 35 points and grabbing 10 rebounds. In the last thirty seconds, he cut the Lakers lead to one with three free throws, but the Sixers were ultimately no match for O'Neal. The Lakers took command of the series with a 96–91 win. As the clock wound down, Brown took Iverson out. The fans rose en masse and serenaded their team with an ovation normally reserved for winners; Iverson clapped back, applauding the fans and his teammates.

Then he stood next to Geiger and gently put his head on his teammate's chest. "It got away," Iverson said after the game. "We had our chances."

Los Angeles went on to close out the series, four games to one. O'Neal was named the play-off MVP, but Iverson had left an indelible mark. He scored more than 35 points a game on 40 percent shooting, but measuring his game by his statistics was akin to judging Martin Luther King Jr. on his administrative skill. Iverson had played with a passion and a defiance seldom seen on the public stage. He'd spent the long play-off run battered and bruised but not beaten, spent it talking about "heart"—his and his team's—in a way that only boxers, alone among athletes, commonly did. Because that's what he was, Iverson would tell you: a basketball player with a pugilist's spirit.

When it was all over, he came into the interview room with Tawanna and the kids. Shaq was at the podium. Unbeknownst to Iverson, Bryant was on the other side of the room, awaiting his turn to face the press. When Shaq got up and left, both Iverson and Bryant started for the microphone—with Bryant getting there first. Iverson about-faced, suddenly pissed, muttering to Tawanna, "Let's get the fuck out of here." Exiting the room, someone called to him, "A.I., what about the interviews?"

"Fuck that, man," he said. And then he was off for the summer.

As always, the now abbreviated off-season would be action-packed for the Sixers. First, Croce announced he was resigning as team president. In a series of highly publicized negotiations with his senior partner, Ed Snider, he had sought assurances that he'd be Snider's heir apparent as chairman of Comcast-Spectacor. When nothing could be worked out, he stepped down in an awkward press conference, claiming that "the keys to the kingdom" had been "dangled" before him; Snider claimed Croce had misunderstood him. (Though, three years earlier, Snider had publicly fantasized about Croce eventually taking over for him; that was before their relationship soured. As time went on, Croce felt Snider treated him more like an employee than a partner. For his part, as the Sixers' fortunes turned around, Snider seemed irked that Croce was often referred to as "the owner" of the Sixers.)

Once Croce announced his resignation, Brown felt compelled to come back and coach again. He'd been 90 percent certain he was going to retire. But once Croce left, he didn't feel he could leave Ed Snider in the lurch.

August 4, 2001: Iverson and longtime girlfriend Tawanna Turner tie the knot.

One of Brown's first acts in preparation for the next season was the trading of Tyrone Hill—who had disappointed in the play-offs—to Cleveland for six-foot seven-inch Matt Harpring.

Over the summer, Iverson was named *Time* magazine's Athlete of the Year. But his attention was far from the basketball court. He was busy preparing for the social event of Philadelphia's season: his own wedding, set for early August. He and Tawanna registered at Bloomingdale's ($4,200 in china and stemware) and Williams-Sonoma, where, among their desired items, was a $26 mini-muffin pan and $649 chrome bowl mixer.

Three days before the big day, however, Gary Moore started making calls: the wedding was off. Later, word came again: false alarm. It was just another example of a tumultuous but loving relationship that had lasted close to ten years and produced two children. But before the big night, Iverson had a score to settle. He was waiting in the hotel lobby for Michael Jackson to arrive. Jackson was now getting a Ph.D. in education administration from Ohio State, but to Iverson, he was still that twelve-year-old "Thrilla" who had beaten him in a sprint.

"Let's race now! Let's race now!" Iverson said after the two men embraced. They went out into the parking lot while a lobbyful of guests looked on. Iverson, in Timberlands and droopy jeans, won.

Two days later, on Saturday, August 4, the bad boy of the NBA wore a black tuxedo jacket, white vest, and a broad smile in front of 210 guests in a ceremony those in attendance described as "touching" and "spiritual."

It was held at the Mansion in Voorhees, New Jersey, an upscale banquet hall, although the location, despite intense media scrutiny, was kept a secret—even among invited guests, who were shuttled from area hotels. Ann arrived late, so the ceremony started well past its scheduled time of 7 P.M. The wedding program read: "This day, I marry my friend, the one I laugh with, live for, dream with, love . . ."

When Allen saw Tawanna stride down the aisle in her ivory strapless gown, a tear came to his eye. Three-year-old Deuce, seeing his father tear up, started to cry himself. Smiling, Iverson's groomsmen, among them Gaskins, Ra, and uncles Gregory and Stevie, patted the man of the hour on the back. The best men were Gary Moore, Michael Freeman, and Arnie Steele. Iverson, as on the court, was fully in the present, nodding his head solemnly when Reverend Barber from back home intoned, "When times are hard, don't call on others to make things right. Call on

God." The couple kissed and marched off to "Ease on Down the Road" from *The Wiz.*

Afterward, during the elegant affair's cocktail hour, Iverson sought out Sue Lambiotte. She'd never met Tawanna. "This is what I've always wanted to see," Allen said as the two women—who had long heard about each other—hugged. Later, there was a two-foot-high wedding cake and a seafood buffet. In attendance, seated at tables identified not by numbers but by names such as "Hope," "Faith," and "Commitment" were Allen's teammates and their wives, Larry and Shelly Brown, Pat and Diane Croce, and Billy King.

At 2:40 in the morning, the newlyweds emerged outside onto the street, with Allen holding a bottle of champagne. Several days later, Allen and Tawanna escaped to a tropical locale for their honeymoon—but not alone. Que and Cindy Gaskins and Ra and his fiancée, Sherri, all joined them, at Allen's urging; the only way he could make sure he'd stay on the trip for a whole week was if he broke up how he spent his time, he explained. This way, during the day, he, Que, and Ra could ride jet skis while the girls got manicures and pedicures. At night, the couples could go do their couple things.

In two months, and for many thereafter, Allen Iverson would be unable to stop picturing his friend Ra's smiling face on his honeymoon.

chapter | 12

HOLD MY OWN

I was at the tattoo place and I said to myself, "who can look out for me better than me?" so I came up with "hold my own" 'cause so much of life is up to me.

It was, Allen Iverson would later recall, a real bad feeling. A sinking, short-of-breath, empty feeling, like when he used to get hit on the football field and the air would be crushed from his body. That was the feeling of September 11, when Tawanna came upstairs and turned on the TV, waking him up by softly saying, "I cannot believe what just happened."

A lot of people he knew watched the TV all day. They saw the buildings fall, they saw city streets morph into war zones. After an hour, Iverson clicked it off. He'd seen more than his share of bad shit; he knew early on when something sure as hell wasn't about to end well. "All those innocent people who woke up that morning just like me and went to work like any other day, for them to just die like that?" Iverson would later say. "If that can happen, that tells you that anything can happen. I didn't know anybody in there, but it hurt so bad thinking about those people's families."

Four weeks later, the feeling was back, though this time it didn't just remind Iverson of having the wind knocked from him. This time, when the news came, it was worse than any hit he'd ever taken. It was worse than when Tony Clark was killed, because at least that was back in the day when corpses and chalk outlines were everyday sights. Word came that Ra, the most affable Cru Thik member, had been murdered back in Virginia, shot outside a bar, left leaking in the street.

On the night of October 13, Ra had been with friends at the MVP Sports Bar in downtown Newport News. So had somebody named Gregory Fox. Iverson was hearing that Fiend was there, too, a guy known to both Iverson and Ra. Fiend knew Fox, too—and now Fiend was nowhere to be found. Inside the bar, Ra may have teased Fox about having a lazy eye. There was speculation that after the two groups had left the bar, Ra and Fox argued over which one was the better rapper. Then there were eight gunshots. And Ra was no more.

Ra, the court jester of Cru Thik. The one who'd tease the others unmercifully, who'd say, "Oh, so I'm the scapegoat tonight, everybody gonna crack on ol' Ra," when the barbs were shot right back at him. Ra, the best father of the bunch; some of the other guys, you'd meet their kids on the sly. Ra was always with his three kids. He'd tell Allen he was heading back to Virginia to see his kids and Allen would instead send for them, just to keep Ra around. Because Ra always made things better. "I went to bed with two kids and woke up with five," Iverson told Royster when he called him with the news of Ra's murder. "Now I gotta take care of these kids and let them know what a great father they had."

At the funeral, just two months after he officiated at the Iverson wedding, Reverend Barber eulogized Ra and again put things in perspective for a grieving Allen. "Look at your life as a book," the reverend counseled. "And stop wasting pages complaining, worrying, and gossiping."

Iverson's mourning was made all the more painful because he didn't have his customary refuge available to him. He couldn't escape his pain on the basketball court because he'd delayed undergoing arthroscopic surgery on his elbow all summer. In the past, his body had always healed itself. In fact, this very elbow, which had been a problem at least since Georgetown, had always come back on its own after a summer of rest. That's what he was banking on all summer, even while the doctors were telling him he'd need surgery. Easy for them to tell a guy to go get himself cut. Friends would later say that on a certain level, Iverson's reluctance to go under the knife had something to do with a cultural predisposition, a reaction to the often exclusionary nature of the medical establishment in general—an establishment with a storied history of treating black people poorly or not at all (or even maliciously, as with the infamous Tuskeegee experiments).

He reluctantly went under the knife just before training camp. (As did his teammate McKie; the last act of Croce's presidency of the team had been to call McKie in July to congratulate him on his new, lucrative contract and to urge him to get the surgery he needed. Given Croce's penchant for attending to details, many connected to the Sixers doubted that the surgeries for Iverson and McKie would have taken place so late had Croce still been with the team.) An arduous rehab process followed, one that Iverson wasn't always diligent about.

Already, the new season differed significantly from a year before. Then, Iverson had come to training camp with something to prove and, when the rap CD imbroglio hit, was more deeply committed to his team than ever. Now his prevailing mood was grief, not determination, and, as he was unable to play, the court was suddenly no longer his sanctuary.

There were other differences as well. This year, because of injuries, McKie and Snow missed training camp along with Iverson. (Snow would begin the season on the disabled list with an injured thumb.) In addition, unlike a year earlier, when Geiger's refusal to waive his trade-kicker had certified that the off-season roster changes would be minimal, Brown made sweeping moves. Gone were Tyrone Hill, Jumaine Jones, and backup center Todd MacCulloch.

With Croce gone, the setting was ripe for Derrick Coleman's return. In Charlotte, Coleman was coming off his worst season as a professional. His relationship with his coach and onetime mentor, Paul Silas, had deteriorated. Charlotte would have been happy to give him away. But Brown traded starter George Lynch for him because Lynch felt underpaid by the Sixers and Brown knew Charlotte had the money to take care of him. For those who feared that Coleman's lackluster practice habits might rub off on Iverson, Brown said, "When Derrick was here before, he didn't have to practice all the time. This time, I've made it clear what will be expected of him."

Suddenly Iverson was on a vastly different team. Instead of the ego-less, defensive-minded Lynch and Hill up front, there would be Harpring, a hustling player with an inconsistent outside shot, and Coleman, with his proficient offensive game and slow-footed defense. The combination of Mutombo and Coleman up front helped turn the Sixers from a young, athletic team into an older, plodding one.

The league was different as well, having finally legalized zone defenses. (In a zone, defensive players play an area of the floor rather than a man.) Now opposing teams could dedicate themselves to stopping Iverson with impunity. They could double-team him all over the court, whether he had the ball or not. Other coaches, like Flip Saunders in Minnesota and John Lucas in Cleveland, would adopt zone defenses early in the season with some success. Brown not only stuck with his tried-and-true defensive principles, he also refrained from adding an offensive "zone buster" to the team, someone who could score over packed-in defenses.

Without Iverson, the Sixers started the season 0–5. With his elbow still hurting, Iverson made his season debut at Dallas; before the game, Gary Moore gave him a black armband with the name Rasaan inscribed on it. Moore had been like a father to Ra; neither man said a word to the other as Iverson somberly placed the armband on his left elbow. (The right elbow was already encased in a black protective sleeve, as it would be all season.) Iverson vowed that before every free throw for the rest of the season, he'd tap the armband in a symbolic show of love for Ra.

On the court, Iverson scored 18 points on 7-for-28 shooting with nine assists in forty-four minutes. "Allen makes us a totally different team," Brown said afterward. "To play as many minutes as he did without that much practice time is incredible."

With Iverson back in the lineup, the Sixers ran off seven straight wins, a streak promptly followed by losses in seven of their next eight games. Iverson appeared to be playing with as much passion as ever. But off the court, the trauma of his friend's murder lingered. At Miami, Iverson missed practice the day before the game, telling the Sixers that Royster's mother had passed away and that he had to be with his now former bodyguard, who was from the Miami area.

Late the previous season, Royster had intervened when Iverson couldn't find about $300,000 worth of jewelry. Through police contacts, he traced the jewels to a pawnshop back in Virginia; a couple of Iverson's friends had apparently stolen and pawned the goods. As prominent a member of society as he had become, Iverson had never shed his belief, instilled by the social chaos in which he was reared, that the police were simply not to be trusted under any circumstances and that matters of justice were always to be handled "in-house"—within the community. (Iverson's outrage over Brown's public airing of their spats had similar roots; "family business," he maintained, ought to be handled internally.) When Royster used his police contacts to find out what had happened to the jewelry, it was as though he were *informing* on Cru Thik—a more grievous betrayal, at least in Iverson's eyes, than that of the friends who had stolen from him. After all, no human connection in this world, save that with his mother, was more essential to Iverson than the one he shared with Cru Thik. After Royster solved the mystery of the missing baubles, he was told his services would no longer be needed.

While it was true, now, that Royster's mother had passed away, it wasn't the case that the bodyguard was in Miami. He was in North Carolina, where Iverson reached him to express his condolences. Iverson, according to Royster, was "torn up" about Royster's loss, and spent a long time talking about how to deal with such tragic losses.

The next day, some two hours before game time, Iverson sat in the trainer's room, getting treatment on his elbow. His shooting percentage—never great—was way down, thanks in part to his continuing inability to fully extend the elbow on his shot. The malady would haunt his game all year and underscore in Iverson a distrust of those who had urged him to have the surgery.

But on this night, as on so many others of late, whether the subject was his elbow or his team's chances, the conversation always circled back to his dead friend. "It's always on my mind, except when I'm on the court," Iverson said; in a couple of hours, he'd score 25 points and lead the Sixers to a road win, but now he sounded morose and sapped of energy, as if to compensate in advance for his later expenditure. "I think about the good times we had, the things we went through. Most of all, I keep telling myself that he did his job with helping somebody—me. He helped me so much just by being a real friend and always telling me when he thought I was wrong. And I needed that in a friend, instead of a bunch of people telling me everything I want to hear. I feel good about the friendship I had with Ra. He saw things he might never have seen, he been to places and he experienced things. I know he had fun, because he was a happy-go-lucky guy. I just miss laughing with him. I even miss arguing with him, and me and him used to argue damn near every day."

Gary Moore came in. "You okay?" he asked.

"I'm cool, cat-daddy," Iverson said. In about fifteen minutes, he'd morph into what he'd always been, a chirping, class clown of a teammate. Turns out, Iverson's rookie teammate Samuel Dalembert had spray-painted a pair of his own sneakers, and after this therapy session, Iverson relentlessly rode the rookie: "This the NBA, man! You can call up a shoe company, say you in the NBA, and they'll send you boxes of the shit—in all colors!"

But first, after a moment of silence, his thoughts returned to Ra. "I know I'll see him again, and we'll have fun just like we always had," he said. "That's why, you watch me on the court, and you tell me if that guy is good or bad. I think you can tell who I am. I think you can tell I'm trying to get better as a person. Believe that. Because I want to go to heaven. When I die, I want to go see Ra, man. I know he's in heaven, and before I die I want to know that's where I'm going. I don't want to have to guess."

In November 2001, Reebok tore up Iverson's existing endorsement deal and announced it was signing him to a lifetime contract. No details were reported, but one industry source placed the amount at $121 million. It was just in time, too, because Iverson was feeling a cash crunch, thanks to all the houses and cars and living expenses he was having Woody's office dole out to some thirty-odd people (many of whom had kids to support). From Reebok's perspective, the new deal tied up their top endorser forever and gave the company final say over all his marketing plans. From now on, all of Iverson's business interests would dovetail with the image the company was promoting.

As November gave way to December, the Sixers' woes continued. Eric Snow was still sidelined with a thumb injury. Geiger's knees were worse, but the Philadelphia fans were unsympathetic. Their booing of him, he said, "at times broke my spirit"; he retired and swiftly moved back to Florida, leaving the Sixers without a backup center. McKie missed multiple games with an irregular heartbeat and back problems, Coleman sat out after hyperextending his knee, and Iverson missed games with a sprained left thumb.

But it wasn't just injuries plaguing the Sixers. The team suddenly seemed much older; Mutombo, in particular, seemed to have aged considerably since the play-off run last spring. Chemistry was also an issue. Coleman's physical problems were limiting him from practicing, and Iverson began to sense a double standard. Coleman was always talking basketball with Coach, sometimes dissecting tapes of games on the team plane with Brown and his assistants. Iverson saw that Coleman was able to go half speed, if need be, during practice, or take practices off when his knees swelled, and he began to complain within the confines of the team that Coleman was being afforded "franchise player" status.

The coaches felt it was a ridiculous argument, that Iverson was equating being a "franchise player" with getting away with special privileges. It never occurred to them that, in his own unique, and typically macho way, Iverson might have actually been jealous of Coleman's favored status in Brown's eyes. Maybe Iverson wanted to be the player Brown continually praised to the media as someone "who will make a great coach someday," as he often said of Coleman.

Meantime, Brown felt Iverson was reverting to his old habits. On December 17, Royster, seeking a security gig with the team, met with

Brown before practice and heard his complaints. "I've been in this business thirty-one years and I've never gone through something like this," Brown said. "I can't take it. He comes to the team plane late. He came to practice yesterday reeking of alcohol. I took one look at him and said, 'He's not going to make it through practice.'"

Three days later, the issues between the two men became public. The Sixers had lost the night before to Charlotte at home, dropping their record to 10–15. Iverson, bothered by the pain in his right elbow, left while practice was in midsession. "We had everybody here but Allen, which is typical," Brown said to the media afterward. He also returned to a pet peeve when it came to Iverson's game: "Everybody tells me we need a shooter," he said. "But we don't have anybody that will pass it to a shooter."

Iverson's response? He missed the next day's shoot-around before a win over Atlanta. At the end of December, the team left on a seven-game, thirteen-day West Coast roadtrip. While the team was on the road, rumors started swirling that Brown was about to resign. In Denver, he was asked if he'd be interested in coaching the Nuggets, who had named Mike Evans interim head coach after Dan Issel resigned the day after Christmas. Brown was circumspect and didn't rule out returning to coach in Denver someday. His coy response, plus his longtime friendship with Denver general manager Kiki Vandeweghe, helped give the rumor legs.

On the morning of the game against the Nuggets, Brown pulled Iverson aside for a lengthy, and overdue, heart-to-heart. "We've got to do this together," he said. "If we don't, with Pat gone, everybody's going to blame the two of us."

It was a productive clearing of the air, but it was undermined come game time when Iverson learned that Brown wouldn't be on the bench. Brown reportedly had taken a muscle relaxant for back and neck pain before the game; he was in no shape to coach. He stayed and rested in the training room instead. After a heartbreaking loss (Coleman, who had otherwise played well, failed to block out power forward Raef LaFrentz on a critical offensive rebound put-back late in the game), Iverson was despondent. His team had lost, and from his perspective, a father figure had once again reached out to him—only to disappoint. "If he's not coaching tomorrow night," Iverson grumbled on his way to the team bus, "he better just quit." It was no secret that Brown had wanted to retire after last season; Iverson believed that his coach's heart wasn't in the current season. "If he doesn't want to be here, he shouldn't have come back," he said.

On January 10, 2002, after the Orlando Magic came to Philly and manhandled the Sixers, 102–91, dropping the Sixers' record to 15–20, Iverson's team was eight games behind first-place New Jersey in the Atlantic Division. He spoke out after the game. "A lot of stuff that goes on on the court didn't go on last year, and nothing's being done about it," he said. "I don't know what the plan is, night in and night out, as far as the offensive end. At the defensive end, it should be obvious. We need to get stops and hustle, scramble like we always did. But we don't have that team no more." Later in the same media session, Iverson said, "Sometimes, if it ain't broke, don't fix it." Brown was reportedly angered by the comment, interpreting it as a reference to all the off-season moves that had changed the team.

Two days later, Iverson was a couple of minutes late to shoot-around. Brown told him to leave. That night, the mighty San Antonio Spurs were in town. Of course, they didn't stand a chance, not with Iverson having been kicked out of the shoot-around, not with the coach and player feuding once again. Iverson scored 37 points to go with 6 assists and 4 steals in forty-three dominant minutes. The Sixers won, 101–84. Mutombo, who had yet to see this once commonplace type of rift between his coach and teammate, observed that this spat "was like a father and a son."

By the end of January, the Sixers climbed back to the .500 mark after a 106–90 win at Boston, thanks to Iverson, who had 47 points. Though a Sixers insider described the relationship between Brown and Iverson as "beyond repair," the coach heaped affectionate praise upon his star player. "The little kid was sensational," he said, referring to Iverson by a moniker that some close to the team felt infantalized the player. "He took it to another level."

Iverson was leading the league in scoring again and his team might have been on a modest upswing, finally. The all-star game loomed, but it wouldn't be just any all-star game. It would be in Philly, and Allen Iverson was real serious about being a proper host.

He was everywhere. The Cru Thik guys threw two massive parties in his name at The Gallery, an inner-city Philadelphia shopping mall. Iverson was there the first night, in a VIP area, looking out over the crowd that had gathered to catch a glimpse of him. Then it was on to the jazz club Zanzibar Blue, where, along with hip-hop impresario Russell Simmons and comedian Chris Tucker, Iverson was one of the hosts for a bash benefiting Inner-City Games, Arnold Schwarzenegger's charity.

Simmons, Tucker, and Run-D.M.C. may have been in the house, but it was Iverson the crowd had come to see. Though he normally shied away from crowds—"People look at you like you ain't even human, like you need to be caged up or something," he said—Iverson found himself standing against a wall with Gaskins and Moore while a packed room of fans and media turned his way, watching his every move, camera lights glaring into his eyes. There he stayed for much of the evening; fans would approach with kind words, and he'd respond with shy thanks. Unlike, say, Charles Barkley or Magic Johnson, both of whom would work a room like this with the smooth skills of practiced politicians, Iverson stood, back against the wall, eyes downcast, forcing himself to adopt a public persona. After a few hours at Zanzibar, it was on to the center-city lounge Gaskins had rented for an all-night, laid-back after-hours party.

Meantime, the Philadelphia media seemed unimpressed that Iverson was spending time among the fans during all-star weekend. On talk radio, he was criticized for putting in brief appearances at parties thrown in his name; in fact, that was part of the plan. Iverson tried to hit as many parties as he could, to be with as many fans as he could, instead of spending all his time at just one venue.

The big story was that he'd blown off Friday's mandatory media session, as had Michael Jordan, whose stirring comeback at age thirty-nine had become a major story. Both were fined $10,000. When the two did meet with the press together, Jordan praised his younger rival. "I see traits of me in him in terms of just a competitive nature," Jordan said, while Iverson beamed sitting next to his childhood idol on the podium. "[He has] overcome any negative outlook from anybody. And he's taken it as a challenge to prove people wrong. And those are things you just can't teach."

Game day began with Iverson as a guest on Tim Russert's *Meet the Press.* Asked about September 11, Iverson paid homage to the New York City police without pointing out that he'd once been, in his view, unfairly prosecuted by police. The game itself was proof of just how integral the

NBA product had become in terms of showcasing African-American culture. Stars lined the court. Angie Stone and Alicia Keys movingly performed the African-American national anthem. Even if the game was anticlimactic, it had become a pop-culture happening.

Come game time, Iverson seemed listless, prompting more criticism from the talk-show snipers, who complained that his partying interfered with his play. Kobe Bryant dominated the game and was named MVP. Much to Iverson's chagrin, Bryant was booed mercilessly throughout the game, especially when he was awarded the MVP trophy.

Of course, the lack of hospitality afforded Bryant in his hometown made national news. Defenders of the Philadelphia fan noted that the Sixers got only a few thousand tickets for local fans; most of the crowd was made up of NBA heavy hitters from out of town. But this was Philly, after all, where a few thousand irate leather-lungs could sound like an arenaful.

After the game, Bryant said he was "upset" and "hurt" by the fans' reaction. Iverson rose to his defense. "I think [the booing] was wrong and I feel bad for him," he said. "I think a lot of people should take the time and think, what if that was their kid up there? But that's the way this profession is. You want to bring up a reason for it, but for something like that, you just can't find a reason."

Of course, the reasons were there. Just seven months before, Kobe had marched into Philly, his self-proclaimed assassin's game-face on, saying he'd come to "cut [the Sixers'] hearts out." And then he had. But something else was very likely afoot, too. Iverson had long since supplanted Bryant in the collective heart of the City of Brotherly Love—a nickname that, originally, at least, was not meant to be taken ironically. In the Age of Iverson, Bryant had become the unreal. Iverson was the player who kept it real, who showed up with a kid on each knee at the same indoor press conferences for which Kobe donned expensive sunglasses.

Maybe the fans booed Kobe because, on some level, they suspected Bryant had "gone Hollywood." To Iverson, such a view overlooked what Bryant's game said about him. He knew that Bryant worked his ass off. He knew that when Bryant's rookie season ended with a procession of play-off airballs, Kobe awoke the next morning, procured the key to the Pacific Palisades High School gym, and spent the afternoon and evening there, taking the same shots he'd blown the night before over and over again, willing himself into a clutch player.

Iverson knew that he and Bryant differed in approach and style. But when it came to the substance of his game, the man deserved respect. He tried to cheer up his rival. "I've played in Philly for six years," Iverson said, "and they boo us in the first quarter if things aren't going right."

In the second half of the season, injuries continued to decimate the Sixers. They hovered around .500 for much of the season's remainder, while Brown and Iverson maintained a steady truce. There were flare-ups, of course.

After a late February loss to Portland, Iverson spoke publicly about "some players not knowing the plays at the end of the game." He didn't name him, but he was talking about Mutombo, whose level of performance was waning as the season wore on. From Iverson's perspective, he was exhibiting leadership. He'd never single out a teammate for criticism by name, as Jordan had been known to do. (Jordan, who'd refer to his teammates as his "supporting cast," used to shout at Phil Jackson the names of the players he wanted to go back in for when he was on the bench.)

Mutombo was offended, however, as were many in the media. Mutombo was on the local news, saying Iverson had "pointed fingers." Before the next game, against Miami, Iverson confronted his teammate in the training room.

"You say shit about pointing fingers, that's a fuckin' slap in my face!" he shouted.

Mutombo was stunned. "Shut up! Shut up!" he yelled, in a hoarse baritone.

Days later, Iverson showed up a couple of minutes late for shoot-around. That night, with the first-place New Jersey Nets coming to town, Brown did not start Iverson. After five minutes and fourteen seconds of play, he entered the game to stirring applause and drained his first two jumpers. He scored 43 points and the Sixers raised their record to 29–28. After the game, Iverson was philosophical.

"I broke a team rule," he said. "You break a rule, so you've got to pay for it. But I wonder, what do you do when a player that doesn't start comes late? What's his punishment? I guess that rule was made for me."

The press pack laughed. But Iverson was still having a tough time. Though he played with undeniable zeal, he privately talked about how, all season, he'd been having trouble "finding the love." Unlike in past years, he was having difficulty putting a lot of off-court stuff aside.

"It's been hard, man," Iverson said one late-season day, stretched out in front of his locker, his elbow encased in a bulky ice pack. "I still can't straighten my arm out. But I ain't gonna use that as an excuse. It's just been hard, man."

Off the court, it had been a season that began with surgery and his best friend's murder. Another friend from back home, Jamil Blackmon, had filed a lawsuit against Iverson seeking a quarter of all proceeds Reebok derived from the nickname "The Answer," which Blackmon had given to Iverson. With Ra gone and Blackmon now turned against him, Iverson was face-to-face with the downside of the posse phenomenon. Having a crew might have been a necessary survival mechanism on the streets, but it lost its traction and very tenability once Iverson began moving in the "real" world. In Newport News, Cru Thik held its center because there *were* real threats, real enemies who needed to be kept at bay. But once Iverson moved on and up, those threats were no more; could it be that the psychic energy the posse had once directed toward outsiders was now, inevitably, turning inward?

Lately, one friend of the Iversons had even speculated that their marriage had hit a rough spot, owing to Tawanna's efforts to get her husband to cut at least some of his friends from the payroll. (Some of those friends were actually closer to Arnie Steele than to Iverson.)

Add to the mix a season of tough losses and problems with Brown that Iverson had thought they'd gotten behind them a year ago. "A lot of shit has gone down within the organization that's been tough," he said.

As the Sixers made a late-season run, there were moments, though. In a game at Toronto, Iverson scored 42 points and emitted an open-mouthed, openhearted warrior roar after sealing the game with back-to-back steals and driving layups.

"Maybe I'm getting the love back," he said shortly after the Toronto game, before again showing that heartache still haunted him. "I know that Ra is with me and that he wouldn't accept anything but me loving it out there, like I always have. I mean, it's a feeling you get. And you can't force it. Maybe it's coming back. I mean, the play-offs are coming. You know what Ra would say, right? He'd say, 'It's the play-offs? Well, let's get this party jumping, man.' "

But just when it looked like Iverson was getting into his groove, his regular season ended prematurely. In the first half of a game against Boston, Tony Battie chopped down on Iverson's left hand, fracturing the second metacarpal. On the bench, Iverson told Snow his hand was broken. Yet he played until he could undergo X rays at halftime—scoring 20 points *after* the injury.

The doctors said he could have surgery or try to let the injury heal on its own. Successful surgery might get him back a week sooner. This time, there was no hesitancy. The talk-show mavens could blather on all they wanted. Nobody was about to cut on him again. His regular season over early, Iverson won his second scoring title (31.1 points per game) on a career-low 39 percent shooting. He'd be back for the play-offs, which the Sixers qualified for as the number six seed, with a 43–39 record. A first-round, best-of-five matchup against the up-and-coming Celtics awaited them.

When the Sixers practiced at Harvard University the day before game one of the play-offs, it marked the first time all year that Brown had every one of his players available to him in the most injury-plagued season he'd ever coached. With the benefit of just one practice, Iverson pronounced himself ready. "I feel great," he said.

The matchup between the Sixers and Celtics marked a renewal of basketball's most-storied play-off rivalry. In the past, Wilt did battle with Bill Russell, Dr. J with Larry Bird. This series promised to be a war between Iverson and Paul Pierce, the sharpshooting small forward Brown had passed on in the 1999 draft in favor of Larry Hughes.

Five seconds into game one, Iverson buried his first shot, a jumper. In fact, he made four of his first five attempts, but as the game went on, his shooting touch went south. He missed his last 10 shots, finishing 4 for 15 for 20 points. The Sixers lost, 92–82. With their expert outside shooting, the Celtics spread the floor and pulled Mutombo out from beneath the basket. On the perimeter, he was rendered ineffective. Late in the game, they sent cutters behind him for backdoor baskets.

Iverson was unable to take over the game, conceding afterward that he'd been "kind of hesitant." Players often speak of "letting the game come to them," but that had never been Iverson's style. He had always stubbornly stamped his imprint on the game, always been an instigator of action.

The day before game two, according to the Sixers' public-relations staff, Iverson didn't practice. He vociferously denied the report. Brown said he "ran up and down the court a few times" but had mostly sat out with a "sinus infection." In any case, Iverson was thinking ahead to game two. "I'm all about bouncing back," he said.

In that game, with Iverson resting on the bench, the Sixers went on a 14–2 fourth-quarter run to go ahead 75–71, behind 10 straight points from McKie. But with seven minutes left, Iverson checked back in and McKie came out. With the Sixers up four, Iverson missed two jumpers; the Celtics went ahead to stay and won, 93–85.

Iverson had hit 11 of 30 shots for 29 points, but he missed five of his last seven shots, including the two with the Sixers ahead by four. After the game, Iverson reacted angrily when a reporter asked if, in retrospect, the decision to take those two shots was a "smart" one. "That stuff happens in the flow of the game," he said, annoyed at the second-guessing and, perhaps, the racially charged insinuation about intelligence. "I don't care about that. They were shots that were missed."

Meantime, in his postgame comments, Brown set off a couple of days' worth of controversy. "I think their star players are thinking about winning the game and not dominating the game," he said.

By now, Iverson had grown accustomed to his coach's none-too-subtle public digs. There was that time early in the season, after a loss to Toronto, when Brown observed that "[Toronto's] superstar is unselfish." Iverson had held his tongue, but he felt it was Brown's way of name-calling and finger-pointing.

At practice the day after the Celtics loss, Iverson responded. "I don't know why he would want to think that I don't want to win," he said. "I want to be dominant and I want to win. You should've asked him, did he feel like I want to win? Because he'll tell you I want to do both."

Brown offered a strange pseudo-rebuttal: "I think I'd rather have him say he wants to win and then dominate," he said.

The back-and-forth—carried out through the indirect agency of reporters—typically glossed over some critical points. Iverson believed that the odds of his team winning were *enhanced* if he dominated—no matter what order you put the terms in. Otherwise, the Sixers' record in games without him this season wouldn't have been 7–15. (For his career, his team is 22–34 when he wasn't in the lineup.) More important, from Iverson's perspective, the "is he more interested in dominating than winning" question was further proof of a lack of respect accorded him—a disrespect no other player of his stature seemed to receive. It led Iverson to declare, somewhat mysteriously, that he is not "a franchise player."

Over the next couple of days, many in the Philadelphia media interpreted the remark as a sign that Iverson was shrinking from his responsibility as the team's go-to man. Instead, Iverson meant to say he wasn't being *treated* as a franchise player by management. All season long he'd voiced this complaint, whether it was in observing that Coleman got away with missing practices he'd have been disciplined for skipping or in pointing out that when his shots didn't fall at the end of games, his coach got on him—something few "franchise" players had to tolerate.

Iverson even entertained the notion that he could be traded. Since jettisoning Falk, he hadn't had—or needed—an agent. But that would change if he were suddenly on the trading block. His lawyers weren't known in NBA circles. So he hired Leon Rose, McKie's agent, to start representing him on basketball matters, and now, on the eve of game three, he raised the issue of a trade.

"I mean, after going to the Finals last year, you see how many changes we made, so anything can happen," he said. "I could be gone this summer. I know it's a business. And I know once things start going bad, the first thing you think about is making changes instead of just trying to get better . . . I've always said from day one, I want to be a Sixer. I want to remain a Sixer for the rest of my career. And I'm not going to let anyone drive me out of here. But if people think me leaving is the best for the team, then make that decision."

In the first two games of the series, Iverson shot a paltry 15 for 45, while his backcourt mate Snow was a chilly 4 for 25. And now, thanks to Iverson and Brown's latest Kabuki dance, the pressure was palpable. *Philadelphia Inquirer* columnist Stephen A. Smith went so far as to suggest that if Iverson didn't single-handedly stave off the Sixers' elimination by playing like a superstar, he ought to get ready to pack his bags—because he'd be as good as traded. "Iverson has had many challenges in his basketball career," Smith wrote, "but maybe none as tough as this one."

Perhaps predictably, Iverson not only responded to Smith's challenge—he proved that, when he dominates, the Sixers win. The final score was 108–103, and he had 42 points, connected on 19 of 20 free throws, and made 5 steals. In a close fourth quarter, he scored 13 points. Snow helped keep the defense honest by nailing 9 of 14 shots. "Pressure is in tires," Iverson quipped after the game. "Basketball is what I love to do. It's not supposed to be any type of pressure. It's supposed to be fun."

For his part, Brown was contrite about the controversy leading up to game three. "Our stars the last two games are trying to do it the right way," he said. "I've got to be real careful the way I word things. This is typical of what goes on with us when things go bad, and I think people equate 'things go bad' with when you lose a couple games."

Game four had a different feel. The teams were tied with less than two minutes remaining; Iverson had spent much of the game missing shots, hitting only 5 of 21. Miraculously, he scored eight points in the final seventy-seven seconds. First, he snared an offensive rebound off a McKie missed foul shot and drove the lane, lofting a high, soft shot that bounced around the rim and finally through it. After a McKie steal, Iverson knifed through the lane for a driving layup. When Boston's Rodney Rogers tied the game at 79, Iverson raised up and hit a twenty-foot jumper while falling to his right. That proved to be the game winner. When his two free throws iced the game with seconds left, the crowd chanted "MVP! MVP!" while Iverson, childlike, skipped off the court.

"I've been around stars," McKie said after the game. "But he's in a league by himself."

The deciding game five in Boston, however, was a disaster. Paul Pierce riddled the Sixers' defense for 46 points, including 8 of 10 three-pointers, in a 120–87 Boston blowout. Defensively, the Sixers—particularly Mutombo and Coleman—were unable to cover Boston's perimeter shooters. On offense, Mutombo was again a nonfactor and Snow hit only 2 of 12 shots, making him 18 of 56 (32 percent) for the series. Alone among the Sixers, Iverson, who liked to boast that he "plays every game like it's my last," played with urgency. He hit 11 of 24 shots for 31 points. But it was Celtics point guard Kenny Anderson who summed up the Sixers' season best after the game: "They are nothing like the team I saw last year," he said. "They have Allen Iverson. Everything else was so different."

Their season was over, but—this being Brown, Iverson, and the 76ers—the drama was just starting.

The day after the end of his team's season, Larry Brown met individually with all but one of his players. When Iverson was a no-show, Brown would later say, he was "crushed." And so he told members of the press what Iverson might otherwise have heard in private.

"My problems with Allen have been the same for five years," Brown said. "I love him, I love his competitiveness. The issues I have are all the things he has control over. He'll have a problem if that doesn't change. I'm looking at a kid that tells me he wants to win. I've heard him say it to the media, he doesn't have a selfish bone in his body, that he's going to be the first guy to practice and last to leave. He said that publicly. Now let's do it."

Brown's comments filled a gaping sports-news hole in Philadelphia. The Sixers' and Flyers' seasons had both just ended, it was two months until football's training camp, and the Phillies were already mired in last place. The big story became: Was Allen Iverson about to be traded? WIP, the all-sports talker, debated the issue around the clock and the newspapers were filled with speculation. On Tuesday, May 7, 2002, Iverson finally had a meeting with Brown. Sixers sources said it went swimmingly; afterward, Iverson held a press conference at the arena that would be carried live on TV in Philadelphia. When the fireworks started, ESPN2 would jump to the story live as well.

Iverson began the session talking about the meeting he'd just had with Brown. "I just let him know I'm that pit bull in his yard, and if anybody tries to intrude, I'm going to be the one that's going to bite and protect his home," he said. But he was also upset by Brown's public comments. "No question," he said. "[We're] not as tight as I thought we was by this shit happening right now . . . If you're going to get rid of Allen Iverson, then get rid of Allen Iverson. Do a trade. But you don't have to assassinate his character."

The words started coming faster now, tinged with fury. He couldn't believe he was here, facing the judgment of a roomful of journalists—when his teammates were long gone. "I know I do all I can for this city, for this team, for my teammates. I know don't nobody in the world plays harder than me. And for me to go through this is just tough, man. Everybody in Philadelphia know, all y'all know I want to be here. That ain't no secret. Everybody knows I want to be a Sixer for the rest of my career, but I'm tired. I'm hurt, too."

Someone asked about missing practices. For a brief moment, he was silent, staring at his questioners. "If I can't practice, I can't practice," he said. "If I'm hurt, I'm hurt . . . I know I'm supposed to be there. I know I'm supposed to lead by example. I know that. I know it's important, I honestly do. But we're talking about practice."

And then he was off on what would commonly be referred to in the press as a "rant" about practice. He would use the word seventeen times, prompting Brown to joke that Iverson *said* "practice" more than he came to it. "I'm supposed to be the franchise player, and we're in here talking about practice," he said. "Not a game. We're talking about practice. How silly is that? . . . I don't feel like the franchise player because—look at this press conference, look at what we're talking about . . . Practice. Franchise players don't go through this. Franchise players' daughters don't have to go to school and hear, 'Is your daddy coming back? What's going on with your daddy and Coach Brown?' She's seven years old and that's what she's got to deal with. It hurt."

Iverson scoffed at the notion that he could make his teammates better by practicing. "How the hell can I make my teammates better by practicing?" he shot back. "So my game is going to deteriorate if I don't practice with those guys? Is my game going to get worse?"

He sat on the edge of his seat, ready to do battle. Off in the wings, Sixers general manager Billy King reached for his cell phone with a worried look. Meantime, Iverson turned the tables on his questioners. When Comcast SportsNet's Michael Barkann suggested that such criticism comes with the territory of being paid $11 million to play a game, Iverson waved away the Sixers public-relations official who tried to intervene and shot back: "Don't you get paid to do what you do? I don't go around saying I don't like the way you mispronounced this or that word, man." When Phil Jasner, longtime beat writer for the *Philadelphia Daily News*, posited that, if Iverson worked out with weights, maybe he could increase the strength in his legs and, thus, his shooting percentage by a couple of points, Iverson said: "You ever play basketball?"

"Yes," Jasner muttered.

"Well, I don't know Phil Jasner as no basketball player," Iverson said, smiling slightly. "I know Phil Jasner as a columnist." (The next day, the *Daily News* would run a photo of Jasner playing pickup basketball.)

Later, members of the media marveled at Iverson's aggressive defensiveness. From his point of view, however, his work ethic and character were on trial—and he was particularly sensitive to being on trial. Moreover, on a practical level, Iverson believed his low shooting percentage wasn't a function of weak legs; he'd always known his body, always had preternatural energy and stamina and strength. No, he shot a low percentage because he took low-percentage shots, which had been part of Brown's system for five years now. Without another scorer capable of drawing a double team, paired in a backcourt with a guard who couldn't consistently hit open jumpshots, Iverson had long been relegated to leading the league in scoring, yes, but also in degree-of-difficulty shots.

But he said none of this—why should he have to? He railed on and on, about practice—"we talkin' 'bout *practice,* man,"—but beneath the lashing out was a tension born of his own dawning, but not yet fully conscious, knowledge. He'd improved every year of his basketball career—until this one; perhaps he was advancing to the point in his career where talent alone was no longer sufficient to cut it. Could Iverson's anger have had something to do with a nascent realization that, to continue being a brilliant grasshopper, he'd have to change his ways and become a worker ant, too?

But the pundits saw Iverson's performance as a defiant announcement that he'd never change. There you have it, they said: he's as much as told us he'll never consistently come to practice. In fact, he'd explicitly said the opposite, beginning by saying, "I know I'm supposed to lead by example" and by acknowledging his missteps: "I got some shit that I need to get better in." No, as Iverson kept upbraiding the press pack for its focus on "practice," it was clear, in his own unique way, he was serving up a media critique. They'd taken his coach's bait and scapegoated him, he seemed to suggest, after a series in which—though he'd never name his teammates—Eric Snow couldn't hit an open twelve-foot jumpshot and Dikembe Mutombo couldn't catch a simple entry pass into the post. "We talking 'bout *practice"* was nothing short of Iverson's way of stating the obvious: "I'm not the problem with this team."

The media didn't get it. There were comparisons to Mike Tyson; the press conference was more than once referred to as a "meltdown." One columnist called for Iverson to be immediately traded, describing the event as the "truly bizarre ramblings of a scolded, wounded and obviously confused Iverson." But the public reaction, in interviews and anecdotal evidence, seemed much less reactionary. Fans had seen the series, they'd seen game five, when only Iverson seemed to be hustling in the fourth quarter. They heard him respond to being dissed by his coach by proclaiming his love for the man and reiterating his desire to stay a Sixer throughout his career.

Most of all, after all the deadening postgame clichés served up by athletes over the past couple of decades, they'd been treated to a raw, heartfelt exhibition. You wouldn't find Kobe Bryant holding such a press conference. The next day, Brown held a press conference of his own. He said that, in his meeting with Iverson before the player's press conference, he'd told him, "You can tell your daughter not to worry about it: Daddy is going to be living in Philadelphia and we're going to see him at training camp at Penn State and move on and try to figure out a way we can get better."

"The way you saw him act is maybe why he does so many special things on the court," Brown continued. "Maybe why every time I take him out of a game he dresses me down publicly . . . It's my responsibility to teach him the right way without inhibiting him. I have to let him grow; I've got to grow myself."

Watching Iverson's news conference, Brown suggested, was like watching "a young kid reaching out for help." In that sense, maybe it was all a fitting end to a turbulent, wrenching season. At one point during his press conference, Iverson had lowered his volume and taken a step back. "You want to know why I'm upset? I just didn't want to have to be here, that's all," he said. "My best friend died, my team lost, and this is what I've got to go through for the rest of the summer until the season starts over again. This is what I've got to go through. This is my life, in a nutshell."

Just before the curtain closed—only temporarily—on the drama that is Allen Iverson, he stood up and said, "Y'all have a happy life," and then he was gone, scaling a fence outside the arena en route to one of his three Cadillac Escalades, pausing only to hug Comcast SportsNet's Barkann, with whom he'd just tussled, when Barkann called to him, "A.I., have a great summer." Looking back at the tailing media over his shoulder, he called, "It's going to be a happy ending," a note of reassurance in his voice, as though he were suddenly comforting his chroniclers. Then he slapped hands with the black parking-lot attendant before peeling out of the lot. Finally, summer.

Event#:   181174087
PID#: 948473
Name: IVERSON
          ALLEN
Arrest Date: 07 / 16 / 02
Age at Arrest: 27
Height: 6'00"
Weight: 165
Hair Color: BLACK
Eye Color: BROWN
Phila. PD ARREST

epilogue

These are tough times, man. Everybody's
taking the chance to throw their darts at me.

In Tom Wolfe's *The Bonfire of the Vanities*, the protagonist, an uppity yuppie named Sherman McCoy, is unaware that he is surrounded by people itching for his comeuppance. He finds himself in an altercation. At first, it doesn't seem like a big deal. The fallout, however, is anything but minor. McCoy's life spirals into an absurd nightmare peopled with self-interested politicians, Kafkaesque denizens of the criminal "justice" system, and tabloid hacks out to make a quick buck. It is more than a novel; it is a deconstruction of a singularly modern development: the all-consuming media feeding frenzy.

Allen Iverson never read Wolfe's book, but as Iverson's life blew up in the summer of 2002 and made headlines the world over, it was as though Wolfe were workshopping a sequel. Within a matter of weeks, Iverson found himself at the center of a narrative that featured a stranger-than-fiction cast of characters.

There were the cops, with their pronouncements straight out of *Dirty Harry*. There was the tabloid paper, running Iverson's image on the cover for seven straight days—and seeing an average increase in sales of five thousand papers per day. There was Iverson's flamboyant accuser, who wore revealing, high-cut "poom-poom pants." There was a city's black mayor, whose spokesman publicly tried to rein in the police. There was a rabid radio talk-show host, unleashing incendiary charges of "cover-up" early on. There was the pricey, hotshot lawyer Iverson would turn to. There were the TV stations camped outside Iverson's mansion around the clock. There were the gay-rights groups who wanted to know just why the accuser's sexuality—not to mention the type of pants he wore—was relevant.

In Wolfe's novel, a fictional character stood at the center of the storm. Now it was Iverson's turn.

Over the July Fourth weekend, the cops started to leak the news. They were looking into a complaint regarding Allen Iverson and a home invasion. Something about Allen and Tawanna having a fight, and Allen searching for his wife late at night in a West Philly apartment.

It had been a slow news summer in Philadelphia; the specter of an Iverson scandal instantly energized the fourth estate in the nation's fourth largest media market.

The apartment in question belonged to Iverson's first cousin Shaun Bowman, Aunt Jessie's twenty-one-year-old son. Tawanna often turned to Shaun when she and Allen argued. After a quarrel, Tawanna stormed out and headed over to Shaun's. Later, Iverson, accompanied by his uncle Greg, went to find his wife. Only Tawanna and Shaun weren't there. Charles Jones, Shaun's roommate, was in the apartment with seventeen-year-old Hakim Carey, an upstairs neighbor.

Iverson would later tell friends that shortly after he entered the apartment, Jones, who is gay, gave him some finger-snapping, head-bobbing attitude. Iverson, ever the mimic, would even crack up friends with his impression: "Listen here, Mr. Allen Iverson," he'd screech. "Don't be coming in here like you're all that!"

No doubt, words were exchanged. Jones and Carey alleged that Iverson locked the apartment door behind him, forced them to call Bowman, and picked up his shirt so they could see a gun tucked into his waistband. "Either I'm going to die or I'm going to jail, and I guarantee that I am not going to die," Jones and Carey claimed Iverson said. They alleged that he wiped his fingerprints off of the phone and made more threats before leaving.

By midweek, WIP sports talk-show host Howard Eskin was raising the stakes, turning a routine criminal complaint into a political football. He claimed the mayor's office was trying to orchestrate a cover-up, and none too subtly implied a racial cabal, referring to both Mayor John Street and Iverson as "brothers."

Eskin was a longtime Philadelphia broadcaster known for a bombastic style and short fuse. He also had a reputation as a reporter; he didn't just opine, he dug around a story. Ironically, Eskin had long championed past controversial Philly sports stars such as Charles Barkley and Mike Schmidt, cultivating friendships with both men. But for some time, he'd been a fierce critic of Iverson's. (Schmidt, in fact, once explained Eskin's methods: "If you're his buddy, he'll never rip you," said the Hall of Famer. "Like Barkley—for the most part, he'll support everything that Barkley does, because Barkley's his buddy. Same with me.") In the aftermath of the CD controversy in the fall of 2000, Iverson, offended by something Eskin had said about him, ceased to speak to the broadcaster. Once, when Eskin tried to say hello in the locker room, Iverson snapped, "Kiss my ass," and brushed by him.

Ann defending her son in July 2002 as she is driven up to Iverson's estate. "I'm not frontin' no games," she said.

At his 2002 Celebrity Summer Classic, Iverson listens to Pat Croce.

Now Eskin filled the airwaves with invective, calling Iverson a "thug" with "a drinking problem." When African-Americans called in, he'd tease them by breaking into Ebonics—"wassup, dawg?"—or an impression of Iverson's "we talkin' 'bout practice" screed. The problem, Eskin said, was Iverson's friends—though he glossed over the fact that, in this case, Iverson's friends weren't alleged to have been involved. In any case, Eskin argued, Iverson was receiving preferential treatment. If it were anyone else, he argued, the suspect would already be in jail.

Shortly thereafter, mayoral spokesman Frank Keel called into the same station's morning show and rebutted Eskin. "I can tell you that it's going in the opposite direction," Keel said. "There are some detectives within the rank and file of the police department who may actually be a bit overzealous about nailing Allen Iverson in this thing."

Now, with the mayor's office publicly chastising the police, the case—like any cause célèbre—took on a life of its own. Time and again, innuendo and hearsay were repeated as fact; the *Inquirer* printed the transcript of Jones's 911 call, which took place some eleven hours after Iverson had been in the apartment. In the call, Jones told the dispatcher that earlier in the night, Iverson had thrown his wife "out the house naked." Within days, national news outlets were repeating the allegation as though it had been independently reported: "According to published reports, Iverson threw his wife out of the house naked."

The police—challenged now by the mayor's office—leaked to the press that blood had been found in one of the Iversons' cars. Later, it turned out to be jelly from one of the kids' sandwiches. Nothing could stop the media circus. *Nine* detectives were sent to the Iverson mansion to execute a search warrant in search of a gun while news choppers hovered above. The ABC affiliate broadcast Iverson's address. The CBS affiliate led off one newscast with "exclusive" still photos of Iverson stepping onto his patio to rescue his dog, whose head had gotten caught in the porch's wrought-iron gate.

The police couldn't find a gun, but publicly announced they had probable cause for an arrest. The district attorney asked for further investigation. "This isn't over yet," lead detective Lieutenant Mike Chitwood said into the cameras. "Stay tuned." It was a telling choice of language, for the case had quickly morphed from legal issue into *show.*

Iverson was charged with four felonies—two counts of criminal trespass and one each of conspiracy and violating the Uniform Firearms Act—and ten misdemeanors. From a legal standpoint, there was unanimity from former prosecutors and defenders alike: there was no case here. Even former Philadelphia district attorney F. Emmitt Fitzpatrick was quoted in the *New York Times* as saying that "An arrest should never have been made."

Both Ira Berkow and William Rhoden of the *New York Times* weighed in; both mentioned Iverson's "record" and cited the bowling-alley-brawl conviction—without mentioning that an appeals court had overturned it. In the *Chicago Sun-Times*, Rick Telander wrote, "[Iverson] never expresses remorse, or even regret, for the things he does." In the *Philadelphia Daily News*, John Baer wrote that Iverson was "thug-prone," with "too much money, too much freedom, too much talent to hear the word 'no.'" Tom Knott in the *Washington Times*, before comparing Iverson to O. J. Simpson, wrote that, "America cannot say it was not warned if something truly bad ever happens to Iverson's naked wife . . ." The headline on the column by *Washington Post* media writer Howard Kurtz read FEW BOOS FOR GUN WAVING ATHLETE—despite the fact that not even Iverson's accuser claimed he waved a gun. Even Jay Leno got in on the act, unveiling the new Iverson signature shoe from Reebok. "It's called 'The Incarcerator,'" he cracked, pulling them from the box to show a chain link connecting one shoe to the other.

Iverson hired high-powered Philadelphia attorney Richard Sprague, a former prosecutor himself, to defend him. Sprague was out of the country, so the police allowed Iverson to turn himself in for arraignment upon his lawyer's return. In the meantime, they said, he wasn't under house arrest—but if he left his house, he'd be arrested. Iverson's critics howled about the special privileges being afforded him. Who else but a celebrity gets to make an appointment in advance to turn himself in? Actually, in Philadelphia, plenty of suspects. What was unusual here was the de facto house-arrest conditions.

So what did Iverson do? On the Saturday night before his Tuesday-morning arraignment, he threw an all-night party at the mansion while the gaping media looked on. "That's not guts," wrote Jim Spencer back home in the Newport News *Daily Press*. "It's not even arrogance. It is pure contempt—contempt for which Iverson will never be punished . . .

If the [rest] of us did what he does, we'd be behind bars or hanging on the street corner with no money and no prospects."

Just as passionate, on the other side, were Iverson's defenders. Reebok went far beyond the cautiously-supportive-PR-statement standard in such situations. "It is Allen's celebrity status, not the facts, that continues to fuel these proceedings," the company said in a statement. Interestingly, the *Wall Street Journal* reported anecdotal evidence indicating that Iverson's shoes sales were way up in the aftermath of his arrest. According to a Wells Fargo analyst, East Coast retailers had been "unable to keep the Iverson product in the stores."

Outside the Philadelphia Police Roundhouse, Iverson's arraignment was soundtracked by the cheering of fans, some of whom sold T-shirts proclaiming FREE IVERSON and THE ANSWER IS NOT GUILTY, just as had been done a decade earlier outside the courtroom in Virginia.

At one point, Ann came outside the mansion to confront the media horde. She counted five men standing around her with rings on their fingers and talked about how all couples have their ups and downs. "Do those ups and downs include throwing your wife out of the house naked?" asked one female TV reporter.

Ann let loose. "Get outta my face with that crazy stuff," she said while Aunt Jessie, next to her, shouted: "That's hearsay!"

"That's rumors," Ann continued. "Where you get that from? Did Tawanna tell you that? If you want to keep it real, keep it real with me, because I ain't frontin' no games."

Howard Stern had a lot of fun playing that audio clip over and over. But Ann had a point: Tawanna wasn't the complainant in this case. Plus, if the parade of lawyers-turned-pundits were right and the case against Allen was leading nowhere, and if the allegations—even if true—paled in comparison to a host of recent athlete transgressions, it begged the question: Why Iverson? Why this frenzy—again?

The way this country plays out its race traumas is—pardon the pun— very black-and-white. There is victim, and there is victimizer. Iverson's travails in the summer of 2002 were no exception.

Those reflexively denouncing him as a thug, just as those reflexively defending him as a victim of police harassment, might ostensibly have been talking about the case's evidence. But make no mistake: they were all trying to wrest control of what Allen Iverson symbolizes, what his story should *mean*. Many of us, whether we consciously realize it or not, similarly comprehend Iverson as symbol, which necessarily means we *invest* in him—either as a victim or as a victimizer. Those who demand the book be thrown at him today? Invested. Those who ten years ago beheld him as the catalyst for a "Rosa Parks" type movement? Invested.

It's not about the facts. In both the bowling-alley case and this most recent one, observers could sift through the testimony and appear impartial. And yet when people came down on one side or the other, they did so, almost to a person, along racial lines. Allen Iverson has now become a walking, breathing legacy born of the O.J. case; where you fall on Iverson depends on where you've invested yourself. (And in all likelihood, you invested yourself where you did long before Iverson came onto your radar.)

After all, it can't be about substance. Iverson's much-talked-about "record," his "rap sheet," consists of precisely one incident: the 1997 probation for having a legally registered gun under his seat. Those who refer to his litany of transgressions are inevitably including the overturned bowling-alley conviction, the missteps of his friends, and even his run-ins with Larry Brown.

So if it's not the substance, it's got to be the style. Sports' groundbreaking social characters, after all, always engender backlash: Jackie Robinson, Muhammad Ali, Joe Namath. Iverson burst onto the scene as the first athlete to wear cornrows, the first to so widely tattoo his body, the first to fire David Falk, the first to record gangsta rap, the first to cross over Michael Jordan and then say he didn't have to respect him. He instantly supplanted the likes of Mike Tyson as public enemy number one; to some, he represented the worst fears of white America, the latest and maybe best embodiment of what poet Amiri Baraka (then LeRoi Jones) wrote over thirty years ago of boxer Sonny Liston: "[Liston is] the big black Negro in every white man's hallway, waiting to do him in, deal him under for all the hurts white men, through their arbitrary order, have been able to inflict on the world."

For those who came down on his side, there was an appreciation for his ballsy nonconformity. But there are those, too, who reacted defensively when confronted by his unwillingness to sign on to the assimilation script. They are the ones who tend to see Iverson as a grenade with the pin pulled, as a kind of Tyson Redux.

But where Tyson is sideshow material (the cannibalistic threats, the *actual* cannibalism, the overall Poe-like derangement), Iverson is a threat. For Iverson succeeds. Born and raised in chaos, he thrives in it; depending on how you're invested, you can laud him for his survival skills and see him as a classic American figure, someone who succeeded not by overcoming the circumstances that spawned him—but *because* of them. He hasn't overcome the ghetto; he's taken it with him. Or you can see him as a walking refutation of all your own choices. Allen Iverson has never chosen safe or stable or comfortable.

Allen Iverson showed up for his July 29 preliminary hearing wearing a T-shirt, but not just any T-shirt. On the chest was Ra's picture, under the words CRU THIK SUPERSTAR.

In the six-hour hearing, Iverson's lawyer, Sprague, eviscerated the key witnesses against him. Hakim Carey, the upstairs neighbor, testified that when he saw that the man knocking on the door was Allen Iverson, he rushed to get paper and pen for an autograph. Iverson, Carey testified, demanded they get his "cocksucking wife" on the phone. Carey went on to say he didn't see Iverson with a gun and that Jones had urged him to go along with the story that Iverson had one.

Iverson's cousin Shaun testified that Iverson paid the rent on the apartment and had permission to come and go as he pleased. He also alleged that Jones had offered to drop everything for $100,000.

Jones was no match for Sprague, who quickly painted a portrait of Jones as a cocaine-snorting ex-con who couldn't even say where he'd gotten his cell phone from. It was a gift, Jones said, "from some guy Maurice." Sprague read aloud the numbers Jones had called in the ten hours before he dialed the police. The last of these was a twenty-one-minute call to a personal-injury lawyer that ended eighteen seconds before Jones called 911.

The judge had heard enough. He tossed the four felony charges and all but two misdemeanor counts for making terroristic threats. (The remaining misdemeanors were dropped in September.) "It sounded like you had a relative, looking for a relative, at the house of a relative. And you had the door opened by the guest of a guest," said Judge James DeLeon, a

Philadelphia Municipal Court judge, who determined there probably had never been a gun.

That didn't stop those who had already invested in Iverson's guilt from looking askance at the ruling. Eskin, for example, was unbowed. "He *had* a gun!" he shouted on the air, upbraiding the judge for admitting he was a fan of Iverson's and for showing deference to Sprague.

It's true that the judge may have been a bit cowed by Iverson's venerated counsel, but there was unanimity among legal observers when the ruling came down. "The case was dead on arrival," said Philadelphia lawyer George Bochetto, a former Republican candidate for mayor who secured the plum gig as ESPN's on-air legal analyst at the height of the Iverson story. "Before the first witness, the ability to prosecute that case was zero because of the nature and character of the witnesses, the star power of Iverson, and the complete absence of any victim or any harm."

To some, Iverson had evaded justice again. To others, he'd once again escaped the clutches of an unjust system.

The Sixers, who offered sound bites of support for Iverson through the ordeal, followed up the ruling by seeing to it that the headlines soon reverted back to matters of basketball. They let Matt Harpring go as a free agent to Utah and traded center Dikembe Mutombo to interdivision rival New Jersey for former Sixers center Todd MacCulloch (who suffered from chronic foot problems) and former Sixers draft pick Keith Van Horn. The remake raised all sorts of potential pitfalls: Could a front line of MacCulloch, Coleman, and Van Horn play anything but matador defense? Could Brown coach them if that were the case?

But lost in the summer talk of the Sixers' latest makeover, not to mention the fixation on Iverson's legal travails, was a simple fact that might have suggested positive developments for the player and his team: the Sixers consulted Iverson before trading Mutombo. Presumably, he'd signed off on the acquisition of Van Horn, someone with the potential, at least, to be the secondary scorer Iverson has always yearned for. Even if that turns out not to be the case, Iverson was afforded the respect of consultation. That, combined with the resentments of his summer experience, might be bad news for opposing teams in the NBA. If history repeats itself, on every drive to the basket, Iverson will not be seeing the faces of his defenders, but those of the cops, the prosecutors, and his poom-poom-pants-wearing accuser instead.

Just before the preliminary hearing, Iverson went ahead with his annual Summer Celebrity Classic. This time, the charity event took the form of an all-star softball game in Camden, New Jersey, just outside Philly. Before the game, Iverson showed up wearing a Phillies jersey, but not just any Phillies jersey: he was wearing Pete Rose's number fourteen.

Those around Iverson knew it was not coincidental. Iverson was always aware of the messages being sent by his style choices, by his game, by his tattoos. Together, they compose a plea to be taken at face value, to be taken as an athlete rather than as a symbol we manipulate in complicated ways, and for our own purposes. It's as though he has made himself a pictogram, and his tattoos, especially, speak for him.

On another level, while purporting to say, "This is who I am," the tattoos can also suggest a historical context. The branding of his black skin references a time when branding a black man's name onto his body *identified* him. Seen this way, Iverson's tattoos—and whole vibe—might just be a way to get in our face and say: "You don't know me. And you never will."

By the same token, when he didn't clean up for his mug shot, it was one part defiance, one part irony. "This is how you see me, this is what I'll give you," he seemed to be saying. Likewise, the choice of Rose's jersey resonated. Rose's style of play bore a striking resemblance to Iverson's. No one hustled more. Both men evinced a willingness, to put their bodies in harm's way on each and every play.

Rose's career ended in controversial disgrace, banned from baseball for allegedly betting on the game. He was also barred from the Hall of Fame despite the fact that his on-field exploits qualified him as a no-brainer inductee. Iverson believed wholeheartedly in merit; for him, there was a logical connection between him and someone who had been denied the accolades his heart and God-given talents had earned him.

Rose, who led the Phillies to the 1980 World Series championship, had always been a Philadelphia hero. In particular, he enjoyed a stellar relationship with the Philadelphia press, including a close friendship with, among others, Eskin. Could it be that, to Iverson, the media's embrace of Rose, compared with its hassling of him, had something to do with one of the few differences between the two icons—the color of their skin? Philadelphia, after all, has a history of being toughest on its black athletes, from Chamberlain to Dick Allen to Barkley to Randall Cunningham.

There Iverson sat in his Rose jersey, two hours before his charity game, signing posters of himself for a long line of kids from the Boys and Girls Club. They'd come up and shake his hand or shyly ask to hug him and he'd just as shyly oblige. Through it all, though, he was beaming and joking with his friends. This wasn't the Iverson who, when he grudgingly attended adult functions, would be bashfully distant. Instead, he was basking in the unconditional love of mostly disadvantaged black kids.

In line, however, was an adult black woman. When she got to him, she said, smiling, "Can I ask you a question?"

Iverson smiled. As he looked the woman up and down, though, the smile slowly dissipated. "You with the media?" he asked.

"Yes," she replied.

Iverson's shoulders slumped. Cru Thik instantly stepped in.

"No questions!"

"No media!"

"This is for the kids!"

After she was ushered off, it took Iverson a few moments to recover from the buzz-kill. Then he looked up and noticed, for the first time, that virtually all the kids were wearing white headbands that read RA.

"Where'd you get that?" an incredulous Iverson asked one tongue-tied eight-year-old.

"Th-th-they're giving 'em out," he said.

Iverson looked up to his left, where Gary Moore stood. "I had Reebok make some up," he said.

Iverson smiled and looked down the line, at a sea of kids showing love for him by honoring his man.

The locker room before the charity game had a party vibe. There was an elaborate buffet. There was Kevin Garnett chatting up Bow Wow—at fifteen, he no longer wanted to be called *Lil'* Bow Wow. There was Pat Croce, greeted earlier by Iverson with a hug and kiss on the neck, high-fiving Houston Rockets guard Steve Francis. Just outside the locker room, Aaron McKie was talking to the press about his teammate—who, owing to the legal case, would not be speaking publicly tonight.

"When we go to play road games, there are more of his jerseys in the stands than a lot of guys from the home team," McKie said. "His style of play, and him on and off the court—a lot of people would like to be like him, to be a free spirit, to live your life, to not think twice about what other people think of you."

Inside the locker room, the only person not seeming to partake of the party was Iverson himself. He stood in the corner, alone, hunched over a heaping bucket of chicken wings, gnawing away. "These are tough times, man," he said between bites. "Everybody's taking the chance to throw their darts at me."

He spoke softly, as though the weight of everything—the controversy, the allegations, the thirty-some-odd friends and family he supports—had sapped him. Royster, who had once marveled at how responsible Iverson was—who else takes it upon his shoulders to lift up so many people?— also saw the effects of the burdens Iverson bore. "He jokes around a lot, but the only time that man is happy is when he's on the basketball court or up in some pussy," the now former bodyguard had once observed.

I pointed out that so many people seem to be invested in a cut-and-dried view of him: victim or victimizer. "That's how it's always been," Iverson said. "I've always said, there are a million people who love Allen Iverson and a million people who hate Allen Iverson. It's just important for me to concentrate on the ones who love me."

But if you're neither sinner nor saint, is there a third option? "Man, I'm just a guy trying to do better, and sometimes I fuck up," he said. "But because of this talent, it's like I ain't allowed to."

"So who are you?" I asked.

Allen Iverson dropped a gnarled wing into the bucket before him. "Man, if someone's smart, they know," he said. "I'm that guy that you see out there."

Later, the crowd, some 4,500 strong, exploded when Iverson took the field. It was more than just applause; as he raced across the diamond to the dugout, the screaming and shouting bordered on hysteria, reminiscent of a time long ago when four other young pop-culture icons—John, Paul, George, and Ringo—raced across a stadium field. Call it Iverson-mania.

Then Iverson stood just behind the pitcher's mound and listened as, to the crowd's delight, speaker after speaker spoke of him in the most reverential way. Camden mayor Gwendolyn Faison handed him a key to the city and said, "We are not going to worry about all those people and what they say happened!"

After scoring 33 points to eliminate the Indiana Pacers in the 2001 play-offs, Iverson celebrates while holding three-year-old Deuce (Allen Jr.).

State Senator Anthony H. Williams whipped the crowd into a frenzy. "All you people who look at this young man because he wears his hair differently, wears his clothes differently—that does not mean he's a thug," he shouted. "Everybody has a crew. A CEO has his board of directors; that's his crew!"

"We cannot allow another young African-American millionaire to be taken down by a system that can't bear to see young African-American men who take care of their families," chimed in Philadelphia community activist Novella Williams.

Another speaker shared how Iverson had visited his leukemia-stricken nephew in the hospital. Shortly after the visit, the speaker solemnly intoned, the boy's cancer went into remission. The crowd roared; Iverson just looked down and shuffled his feet.

But then it was game time and Iverson seemed to respond to my earlier question—"Who are you?"—on the field. He was on third base, Bow Wow on second, when the batter cracked a shot in the right-center gap. Blaring over the PA system came Bow Wow's rendition of the Kurtis Blow classic "Basketball." Iverson took two steps toward home and stopped, struck by the music. And then he started grooving, moving his shoulders languidly, his feet approximating something close to a Michael Jackson moonwalk. Though Iverson never deigned to dance in the clubs, here he was, the center of attention, unable to resist. The crowd went nuts and Iverson seemed charged by the reaction, continuing the boogie.

After all the highfalutin accolades and shrill denunciations, there he was, finally. As had so often been the case, he was embattled, but intent on joyously expressing himself. He was dancing—the urge no doubt spurred by the same mysterious source as his drawing, rapping, and crossover— and the crowd rose up and joined in. Once again, all eyes were on him as he brought people to their feet.

Bow Wow approached and tried to run past him en route to scoring, but Iverson grabbed him and together they paused on their way home to bask in the music and the moment. It was as though Allen Iverson were saying, *Fuck all the talk. I am what I show myself to be.*

AFTERWORD

Allen Iverson's 2002-2003 season—his seventh in the NBA—got off to an inauspicious start. The team tailspinned in December and January, losing, at one point, 9 of 10 and 14 of 18. Mutombo had been jettisoned to New Jersey for Keith Van Horn. But the Sixers were having trouble integrating Van Horn into the offense, and it didn't help that Iverson at times seemed lost on the court.

"I think I might be playing the worst I've played in my career," Iverson said in mid-January, after his team's sixth straight defeat. "For some reason, I'm a step slower."

Indeed, it appeared that Iverson's partying ways, his nonexistent off-season workout regimen, and the toll six seasons of pounding had taken on his frail frame had finally combined to make him a mere mortal on the court. The whispers started: At all of twenty-seven, was his career's downside already upon him?

At the all-star break, though he was scoring more than 27 points per game, he was shooting just 39.9 percent from the floor and averaging just shy of five assists per game. Meantime, hanging over his head was his possible upcoming exclusion from the 2004 Olympic team—a team that would be coached by Brown, who implausibly maintained that he had no input over the squad's roster. While others—Kobe Bryant and Ray Allen among them—were named to the team, Iverson felt his own coach was playing a role in letting him twist in the wind. But when asked about the topic, Iverson argued his case on the merits. "I know it [his possible exclusion] has to do with my image and not my game," he said. "I know I'm one of the twelve best players in the league."

As in the past, Iverson decided to let his game be his most eloquent argument. He dominated the all-star game, scoring 35 breathtaking points: Finally, he'd found his fifth gear. (Some close to him believed it had simply taken him until then to play himself into shape.) The second half of the year was arguably Iverson's finest stretch as a professional. Not coincidentally, the Sixers had the NBA's best record after the all-star break. Iverson shot nearly 44 percent and averaged nearly seven assists over the team's final 33 games, leading the Sixers to 48 regular season wins. In mid-April, Iverson was named to one of the final Olympic spots, though Brown reportedly was not pleased by the selection.

Meantime, he continued making headlines off the court. A friend was shot in the leg outside a Philly club in the wee hours; police speculated that the shots were intended for a nearby Iverson. At home, Tawanna was pregnant for the third time. And on the court, the Sixers were eliminated from the playoffs by the Detroit Pistons, after Brown had publicly admitted that, had he been asked, he would have taken the recently vacated University of North Carolina head coaching job. For Iverson, this latest betrayal was made worse by the fact that it came while the team was, in his words, "in the trenches." Brown had spent six years preaching team loyalty, but Iverson sensed once again that it was all talk.

Within weeks of the Sixers' ousting from the playoffs, the Iverson-Brown saga, one of sports' most interesting psychodramas, came to a sudden close. Brown resigned and abruptly signed with none other than Detroit, which had just fired its successful coach, Rick Carlisle. At the press conference to introduce the new Pistons' coach, Brown took some swipes toward Iverson's practice habits. (Iverson refrained from commenting in return, but Pat Croce told a Philadelphia radio station that Brown was "full of feces.")

But Iverson was determined to respond—in his way. On some level, he'd spent the past six years imagining (some would say orchestrating) the inevitable: Brown's abandonment of him. As had so often been the case, Iverson would turn what he saw as his victimization into fuel. He would finally get into the gym and pump himself up, or, as he once put it, he'd "get all swoll." At the press conference to announce that Randy Ayers, Brown's assistant, would be his new coach, Iverson was a surprise attendee, dressed in a throwback Houston Astros jersey and matching cap. And he wasted no time in hinting at his newfound motivation. "I can't wait for Coach Brown to see me at the Olympic workouts [in August]," he said, smiling. "I can't wait for him to see me take my shirt off and see how big I've gotten." He didn't have to say what everyone in the room could see him thinking: *I'll show you, Larry Brown. I'll show you.*

Everyday PALEO

Sarah Fragoso

Victory Belt Publishing

LAS VEGAS

First Published in 2011 by Victory Belt Publishing

ISBN 10: 0-9825658-1-X

ISBN 13: 978-0-9825658-1-0

This book is for educational purposes. The publisher and author of this instructional book are not responsible in any manner whatsoever for any adverse effects arising directly or indirectly as a result of the information provided in this book. If not practiced safely and with caution, working out can be dangerous to you and to others. It is important to consult with a professional fitness instructor before beginning training. It is also very important to consult with a physician prior to training due to the intense and strenuous nature of the techniques in this book.

Cover Design by Brian Rule

Printed in USA

Table of Contents

Foreword

by Robb Wolf

Hi, I'm Robb. I'm a former California State power lifting champion and a research biochemist. I own NorCal Strength & Conditioning, which was named one of the "top 30 gyms in America" by Men's Health. I've written a *New York Times* bestselling book, *The Paleo Solution*, and I've talked to hundreds of thousands of people around the world about paleo nutrition via my podcast and seminar.

I don't have kids. Yet.

My lack of kids would cause you, as a parent, to take all of my aforementioned credentials and add them to the burn pile if you heard me talk about feeding kids and dealing with the challenges of raising a family. People without kids lack the credibility to change a tire around folks who *do* have kids. I get that. And that's a large part of why this book exists.

The author, Sarah Fragoso, has the "mommy cred." I most certainly do not. She is the mother of three boys, a trainer at a pretty damn good gym (mine), and she owns not one but two little yipper dogs (one a

Chihuahua, and the other I can only describe as "fishing bait"). Oh yeah, she is also a wife.

Sarah had her first son in high school, helped support her husband through chiropractic school, and lost her mom to a protracted bout of breast cancer. She helped her husband build his practice, and they have had two more sons. Sarah then finished her undergraduate degree—and now she has written this book. I'm tired just reading all that. Sarah has lived it. The reason why I mention all this is because some of you will come to this party with a stack of these things called "excuses." You are going to feel like you are the only one who has dealt with trying to help the family eat better, the only person who might be eating a little "differently," the only one who may not know how to start exercising. Or cooking. Well—how do I say this tactfully—if you want your family to be healthy, if you want things to change, the answers are in this book. If you think your life is too complex/difficult to accomplish these changes, you better have a really impressive story, because Sarah has done it, and tens of thousands of her (and my) blog followers have made these changes. The thing that really separates people like Sarah from so many other folks is she made a decision to forgo the excuses and to *do*.

So, just to answer a few of the big questions up front: Yes, you *can* do this, and yes it *is* the healthiest way to feed your family. Tackle it in steps, do what Sarah tells you to do, and it'll be easier than you think. What will you get from this book? Well, it is actually three books in one:

1. You have some basic theory about the paleo diet written from Sarah's perspective. You also get the story of how she reversed some serious health problems via paleo eating, and how she got the rest of the family (dog included) onboard.

2. You get a comprehensive exercise plan with detailed "how-to" photos and instructions. Never exercised? Don't want to join a gym? Perfect, Sarah's program will take you from the couch to beating your kids at push-up contests. Really.

3. You also get a full cook book (photos included). Breakfast, lunch, dinner, snacks, traveling, sending lunches to school.

You see, Sarah has *done* it, so she has covered all the bases. Again, all you need to do is actually do it.

I know, I'm kind of a smarty pants. I'm trying to be funny, but the topic of feeding the kiddos gets quite serious. You want to do the right thing; you want to do right by your family. Awesome, I want that too, and so does Sarah. This book covers the how-to of eating, exercising, and living for the whole family. Make the process easier on everyone and just give it a shot. Commit 100 percent, see how it goes, and I suspect you will be impressed.

You may find that the most frustrating thing about this book is that it really leaves you, in the words of my good friend Kyle Maynard, "No Excuses." That's OK though, because the flip side of that is it virtually guarantees your success.

—Robb Wolf

Acknowledgments

From an early age I have enjoyed putting my thoughts and feelings into words. Now I have the chance to lay it all out there and to shower love on those who make "me" work, but as I sit here typing, I'm afraid that a few words on a page will never do justice to the people in my life who have shaped me, helped me, loved me, encouraged me, supported me, and taught me over the years. This book is not "mine," but rather a culmination of events, people, and experiences that have led to my dream becoming a reality. Please know that as I express my gratitude, in my heart there is so much more appreciation than these written words could ever express.

With that being said, holy cow, I love my blog readers! Without your comments, questions, and encouragement, Everyday Paleo simply would not exist! Above all else, I have learned so much from each of you, and my depth of thanks for your continued support, comments, and input is immeasurable.

Thank you to Moita Lindgren of Ten Toes Photography for taking the beautiful photos for the book cover!

Thank you to my friends, clients, and coworkers at NorCal Strength & Conditioning. You all have carried me through my worst and lifted me up at my best. A special thank-you to Chrissy, Shawn, Katie, Glen, Natalie, Andy, and Karina. Your continued support and friendship are truly amazing, and I am so grateful for all of you! Oh, and I cannot forget little Kayden—his big hugs helped immensely on several occasions!

Robb Wolf and Nicki Violletti. From the very first day that I met both of you, I had a crazy feeling that my life was going to change forever. Robb, there you were with your beautiful girlfriend, Nicki, and the two of you together had this amazing glow (this is where I get all "hippy," which I know Robb loves), and it was as if you just plopped down out of the sky on a day that I needed answers more than ever. You both have literally saved my life more than once! Nicki, thank you for encouraging me to start my blog, and Robb, thank you for going on that walk around the gym almost eight months ago and telling me in not so many words to just freaking (I'm sorry, "fracking") write a book already! Guess what? I did it! There are a million more reasons to thank you, but please know that I am eternally grateful for all that you both have done for me.

A very special thanks goes out to Laura Harren. You are my angel. I will forever cherish you with love and fondness, and I could not have made it through my cooking marathon, or life in general, without you!

Erich Krauss, you are impressive. As my editor, publisher, and now friend, you have made my dream book a reality. So many nights during this process I have closed my eyes and envisioned how I wanted the Everyday Paleo book to look, and I have you to thank for making my vision vastly brighter, better, and more amazing than my wildest dreams. This book would have never happened without you, and for that I give you my deepest thanks.

I owe a huge thank-you to Dain Sandoval. Out of the kindness of Dain's heart he has supported and helped to create Everyday Paleo. My website is truly his genius at work, and he has kept the EverydayPaleo.com boat afloat from day one. Without Dain I would still be wondering how the heck I am supposed to work just about everything! Thank you to Dain and to your beautiful family.

My love and thanks to my brother, Mark, and to my sister, Laura, my brother-in-law, Eric, and my precious niece, sweet little Shaela Sullivan. My thanks also to my 10 million in-laws; I would name you all, but that would be a whole other book! You know that I love each and every one of you with every fiber of my being. You all have encouraged and supported me through these last few whirlwind months, as well as through life. We have made it through so many triumphs and trials together, and we have only grown closer and stronger as a family.

A special note from my heart to Laura and Mark. I have told you before and I will tell you again—I would most likely be crazy without you. Or maybe I already am crazy, but at least you are the two people I can always count on to bring me back to reality and to keep my head above water: unless, of course, Mark is driving the boat. I love you guys.

Mom, I know you would be proud. Your love carried me through life and carried me through this project, and I forever will cherish, love, and miss you.

Dad—over the years you have loved me more than any dad I know, and for that I am eternally grateful. Your constant support and excitement about this project has meant so much to me. I have always cherished hanging out with you; singing along to your guitar, hearing your stories, and just talking with you about anything and everything. Thank you for always cheering me on and reminding me when to slow down; you are my hero.

Thanks to Sandy for jumping into this crazy family and loving us anyway! Your constant cheerful demeanor and wonderful ideas have helped me tremendously as I developed my blog and book. Thank you!

My boys . . .

Coby, you and I have been partners way before anyone else climbed on board our little train, and you are my daily inspiration. Thank you for hanging out with me at Starbucks on all those nights I had to escape from your little brothers to get some writing done. Thank you for always being willing to help, for always making me laugh, and for being one cool kid.

Jaden! Where the heck did you come from kid? You are such an incredible guy, and you already know way more than your mom about almost everything! Thanks for all your help with our book—you did such an awesome job! Please never change; keep that inquisitive mind, keep asking questions, never stop wondering why, and since it's obvious I'll never learn how to speak Spanish, promise you'll always come with me to Mexico.

My little Row Row! You help me stir, you make the hugest messes, you brighten every single day of my life, and I just love you—big punches and all.

A million years ago, I met this guy named John. He was incredibly hot, but way too nice and not at all my type. You see, he had all the right things to say, and wore this perfectly tucked-in shirt, and it was all a bit too much for my not-so-perfect self. Fast-forward a million years later and every single day I am insanely glad that I took my friends' advice and looked again. John, you amaze me, encourage me, and nothing I have accomplished would have ever happened without you. Thank you for loving me tirelessly and without question. Thank you for always supporting my wild ideas with a passion and giving up any of your spare time to do things like take amazing photos of every single recipe in this book! My world rests safely in your arms, and you know how the story goes: all my heart, all my soul. I love you.

What Is Paleo?

Eating Paleo is an easy concept: We should eat as our ancestors once did, we should eat based on how we are genetically wired to eat, and we should eat foods that are not processed, modified, or tampered with in any way, shape, or form. It is not a "fad" diet or the latest trend in Hollywood. It's how our bodies are meant to be fueled.

There is an obvious problem with the standard American diet. It has made the majority of our society sick, fat, out of shape, and unhappy. It has disabled our children and changed everything about who we are and what we are capable of doing. This diet needs to change, and not in the form of counting calories, measuring and weighing, or reducing the crappy foods we eat. We need to eliminate the crappy foods. We need to eat that which heals the body and supports the immune system, musculoskeletal system, cardiovascular system, brain function, and all major organs. This is what the paleo diet accomplishes. In a nutshell, it's a food prescription for life.

I know what you are probably thinking: *That sounds fine and dandy, but what foods can I eat on the paleo diet?* Well, you can eat meat, seafood, eggs, vegetables, healthy fats (nuts, seeds, olive oil, coconut oil, avocado), and fruit. Why these foods? Because they are the foods that our Paleolithic ancestors consumed, the foods that we are genetically wired to consume. What type of person did our ancestral diet produce? Our hunter/gatherer predecessors had lean, agile, and athletic bodies with no recognizable signs of the modern-day illnesses that currently plague us. Not bad perks, am I right?

Anything that I did not list above should be eliminated—meaning all processed foods, dairy, legumes, any form of sugar, and grains! Grains you ask? Grains might be the biggest part of our food pyramid, but they are also scientifically proven to be the biggest problem with the standard American diet. Grains are gut irritants, especially grains containing gluten such as wheat, barley, and rye. When our gut lining gets irritated, we are unable to properly digest our food, which leads to inflammation in our bodies. Inflammation is the source of a host of different health problems. If that isn't enough of a deterrent, eating processed foods screws with our hormone levels, and our hormones control and manage just about everything important in our bodies. For example, a diet high in grains and sugars causes spikes in insulin levels, and messing with insulin levels is the precursor to one of humankind's worst and ever-growing enemies: diabetes. When your hormone levels go bonkers, you risk all sorts of health problems, from various forms of cancers to autoimmune disease. So, in a nutshell, eating paleo is eating unprocessed foods that were eaten by our ancestors long before the introduction of agriculture.

I am not a scientist, but a realist, and what was more convincing for me than any research or scientific data was my own experiment with eating paleo. I urge you to simply try eating paleo for thirty days. What's the worst that can happen? If you do not have any positive changes due to eating this way, you can simply go back to your old ways and trash my book. But if you are like me and thousands of others who have given the paleo diet a shot, the lifestyle changes presented in this book will make you happier and healthier than you ever thought possible.

It is important to note that my intention with this book is to help you and your family successfully make the transition to a paleo lifestyle. Walking up and down the aisles of a grocery store, reading the ingredient labels, and trying to decipher what you can and cannot eat, can leave you with a terrible lost feeling. Standing in your kitchen in front of an empty pan, wondering how you can combine whole foods into a delicious meal can make you more than a little frustrated. Squatting in your living room in your sweats, wondering what exercises you should do and how to perform them correctly can make you confused. And wondering how to lead your family into this new charge toward a healthier life can make you feel downright angry. My goal with this book is to offer you a roadmap to eliminate that lost feeling, frustration, confusion, and anger. My goal is to help you and your family turn over that new leaf so you don't abandon the most important thing in your life—your health and longevity.

If you need to know the science behind the paleo diet before giving it a shot, I recommend that you pick up a copy of Robb Wolf's book, *The Paleo Solution*, as well as follow his life-changing blog and podcasts, which can be found here: www.robbwolf.com.

everyday paleo

My Life
before Paleo

I was born into a family of health nuts. My grandparents were doing yoga in slinky outfits way before it was cool, and grandma was putting bone meal in my oatmeal cookies, which never became cool. For their generation, this behavior was considered baffling, new age, and wacky. The "wackiness" continued as my grandparents' fixation on good health transferred on down to my mother, and needless to say I ended up being the only child in first grade who brought for lunch a whole wheat tortilla smeared with tahini and topped with organic sprouts and heirloom tomatoes.

A large part of my childhood centered on the healthy concoctions that my mom was constantly creating in the kitchen, and I was always one of her unassuming "come on and try this" guinea pigs. However, as strange as our food often was, my mom always included us in her culinary adventures. One of my earliest and fondest memories is of my mom hoisting me up into her arms, plopping me on the counter, and handing me her favorite wooden spoon so that I could help her stir. At a very early age, my mom instilled in me a lifelong love and curiosity for health and a genuine appreciation for food, fun, and family. I have never been afraid to try new foods or to create new dishes. My mom gave me an invaluable gift, and for this I am eternally grateful.

Besides the fun we had together creating crazy cuisine, what my health food–induced childhood led to was the lingering need for a greater understanding. I realized the importance of knowing where one's food comes from, that what you see on TV is not always good for you, and eventually this lesson: even when you think you are doing everything you can to be healthy, it does not make you invincible.

Although "living healthy" was always a part of my life, I went through several years of going bananas experimenting with every kind of food and diet imaginable, but thanks to my mother's influence, I always preferred food that was fresh, close to its source, and what I considered natural.

After leaving the nest and encountering a few years of being young and silly, I settled down like most of us do, got married, had some babies, and landed somewhere in the middle of what I assumed to be "healthy." I ate whole grains, lots of veggies, some meat now and then, loads of dairy for calcium, and pretty much cruised along through life.

Despite my supposed health-conscious ways, I had weird stuff happening: chronic swelling in my legs during my pregnancy, and after the birth of my second child, weight gain that no matter what I did would never entirely go away. I was also suffering from a constant gassy, bloated feeling after eating, headaches, some mild depression now and then, acne, and chronic yeast infections. I still have a poignant memory of being only three months pregnant with my second child and having my father-in-law ask me if my ankles were already swelling or if they were just fat. His exact words, "Sarah, do you have cankles?" Awesome!

My health problems were not fun to deal with, but I perceived these nuisances to be minor afflictions that were a normal part of life. I probably would have continued to trot along this way, but life decided to deal one of its shocking blows. In the beautiful and what seemed hopeful spring of 2005, I lost my beloved mother to breast cancer. It was unexplainable, overwhelming, and undeniably the most confusing time in my life. My mother never drank, never smoked, ate only organic foods, tons of whole grains—even grinding her own wheat into flour—and yet she died right in front of our eyes with no real explanation as to why, except for cancer does not care.

One month after my mom's death I dragged my defeated and saddened self to the local Relay for Life, which was my mom's favorite fundraiser and the event that she had hoped to attend one last time. I marched relentlessly and with purpose around the track, pushing my eighteen-month-old baby boy in his stroller and holding the brave little hand of my nine-year-old son, looking around into people's faces for some sort of answer. Well, I found one. I practically fell over a man doing a handstand on parallel bars made of PVC pipe and a woman easily tossing a twenty-pound medicine ball into the air.

Fascinated, I stopped to ask what the heck they were doing, and Robb Wolf introduced himself to me along with his girlfriend, Nicki Violetti. My husband had just opened his chiropractic business and, as we chatted, Robb mentioned that he and Nicki had just opened a fitness facility based on full functional movement and high-intensity training, which is why they had their strange equipment out at Relay for Life. During our conversation, Robb mentioned that they happened to be looking for a chiropractor to refer their clients to. Excited about the possibility of networking with these interesting folks, we made a date for breakfast.

As the months went by and our relationship with Robb and Nicki grew, my husband, John, and I began to train at their gym, and they taught us about eating paleo and the health benefits associated with this lifestyle. Although I loved Robb and Nicki and valued our relationship, I was still in such a rough place emotionally that I simply could not see the gift that was being given to me. The answer to true health and wellness was in my lap, but I missed my mom terribly and I was living in a haze of grief. Instead of dealing with it, I gave all I had of myself to everyone and everything else around, resulting with nothing left for me. I worked out sporadically at Robb and Nicki's gym and ate a "normal healthy diet," which helped in no way but to up the scale a few more pounds. I soon found out that I was pregnant with our third child, stopped my already infrequent workouts, and of course continued to bury myself in all sorts of distracting projects. After nine months of pregnancy and eating everything on the planet, I had my third little boy, looked in the mirror, and did not even recognize myself.

In the two years that had passed since I lost my mother, I had turned myself into a blubbery ball of misery: unhealthy, sad, and frustrated. I had these three amazing little boys, one incredible, dedicated, and loving husband, and yet I was just floating along through life, slapping on my smile, but in reality feeling miserable, unhealthy and alone. I had to get serious.

I was ready for a change, and I made a commitment to work out twice a week at Robb and Nicki's gym. About a month into my consistent workouts, I felt a bit better, but I still suffered from the list of complaints I had been suffering from for years, and I hadn't really lost any weight.

After complaining to Nicki (never a good idea by the way), she challenged me. Nicki calmly and coolly said to me, "Sarah, try eating strict paleo for thirty days; if you do not feel, perform, or look better, then go back to what you were eating before, simple as that." Somewhere inside me, a fire was lit. The old me used to like a challenge, and I knew I could do it. I was so incredibly ready to see if I could feel "normal" again that I dove in headfirst, and at the end of those thirty days, there was no turning back.

Almost immediately after changing my diet, the chronic swelling in my legs literally disappeared (no more cankles!). I lost an easy ten pounds in the first month, no longer felt gassy or bloated, and to this day I have not had a single yeast infection. All the inflammation and discomfort that had been plaguing me for years was gone. Besides feeling better, it was as if my body just knew that what I was eating before was bad for me. I did have a couple of weeks of carb and sugar withdrawals that I'll talk about later, but soon my body began to crave meat and veggies drowned in coconut milk, while the sight of a sandwich would almost repulse me. I had no desire to ever drift back to how I used to look and feel. Never had a diet done such amazing things for me. Everything else I had ever tried left me feeling cheated, deprived, and always hungry. It was clear to me early on that by eating paleo I was not dieting; I was *living*!

I remember clearly my "light-bulb moment." About three weeks into my paleo challenge, I was standing in my kitchen making lunch and suddenly started crying tears of gratefulness, relief, grief, and thanks. I felt so appreciative to my precious mom, and although I had lost her, she somehow gave me the gift of meeting Robb and Nicki at that fateful Relay for Life. It was *my* Relay for Life that day, and I was given the answer I had been searching for. I had found a way to truly be healthy, to really find wellness, and I was finally at peace both physically and mentally.

After successfully wrapping up the first thirty days of my paleo challenge, I became really focused. In seven short months, I was fitter than I ever had been in my life, even before having children. I felt vibrant, alive, and invincible, and yet I continued to feed my little boys and my husband the same old crap that made me feel so awful while I sat at the same table eating my paleo meals. Something simply did not jive. Why would I feed the same foods that used to make me so unhealthy and miserable to the ones I loved the most? Why was I not sharing with my own family the joy of feeling great after every meal? The very next day I tossed the entire family onto the paleo wagon.

My husband was easy to get on board. Being a chiropractor, an athlete, and a scientist, once he took the time to research the benefits and the "whys" of eating paleo, he was willing to give it a try. Even with all of his doctor's smarts, like any other dude, the real proof was in his ego. He always looked good, but after consistently eating paleo, he looked even better. He achieved more personal records at the gym, and although he was dang strong before eating paleo, he became unbelievably strong after tweaking his way of eating.

Feeding my two youngest boys paleo was easier than convincing my oldest son that this was the way to

Sarah Before Picture: February 2008

Sarah After Picture: August 2008

go, but it did happen, and it happened successfully. I will fill you in later on the secrets to getting the whole family on board, but for now I can confirm that a family eating paleo is entirely possible, and the positive changes I continue to witness in my family are well worth the initial effort.

For example, my children's behavior became more manageable. I am truly blessed with three amazing sons, but let's be honest—all kids can be difficult. My middle son, who was particularly sensitive, cranky at best, and the temper tantrum king, became much more mild-mannered and gained the ability to better control his little emotions. Maybe it was the lack of insulin spikes and dives throughout his day—his little body just couldn't handle the sugar rushes and crashes that were brought on even with his previously "healthy" diet of oatmeal breakfasts and whole wheat sandwich lunches.

The next most notable sign was the baby. During his first year of life, he literally never got sick, except for a few minor sniffles. He was just goofy, happy, and easy going, and ate whatever I put in front of him, from salmon to sweet potatoes and Brussels sprouts to spinach frittatas. He was my paleo baby guinea pig, and what a discovery I made. If you avoid introducing the foods that you do not want your little ones to eat, they will have no choice but to like the healthy foods you offer!

After converting my family to paleo, the most significant change transpired in my oldest boy. He began to exhibit a significant increase in his interest in academics. Before eating paleo he was an average student. But for the first time, he made the honor roll with no pressure from his parents beyond encouragement, support, and paleo living. *Hmmm*, can you see any possible correlation between his shift in diet and his shift in focus, enthusiasm, and academics?

As we continued on our paleo journey and I witnessed the remarkable changes in my family, I also began to realize more the significance of my own behavioral changes. I was happy—really, really happy for the first time in years. I felt as if the fog had finally lifted. As I felt better physically, I was able to make other significantly positive changes in all aspects of my life. Don't get me wrong, life is hard. My life story is much longer than the little bit I have written about here. I could bore you to tears with the challenges I have faced. But you know what? If you are eating paleo, exercising, sleeping enough, and finding time to play, all the other difficult stuff does *not* disappear, but it does become more manageable. There is no such thing in life as a bulletproof vest, but I would like to think that there is a viable and sensible way to do all that we can to be truly healthy. If you are with me, let's get started!

everyday paleo

Getting Started

Since you picked this book up, I will assume that you are convinced enough to give this paleo thing a try and you're looking for some assistance. I hope my assumptions are correct, because a starter guide is exactly what I will give you, but before we head down that road, let's chat for a moment.

Everyone is different, I know, but we all have one thing in common—we are human. Relying on will power alone to stay on track is crazy. It's the reason why so many people fail when "dieting." Anything worthwhile takes hard work, and my advice is to make a real commitment to do this. The shift to paleo eating should be looked at as a lifelong commitment rather than a few weeks of hell so that your jeans fit better for that important night out. Making any sort of change is about what you choose to do, not what might simply happen. If you don't hold yourself accountable or you make excuses such as, "I don't know what to do" or "It's too hard," you are setting yourself up for failure. If you are ready to change, you'll do it, plain and simple.

After a few days of conquering eating paleo, you will begin to gain some confidence in your ability to handle and maintain change. This is the time to start gathering resources and educating yourself. Having support and a community is very important when trying to obtain a goal. No one should have to be alone on this journey, and with the vast and constantly growing online paleo community, you always have a paleo friend nearby. Visit blogs of those who will support and encourage you, like mine and like Robb Wolf's (www.robbwolf.com). Understand why you are eating paleo so that when you decide (because it is always a choice) to fall off the wagon, you won't stay off. Instead, you shake the dirt out of your pretty white petticoats and hop the hell back on.

It is also important to note that if you *do* fall off the wagon, do not fall off into anything that contains gluten. We will talk later in the book about "cheating," but please understand that eating gluten will set you back farther than you thought possible in regard to your health. It takes fourteen to fifteen days for your body to recover from a dose of gluten, and especially during the first thirty days of eating clean, you want to give your body a chance to heal and recover from any previous damage done.

Table A: What Sarah Wants You to Have

IN YOUR PANTRY

- **Coconut milk**
- **Canned organic diced tomatoes** (no salt added)
- **Organic tomato paste**
- **Organic free-range gluten-free chicken broth** (Trader Joe's carries a great brand)
- **Coconut flakes** (keep in the fridge after you open them)
- **Coconut flour**
- **Almond meal**
- **Raw almonds**
- **Raw pecans**
- **Raw walnuts** (all nuts actually keep better in the freezer after you open the bag)
- **Almond butter** (again, in the fridge after you open)
- **Beef jerky** (gluten and soy free from Paleo Brands or Trader Joe's is best)
- **Canned wild-caught Alaskan salmon**
- **Canned tuna**
- **Olives**
- **Artichoke hearts**
- **Dried unsweetened Bing cherries**
- **Dried unsweetened figs**
- **Dried unsweetened apricots**
- **Olive oil**
- **Coconut oil**
- **El Pato hot sauce and enchilada sauce**
- **Jalapeños**
- **Canned diced green chilies**
- **Sun-dried tomatoes**
- **As many freaking spices as you can get your hands on!** With spices you never have an excuse to eat a boring meal!

IN YOUR FRIDGE

- **Eggs**—preferably free range (not fed soy) or omega-3 enriched
- **Grass-fed ground beef**
- **Free-range chicken** (thighs are my favorite, or the whole darn bird is my next favorite—you can make my amazing roast chicken and then boil the carcass for soup. Chicken is so versatile it should always be around)
- **Nitrate-free deli meat** (great for on the go, kids' lunches, and fast snacking)
- **Bacon**
- **Mustard**
- **Salsa**
- **Hot sauce**
- **Chili oil**
- **Thai fish oil**
- **Thai curry paste**
- **So Delicious brand unsweetened coconut milk**
- **Spinach**
- **Kale**
- **Carrots**
- **Cucumber**
- **Organic lettuce mix**
- **Romaine lettuce**
- **Apples**
- **Blueberries**
- **Lemons**
- **Limes**
- **Any veggie and fruit that you can get your hands on that is as fresh as possible and in season!**

everyday paleo

During the first week or two of changing your diet, you might have moments of feeling sluggish, tired, and totally done with paleo. These symptoms are you coming out of the carb- and sugar-induced coma you probably have been in for many, many years. It will get better. Soon you will have boundless energy and a brand new lease on life. Even better, real food will start to taste really good, and the desire for junk food will begin to disappear or drastically diminish—but only if you are consistent and stick with it. You have the power, and if you really want this, you *will* make the choice!

Life in the twenty-first century is crazy, hectic, and stupid busy, and women especially are known to not make themselves a priority. For once in your life, be selfish and lose the guilt. Make the conscious decision to not give in to the bagel breakfast mornings with your girlfriends or the pumpkin chocolate chip muffin fests at your playgroups. If you show up to these events full from your eggs and avocado with your goal in mind and a plan for success, you will not feel pressured to partake. It takes a bit of planning ahead, but cutting out something like one hour of mindless TV to be ready for your week is part of the importance of taking care of you.

For some, the transition to paleo living might be difficult at first, but it will become easier. Just because I was able to dive in headfirst and never look back doesn't mean I wasn't crying into my empty cereal bowl for the first couple of weeks, dreaming of my banana nut clusters and frosted flakes. Because I have lived through the transition of eating paleo for not only myself, but also for my family, I have insight into the reality of the work that it takes to get there. I have also successfully helped countless others make the transition over the last few years, and using that knowledge, I'll walk you through how to survive when faced with that awful choice at 10:00 PM, when all you really want is what you should not have.

The Prepping Process

Step 1: Rid your house of everything that is processed. Take a giant box or garbage bag and start in your cupboards. Remove all grain-based food products and anything containing sugar or any type of sweeteners.

Step 2: Move on to the fridge and start the purge. The only items left should be fresh veggies, fruits, eggs, unprocessed meats, and condiments that do not contain sugar, such as mustard and salsa. Out with all the dairy products, too.

Once steps one and two have been accomplished take a big breath of air and let it out—you have made your first leap forward, so be proud! Now, unless you make the conscious decision to go out and purchase a non-paleo food item, the temptation will no longer exist and you won't have to worry about "will-power." I offer a more extensive shopping guide later, but for now, after you clean out your cabinets and fridge, the items listed in table A are what I always want you to have on hand.

When getting started, it is important not to overwhelm yourself by looking deep into the future. Don't think about how you may never eat another bagel. Don't get stressed about what you will do at parties. And don't get your heart palpitating by thinking that your grandmother will never forgive you for shunning her famous apple pound cake. Simply take your paleo journey one meal at a time. Focus on what you are doing right now, not on what might happen two weeks from now at the monthly moms' night out. Realize that you have the tools to make this work, and you have made a wonderful decision that will change your life only for the better. Remember, anything worth something takes hard work. Take it one meal at a time, be prepared, and enjoy the ride.

An Easy Start

Let's start with breakfast. I know it's an old adage that breakfast is the most important meal of the day, but that old adage is right. The first meal of the day is really what gets you going.

The prescription is quite simple; eat a fist sized portion of good protein like omega-3-enriched eggs, add in a small handful of good fat like half an avocado, and maybe toss in a bit of veggies like steamed spinach. Keep those first few paleo mornings simple. We've all eaten eggs for breakfast before; this is not rocket science. In fact, there's nothing weird about it. All you have to do with this common meal is leave out the English muffin!

As you go about your day, survey how you feel, and I promise you will be amazed. You will be full until lunch or later, you will not crash and burn, and you'll probably even like it. I will not lie to you, you'll still wake up craving your bagel and your latte, but be brave, because you can do it. Those crazy, carb-induced cravings will pass, and this will become easy.

Once you have conquered your first paleo meal, you will most likely be excited about trying lunch. Lunch can look like a million lunches you've had before, minus the bread and cheese. Most folks find it easy to make or buy a salad that fits perfectly into a paleo lifestyle. Think lettuce, chicken, bell peppers, olive oil, and a splash of balsamic vinegar. Delicious, satisfying, and no need to add up points, bring a scale with you to work to weigh your portions, or lug out the calculator to figure calories. Just eat some chicken on a salad with some olive oil and smile.

Now dive back into your day and forge on toward dinner. Again, dinner does not have to be weird to be paleo. How about some salmon and asparagus? Maybe a steak, some broccoli, and a nice salad; doesn't that all sound easy, delicious, and pretty darn normal? Congratulate yourself because you made it through day one and your journey has begun!

Shopping Paleo

To be successful with the paleo diet, you need to learn what your food options are and how to shop for them. Before we dive into specifics, here are a few terms I suggest you make yourself familiar with:

Macronutrients: Food is composed of three main nutrients—protein, carbohydrate, and fat. Each of these nutrients is critical for different functions in the body. The primary macronutrient in a food determines what category we place it under. For example, nuts have protein, carbohydrate, and fat. However, the primary macronutrient is fat, so we place nuts in the fat category.

Protein: A protein is a macronutrient that comes primarily from animals. For paleo eating purposes, your protein sources need to have had a mommy and a daddy. From now on, please remember that protein does not mean the "perfect" combination of beans and rice, nor does it mean dairy sources such as yogurt. I have never witnessed a bean give birth, so therefore, not an adequate source of protein. Remember, the protein that you must eat should come from a source that had a face (or would have at some point, i.e., eggs).

Carbohydrate: This macronutrient is the hardest one for most folks to wrap their brain around. The food pyramid suggests that carbohydrates only come from grain-based food items, so those of us who want to load up on carbs after a tough workout typically think of a plate full of pasta or a nine-grain bagel. Starting now, erase this notion from your memory and put this fact in the empty space—if it grew in the ground, it's a carbohydrate!

All fruits and vegetables are primarily carbohydrate. Some are higher in sugar and starch than others, but all plant-based foods are carbs. It is wise for those folks who want to lose weight to choose an abundance of vegetables before stuffing themselves with fruit. This will help to limit overall sugar consumption, and therefore will help improve body composition. When you hear folks say they simply cannot live without carbohydrates, they are correct. No one can live without vegetables and fruit, but we can live, and live well, without the traditional notion of carbohydrates. So please say goodbye to your pasta and bagels and hello to your broccoli and melons.

Fat: Oh, boy, are you ready—you might want to brace yourself for this one: you must eat fat and, most importantly, fat does not make you fat! This message might feel like a meteorite just hit you square in the forehead as visions of your nonfat sugar-free latte disappear into space, but I am telling the truth. Our bodies need fat. Think about the thirty-plus-year trend of the nonfat, high-carb diet and ask yourself: Has it freaking worked? Look around you. Overweight, unhealthy, and muffin-topped is the new normal.

Being lean, fit, and in shape is now a bit odd. This new "trend" is very and incredulously wrong. Think about why fat-free foods have any taste at all—*sugar*! In order to make fat-free anything edible, one must process the living hell out of it, add a billion additives and flavors, and strip whatever is left of any nutrients that might be remotely beneficial. Thanks to our lovely food pyramid, the majority of our country is really sick and out of shape, and by taking away our fat consumption, we have added on the sugar-free pounds, topped with a nonfat blob of heart disease and a side of diabetes.

Let me take this chance to reintroduce fat into your life. The media has made the word fat sound ugly, but as you continue on your paleo journey, you will really grow to love the healthy fats that fuel you. You'll also love watching the unhealthy fat that hangs off you melt away.

Still not convinced? Fat is a macronutrient that is found in both animal and plant products. It's a great source of energy, it helps you digest fat-soluble vitamins, and your brain and your heart depend on fat to function. Unfortunately, the lack of fat in our diets and the consumption of too many processed foods and carbohydrates have a devastating effect on hormone balance. For us women, especially, eating fat aids in regulating hormone balance, which determines everything from mood to disease prevention. Scary side note—woman with hormone imbalance are more likely to experience devastating illnesses such as cancer, autoimmune disorders, and hypothyroidism, to name a few. As the incidences of these diseases continue to rise among women, correlating this frightening fact with our low-fat diets is only obvious.

Now, this section on fat does not give you the freedom to dive into a trans-fat-laden bowl of deep-fried potato chips; you must choose your fats wisely! Fat that comes from nature is permitted. The shopping guide listed in table B will help you determine what those healthy fats are, as well as give you a head start on all the other paleo food essentials you will want to stock up on.

Along with the following basic food guide, I also offer a family-friendly thirty-day meal plan and weekly shopping lists immediately following the recipe section of this book. This list is a great way to get things started and nice to have on hand when clearing out the kitchen and restocking with paleo food items.

Get Creative

This list in table B is just the beginning of what is possible, so feel free to explore the vast empire of vegetables and spices. After all, always having a variety of spices will ensure you never get bored or tired of food.

When you enter a grocery store with list in hand, pretend that the only part of the store that is accessible is the perimeter and the aisle in which you will find the oil and nuts. Pick a day on the weekend and plan your meals. Think about the foods that you love and how you can modify them to make them paleo. For example, vegetables are an excellent substitute for pasta. Thinly sliced zucchini sautéed quickly in coconut oil makes a wonderful base for your favorite marinara sauce. Throw on top a homemade paleo meatball, and you have a bit of heaven. The possibilities truly are endless.

Look at cookbooks and start revising recipes. Check out paleo blogs and become inspired. If you hate to cook, you have to simply get over it. Take a cooking class and decide you will like it because what you put into your body is what keeps you alive.

Another great way to shop is to find local resources. Check to see if you have a farmers market and visit it. Bring your family and get the kids involved. Let the kids see where real food comes from, introduce them to the farmers behind the stands, and let them choose a different and interesting vegetable or fruit to try. Making it a family affair can get everyone more excited about eating healthy, and you will feel closer to the source of where your paleo food is coming from.

What About?

Before we move on, I want to cover a few "what about" food items that people often wonder about when getting started on a paleo lifestyle. I first want to start with the most common "what about" that I hear among paleo beginners.

Table B: Basic Food Guide

Meat
(Protein)
(Lean/organic/grass-fed cuts are best)

- Chicken
- Turkey
- Duck
- Beef
- Pork
- Lamb
- Veal
- Bison
- Venison
- Elk
- Omega-3-enriched eggs
- Jerky (gluten-free and not marinated in soy)

Fish and Seafood
(Protein)
(Low mercury, wild caught if possible)

- Salmon
- Tilapia
- Crab
- Shrimp
- Tuna
- Cod

Vegetables
(Carbohydrates)
(Organic, if possible)

- Artichoke
- Asparagus
- Beets
- Broccoli
- Brussels sprouts
- Cabbage
- Carrots
- Cauliflower
- Celery
- Collards/mustard greens/kale
- Cucumber
- Eggplant
- Endive
- Lettuce, spinach
- Mushrooms
- Onions
- Parsley
- Parsnip
- Peppers
- Radish
- Seaweed
- Squash (all types)
- Yams (in moderation, unless you are a kid)

everyday paleo

Fruit
(Carbohydrates)
(Organic, if possible)

- Tomato
- Lemons/limes
- Apple
- Apricot
- All berries
- All melons
- Fig
- Grapefruit
- Kiwi
- Nectarine
- Orange
- Peach
- Pear
- Plum
- Pomegranate
- Tangerine
- Watermelon

IN MODERATION

- Dried fruit (no sugar added)
- Tropical fruits such as:
  - Banana
  - Mango
  - Pineapple
  - Guava

Fats

- Avocado
- Olive oil
- Coconut oil
- Coconut milk
- Coconut flakes (unsweetened)
- Almonds
- Brazil nuts
- Chestnuts
- Hazelnuts
- Macadamia nuts
- Pecans
- Pine nuts
- Pistachios
- Walnuts
- Pumpkin seeds
- Sesame seeds
- Sesame seeds
- Almond butter
- Cashew butter
- Organic grass-fed heavy cream (unless you have an autoimmunity issue)
- Organic grass-fed ghee (unless you have an autoimmunity issue)
- Organic grass-fed butter (unless you have an autoimmunity issue)
- Lard, tallow

Spices

- Allspice
- Anise
- Basil
- Bay leaf
- Caraway
- Cardamom
- Cayenne powder
- Chili powder
- Cilantro
- Cinnamon
- Cloves
- Coriander
- Cumin
- Curry powder
- Dill
- Fenugreek
- Garlic
- Ginger
- Marjoram
- Mint
- Mustard
- Nutmeg
- Oregano
- Paprika
- Parsley
- Pepper
- Rosemary
- Saffron
- Sage
- Tarragon
- Thyme
- Turmeric
- Vanilla

Milk Substitutes?

1) **Coconut Milk:** We all love cream in our coffee, but with dairy not being a part of the paleo diet, what's a coffee-loving mama to do? I personally love coconut milk. It goes great in my morning cup of Joe, and it goes just as good in my afternoon cup of black tea. I use the So Delicious brand of unsweetened coconut milk. It has been watered down a bit, so I do not rely on this milk substitute as my only fat source, but it tastes just like the brand name implies. Personally, I find that it gives a great texture to the coconut milk smoothies I make for my kids. If you like smoothies, you've got to try it:

Awesome Smoothie:
1. Fill a blender half way up with 1 banana, frozen blueberries, and ½ a mango.

2. Add So Delicious coconut milk until it's just covering the fruit. Blend until smooth.

My kids love this smoothie, along with scrambled eggs, for a quick breakfast on those rushed-to-get-to-school-on-time mornings.

Canned coconut milk is a perfect substitute for any recipe that typically calls for heavy cream, half-and-half, or milk. I use canned coconut milk for curries, soups, stews, and in several other recipes that you will find in the recipe section. Coconut milk is extremely healing to the gut lining and an amazing source of lauric acid, which does wonders for the immune system and is one of the most beneficial essential fatty acids.

2) **Almond Milk:** Almond milk is preferable to cow's milk, but it's not my favorite milk substitute because of its high levels of omega-6 fatty acids. Most folks new to the paleo diet have extremely high levels of omega-6 fatty acids and very low levels of omega-3 fatty acids. We want those levels to be a bit more even in order to obtain optimum health and lessen inflammation in our bodies; therefore, if you are using a tablespoon or two of almond milk in your coffee, that's probably OK, but I would not recommend drinking almond milk everyday by the glassful.

3) **Heavy Cream:** Yes, it's dairy, but heavy cream is mainly fat, and by buying grass-fed organic heavy cream, you benefit from some of those good omega-3s I was talking about in the last paragraph. If you allow a tablespoon or two of heavy cream in your coffee in the morning, and are otherwise healthy, see how you feel. Some folks do fine. However, if you have any sort of autoimmune issue, I recommend staying away from all dairy products. I love heavy cream, but I find that it makes me feel really full and kind of sluggish if I have it every day, so I use it more as a treat in my coffee now and then or for homemade whipped cream to put on top of my paleo pumpkin pie on holidays. However, overall I rate coconut milk as the number one milk replacement.

Yams or Sweet Potatoes:
Depending on where you live, you might call them yams or you might call them sweet potatoes. Whatever you end up calling them, make sure you eat potatoes that are orange on the inside. I love yams, but living off of them is not my recommendation. Nor would I recommend yams as a daily staple to someone trying to lose weight. They are best consumed after a workout as a carb "recovery fuel." Kiddlets, however, burn a heck of a lot more calories than we adults, and they are typically healthier than us as well. As a result, they can oftentimes use more dense carbs than mommies and daddies.

If you are healthy, I would suggest playing with yams in your diet. You have to figure out for yourself what your body likes best as far as fuel sources. Some people can eat yams every day and feel, look, and perform just fine. Other folks find that if they eat a ton of starchy tubers they have a more difficult time losing weight and feel a bit more sluggish.

Butter:
My answer to butter will be very similar to my answer about heavy cream. Organic, grass-fed butter does have some healthy properties, and can be a good source of fat for some folks. I love butter, but the health benefits of coconut oil outweigh those of butter, so I recommend folks stick to coconut oil for high-heat cooking and olive oil for low-heat sautéing and for salad dressings. However, if you do not suffer from any sort of autoimmune issue and are otherwise healthy, scrambling those eggs in butter occasionally is fine as long as *you* continue to look, feel, and perform at your optimal level. A side note, if you are going to eat butter, it's best to purchase already clarified butter. This is called ghee, and it can be found at most health food stores. The clarification process removes most of the remaining milk solids, which contain lactose, making clarified butter the optimal choice.

Bacon:

"But Sarah, you said *lean* meats, and so does everyone else who preaches paleo." Here's the skinny on the fat. Most of our meat supply comes from grain-fed, commercially raised feedlot animals. The fat in these animals is high in omega-6s, those fatty acids that we want to cut down on. If you are eating grass-fed, pasture-raised animals, the fat in these animals is really good for you! Animal fat is not bad, it's the bad stuff found in most conventionally farmed animal fat that is bad for us.

Some are fearful of the nitrate content in bacon and other cured or deli meats, but several grocers are now selling nitrate-free bacon, sausages, and deli meats. Furthermore, studies now show that nitrates are not as fearful as once thought, and that the nitrate amounts found in cured meats are much less than in previous years and not as harmful as previously suggested. The best bacon would be from pigs raised on food sources other than grains, and raised humanely. I love bacon, support bacon, and want you to enjoy your bacon too. Go to www.eatwild.com to find local sources for grass-fed beef and pasture-raised hogs and poultry.

Fruit, Dried Fruit, and Paleo "Treats"

Many people want a solid list of what "is and isn't paleo." We know the obvious answer to what we should not eat to obtain true health—grains, legumes, and dairy—but there are many tweaks that we can make to our diet that will hinder or progress our optimal goal of health. This entire "what about" section is me giving you the freedom to determine for yourself what will and will not make your "what is paleo" list.

For me, lots of fruit in my diet is not paleo at all. If I eat too much fruit, especially in the morning, I feel terrible. I am hungry by 10 AM and I tend to gain a bit of weight. The same is true for dried fruit and "paleo treats" like my Great Date Balls found in the recipe section. Treats should be treated as the name implies, a "treat"!

I have found for myself that I can eat a few blueberries or a bit of diced apple in my salad or some cooked fruit in moderation with my protein and do fine, but if I eat fruit with every meal or for snacks, I do not look, feel, or perform like I want to.

You will have to determine what works best for you when it comes to fruit and paleo treat consumption. During those first thirty days of eating paleo, especially for those folks wanting to lose weight, I suggest you keep your fruit consumption to a very small amount and combine it with some protein and fat. Better yet, save your fruit consumption to post-workouts. If you are otherwise lean and healthy, you might be able to get away with a bit more fruit consumption, but base it on how you feel.

The same protocol is true for dried fruit and paleo treats. Anything in the recipe section that looks like dessert should be considered something for a special occasion. Kids might be able to eat a few more of my Nutty Cookies than you or me, but just because they are not made of grains does not mean that these treats should be an everyday occurrence. As with anything you choose to eat, if you begin to gain weight, have a hard time losing weight, or simply do not feel as great as you know you can, look back on what you have been eating and consider if you need to cut out some fruit or dial back a bit on the paleo treats.

Nuts:

When you hear about eating Paleo, nuts are usually high on the list, but let's get real. Nuts are pretty high in calories, and some nuts, like almonds, are particularly high in omega-6 fatty acids. Think about how we used to eat nuts. We had to gather them first, and then shell them one by one. That's a lot of work for a handful of nuts. Today, we can conveniently buy them prepackaged and ready to go, but if you are consuming nuts by the tubful, this probably is not the best choice for reaching optimal health. I love nuts as an emergency food supply and always keep trail mix handy in my car, but I do not recommend nuts as your only source for healthy fats. Look more to avocado, olive oil, and coconut products for your sources of fat and see how you feel. As you will see in the recipe section, I personally use nuts as a filler in a few recipes and as convenient snacks.

Salt:

Processed foods are filled with salt, which puts stress on the kidneys. If your diet lacks alkaline foods such as vegetables and fruits, this can be a problem. Cutting out all processed foods is a huge step in the right direction. With that being said, adding a bit of sea salt to one's healthy paleo foods should not pose a significant health risk. However, you should use Celtic sea salt, and not table salt, which has no health benefits whatsoever. I'm not saying to go crazy. Keep your salt intake to a minimum, but by no means force down a plate of steamed veggies if you know you would enjoy them if drizzled with a bit of olive oil and a sprinkle of sea salt. For athletes, the total absence of salt can actually lead

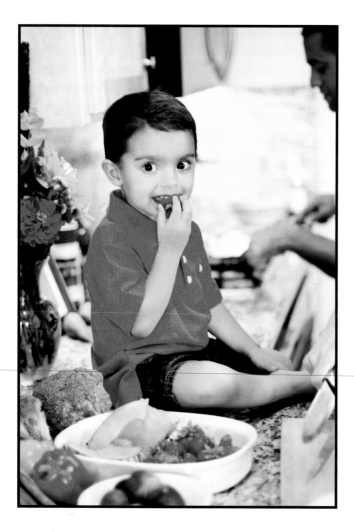

Supplements:
For detailed supplement recommendations, read Robb Wolf's book, The Paleo Solution, or visit his blog and search for "supplements." In the meantime, think about getting more sun or taking a vitamin D supplement along with some extra magnesium and fish oils.

Wrap Up

To wrap up getting started, remember that small changes make the big changes more manageable. If you falter, don't throw in the towel. Instead, dust yourself off and keep on going. We are all human, after all, and this should work with your life, not against it. Always be prepared, shop smart, and plan ahead. By now you should have your fridge stocked with plenty of lean meat options, eggs, loads of veggies, and fruit. Your pantry should hold cans of coconut milk, tons of spices, olive oil, and coconut oil. By now you should have rid your house of everything that is not paleo. Remember, what you do not have, you cannot eat. Do not for a minute think that having junk food around is manageable, because, especially in those first thirty days, it's just plain mean to do that to yourself. Here are a few more tips for being successful during the most important meal of the day; breakfast.

Breakfast tips for success:
Plan, plan, plan ahead—there are no excuses when you are prepared! Here is a list of breakfast items you should always have on hand for when there is no time for cooking and no leftovers:

- 1 dozen hard-boiled omega-3-enriched eggs
- Frozen blueberries.
- Sliced raw almonds.

In a pinch you can grab a couple of hard-boiled eggs, toss some blueberries and a small handful of sliced almonds in a Tupperware, and breakfast is served and portable. Kids love the blueberries still a bit frozen; it's like having a dessert in the morning.

to dehydration, and having a bit of sea salt in their diet can help prevent this.

Alcohol:
Some folks do like to live it up now and then, and alcohol is often involved in these merrier moments. I do not recommend making a nightly booze fest part of your routine, but if you are going to drink now and then, here are some guidelines. Stick to drinks that are not mixed with sugary cocktail concoctions or soda. Have a glass of wine with dinner or a shot of vodka over ice, mixed with soda water and plenty of fresh-squeezed lime. Of course, there is always the infamous NorCal Margarita, created by Robb Wolf, which contains two shots of good tequila poured over ice followed by the juice from 1 whole lime and a splash of soda water. If you are going to drink, use your head, keep the alcohol intake at a minimum, try to avoid drinking right before you go to bed, as alcohol intake tends to disturb your sleep, and stay away from the sweet stuff!

The Mental Mind Game of Managing Change and Tossing the Family on Board!

Before we dive into getting the family on board, let's talk a bit about managing all of these changes. After all, you must change your own thinking patterns, habits, and choices before trying to influence change in those around you. I know, change can be absolutely terrifying. Change is something in life that we often have no control over, and yet the things we *can* control often come around to bite us in the behind, or make our behinds bigger and very unhealthy. If you get what I am saying, you realize that food is one of those things in life that we *do* have control over. This fact can be pretty darn comforting in a crazy world in which we have no earthly idea what the heck might happen next. Will we still have our job tomorrow? Will our relationships stay stable? Will my kids stay out of trouble? Will you still love me if . . . ? Will the sky fall if I *decide* to make a change?

Although having control over what we eat might feel good, along with having that control comes re-

sponsibility and accountability. We often eat to comfort ourselves, to celebrate, to ditch boredom, and to mask our emotions. If eating has become more habitual and therapeutic than life sustaining, you will need to refocus on what continually feels good, which, over all else, is the wonderful feeling of being healthy. Yes, the initial feeling of comfort that we receive from eating a doughnut is pretty delightful, but the long-lasting effects of self-medicating with food is debilitating and depressing, and it will eventually kill you. Remember, if you feel better physically, guess what—you will feel better mentally—and what might have begun as a scary and somewhat difficult change will catapult you into a whole new existence.

Living a life of health makes everything else so much more manageable, and being healthy can really, honestly, not kidding bring happiness and contentment in other areas of your life as well! You have the power to break a vicious cycle; you simply have to be ready, stay focused, and make the decision to change.

Look into the future for just a minute and imagine how it would feel to wake up in the morning with energy. You throw on your jeans, and dang they fit so nicely. You eat breakfast and feel a sense of confidence that the morning is conquerable. You do not need to take pills for what ails you; you simply grab your paleo lunch and head out the door. Tough stuff comes up, but you are physically in check, balanced, clear headed, awake, and able to make sense of all the madness.

Eating paleo does not erase the hard times, the stress, or the difficulties, but it will give you a chance to have the physical and mental capacity to better cope with what obstacles might be in your way. Remember, only *you* are able to control what you eat, and I urge you to take control and stay committed to your choice to change.

You must tell yourself and believe that eating paleo is not a "diet" that you might "fail" at, but rather a way of life that will keep you healthy and alive a lot longer than your previous way of eating. Keeping this thought in the forefront of your head will help you when you want to dive into a bowl of cereal-topped ice cream cake. If I offered you a pill and told you it would comfort you for a moment but most likely kill you thirty years down the road in a most uncomfortable fashion, would you take it? I sure do hope not.

I have tons of compassion for those struggling to make the transition to a healthier way of living, but I also feel strongly that our easy-to-access, whatever-we-want lifestyles have brought some of us to a place where we do not want anything to be hard unless it *has* to be. The reality check is: In order to get results, look better, feel better, and live better, it takes hard work.

Paleo Kids

Ok, now let's move on to the kiddos! The most frequent question I get is how to bring the family on board, especially children. The majority of parents appear to be faced with "picky" eaters. Either their children simply won't sit down and eat, or if they do eat, it's a lot of one thing, and that one thing is not what the parent wants them to eat.

Does the following scenario sound familiar? Mealtime is upon you and you feel as if you are preparing for battle. Instead of joy, family bonding, and happy conversation, dinner is torturous, twisted, and a time to be dreaded, knowing that you will have to beg and plead with your little ones to eat even one bite

of protein, much less anything that looks like a vegetable. OK, so maybe that description is a little over the top and some folks land somewhere in the middle, but either way, introducing paleo does not have to be another battle. In fact, switching the family to a paleo lifestyle should be the end of any previous food wars, and your food life will eventually become incredibly easier to manage.

Before I unveil the secrets to paleo kid success, let's talk about why kids and paleo are important. The health and longevity of your children depend on your decision to feed them a paleo diet. The above statement is not meant to make you feel guilty or wrong, it's purely factual. According to the Centers for Disease Control and Prevention, the rate of childhood-onset type 2 diabetes has increased at an alarming rate over the last two decades. Type 2 diabetes was originally called "adult-onset diabetes" because it was typically only diagnosed in adults over the age of forty. Today, one in three children are at risk of developing this devastating condition. Furthermore, if you have not noticed with your own eyes, childhood obesity has been on an overwhelming climb over the last twenty years (seeing any correlation yet between the high-carb/low-fat trend and the certain near-future death of our youth?). With childhood obesity, besides upping the risk for type 2 diabetes, our kids are also facing a much higher likelihood of suffering from lots of other illnesses early on in life, such as heart disease, stroke, cancer, and depression. In fact, we are looking at a generation of children in which a large majority might die due to obesity-related diseases even before we do! What happened to worrying about our kids' first kiss, whether or not they make good grades, or how late they stay out with their friends?

The statistics are frightening, but this happens to be our current reality, so let's get started together on getting the kids on track.

Your first concern might be that by switching your children to a paleo diet, they risk the chance of missing out on all the essential nutrients necessary to support a developing body, brain, and immune system. The truth is, with a paleo diet, a child is actually *more* likely to obtain, absorb, and utilize all the necessary macronutrients essential to health and longevity. By eating paleo foods—remember, the foods our bodies are meant to run on—you and your child will be consuming more nutrient-dense foods than before, and no matter how you look at it, foods that are more nutrient rich always win.

If one were to compare a standard American meal to a paleo meal, the paleo meal will prove to be more nutritious. And by removing gut-irritating, inflammation-causing grains, legumes, and dairy products from your child's meals, you will enable your child to adequately digest and use the nutrients consumed through the optimal paleo diet.

As important as it is to understand why your child should eat paleo, it is just as important to understand how their little minds work so that switching over to the paleo diet is a successful venture. Please understand that kids live for attention. Getting attention, either in a positive or negative manner, is why kids wake up in the morning and why they refuse to go to bed at night. This is totally normal, and how we manage their needs for attention will determine whether or not change, whatever it might be, will result in monumental tantrums or a rewarding journey together.

When transitioning your family to paleo eating, this is the first fact that I suggest you keep in mind: The more attention you give to the reality that you are changing what you all are eating, the more resistant your kids will be to your efforts. Just as I suggested in the first chapter, you must also make the "fun kid food" and the processed and grain-based foods disappear. Do not make the disappearance of these foods a production. When the kids are sleeping or away at school is the optimal time to remove these food items from the home. Tossing out the fruit loops in front of the brood could cause an instant uprising, but if these choices disappear without commotion, it will not be as noticeable or disturbing to the little ones.

Introducing Paleo to the Kids

Everyone is typically hungry at breakfast, so this should be the first paleo meal you introduce to the family. Put the food on the table and do *not* make a fuss about how "different" the food is. Make it appear as your normal routine because it will become your normal routine. Kids always do so much better when there is some sort of routine.

Serve up healthy plates to your little ones, and then sit down and eat with them without mentioning or suggesting that anything is different. When you serve the healthy paleo breakfast for the first time, and do not have the non-paleo alternative, most kids will not freak out. This is especially true when you focus on having fun, eating, and socializing, rather than what is missing. After all, most kids really like scrambled eggs, bacon, and fruit. If they do not, that will be OK,

too—we'll work around it. Just remember to be patient. If your child only eats the bacon and the fruit or only the eggs, consider your first paleo breakfast a success and move on. Do not force your child to eat everything. He or she will not starve or suffer from eating an "incomplete" meal.

If you have a kid who does freak out, don't freak out too—this is the reinforcement (the attention) they are looking for, and the tantrums will continue. Some children will miss the toast and jelly or cereal right away, even if they are used to eating protein at breakfast, but giving in or arguing will only prolong the successful transition. Instead, calmly and cheerfully say, "This is all we have!" However, for this to work, you must not have an unhealthy option available. With no cereal in the cupboards or waffles in the freezer, your child will realize that there is no point trying to convince you to serve something you don't have.

Please rest assured that if your child opts to not eat, he or she will not stave. I have had parents tell me otherwise, but after some prying, I typically find out that they tried for one day and ended up giving in and pulling out the hidden pop-tarts. Trust me, your child will not be forever damaged if he or she skips a day of breakfast. If you reinforce your child's behavior by giving tons of attention to it, they will not give up the fight, but if you do not reinforce the behavior, your child will get distracted with something else, be hungry, and at some point eat what you put in front of him or her.

Another important thing to remember: paleo food does not have to "look" like breakfast, lunch, and dinner. My middle child, Jaden, is not a huge fan of eggs in the morning. When he gets tired of eggs, I'll let him choose what he'll have for breakfast for the next few days. Often he'll choose "Karina's Yam Hash," or sometimes he'll opt for chicken sausage and a coconut milk smoothie, or even leftovers from the night before. Giving your child the power to choose is golden, and if you only have paleo options to choose from, you both win!

Another example of switching up mealtime habits would be breakfast for dinner. My oldest son loves to make breakfast for dinner, and when he's in charge of cooking the evening meal, we'll often eat scrumptious omelets before bedtime. The point is if you and your family are eating some protein, veggies, and healthy fat, you are getting the job done. Be creative and not so stringent with how each meal should "look." If eggs are not the protein source in the morning, that is perfectly fine—this is your chance to get creative!

The most important point to remember when transitioning the kids is that food can still be fun, even without the cartoon character boxes. The best way to get your kids excited about the new foods you are offering is to involve them in the process. Kids love to cook, and I urge you to try to make meal prep a family affair. Give each child an important job in the kitchen and talk about what you are making together. Have your children retrieve the required ingredients from the refrigerator or pantry and talk about what you are using. If you are using a vegetable they have never seen before, explore it together. Let them wash the vegetable, touch it, smell it, and break off a piece. Tell them how it grows, how it's harvested, and ask them to describe to you what it smells like and what it reminds them of. Make it a process, an experiment, and an exciting adventure. Allow your children to choose a vegetable or protein source to try at mealtime and decide together how you will prepare it. Do not be afraid of making a mess. Spills can be cleaned, and getting the little ones in the kitchen will be the first step in nurturing and developing their lifelong positive relationship with food. If your children are allowed to be with you at the counter, stirring, tasting, pouring, and creating, they are so much more likely to eat the food they had a hand in making.

Praise your kids for their efforts and make a big deal about how great it tastes because they helped! Remember that attention thing? Giving your kids positive attention and recognition for their efforts in the kitchen is like giving the little ones a magical "I will eat anything you want me to" pill! Another tip is to let your child name the dish you created together, or you can give the dish a name you know your kids will flip over. My kids love Sonic characters, and there is nothing better than Sonic Powered Soup. Of course having the kids help with every meal is not possible, but even getting them involved in some way can be helpful in egging on the excitement at mealtime.

Other suggestions for making mealtime fun include having your kids make placemats that they are responsible for putting on the table before you eat and having them pick out new lunch boxes and special containers to pack paleo lunches in. I have several blog posts talking about certain lunch boxes that are environmentally friendly and fun. Show your kids pictures in this book and on the computer of paleo meals, and let them pick out a meal or two that they want you to make during the week. When they do not like something, just say, "OK," and let them eat more of whatever else is on the menu. You'll find yourself less upset about little Johnnie only eating steak and sweet potatoes but no Brussels sprouts than little Johnnie only eating toast and butter and nothing else at all. If you only have good choices and your kid picks one or two of those good choices, so be it. Look back over your child's week of eating rather than each meal, and you'll be surprised how "balanced" they actually eat when their only options are paleo options.

If your kids are old enough to understand, and most kids *are* old enough to understand, if they ask why you no longer have their favorite non-paleo foods, be honest. Let them know that you are making better food choices for the entire family because you want to do all you can to ensure that your kids are healthy and not faced with scary illnesses later on in life, or even in their upcoming teenage years. More and more children are either obese or have other frightening health problems before they are old enough to drive a car. Something is very wrong with the foods that we are feeding our children, and realizing that we have the power to keep our children safe from the scary statistics should be exciting and relieving. You are in control of the foods that enter your home, and you have the power to let your kids know that you want them to eat the kinds of foods that our bodies are supposed to have.

With that being said, I also firmly believe that you should not use scare tactics to get your kids to eat paleo. Talk honestly and openly about eating healthy foods, but do not threaten your kids with certain death or tell them that they might get fat if they eat less than perfect paleo foods. Eating healthy and controlling what you let into your home does not lead to emotional issues with food. What leads to emotional issues are life circumstances, abuse, and parents modeling unhealthy relationships with food.

Personally, I firmly believe that you should let your kids make their own food choices when faced with social settings such as parties and visiting friends' houses. When your children visit someone else's home, unless they have a life-threatening or severe food allergy, let them eat what they want to. Soon you will see your children naturally making better food choices, even when unhealthy options are available. Why? Because they will notice that they feel better when eating paleo.

My oldest is very sensitive to dairy and grains, and although he will still sometimes choose to eat non-paleo foods when he is away from home, he always comes home to tell me he regretted his decision because inevitably the rest of his day is spent in the bathroom. Currently, he plans on opening a paleo restaurant, and his little brother is begging to be his assistant. I do not doubt it will happen—kids are smarter than we will ever be, and if we are honest, caring, and compassionate, as well as firm and patient, our kids will figure out just as we have that eating paleo and feeling good is the best choice for their little bodies.

Paleo Babies and Toddlers

I often have people ask me about feeding babies and toddlers. How do we get the little ones to eat a balanced paleo meal? The truth is, feeding babies and toddlers is kind of like trying to pin down and feed wild monkeys. Let's first look at babies. If you are exclusively breast-feeding an infant, you are already giving the little one the most important nutrients that he needs. Introducing solid foods to a breast-fed baby should happen when the baby is old enough to sit up on his own and begins to show an interest in food. At this point, eating solids is more about the experience than about eating a well-balanced meal. Remember, your little one is still getting everything he needs from you. The solid food is an introduction to what will sustain him after he is weaned. Sometimes situations arise in which breast-feeding is impossible, but nevertheless, the same rules apply. Introduce solids when baby shows signs that he or she is ready, and rest assured that you are doing the very best that you can for your baby.

Babies do not need rice or barley cereal to thrive. Start your little one with paleo foods that can be easily mashed: yams, bananas, all veggies that can be cooked soft enough, and, my personal favorite, avocado, which seems to have been designed for babies to eat. The best plan is to introduce a variety of veggies, fruits, and proteins when your child appears to be interested, but do not worry about "balanced" meals until your child is no longer relying on breast milk or formula for the majority of his nutritional needs. Remember to avoid introducing eggs, seafood, and nuts until after your little one is twelve months of age in order to avoid introducing possible allergens.

Once babies reach toddlerhood, they will rely mainly on solid foods for their source of fuel. Feed them everything that you feed yourself, but realize that they might have other ideas as far as how much and when they should be eating. I believe in the importance of a family sitting together at the table to eat, but your toddler might be ready for dinner at 4 PM rather than 6:30, and that's OK too. Often toddlers will eat sporadically, and sometimes only choose one thing on his plate. Sometimes a day of eating for the average twelve- to fourteen-month-old will look like this:

Breakfast: Scrambled eggs

Morning Snack: Coconut milk smoothie

Lunch: Turkey chunks and pears

Afternoon Snack: Lots of steamed broccoli and avocado dip

Dinner: Salmon and a fistful of yams

Bedtime Snack: Carrots and almond butter.

If you look back over the entire day of snacks and meals, what's listed is a pretty balanced day of eating. Even though the little one did not have all three macronutrients at every meal, the toddler is still getting what he or she needs, so relax a little. You're offering healthy foods, and at some point your little bugger will get bigger and begin to behave more human and less like a monkey.

Paleo in School

Having a good handle on feeding your little ones at home is a huge accomplishment, but what about the school lunch dilemma? Making a turkey sandwich and throwing in a bag of chips is so easy, but remember, we decided earlier on that a little hard work goes a long way, so again, being prepared is essential to overcoming the school lunch dilemma. Thinking differently about meals is of upmost importance in paleo success. What we assume a child's lunch should look like (sandwiches, burgers, or hot dogs, chips, cookies, and juice) is just that, an assumption. I suggest thinking outside the lunch box and getting a bit more creative and, in time, you'll find that making a paleo school lunch is not as hard or time consuming as you might think.

My seven-year-old has two common requests for his lunch, the first one being chicken salad, grapes, and cashews, and the second being turkey wraps. The turkey wraps are pieces of turkey that I wrap around thinly sliced carrots or a small handful of shredded cabbage or broccoli slaw. These school lunches are just as fast and easy as a sandwich, and if you add in nuts, dried fruit, or sliced apples, you have a perfect paleo, kid-friendly lunch in minutes. Some schools have a no-nut policy, and in this case, shredded coconut flakes or coconut milk smoothies are good fat alternatives, as are avocado slices and guacamole. Also, please remember, if your child does not have every macronutrient at lunch, they will be OK. Look back over your child's day of eating rather than fretting over every meal. To make things a bit easier in the school lunch department, after the thirty-day family meal plan, I offer two weeks' worth of school lunch ideas.

My oldest son, who is in high school, will often pack leftovers in a Tupperware for his lunch, just like his dad, and they will pack their food together in the morning, which is a great routine and brings them together for some conversation and early morning camaraderie. Looking at lunch differently is the first step to overcoming the school lunch dilemma, as well as educating your child about the foods that they are avoiding by eating a homemade paleo lunch.

Congratulations, you did it—you and the kids are getting healthier and it looks like smooth sailing. But what about the significant other?

The Paleo Relationship

Sometimes when one person in a relationship makes a radical change, that person's partner is either totally on board or incredibly resistant. If your partner is incredibly resistant, the issues probably run deeper than what's for dinner. The least that anyone should ask for in any type of relationship is support and acceptance. Furthermore, if *you* nag, complain, whine, yell, and scream at your noncompliant mate, I can guarantee that your lifelong love will never even attempt to eat paleo with you. On the other hand, if you focus on taking care of your own needs while being totally sweet and loving to your noncompliant significant other, I guarantee at some point your partner will show some interest in what you are doing.

As you continue to focus on your health, first you are going to feel better, and then you are going to look better, and next you are going to have a whole new lease on life. As you change any negative behavior patterns associated with health, fitness, and food, you are bound to change negative behavior patterns in other areas of your life as well. In fact, you have to make these changes in order to be successful on the road to health. If you give into negativity in your relationships at home, work, and with friends, it's sure to be a slippery slope back to a negative relationship with your own health.

With children, often the best way to convince them to do as you wish is to lead by example, and I suggest you do the same with a significant other who is not on board with your new path to health. Trying to force change on your significant other is like beating your head against a wall. When you are amazing, people start to notice—when you nag, you will only be met with resistance.

Another suggestion for dealing with a noncompliant mate is to empower them with the opportunity to take care of their own needs as you take care of yours. How can someone argue with you if you do not put up a fight? If your partner does not like what you are making in the kitchen, calmly suggest that they make their own portion of the meal that they believe is missing. Make it a partnership rather than a battlefield.

If you do not have the support of your life partner when you make a choice that is best for your longevity and wellness, please realize that you can only change your own behavior and feelings about the situation. You have no control over changing your significant other. Realizing this can be incredibly empowering and powerful in a relationship. By focusing more on changing who you are rather than changing those around you, you will have a greater impact on others than you realize. After all, people notice when you stop noticing, and this is often the best way to garner the interest of those resistant to change. When you give your significant other a chance to make the decision to change on his or her own, you often see great results.

If you are in a relationship in which your partner *is* on board, now is the time to have fun together. Besides eating paleo together, I also suggest exercising together. Even if schedules are conflicting during the week, the entire family, kids included, can come together to exercise, meal plan, and cook on the weekends. When you start to make healthy living your priority, it becomes a lifestyle rather than a chore and, before you know it, you will be planning weekend trips to farmers markets followed by family outings in the park.

Accomplishing health and wellness as a family is very gratifying and will bring your family closer together. The positive energy that comes from teamwork will help keep everyone on track and eager to explore a new and better way of living. To help you down this road, we'll look at working out as a family in the fitness section later in the book.

Sleep, Stress,
and How to Not Be a Mess

We women, especially moms, tend to take care of everyone except for one very important person—ourselves! The feminist movement did wonderful things for women's rights, and thank goodness for what we women are able to freely accomplish!

Women are amazing, powerful, beautiful creatures. As women continue to fight, we continue to succeed. But we also continue to burn the hell out of ourselves until nothing is left but a shriveled up heap at the end of the day—too tired to laugh, too tired to love, too tired to eat healthy and exercise.

I firmly believe that the time has come for another women's movement, because the sad, cold truth is that we cannot do it all, nor are we intended to. Women and men alike are not naturally programmed to work their tails off all day, only to wake up and do it all over again. We are genetically programmed to work hard, sleep a lot, eat good food, and relax with those that we love. We are programmed to nurture ourselves with positive influences such as nature, good conversation, and satisfying sex. Instead, we often tend to prioritize our lives with everything and everyone on the top of our list besides ourselves, and this leaves us with little energy to truly and honestly give of ourselves.

If we begin to pay attention to our own needs, we will feel fulfilled enough to truly enjoy giving of ourselves to others. We will be more productive at work, nicer to our children, and more satisfied with our love lives. Instead of these items feeling like chores that have to be completed, they will begin to feel like what makes our life worth living. If our glass is constantly running dry, how can we fill up the lives of those around us without feeling bitter, used up, and unappreciated? Along with eating paleo, I suggest that you begin to reprioritize your life, starting with getting enough sleep.

Sleep

What is enough sleep? Most folks need to sleep eight to nine hours every single night, and your sleep should be quality sleep, not simply time spent in bed. Lack of sleep is scientifically proven to cause or contribute to all major and minor health problems, and although it might feel as if there is not enough time in the day, forgoing sleep to tackle what has to be done is counterproductive to success. When you are no longer sleep deprived, your mental clarity and energy will make up for what appeared to be "lost time."

Before you begin reprioritizing, the first question you should ask yourself is why? Why are you burning your candle at both ends? What is the importance of working yourself into a frazzled mess? Are you happy with your lifestyle? Are you feeling cared for and nurtured as much as you feel like you are caring for and nurturing the rest of the world?

If you are in tears by now because you know I am talking to you, I suggest it's time to make a few changes. Start out small. Start by simply putting down whatever you are working on and going to bed. If falling asleep is an issue, think back on your day. What did you eat? Did you exercise? How much caffeine did you drink? Most people do not sleep well at night because of poor nutrition, too much caffeine, and lack of exercise. The truth is, if you are eating a paleo diet and exercising, you will begin to find it much easier to drift into a blissful slumber at night.

Most people feel as if they can "get by" on a minimal amount of sleep, but the truth is, we can actually go longer without food than we can go without sleep. If that did not ring loud and clear in your sleep deprived head, I'll say it louder. You can go a month without eating and survive—if you do not sleep for a week, you'll be *dead*!

Think about all your sleep-deprived nights, add those lost hours of sleep together, and please feel afraid enough to take this section seriously. Studies show that especially for women, lack of sleep contributes to illness and mental imbalance. This is not a great combination, especially when dealing with itty-bitty kids, careers, dogs, laundry, dishes, grocery shopping, exercising, living, laughing, and love making. If you are trying to maintain a paleo lifestyle and yet you ignore your need for sleep, the hormones that regulate appetite control are severely affected. As a result, things like sugar and caffeine cravings become more difficult to curb, making your judgment and decision making hazy, which is just another roadblock to keeping yourself on track.

Lack of sleep also contributes to depression, mood disorders, and anxiety. Well, duh! If you are unable to concentrate, keep falling asleep in your afternoon cup of coffee, find it hard to keep up with life, and fall off the paleo wagon over and over again because you feel as if you need that afternoon sugar pick-me-up, depression pretty much seems like a guarantee! Wouldn't you rather tackle your daily list well rested in the morning, feel satisfied at the end of your day with what you *have* accomplished, crawl into bed at night with still enough energy left to tangle under the sheets with your honey, and know that the pile of bills or unwashed dishes will still be there in the morning?

When I ignore my need for rest, my sanity and health suffer tremendously. As a result, those who rely on my well-being suffer right along with me. It took me too many years of learning the hard way, but now I get it. Many a night I have flopped into bed wishing I could do more, but now I know that doing more means nothing when I am a burnt-out, frazzled mess.

Another contributing factor to lack of sleep is letting light into your room. Sleeping in a darkened room helps your body to produce melatonin, and if there is any light source intruding into your cave at night, whether natural or artificial, it can mess with your ability to make melatonin. As a result, it is more difficult for you to fall asleep, stay asleep, and get the restful sleep you need. Lack of sleep makes your body produce more of the stress hormone called cortisol, and increased levels of cortisol can do all sorts of unpleasant and frustrating things to your body, such as making it impossible to lose that last bit of belly fat, no matter how well you eat or how much exercise you do.

Do you need a bigger reason to run down to the nearest big box store and buy some black out shades? OK, I'll give you one. New research is also indicating that lack of sleep can increase the chance of women developing cancer. So please, black out those windows, cover up your alarm clock with a towel, chuck the night-light, and crawl into bed.

For those of you with kids sleeping down the hall that might need mommy or daddy in the night, keep a flashlight on your nightstand so that you don't fall over the heap of laundry in the middle of your bedroom floor. There is no reason to keep the lights burning at night, and your kids will also sleep better in a darkened room, too. If they want a nightlight to go to sleep, simply unplug it once they are snoring.

The moral of the story is that we all need adequate sleep at night, even when we feel as if we cannot go to bed without finishing that one last project. The truth is, you better go to bed because in no uncertain terms, lack of sleep in one way or another will most certainly kill you, and in that case you will no longer have to worry about those unfinished projects. The folks who live by the mantra "I'll sleep when I'm dead" are actually on a faster road to that goal than they would probably like to admit. For more information on the importance of sleep, I suggest you pick up and read a copy of *Lights Out: Sleep, Sugar, and Survival* by T. S. Wiley.

Stress

Now what about stress? I am not asking you to eliminate stress from your life because that is simply an impossible request. Life *is* stress, good and bad. Stress is what motivates us into action, and without stress we would shrivel up and die. But guess what—just like

everything else health related it seems, with too much of it we shrivel up and die; and fast.

Too much or unmanaged stress, like lack of sleep, is medically proven to do all sorts of wonky stuff to your body. Unbelievable as it might seem, solving your lack of sleep might be all you need in order to bring your stress down to a normal level. If you are sleeping well, eating right, exercising, and still feeling like you want to kick the dog, burn the Dr. Suess books, and have your hubby's name permanently embroidered on the couch as his final resting place, then maybe what's left to change is your *attitude!* Yes, I'm calling you out on your own choice to be miserable.

This book is about eating paleo, but it's also about adopting a lifestyle that is reminiscent of days past. Days when life was a tad simpler. Days when the bills got paid, the dishes got done, and you still had time to play with the kids. Why are things so different now?

We only have ourselves to blame, and like being able to make choices about what we eat, we can also make choices about how we feel and behave. Feelings don't just happen to us, but rather are a state of mind we choose to be in. Situations happen to us and we can choose how we want to deal with them and feel about them. If you are dead-set on being pissed off about life, then you will be. If you are willing to be the one to always see the silver lining, you can be. I suggest that everyone try being that positive "ray of sunshine" person for a few days and simply see what happens.

I am in no way implying that life is a bed of roses, because believe me, I know that it's not. But if you are willing to create your own bed of roses, if you are grateful for the positive things in your life, if you take five minutes a day to appreciate nature (I know I'm sounding really "out there," but just listen!), you will start to see everything in a different light. For example, you can choose to let the dude that cut you off make you so angry that you punch your steering wheel and scream and yell as you feel your blood pressure rise and that weird vein in your neck pop out; or you can choose to smile and wave at him without a care in the world and save your adrenaline rush for the gym.

The Worry

Well, what about those what ifs and the maybes and the many I don't knows? Trust me, I get it. I used to be the biggest worrier on planet Earth. I worried about my health, I worried about my kids' health, I worried about not being able to pay the bills, I worried about the bump on my nose, I worried about not being able to see improvements every time I went to the gym, I worried until I worried myself sick, and then I realized that I have nothing to prove. I am who I am. I have my health, I work hard, and I have great kids. I have a lot of other crazy poop in my life that could make me crazy, but I have decided not to let this stuff take me down the flusher, and this allows me the freedom to cope. We can worry ourselves into a hole or we can do all we can to be healthy and take life one day at a time, knowing that everything else will simply be and we can handle what comes our way because we are healthy, positive, and prepared.

Please, take time to have more fun. When was the last time you were just totally silly? Next time you are rushing around the kitchen, trying to make dinner with crying, hungry, need-a-bath kids racing and fighting around you, instead of trying to fight off screaming, start singing and dancing along to the goofiest kids song that you know. Just belt it out at the top of your lungs. Shake your hips, wave your arms around, and before you know it, your kids will be falling over themselves, laughing and joining in. Dinner will get done, and you will feel alive. Stop taking yourself so seriously and you will start to enjoy yourself by just being you.

Often in life we lose track of what we enjoy because we are too busy simply making life work. Stop reading for a minute or two and sit with this thought. What do you love to do? Shopping online or watching Life & Style are not options. Maybe you need to think back five, ten, or fifteen years to a different time in your life. What used to make you excited to get out of bed in the morning? Whatever comes to mind first, make a date with *you* to do that thing. Maybe it's hiking, knitting, getting lost in a novel, volunteering for your favorite charity, or acting in a play. Whatever that thing might be, try to recapture what used to motivate you. This is not a senseless or time-sucking endeavor. It's a step back to what I was talking about earlier in this chapter, a step back to simpler times, back to when the days did not pass us by with little time left to live, laugh, and love.

We have all become exceptionally efficient schedulers with our handheld gadgets, so use it and schedule in one day, afternoon, or evening a week to do something that really fulfills you. Even if you think it might be silly. After a couple of weeks of your new routine, you will wonder how you ever did without. To top it off, your loved ones will love you more for taking the time to care for yourself.

Next step: do not feel guilty! You will ruin your moment by coming home and apologizing for spending time on yourself. So, my secret to successfully de-stressing is the same as my secret to maintaining a healthy lifestyle—make the choice to do it! We can choose to always wallow in the challenges that life throws at us or we can embrace life's challenges, grateful for all of the good in life that we do have. Bad stuff happens, every day, all of the time, but managing your health first is the most important factor in surviving the bad and coming through it thriving!

Kitchen Essentials
and a Paleo Survival Guide

For lots of folks in the twenty-first century, cooking simply does not happen. Reality check time: you have to cook in order to eat paleo. Cooking does not mean hours upon hours in the kitchen. It means being prepared, planning ahead, staying committed, and, most importantly, having fun. Successful cooking also means having a well-stocked kitchen equipped with the essentials for making fast, easy, and delicious paleo meals. In table C I have included a list of the items you will need to run a well-equipped paleo kitchen.

Once your groceries are bought and your kitchen essentials are on hand, it is time to closely examine what it means to "plan ahead and be prepared." Most of the recipes in this book are designed so that you can make plenty and save for later. For example, slow cookers can usually prepare a large amount of food, so when you see a recipe that is made in a slow cooker, plan to make enough for several meals. Leftovers are lifesavers because they can seriously cut down on the time you spend in the kitchen.

When eating paleo, one must think outside the lunch box. For example, breakfast does not always have to look like breakfast. Oftentimes the easiest breakfast is leftovers from dinner! On the flip side, dinner can just as easily be breakfast. Omelets in the evening taste just as good as they do in the morning, and they are fast, nutritious, and can be made 10 million different ways.

The point is, do not be afraid of breaking the traditional rules. I have heard time and again, "Sarah, I don't know what else to do for lunch but to eat a sandwich!" The truth is, you *do* know. Planning ahead and being prepared is part of holding yourself accountable. Almost every day my husband and I eat leftover dinner for lunch, and I cannot express to you how much time, money, and stress this one simple trick can save you. Most importantly, having those leftovers handy leaves you with zero excuses to eat something unhealthy.

YOUR PALEO SURVIVAL GUIDE BEGINS NOW

Being prepared and planning ahead also pertains to when you leave your home. Every modern-day hunter and gatherer must have a survival kit handy at all times. Our days are crazy and often take unexpected twists and turns, especially when children are involved, and if you have a car full of hungry, cranky children and a hungry, cranky parent in charge, disaster is sure to strike.

The first item in your survival kit should be an emergency stash of food that you either carry with you or in your vehicle at all times. There are several paleo food items that travel well, and making your own paleo version of trail mix is a must. Here is how to do it:

1. Fill a large portable container with 3 cups of raw almonds, shelled pistachios, cashews, and pecans.
2. Add in ½ cup of unsweetened dried cherries, blueberries, or cranberries, and top it all off with 4 cups of gluten-free beef jerky cut into bite-size pieces.

You can portion out the mix into smaller portable containers that fit easily into a purse, backpack, or briefcase, and you should always keep one large container of this mix in your car. When hunger strikes the on-the-go family, there will always be a snack on hand.

The next part of your kit should include other kid- and parent-friendly items. Keep apples, oranges, mandarins, and packages of beef jerky in your car for after-school snacks. Kids are always *starving* when you pick them up, and offering something immediately will help you avoid the habitual drive-through. Other kid-friendly on-the-go snack options include baby carrots, celery sticks, and almond butter. For toddlers, steam a pound of baby carrots on the weekend and have these ready to go in the fridge, along with thinly sliced and peeled apples, mandarin slices, hard-boiled eggs, and small pieces of cooked turkey or chicken.

Table C: Paleo Kitchen Essentials

Slow Cooker—A slow cooker is essential. There is nothing better than taking a few extra minutes in the morning to throw in some protein, veggies, and spices into your slow cooker only to come home to a house filled with delicious smells and dinner ready and waiting. The slow cooker is a must have!

Pressure Cooker—A pressure cooker is another paleo kitchen essential. The pressure cooker allows you to cook food that otherwise takes a long time to prepare in mere minutes. An entire winter squash takes 1 hour in the oven but in the pressure cooker, your side dish will be done in 8 minutes. You can make savory soups and stews in 20 minutes, artichokes in 5, and pork chops in 10.

Food Processor—The food processor allows you freedom and variety, and it's fast! Many of my recipes call for this handy tool and you'll love the freshness of homemade sauces, soups, and dips as well as quickly slicing, dicing, and shredding veggies for different paleo concoctions.

Large Soup Pot—Soups and stews are great paleo staples and although the slow cooker and pressure cooker are great, sometimes there is nothing better than the long slow simmer of a soup pot.

Large Skillet—A must have for your fast meat and veggie stir-fry's!

Small Sauce Pan—Great for everything from poached eggs to my paleo Béarnaise!

Chef's Knife and Paring Knife— You must slice and dice to survive.

Mandolin Slicer—This tool offers a unique way of thinly slicing veggies, which is a great way to replace the pasta!

If you have these items prepared ahead of time, you can easily grab-and-go, leaving no excuses for unhealthy, sugar-laden, gluten-filled, prepackaged baby snacks. Most diaper bags come equipped with a smaller tote to keep milk and formula cold. Use this for your baby's snacks as well, and always have a few ice packs on hand in the freezer to toss in with your snacks. Again, it's all about planning ahead, and although it might sound daunting, in reality the little bit of extra time is worth happy and healthy children.

The key to fast snacking success it to not be empty handed. However, if you do find yourself in a pinch, a fast trip into a grocery store for prepackaged sliced fruit, nitrate-free deli meat (now carried by most major grocery stores), and nuts or coconut flakes will avert the hunger crisis.

SURVIVAL GUIDE: EATING OUT

Feeling prepared brings on a sense of well-being, calm, and self-assuredness, but the truth is, we are often faced with situations in which social pressure is involved, and this often leads to second-guessing and uncertainty. The next part of the "survival guide" is to know what to do when you have to eat food that you cannot prepare yourself.

Let's use eating out as our first example. We all enjoy eating at restaurants with friends and family, so avoiding this scenario altogether is not possible or fun. Once you are eating paleo, looking at a menu can be a daunting task, but again this is when those behavioral changes that you made earlier in the book come into play. You have choices, an entire menu full of them, and you can either ask for what you need or give in and give up.

Almost every restaurant has protein and vegetables in some form, as well as olive oil and lemon wedges for salad dressings. If you are eating at a standard American food establishment, one can typically ask for the grilled chicken with a side of vegetables and hold the potato or the rice. Do not be afraid to make it very clear that you cannot eat anything that contains gluten.

As soon as you sit down, ask the waiter or waitress to not bring the bread (unless, of course, people with you want the bread. In such a case, ignore the bread when it arrives!). If you order a salad, ask to leave off the croutons and cheese, and ask for olive oil and lemon or vinegar on the side. Another option is to order a hamburger without the bun and a side salad. Just make sure you trust the quality of the meat and ask if they mix any fillers like bread crumbs in the patties.

Another great restaurant option for eating out paleo style is Mexican food. I suggest ordering fajitas, which typically include grilled chicken, beef, or shrimp with grilled vegetables. Order this meal without the rice, beans, and tortillas, and instead order a side of guacamole or avocado. Succulently seasoned meat, veggies, and guacamole, topped with some salsa, can be a paleo meal that one only dreams of!

Thai food can also be a wonderful paleo choice. Stick to curries, which are typically made with coconut milk and spices, rather than soy-based sauces, and ask for additional vegetables instead of rice.

Looking a bit farther than what's on the menu in front of you is the best way to navigate the undeniable fact that you will be eating at restaurants now and then. Do not be afraid to ask for what you want, as most establishments are happy to oblige with substitutions.

SURVIVAL GUIDE: PEER PRESSURE

Your paleo survival guide also includes how to manage friends who simply do not understand why you are eating paleo and enjoy giving you a hard time about it. My favorite is when I hear, "Sarah, you're already skinny, why don't you just eat the bread?" Education is the best weapon, but if *you* do not understand why you are eating paleo, you will find it extremely difficult to explain your choices. With that said, in the beginning I would focus on what you are doing for yourself and not worry about what everyone else might be thinking. To be perfectly blunt, we typically imagine that people think or talk a great deal more about us than they actually do. Most people are more worried about what *we* are thinking, talking, or feeling about *them* than they do about us. Second, as you start to look, feel, and perform better, people will notice these positive changes before they notice that you no longer have a turkey sandwich for lunch.

If people do ask questions, simply say you are taking better care of yourself. If you find yourself in a situation in which friends or family members are seriously concerned about the missing grains on your plate, inform these folks about the paleo diet as best you can. Explain that by eating paleo you are hoping to make a positive life change. However, avoid calling it a diet because most folks will not take you seriously if they think you are simply trying this month's latest fad.

If someone really gives you a hard time about not eating grains, and yes some people do, instead of getting into a senseless argument, present this person with a challenge. Ask him or her to try eating paleo for thirty days. If the person does not feel, look, or perform better, promise that you will go back to eating a standard American diet. Third, recommend that people do their own research rather than harp on you for answers. Suggest to your friends the books that you have read, e-mail them links to your favorite and most informative paleo blogs, and introduce them to articles that have supportive research on the benefits of paleo eating. The simple truth is that by eating meats, vegetables, and healthy fats, you are actually getting more nutrients than you ever could from a diet filled with whole grains. Education is your best argument, and suggesting that people find out for themselves leaves you more time to focus on the most important thing, *your* good health and well-being. Last but not least, if you have a person in your life that is extremely adamant, rude, and unsupportive of your endeavor to improve your health, maybe this is the time to reconsider the importance of maintaining your relationship with this person.

SURVIVAL GUIDE: CHEATING

Now that I have hammered home the importance of sticking to your guns and making the best choices for yourself in all possible situations, I must answer the one question that you are probably still pondering. Can I *ever* cheat?

The answer to "cheating" is yes, but I once again want you to reframe your way of thinking. If you think of it as cheating, you are more likely to also experience all those awful feelings associated with the word "cheating." When I think about cheating, I think about betrayal or letting someone down, and when it comes to food and cheating, you are letting yourself down. Start by looking at eating paleo as the ability to eat whatever you want to. For example, you eat this way because you *want* to eat meat, vegetables, a little bit of fruit, and good fats. You want to eat these things because they make you feel good, and I will bet at this point, you honestly love how real food tastes. I personally do not want to eat anything with gluten in it because I know what gluten does to our bodies and I know how awful I feel after eating it.

So here's my personal approach to the matter: I love corn chips, I love enchiladas dripping with cheese, and I really love chocolate ice cream, and every now and then I eat those things because I *want* to, not because I am "cheating." I make the conscious decision to do so, but I do not want to eat these things all the time, because I know better. I like how my jeans fit and know the health repercussions associated with gorging on an entire tub of ice cream and a week's worth of cheese-smothered corn tortillas. If I find myself on a Friday night sharing a margarita with my man along with a plate of nachos, I simply wake up the next morning and move on rather than wallow in a "cheating" pool of nacho misery.

I advise that once you are eating paleo to make the conscious decision to not eat anything containing gluten. I also advice that you eat strict paleo for the first thirty days of your paleo journey in order to reset your body and give yourself a chance to acclimate to your new lifestyle. As outlined earlier in the book, when you eat gluten, it's like having to start the intestinal healing process all over again. Some folks can eat gluten now and then and feel OK—but this does not mean that the damage has not been done. Most people find that after the initial thirty days of eating strict paleo, if they eat something with gluten, they really pay for it. Most folks end up spending a lot of time in the bathroom the next day and usually have a distended and uncomfortable tummy soon after consuming the gluten-containing food product. This experience is usually enough to deter most people from ever wanting to eat it again, and the damage that these foods can do to your body is not worth the moment, especially when there are so many other options available.

So eat wisely, eat well, and eat what you want to, but remember—what you want to eat directly correlates with how you want to look, feel, and perform, so if your "I want to eat nachos" choices start happening more often than not, it's probably time to reevaluate your decision making.

Well, you are now equipped to embark on your paleo journey to true health and wellness. I will continue to support you and answer your questions via my blog (www.everydaypaleo.com). Please remember that you are never alone on your journey. You are powerful, beautiful, and strong, and you are *worth* the hard work it takes to be healthy. You can do this! And, as always, enjoy!

NOTE: Immediately following the recipe section you will find a thirty-day family meal plan, including weekly shopping lists correlating with the meal plan and two weeks' worth of kids' school lunch ideas.

Recipes

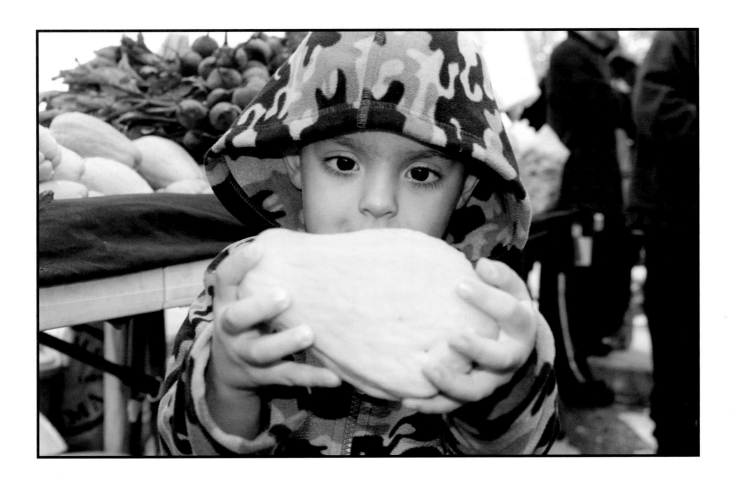

Welcome to the recipe section of Everyday Paleo. To make things easier while reading the ingredients lists, I will explain a few expectations for each of my recipes here rather than cluttering up each page with repetitive details.

1. Please try as best you can to always use organic fruits and vegetables, free-range poultry, pastured lamb and hogs, grass-fed beef, wild-caught seafood, and omega-3-enriched eggs (even better if you can find eggs from a local farm that come from free-range chickens that are not fed soy products!).

2. The few canned items I use include tomatoes, (diced or paste), diced green chilies, and coconut milk. For the

tomatoes and chilies, try to purchase organic with nothing added, just the tomatoes. Trader Joe's carries both canned tomatoes and chilies that are organic and with nothing else added. I have also seen organic canned tomatoes at major grocery stores. There are two brands of canned coconut milk that I suggest: Chao Koh and Mae Ploy. Both are sold in major grocery stores or can be ordered on Amazon. Make sure when using canned coconut milk that you use the full-fat variety.

Do not be discouraged if you find it impossible to always eat organic or free-range. You are still doing what's best for your body by avoiding grains and other processed foods. Be especially careful of meat that is labeled "organic." This usually means that the animals were fed grain. It was most likely organically grown grain, but grain nonetheless, which gives the meat a higher omega-6 ratio. Finding grass-fed is possible, it just takes a bit of detective work. To help you with your detective work visit eatwild.com to find grass-fed meat, and visit localharvest.org to find local farm-share cooperatives. If you aren't able to make use of these resources, do what you can with what is available in your area. In the end, meat—even grain fed—is better than a box of mac and cheese. Just try to buy meat from trusted locations such as Trader Joe's or a local butcher, as these places can usually tell you how the meat was processed. And when it comes to fruits and veggies, stick with what is in season and looks freshest in your grocery store.

It is important to note that a few of the ingredients that you find in some of my recipes are optional, such as sea salt and butter. If you have any sort of autoimmune issues, you would be better off avoiding all dairy and butter and substituting with coconut oil. If you do not want to use sea salt, simply omit it from the recipe.

Also, feel free to be creative with my recipes! Use different vegetables or meat options to make each recipe a "new" one. The beauty of eating paleo is that there are millions of options, and eating should never be boring, dull, or tasteless. Sometimes removing one spice or adding another makes an entirely new and impressive meal!

My serving sizes will reflect how many typical adults the dish will serve. With many recipes, there will be enough for a family of five, sometimes with leftovers. I'll make suggestions on the recipes I feel you should double.

Finally, you may be wondering why I do not include nutritional information for each recipe, such as calories, fat content, carb breakdown, and grams of protein. I left this out for a significant reason. Eating paleo should not be difficult, and it has nothing to do with counting calories or freaking out over fat content. Most of us are programmed to think that fat is bad and that an abundance of carbs is good, and I want to deprogram you from this way of thinking. If every recipe glared at you with numbers, calories, and ratios, you might sink back into the insanity that most "fad" diets offer.

The key to success when eating paleo is to eat a variety of vegetables and protein with every meal, throw in some good fat, and call it a day! Adding the stress of calorie counting conflicts with the paleo mindset. After all, overeating on meat and vegetables is difficult; it's when we add in the grains and sugars to our diet that we are triggered to eat more and more and more. Eating paleo resets our hormones that control satiety, and we learn to stop when we are full. In addition to this, we stay full longer because our insulin levels begin to regulate. Gone are the days of 100-calorie packs, or starving at dinner because you binged at lunch. Now, go have fun, explore, experiment, get the kids involved, and, as always, enjoy!

Poultry

everyday paleo

Pecan-Crusted Chicken

This recipe was inspired, as many of my recipes often are, by what I had left in my fridge and cabinet. I took a look around one evening, did not find a whole lot to choose from, put together what I had handy, and came up with Pecan-Crusted Chicken. It's a reminder that as long as you have some protein, fat, and spices in your kitchen, and get a bit creative, you can always make a tasty meal. This recipe is now one of our family's favorites, and we are never disappointed with the results!

- ½ cup spicy brown mustard
- 2 tablespoons raw organic honey (optional)
- 1 cup pecans, crushed
- 4 boneless, skinless chicken breasts

Prep Time: 10 minutes
Cook Time: 45 minutes
Serves: 4–5

1. Preheat oven to 350°F. In a medium-sized mixing bowl, whisk together the mustard and honey.
2. Toss the pecans in a food processor and pulse until the nuts are finely chopped. Pour the chopped pecans into a large bowl and set aside.
3. Using a paper towel, remove any excess moisture from the outside of the chicken breasts.
4. Taking one chicken breast at a time, roll the chicken in the mustard-honey mixture and coat on both sides.
5. Transfer the coated chicken into the chopped pecans and again cover both sides.
6. Place the crusted chicken into a greased glass baking dish and sprinkle each chicken breast with just a little sea salt if desired. Bake 45 minutes or until the chicken juices run clear.

everyday paleo

Spice Rub Slow-Cooked Chicken

I love this chicken for how versatile it can be! You can eat this meal just as it is, or you can use the meat for lettuce wraps or for filling up a Portobello Mushroom Sandwich (recipe in the snack section). Before eating the chicken, make sure to top each serving with the onions and juices from the bottom of the slow cooker. Note: for those of you with babies and toddlers, meat cooked in a slow cooker is perfect for little ones because of how tender and easy it is to chew.

◇◇◇

- 1 white onion, sliced
- 1 teaspoon sea salt
- 2 teaspoons paprika
- 1 teaspoon cayenne pepper
- 1 teaspoon white pepper or finely ground black pepper
- 1 teaspoon poultry seasoning
- 1 teaspoon garlic powder
- 5- to 6-pound free-range organic chicken, rinsed, and patted dry with paper towels

Prep Time: 10 minutes

Cook Time: 5–6 hours

Serves: 5–6

◇◇◇

1. Cover the bottom of a slow cooker with the sliced onions.
2. Mix all spices in a small bowl and using your hands, rub the spice mixture all over the whole chicken.
3. Place the spiced chicken on top of the onions in the slow cooker, cover and cook on low for 5 to 6 hours. There is no need to add any liquid to the slow cooker—the chicken will cook in its own juices.

everyday paleo

Rockin' Moroccan Chicken

I used a combination of spices commonly found in Moroccan cooking to add some excitement to our family's chicken stir-fry. The duo of subtle sweetness from the cinnamon and just a touch of spice from the cumin, paired with the bite from the green olives, makes this dish pop! This is a good recipe to make a double batch of to ensure leftovers are handy to bring along for lunch the next day.

- 4 tablespoons coconut oil
- 4 boneless, skinless chicken breasts, cut into bite-size pieces
- 2 cups broccoli, chopped
- 2 cups carrots, diced
- 1 tablespoon cinnamon
- 2 teaspoons ground cumin
- 1 teaspoon dried ground ginger
- Small pinch of cayenne pepper
- Black pepper to taste
- ½ cup pimento-stuffed green olives, sliced
- ¼ cup raisins (optional)
- ¼ cup chicken broth

Prep Time: 10 minutes
Cook Time: 15–20 minutes
Serves: 4–5

1. Cover the bottom of a large skillet with coconut oil. Sauté the chicken until no longer pink in the middle (about 7 minutes).
2. Add the veggies in with the chicken and stir-fry for another 5 minutes or until the broccoli and carrots start to become tender.
3. Add the cinnamon, ginger, cumin, cayenne pepper, and black pepper. Once the chicken and veggies are covered with the spices, add the sliced olives, raisins, and the chicken broth to create a sauce. Stir well and bring to a simmer. Cook another 5–7 minutes stirring often. Serve immediately.

everyday paleo

Ginger Citrus Skillet Chicken

When I created this dish, I was once again determined to change the average chicken stir-fry, and there on my counter sitting next to each other was a beautiful orange and some fresh ginger. That's all I needed for a bit of inspiration to create what is now one my favorite go-to chicken recipes. I hope you enjoy this one as much as we do!

- 4 tablespoons coconut oil
- 2 lbs boneless, skinless chicken thighs, cut into bite-size pieces
- ½ cup cremini mushrooms, sliced
- 1 red bell pepper, thinly sliced
- 4 green onions, diced
- ¼ cup organic, free-range chicken broth
- ½ teaspoon fresh ginger, grated
- Juice from 1 medium orange
- 1 tablespoon dried basil
- ½ jalapeño minced (optional)
- Black pepper to taste
- 1 bunch kale, chopped with tough stems removed
- ¼ cup sliced almonds

Prep Time: 10 minutes
Cook Time: 15 minutes
Serves: 5

1. In a large skillet, heat 2 tablespoons of the coconut oil and sauté the chicken for 5–7 minutes.
2. To the chicken, add the sliced mushrooms, red pepper, and onions, and sauté another 2 minutes.
3. Add the remaining ingredients except for the kale and almonds, stir well, bring to a simmer, and cook for another 2 minutes.
4. Remove all ingredients from the pan and set aside. In the same pan add the remaining 2 tablespoons coconut oil and the kale. Sauté the kale until tender, about 4 minutes.
5. Serve the chicken on top of the kale, and add a sprinkle of the sliced almonds on top.

"Breaded" Baked Chicken

One evening soon after we first started eating paleo, Coby, my oldest son, asked me if he could help to figure out a way to make breaded chicken—so together we did! This dish is an awesome way to get your kids excited about eating paleo. Let them help make this dish and they will be amazed that this crispy, succulent chicken is actually very nutritious! It is important to note that this recipe, as well as several others, requires coconut flour, which can be found at most health food stores. You can also purchase coconut flour by visiting my Amazon store at everydaypaleo.com.

- 3 eggs
- 1 cup almond meal
- 1 cup coconut flour
- 1 tablespoon garlic powder
- Black pepper to taste
- 2 pounds boneless, skinless chicken thighs
- Coconut oil

Prep Time: 10–15 minutes

Cook Time: 45 minutes–1 hour

Serves: 4–5

1. Preheat oven to 350°F. Whisk the eggs in one dish and in a separate dish mix almond meal, coconut flour, garlic powder, and black pepper.

2. Dip chicken pieces one at a time into the egg. Next, roll the chicken in the breading mixture until both sides are covered.

3. Place the chicken in a glass baking dish that has been lightly greased with coconut oil. Bake for 45 minutes to 1 hour or until the chicken juices run clear.

Caraway Chicken with Belgian Endive

One day, I happened to pick up some Belgian endive from Trader Joe's, but I had no idea what to do with it. This recipe is what I came up with, and the end result was terrific! If you cannot find any endive in your area, substituting with cabbage is the next best option and just as tasty.

- 2 pounds boneless chicken thighs
- 2 tablespoons caraway seeds
- 1 teaspoon sea salt (optional)
- Black pepper to taste
- 3 Belgian endives
- 1 apple, cored and sliced
- 8 strips bacon, cooked and diced
- ¼ cup chicken broth

Prep Time: 15 minutes
Cook Time: 6 hours
Serves: 5–6

1. Place chicken thighs in the slow cooker and mix with caraway seeds, salt, and pepper.
2. Slice endives in half lengthwise, remove core, and slice into long strips.
3. Layer sliced endive on top of the chicken thighs, and layer the apple slices on top of the endive.
4. Top the apples with the bacon pieces and pour the bacon grease over the dish along with the chicken broth.
5. Cook on low for 6 hours or until the chicken is tender and falling apart.

Chicken Paleo Piccata

I *love* chicken piccata, but the traditional dish is usually dredged in flour, so I set out to make a paleo version. By simply omitting non-paleo food items from your favorite existing recipes, the dish will in fact become better than the original. Again my dear friends—get creative!

- 4 skinless, boneless chicken breasts
- 2 tablespoons organic butter or ghee
- Sea salt and black pepper to taste
- 3 tablespoons extra-virgin olive oil
- 6 garlic cloves, minced
- 3 green onions, diced
- ¼ cup white wine
- ½ cup chicken stock
- Juice from 1 lemon
- 3 tablespoons capers

Prep time: 10 minutes
Cook time: 12–15 minutes
Serves: 4–5

1. Butterfly the chicken breasts by cutting in half lengthwise.
2. Place the butterflied chicken pieces in between two pieces of parchment paper and with the flat side of a meat mallet, gently pound the chicken until the meat is approximately ¼ inch in thickness.
3. Cut the pounded pieces of chicken in half and set aside.
4. In a large sauté pan heat the 2 tablespoons of butter or ghee over medium-high heat. While your pan is heating, lightly sprinkle both sides of the chicken with the sea salt and black pepper.
5. Place the chicken into the hot skillet and cook on both sides for 3–5 minutes, until the chicken is no longer pink in the middle but still tender.
6. Remove the chicken from the pan and add to the same pan the extra-virgin olive oil, garlic, and onions.
7. Using a wooden spoon, quickly sauté the garlic and onions for 2 minutes, scraping any of the chicken drippings off the bottom of the pan.
8. Add the wine, chicken stock, lemon juice, and capers and bring to a simmer for 3–5 minutes.
9. Pour the sauce over the chicken and serve immediately.

Pollo Con Salsa Roja

My mom used to make the most amazing enchiladas, and you could seriously taste the love she would put into her cooking. My mother's influence made these flavors a staple in our kitchen. This chicken is a go-to meal for our family, and pairing it with my Kids Love Cabbage slaw, which you will find the recipe for in the salad section, gives this dish an extra yummy kick!

- 2 cups carrots, diced
- 7 celery stalks, diced
- 1 yellow onion, sliced
- 4 cloves garlic, minced
- 3 pounds boneless, skinless chicken thighs
- Juice from 1 lemon
- 1 (28-ounce) can El Pato Salsa Para Enchiladas
- 2 avocados, diced
- 1 bunch cilantro, chopped

Prep Time: 15 minutes
Cook Time: 6–8 hours
Serves: 5–6

1. In the bottom of your slow cooker, layer the carrots, celery, and onions, and top with the minced garlic.
2. On top of the veggies add the chicken, squeeze the lemon juice over the chicken, and pour the entire contents of the El Pato sauce on top.
3. Cook on low all day (6–8 hours). Serve in bowls topped with the diced avocado and cilantro.

Asparagus-Stuffed Chicken Breasts

This dish looks like it's hard to make, but it's actually pretty darn easy, and stuffing chicken breasts is such a great way to liven up the typically boring chicken option. I made this recipe after simply looking in the fridge and putting together what I had available. Try this one for yourself and explore other options, such as stuffing a chicken breast with sun-dried tomatoes, spinach, and garlic, or whatever else strikes your fancy!

- 16 asparagus stalks
- 4 boneless skinless chicken breasts, butterflied
- 4 tablespoons grass-fed organic butter (or extra-virgin olive oil)
- 1 cup ham steak, cubed
- Sea salt and black pepper to taste

Prep Time: 15 minutes
Cook Time: 20 minutes
Serves: 4–5

1. Preheat oven to 350°F. Blanch the asparagus for 1 minute in boiling water, remove and set aside.
2. Open up the butterflied chicken breast and place in each breast 1 tablespoon of butter (or extra-virgin olive oil), 4 asparagus stalks, and some of the cubed ham (split the ham evenly between all chicken breasts).
3. Pull the two sides of the chicken breast together to enclose your stuffing and secure with a toothpick.
4. Sprinkle the outside of the chicken breast with sea salt and pepper and place the breasts in a glass baking dish lightly greased with extra-virgin olive oil.
5. Bake for 20 minutes or until chicken is cooked all the way through.

Better Butter Chicken

My son Jaden loves Indian food! At our favorite Indian restaurant here in Chico, California, Jaden will fall over himself to get to their amazing butter chicken. After our last visit to this restaurant, I told Jaden that I would do my best to try and make our own version at home. After a quick Internet search to figure out which spices give a classic butter chicken it's special flavor, I created my own recipe by adding depth to the flavor with coconut milk and serving it over a healthy and delicious bed of greens. Jaden claims that this recipe is the "Better Butter Chicken", hence the name!

- 2½ pounds boneless, skinless chicken thighs
- 3 tablespoons coconut oil
- 1 red onion, diced
- 2 garlic cloves, minced
- ½ teaspoon cardamom powder
- ½ teaspoon coriander powder
- 1 teaspoon fenugreek powder
- 1 teaspoon chili powder
- 1 (6-ounce) can tomato paste
- ½ can coconut milk
- 1 teaspoon sea salt
- 4 tablespoons ghee or organic butter
- 1 pound red chard, chopped with stems removed

Prep Time: 20 minutes
Cook Time: 25 minutes
Serves: 5–6

1. Cut the chicken thighs into bite-size pieces and set aside.
2. In a large skillet or soup pot, heat the coconut oil over medium heat. Add the diced onion and sauté until translucent.
3. Turn the heat down to low. To the onion, add the minced garlic, cardamom, coriander, fenugreek, and chili powder and stir well to make a paste.
4. Add the tomato paste to the onions and spices and stir—this mixture will be very thick.
5. Turn the heat back up to medium and add the coconut milk and salt. Use a whisk to blend the tomato paste mixture and coconut milk together into a thick sauce.
6. Bring the sauce to a simmer and add the chicken. Stir well, turn down to medium low, cover, and cook for approximately 15 minutes or until the chicken is done all the way through—stir occasionally during the cooking process.
7. After the chicken is cooked, add the ghee or butter and mix into the sauce until melted. Serve the chicken over the steamed red chard.

everyday paleo

Beef, Pork, and Lamb

everyday paleo

Puerto Rican Beef

I used classic Puerto Rican spices to jazz up our typical ground beef and veggies. After searching through my cupboard for an interesting spice combination, a new family favorite was born!

- 1 pound ground beef
- ½ each green, red, and yellow bell pepper, sliced
- 1 white onion, sliced
- 3 tablespoons extra-virgin olive oil
- ½ tablespoon ground cumin
- 1 teaspoon ground coriander
- ½ tablespoon turmeric powder
- 1 tablespoon dried oregano
- Pinch of saffron threads (optional)
- Sea salt and black pepper to taste
- 1 bunch kale, chopped
- ½ cup pimento-stuffed green olives
- 3 sweet potatoes
- 1 ripe avocado

Prep Time: 10 minutes

Cook Time: 15 minutes

1. In a large skillet brown the ground beef.
2. Add the bell peppers, onions, and extra-virgin olive oil and sauté until the onions and peppers are tender.
3. Add all of the spices and mix well.
4. Add the kale and green olives; continue cooking, stirring often until the kale is tender (about 4–5 minutes).
5. Serve over mashed sweet potatoes with a side of sliced avocado. To quickly prepare the sweet potatoes, peel and quarter them and cook in a pressure cooker for 12–14 minutes. You can also boil the peeled and quartered potatoes for 20-25 minutes, drain, and mash.

everyday paleo

Easy Steak Skewers

All I have to say about this recipe is that it simply does not get much easier than this. No one is ever disappointed by a quick and delicious meal of grilled meat and veggies. If you plan ahead and have these ingredients always on hand, a hectic evening can become manageable! Serve with a big green salad and dinner is ready!

◇◇◇

- 2½ pounds sirloin steaks cut into 1-inch cubes
- 4 tablespoons extra-virgin olive oil
- 1 tablespoon dried basil
- 1 tablespoon dried oregano
- ½ tablespoon garlic powder
- Cracked black pepper
- ⅛ teaspoon cayenne pepper
- 3 zucchini squash, cut into 1-inch chunks
- 3 cups cremini mushrooms
- 1 red bell pepper, cut into chunks

Prep Time: 10 minutes
Cook Time: 15 minutes

◇◇◇

1. Place the chunks of steak into a large mixing bowl, add the extra-virgin olive oil, and generously sprinkle with the basil, oregano, garlic, and cracked black pepper.
2. Add a pinch or two of cayenne pepper and mix well until all the steak pieces are covered with the spices.
3. Take metal or bamboo skewers and alternate skewering pieces of the meat and veggies.
4. Cook over a medium-high grill for 7–10 minutes, turning often.

everyday paleo

Everyday Meatloaf

I will not lie; as a child I was not a big fan of meatloaf. As a result, I never considered making it as an adult until John suggested I try to come up with a paleo meatloaf. John, having no idea that I had a meatloaf aversion, was unaware of the challenge that he had presented me with. Instead of turning down the idea all together, I considered what I would actually put into a meatloaf to make it taste how I wanted it to, and went ahead and gave it a shot. Again, I'm being honest here—after making my meatloaf and tasting it for the first time, I immediately decided that meatloaf rocks! Another true statement: my kids *beg me* for meatloaf. No joke, it's that good. Paired up with my recipe for Brussels sprouts, found in the vegetable section, and some baked yams, nothing beats this total comfort food.

- 2 pounds ground beef
- 1 cup almond meal
- 2 eggs
- 1 (6-ounce) can tomato paste
- 1 red onion, finely diced
- 3 garlic cloves, minced
- ½ tablespoon sea salt
- ½ cup fresh basil, diced
- 1 teaspoon marjoram
- 2 teaspoons finely ground black pepper

Prep Time: 10 minutes
Cook Time: 1 hour
Serves: 5

1. Preheat oven to 350°F.
2. Mix all ingredients by hand in a large mixing bowl.
3. Place meat mixture into a large, glass baking dish and form into a loaf.
4. Bake for 1 hour or until the meatloaf is no longer pink in the middle.

Italian Rib Eye
with Sun-Dried Tomato Topping

I'm not sure if the steaks or the topping make this recipe so great. Perhaps it's just the fact that it's sinfully easy to make. Either way, the first time I made this, Rowan sat on the counter and ate half of the Sun Dried Tomato Topping with a spoon before John could even get the steaks off the grill! Rowan likes to eat half of his food while helping me prepare our meals and the rest at the dinner table, but at least it's all good food! In a paleo kitchen, one never has to worry about kids "spoiling their appetites."

- 1½ cups extra-virgin olive oil
- Juice from 1 Meyer lemon
- 1 tablespoon dried basil
- 1 tablespoon dried oregano
- Ground black pepper to taste
- Sea salt to taste
- 4 big rib eye steaks

Prep Time: 10 minutes
Cook Time: 10 minutes
Serves: 4–5

1. Mix all marinade ingredients together in a large mixing bowl.
2. Add steaks and mix together with your hands to make sure all the steaks are well coated. Leave in the fridge for at least 45 minutes.
3. For medium-rare, broil or grill the steaks for 7–10 minutes per side, depending on their thickness. For rare, cook for 4–6 minutes each side.

Sun Dried Tomato Topping

- 8½ ounces sun-dried tomatoes
- 1 cup canned artichoke hearts
- ½ cup garlic-stuffed green olives

1. In a food processor combine the sun-dried tomatoes, artichoke hearts, and garlic-stuffed green olives. Pulse until roughly chopped and serve on top of the steaks.

Dry Rub Burgers

My husband makes a mean rib-eye with a similar dry rub; therefore, John was my inspiration for this meal. I wanted those same flavors, but with the ease of making hamburgers, so I mixed up some of the key dry-rub ingredients that I knew he used, threw together some burgers, and what we ended up with was a juicy, but crispy on the outside, subtly spicy, and satisfying burger. Serve on crisp lettuce, with thick tomatoes and onions, and who on earth would ever miss the bun! My kids love to wrap two pieces of lettuce around these burgers so they can pick them up to eat them. Hint—make sure you prepare some Yummy Yam Spears (recipe in Veggie section) to go along with this meal.

- 1½ tablespoons chili powder
- 2½ teaspoons paprika
- 1 teaspoon ground cumin
- ¼ teaspoon cayenne pepper
- ¼ teaspoon ground white pepper
- 2½ pounds ground beef (makes about 7-9 medium-sized burgers)
- Sea salt to taste

Prep Time: 15 minutes
Cook Time: 8–10 minutes
Serves: 6–7

1. Mix all dry rub ingredients together.
2. Form hamburger meat into patties and cover both sides generously with the dry rub.
3. Let the burgers sit in the fridge for about 30 minutes before cooking.
4. Either grill or pan fry about 4 minutes each side for medium, less for rare, more for well (sprinkle on sea salt once the burgers are in the pan or on the grill).

everyday paleo

Sirloin Dijon

When I first made this dish, I told John it was my "wannabe" version of beef Stroganoff. However, it's very far from an actual Stroganoff and, in my not-so-humble opinion, much better. I love beef and kale together, and the tender kale paired with the garlic and beef along with the bite from the mustard is oh-so-good!

◇◇

- 1½ pounds sirloin, thinly sliced
- 3 garlic cloves, crushed
- 2 tablespoons coconut oil
- Sea salt and black pepper to taste
- ½ cup chicken stock
- ½ tablespoon dried thyme
- 1½ tablespoons Dijon mustard
- 4 cups kale, chopped

Prep Time: 10 minutes
Cook Time: 10 minutes
Serves: 4

◇◇

1. Sauté the sirloin and garlic in coconut oil until the sirloin starts to brown. While the sirloin is browning, sprinkle with sea salt and pepper.
2. In a separate bowl, mix together the chicken stock, thyme, and mustard. Pour the mustard mixture over the sirloin and bring to a simmer.
3. Add the kale to the pan and cook, stirring often until the kale is tender (about 2 minutes). Serve immediately.

Spicy Speedy Stuffed Peppers

You really can't go wrong with stuffed bell peppers. During our pre-paleo days, I would make stuffed bell peppers with a beef and rice mixture, and of course top the stuffed bells with a mountain of cheese. Those days are over, but that does not mean that we have to say good-bye to an old family favorite! Adding in more veggies in place of the rice makes these peppers a complete meal all on their own, and my kids love the neat little bell pepper package that dinner arrives in.

- 4 tablespoons extra-virgin olive oil
- 1 yellow onion, finely chopped
- 3 celery stalks, finely chopped
- 3 carrots, finely chopped
- 1½ pounds Italian pork sausage
- 1 pound grass-fed ground beef
- 2 tablespoons dried oregano
- 1 tablespoon garlic powder
- Sea salt, and black pepper to taste
- 1 yellow crookneck squash, finely chopped
- 3 cups fresh basil, chopped
- 1 (14½-ounce) can diced tomatoes
- 5-6 bell peppers
- 1 tablespoon hot sauce (optional)

Prep Time: 15 minutes
Cook Time: 35 minutes
Serves: 5–6

1. Preheat oven to 350°F.

2. Fill a large soup pot with water and bring to a boil.

3. While you are waiting for the water to boil, cover the bottom of another big soup pot with the extra-virgin olive oil and over medium heat sauté the onion, celery, and carrots until the onions become translucent.

4. Crumble in the sausage and ground beef and add the dried seasonings and the hot sauce if desired to the meat before it's entirely cooked.

5. Add the yellow crookneck, basil, and tomatoes, mix well, and let the meat and veggies cook over medium-low heat, stirring occasionally for another 10–15 minutes.

6. In the meantime, remove just the tops of the bell peppers, and rinse well to remove all the seeds.

7. By now your water should be boiling. Place the bell peppers gently into the boiling water and submerge them for 5–6 minutes or until the bell peppers are just a little soft but not falling apart.

8. Pull the bell peppers out of the water with tongs and arrange in a large glass baking dish. Fill each bell pepper with the meat mixture (don't be shy, stuff 'em good!) and bake in your preheated oven for 20 minutes.

Steak Chile Rellenos

Why did I first make these? Easy answer: I love chile rellenos. My mom, being the health nut that she was, did not often indulge in the typically battered, fried, and cheese-filled treat. However, there was one little Mexican restaurant that we would visit now and then where my mom would treat herself to their chile rellenos, and she would always share with me. What I loved most about those rellenos was the green salsa that was served over them. Using that as my inspiration, I created a protein-packed and just as delicious paleo version. I know my mom would be proud.

- 4 large poblano or Anaheim chilies
- 2 tablespoons coconut oil
- ½ red onion, diced
- 1 pound tri-tip, diced into small pieces
- ½ tablespoon ground cumin
- 1 tablespoon dried oregano
- 1 tablespoon chili powder
- Sea salt and black pepper to taste
- 1 red bell pepper, diced
- 1 bunch kale, chopped
- 4 garlic cloves, thinly sliced
- 2 Roma tomatoes, diced
- 1 (4-ounce) can diced green chilies
- 1 cup salsa verde
- ½ cup cilantro, chopped

Prep Time: 20 minutes
Cook Time: 15–20 minutes
Serves: 4

1. Preheat oven to 500°F.
2. On a tinfoil-lined baking sheet, bake the whole chilies for 10 minutes.
3. The chilies will be slightly charred when finished; remove from baking sheet and set aside.
4. In a large skillet, add the coconut oil and heat over medium. Add the onions and sauté for 2 minutes.
5. Add the steak and sauté until the meat starts to brown.
6. Add the spices to the onions and meat and stir well.
7. Add the remaining ingredients, except the salsa and cilantro, and cook until the greens are tender, about another 2 minutes.
8. Remove the meat mixture from the heat and set aside. Using a knife, cut a slit lengthwise down the middle of the chilies. Remove the seeds gently with a spoon and place the chilies into a glass baking dish.
9. Stuff each chili with the meat mixture and bake in a 375°F oven for 15 minutes.
10. Top each chili with some salsa verde and fresh cilantro and serve.

Giant Stuffed Portobellos

Jaden was my inspiration for this meal. He loves mushrooms, and we all love spicy, savory food, so why not pair them together? My little boys love to help scoop the meat mixture into the giant mushroom caps and then watch them bake in the oven as our house fills with a yummy, earthy, spicy smell. Delicious!

<><><><><><><><><><><><><><><><><><><><><><><><><><><><><><><><><><><><><><><>

- 4-6 giant Portobello mushrooms
- ½ green bell pepper, diced
- 1 red onion, diced
- 3 celery stalks, diced
- 6 garlic cloves, minced
- 1 pound spicy Italian pork sausage—casing removed
- 1 pound ground beef
- 1 teaspoon paprika
- ¼ teaspoon cayenne pepper
- 2 tablespoons dried basil
- 1 tablespoon dried tarragon
- Pinch of sea salt
- Black pepper to taste
- 1 egg
- ¼ cup extra-virgin olive oil
- ¼ cup coconut flour

Prep Time: 25–30 minutes
Cook Time: 20 minutes
Serves: 5–6

1. Preheat oven to 400°F.
2. Use a moist paper towel to gently clean the mushroom caps. Gently remove the mushroom stems with a small knife and set the stems aside.
3. Using a spoon, carefully scoop out the gills from the insides of the mushrooms. Rub the outsides of the mushrooms with extra-virgin olive oil and place each cap down into a large glass baking dish.
4. Dice the bell peppers, onions, celery stalks, and mushroom stems, and mince the garlic.
5. In a large soup pot, brown the sausage and ground beef, add the bell peppers, onions, celery, garlic, and mushrooms, and cook until the veggies are tender.
6. Move the meat and veggie mixture from the pot into a food processor and add all of the spices, the egg, extra-virgin olive oil, and the coconut flour. Process until the mixture is finely chopped but not mushy—it should be chopped fine but still chunky.
7. Scoop the mixture evenly into each mushroom cap – make them really full. Spoon any remaining mixture around the mushrooms and cook your stuffed mushrooms in the preheated oven for 20 minutes or until brown and bubbly.

everyday paleo

Garden-Fresh Meatballs

When I first made these meatballs, I was trying to get as many nutrients as I could into one easy-to-eat package. With my kids always on the go, these meatballs are great because they are easily portable and you can eat them with your hands (once they are cool). They're an entire meal in one little meatball!

◇◇

- 2 zucchinis, grated
- 1 yam, grated
- 4 cups fresh whole-leaf spinach
- 12-ounce jar roasted red peppers
- 2 cloves garlic
- 1½ pounds ground turkey
- 1 pound ground beef
- 2 eggs
- ¼ to ⅓ cup almond meal
- Sea salt and cracked black pepper to taste

Prep Time: 20 minutes
Cook Time: 40–45 minutes
Serves: 6–7

◇◇

1. Preheat oven to 375°F.
2. Grate the zucchini and yam and place into a large mixing bowl.
3. In a food processor, finely mince spinach, roasted red peppers, and garlic, and then add this mixture to the grated zucchini and yam.
4. Add the meat and remaining ingredients to the bowl as well and hand-mix all ingredients.
5. Form into meatballs, a little bigger than golf-ball size.
6. Bake in a large glass baking dish, tightly covered with foil, for 40–45 minutes. Makes 20–25 meatballs.

Marvelous Meatballs

There is nothing better than coming home to a house that smells like the best Italian restaurant you have ever been to. Actually, the one thing better than that is coming home to dinner already ready! I love the slow cooker for just that reason. With a little planning ahead and a few extra minutes in the morning, you can rest assured that the entire family will have a healthy and delicious meal waiting for them!

makes 60-70 meatballs

½ recipe—

- 2 pounds ground beef
- 1 pound mild Italian pork sausage
- 3 celery stalks, diced
- 1 white onion, diced
- 2 carrots, diced
- 3 eggs
- ½ cup almond meal
- 2 tablespoons dried oregano
- 1 tablespoon garlic powder
- Pinch of cayenne pepper
- Sea salt and black pepper to taste

Prep Time: 15 minutes

Cook Time: 6–8 hours

Serves: 6

1. Using your hands, mix all ingredients together. Form the mixture into large meatballs (baseball sized) and place them into the bottom of a slow cooker, stacking them if necessary.

The Sauce

- 16-ounce can diced tomatoes
- 1 can tomato paste
- 3 cups fresh basil, chopped
- 5-6 garlic cloves, coarsely chopped
- Sea salt and black pepper to taste

1. Cover the meatballs with the tomato sauce and cook 6–8 hours on low.

Everyday Paleo Spaghetti

Discovering ways to make "old favorites" into a paleo meal is another wonderful way to get the kids involved with meal planning and preparation. Coby, being my oldest, remembers those limitless pasta days, and he really loves spaghetti. Who doesn't? Coby and I had a great time coming up with this recipe, and putting Coby in charge of seasoning always results in deliciousness. As far as the splash of wine for the sauce, I have my big brother Mark to thank for that. My brother shares my love for cooking and the last sauce we made together had that little splash of wine that I swear makes all the difference. Feel free to leave it out, but for me, that bit of love from my awesome big brother is a must for my spaghetti sauce experience.

- 2 pounds ground beef
- ½ red onion
- ½ cup Italian parsley
- 3 tablespoons fresh rosemary
- 3 heirloom tomatoes
- 2 teaspoons sea salt
- ½ tablespoon garlic powder
- 2 tablespoons dried basil
- Pinch of cayenne pepper
- 1 bay leaf
- Splash of red wine
- 5 zucchini squash, sliced lengthwise with a mandolin slicer or 1 spaghetti squash
- 3-4 garlic cloves

Prep Time: 15 minutes
Cook Time: 20 minutes
Serves: 5

1. Brown the meat in a large soup pan.
2. While the meat is browning, combine the onion, parsley, garlic, and rosemary into a food processor. Process on low for about 15 seconds.
3. Add the tomatoes and process again until the tomatoes are broken down but still chunky.
4. Once the meat is cooked through, add all of the dry spices and mix well.
5. Add the tomato sauce from the food processor, the bay leaf, and the red wine, mix well and bring to a simmer. Simmer for 20 minutes.

For the Pasta

1. In a large pot, bring about 10–12 cups of water to a boil. Add the thinly sliced zucchini to the boiling water.
2. Cook for 3 minutes and drain.
3. Serve the spaghetti sauce over the cooked zucchini pasta.

If using a spaghetti squash for the "pasta," cut the squash in half lengthwise, remove the seeds, and cook in pressure cooker for 10–12 minutes. Using a fork, scrape the insides of the squash out of the skin and serve the sauce on top of the squash.

Everyday Paleo Pizza

The best part about this pizza is getting creative with the toppings! The rosemary and garlic in the crust make it really special, and I love the fact that when we eat this pizza, I know my little guys are getting everything they need to keep them going strong, rather than a dose of gluten-filled dough that has zero nutritional value. I always laugh when little Rowan asks for PIZZZZAAAAA—knowing that what he wants is my Everyday Paleo Pizza!

Crust:

- 2 cups almond meal
- 2 eggs
- 3 tablespoons extra-virgin olive oil
- ¼ teaspoon baking soda
- 1 teaspoon garlic powder
- 1½ tablespoons fresh rosemary, finely chopped

Toppings:

- 1 pound mild Italian pork sausage
- 2 crookneck yellow squash, diced
- 3 green onions, chopped
- 1 cup fresh basil leaves, chopped
- 2 small tomatoes, diced
- ½ cup jarred roasted red peppers, diced
- ½ cup sliced black olives
- 1 cup organic, gluten-free marinara sauce

Prep Time: 20 minutes
Cook Time: 45–50 minutes
Serves: 5

1. Preheat oven to 350°F.
2. Using a spoon, mix all crust ingredients together until it becomes very thick. Using your hands, form the dough into a ball.
3. Lightly grease a pizza pan or a cookie sheet with extra-virgin olive oil. Place the ball of dough in the center of your cookie sheet or pizza pan and using your hands, push and pat the dough down into the shape of a circle, making the dough as thin as possible. Your pizza will be about 12 inches across.

4. Bake just the crust in your preheated oven for 20 minutes.

5. While the crust is cooking, prepare your toppings. Brown the sausage in a large skillet and chop all veggies.

6. After the crust is done, remove from the oven and evenly spread the marinara sauce over the crust.

7. Add the sausage and all remaining toppings evenly over the sauce and bake again for an additional 25–30 minutes.

8. Get creative and use whatever toppings you might like—I also suggest trying chicken, artichoke hearts, and broccoli!

Hasta La Vista Pasta Lasagna

My mom again . . . When she wasn't coming up with a new health food to feed us, she would sneak in a few amazing dishes that we all still laugh and talk about. Her lasagna still brings tears to my eyes when I think about sitting on the counter, helping her layer the flavors into her big lasagna pan. I'm so glad my mom always had me with her in the kitchen, so glad that I learned from her that the best place for babies to be is next to you, arms wrapped around tight, plopped on the counter, watching in wonderment while mom makes magic happen in the kitchen! Yes, my life is messier because my kids always have a hand in what's happening in the kitchen, but the memories I have with my own mom, and the memories I am making with my kids by my side, are priceless and will last a lifetime. I love this lasagna because the zucchini stays a bit crunchy during the cooking process. It adds great texture to the dish and helps the lasagna hold together nicely.

- 1 red onion, diced
- 4 cloves garlic, minced
- 2 tablespoons extra-virgin olive oil
- 1 pound ground beef
- 1 pound mild Italian sausage
- 2 tablespoons dried oregano
- ½ cup fresh basil, chopped
- ½ teaspoon cayenne pepper
- ½ teaspoon sea salt
- ½ tablespoon black pepper
- 1 (14½-ounce) can diced tomatoes, juices drained
- 1 (6-ounce) can tomato paste
- 5-6 zucchinis, thinly sliced long way with a mandolin slicer
- 1 cup sliced black olives

Prep Time: 20 minutes

Cook time: 40 minutes

Serves: 6

1. Preheat oven to 350°F.
2. In a large soup pot sauté the onions and garlic in the extra-virgin olive oil for about 3 minutes.
3. Add the ground beef and sausage, and brown.
4. Season the meat mixture with all of the dry ingredients, add the drained diced tomatoes and tomato paste, and mix well.
5. In a 9 x 11 glass baking dish place a layer of sliced zucchini, making sure to overlap the long slices, ladle on a thick layer of the meat mixture, and top with the sliced black olives.
6. Top meat and olive layer with another layer of sliced zucchini, and top with a final layer of the remaining meat mixture. Cover tightly with aluminum foil and bake for 30 minutes. Let the lasagna sit for 10 minutes before slicing and serving.

Grilled Lamb-Burgers

I would highly recommend doubling this recipe. Ground lamb used to scare me because I honestly had no clue what to do with it. After some experimentation, I have come to discover that lamb tastes great with mint, rosemary, garlic, cinnamon, and cumin, and paring some of these spices together, mixing and matching, and again—getting creative—I now *love* ground lamb and its versatility. These little burgers are mind-blowing good!

- 1 pound ground lamb
- ½ cup red onion, minced
- 2 garlic cloves, minced
- 1 teaspoon sea salt
- 1 teaspoon black pepper
- 1 teaspoon ground cumin
- 1 teaspoon paprika
- 2 tablespoons parsley, chopped
- 2 tablespoons fresh mint, chopped
- 1 egg

Prep Time: 10 minutes
Cook Time: 8 minutes
Serves: 2–3

1. In a large bowl, mix all ingredients by hand and form into palm-size patties. Place in refrigerator for 20 minutes.
2. Heat a grill to medium high and grill the lamb-burgers for 4 minutes on each side.

everyday paleo

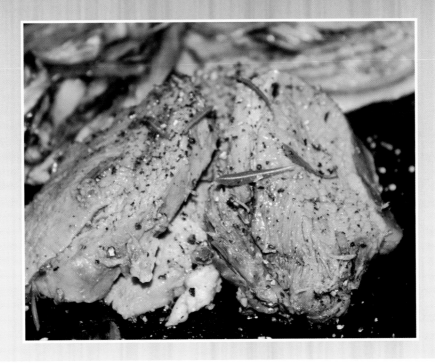

Lamb under Pressure

If time allows, feel free to roast this lamb recipe in the oven. Preheat your oven to 400°F and cook the lamb at this temperature for 20 minutes. Lower the temp to 325°F and roast for an additional 6–10 minutes per pound, so in this case for about another hour. For extra flavor, cut little slits all over the lamb and stuff the slits with whole garlic cloves! I love this lamb served with my Roasted Fennel recipe found in the veggie section.

- ¼ cup extra-virgin olive oil
- 2 tablespoons fresh-squeezed lemon juice
- ½ tablespoon garlic powder
- 1 tablespoon dried oregano
- Sea salt and black pepper to taste
- 4½-pound boneless leg of lamb
- 2 cups chicken stock

Prep Time: 25 minutes

Cook Time: 45 minutes

Serves: 7–8

1. In a small mixing bowl, whisk together the extra-virgin olive oil, lemon juice, and spices.
2. Using your hands, rub the extra-virgin olive oil mixture into the leg of lamb.
3. Place the lamb into a pressure cooker and over medium heat; sear the lamb for 4–5 minutes on each side.
4. Add the chicken stock, lock the lid in place, bring to pressure, and cook for 45–50 minutes.

Karina's Sausage Hash

My dear friend Karina Bangay, an awesome trainer at NorCal Strength and Conditioning, is masterful in the kitchen, and I am so happy that she shared this recipe with us. My family loves this quick and easy meal. I usually scramble or poach up some eggs to go along with it, and everyone is full and happy for the busy morning ahead. This is also a wonderful post-workout meal. Thanks Karina!

- 3 yams
- 1 pound ground pork sausage
- 3 tablespoons coconut oil
- 2 tablespoons cinnamon

Prep Time: 5 minutes

Cook Time: 10 minutes

Serves: 4

1. Grate yams with a cheese grater or in a food processor with the grate blade.
2. In a large skillet brown the sausage.
3. Add the coconut oil and yams, continue cooking for another 7–10 minutes or until the yams are soft.
4. Add the cinnamon, mix well, and serve.

everyday paleo

Pork Tenderloin with Cherry Sauce over Mashed Cauliflower

I love a little bit of sweetness paired with pork, so adding the dried cherries into this dish really gave it flavor. This is a great meal to impress your dinner guests with who might have the misconceived notion that eating paleo is boring and tasteless. Impress them with this one!

- 1 tablespoon extra-virgin olive oil
- 1½-pound pork tenderloin
- Sea salt and pepper to taste
- 1 cup chicken broth
- ¼ cup balsamic vinegar
- 1 cup unsweetened dried cherries
- 1 sprig rosemary
- 1 head cauliflower

Prep Time: 5 minutes
Cook Time: 35 minutes

1. Heat the oil in a large skillet, season pork tenderloin with sea salt and pepper, place in pan, and sear on all sides for about 5–8 minutes or until browned all over.

2. Add the chicken broth, vinegar, dried cherries, and rosemary, and cook for about another 20–25 minutes, turning pork occasionally.

3. Meanwhile, cook the entire head of cauliflower in a pressure cooker for 3 minutes.

4. Remove the cauliflower and mash with a potato masher, cover and set aside.

5. Transfer the pork to a cutting board, cover with tinfoil, and let it rest for 5–7 minutes.

6. Reduce the sauce while stirring for another 3 minutes or so or until it becomes like syrup. Discard the rosemary.

7. Slice the pork tenderloin and serve over the mashed cauliflower, topped with the cherry sauce.

Perfect Pork Pot Roast

This meal is a bit more labor intensive than most of my recipes, but so worth it. I came up with this recipe when my son graduated from eighth grade and we had family over to celebrate. Now I'll make it whenever I find a good pork roast; in fact, there is nothing else I even want to try with a pork roast, this recipe is so good! Serve this with my Fancy Pear Salad found in the salad section!

- 2 tablespoons coconut oil
- Sea salt and crushed black pepper to taste
- 4- to 5-pound pork loin roast
- ¼ cup coconut flour
- 6 carrots
- 5 celery stalks
- 2 leeks
- 2 yellow onions
- 2 cups red wine
- 1½ cups organic free-range chicken broth
- 2 (14-ounce) cans of diced organic salt-free tomatoes
- 6 fresh thyme branches
- 6 garlic cloves
- 4 tablespoons organic butter

Prep Time: 30 minutes
Cook Time: 4–5 hours
Serves: 6-7

1. In a large soup pan or Dutch oven add the coconut oil and heat over medium heat.
2. Sprinkle a bit of the sea salt and the crushed black pepper all over the roast.
3. Roll the seasoned roast in the coconut flour.
4. Sear the roast in the large soup pan for 4 minutes on each side (make sure you get the top and bottom of the roast seared as well).

5. While the roast is searing, chop the veggies into large pieces. When cutting the leeks, make sure to cut them in half lengthwise and rinse well because they are often full of sand and dirt in between the layers.

6. Remove the roast from the pan, add all the veggies, and cook in the drippings from the roast until the onions and leeks become tender.

7. Add the wine, chicken stock, canned tomatoes, thyme branches (tie them together with some cooking twine so they are easier to remove later), and a bit more pepper.

8. With the flat part of your knife blade, crush the whole garlic cloves and toss those in as well. Stir well and bring to a boil.

9. In the meantime, place your roast in a slow cooker. Pour the vegetable mixture over the roast, cook on high for 4 hours, and then on low for 1 hour.

10. After the roast is done, remove the roast from the vegetable mixture.

11. Remove the thyme branches from the vegetable mixture and pour half of the veggie mixture into a food processor or blender, add the butter, and blend until smooth.

12. Place the sliced meat on a large serving platter, top with the remaining cooked veggies, and pour the blended sauce over all of it.

Apple Shallot Pork Chops

I have mentioned in my blog that friends of our family have a pig farm, and they feed their pigs great stuff like apples and veggies. The pork from these pigs is so amazing, beyond words really. Paring apples and shallots with these chops just felt right, and I love the smell of the coconut oil as the chops, smothered in cinnamon, sear in the pan.

- 1 apple
- 2 shallots
- 5 tablespoons coconut oil
- Cinnamon and sea salt
- 4 big pork chops
- ¼ cup white wine
- Slivered toasted almonds

Prep Time: 5 minutes
Cook Time: 16–18 minutes
Serves: 4

1. Slice the apple as thinly as possible and then cut the slices in half.
2. Thinly slice the shallots.
3. In a large skillet, heat 4 tablespoons of the coconut oil over medium heat and add the apples and shallots. Sauté for 5 minutes or until the apples are tender but still a little crisp.
4. Remove the apples and shallots from the pan and add the last tablespoon of coconut oil.
5. Generously sprinkle cinnamon on both sides of the pork chops and lightly sprinkle on sea salt if desired.
6. Rub the cinnamon and salt into the pork chops and place the chops in the hot oiled pan. Sear on each side for 2 minutes.
7. Add wine to skillet and make sure you bring the wine to a boil to cook off the alcohol.
8. After adding the wine, add the apple-shallot mixture back to the pan, cover and cook over medium heat for 6–8 minutes. Depending on the thickness of your pork chops, it might need more or less time.
9. Serve the pork chops with plenty of the apple and shallot mixture, and add a sprinkle of slivered toasted almonds on top.

Seafood

everyday paleo

Collard-Wrapped Tilapia

How do you make fish exciting? There are 10 million ways, so do not get me started, but this recipe is simple, fun, and surprising. It will be a sure way to get your little ones interested in eating seafood.

◇◇◇

- 4 collard green leaves
- 4 tilapia fillets
- Sea salt, paprika and black pepper to taste
- 2 tablespoons coconut oil

Prep Time: 20 minutes
Cook Time: 20 minutes
Serves: 4

◇◇◇

1. Preheat oven to 375°F.
2. Blanch the collard green leaves in boiling water for just a few seconds, remove and lay flat.
3. Cut off the tough end piece of the collard greens and place one tilapia fillet in the center of each collard green, season the fish with the salt, paprika, and pepper, top with ½ tablespoon of coconut oil, and wrap firmly in the collard green.
4. Place all the wrapped fish in a large glass baking dish and bake for 20 minutes. Serve with a lemon wedge.

Spice-It-Up Salmon

This recipe belongs to John. When I first met him, he was living off white rice and burnt chicken (the first meal he ever made me), and I must say I am more than impressed with how his cooking skills have improved over the years, and now I am happy to let the man cook for me. Maybe John will author the next *Everyday Paleo* cookbook from a man's perspective?

- 4 garlic cloves, crushed
- 2 pinches of sea salt
- Ground black pepper to taste
- 1 tablespoon fresh thyme leaves
- ½ teaspoon fresh ginger, grated
- 2 pinches of cayenne pepper
- 2 pinches of cumin
- Extra-virgin olive oil, enough to make a paste
- 2 wild-caught salmon fillets

Prep Time: 10 minutes
Cook Time: 10 minutes
Serves: 2–3

1. Heat your grill to medium.
2. In a small bowl add the crushed garlic cloves and all other spices. Add enough extra-virgin olive oil to make a paste—a couple tablespoons typically.
3. Place the salmon fillets skin down on a large sheet of tin foil. Fold the sides up on the tin foil to make a tin foil "tray."
4. Rub the spice mixture on top of the salmon fillets and place the tin foil tray on the bottom rack of your grill. Cover the salmon loosely with more tin foil and close your grill.
5. This is where you have to be careful because all grills cook differently, and all salmon fillets are different. It will typically take about ten minutes of cooking time. Make sure that the salmon is warm all the way through but still a bit pink in the middle.
6. Serve with lemon wedges.

everyday paleo

Skillet Salmon with Baby Bok Choy

Here's another "what the heck is in my fridge" meal that turned out better than good. I made this for John when he came home for lunch one day, and he stood at the kitchen counter and ate it until it was gone, saying nothing. That's the best compliment I can get! Thanks John for always being my biggest fan.

◇◇

- 1 tablespoon premium fish sauce
- ½ teaspoon chili oil
- 1 tablespoon toasted sesame oil
- 1 tablespoon raw organic honey
- 2 tablespoons chives, chopped
- 2 wild-caught salmon fillets
- 3 baby bok choy, stems removed and washed
- 4 tablespoons cashew halves

Prep Time: 5 minutes
Cook Time: 10–12 minutes
Serves: 2–3

◇◇

1. In a large mixing bowl, whisk together the fish sauce, chili oil, sesame oil, honey, and chives. Cover the salmon fillets with the sauce and set aside.
2. Cut off the ends of the bok choy, leaving some of the stems remaining, wash, and pat dry with paper towels.
3. In a large skillet, cook the salmon fillets along with any remaining sauce for 2 minutes per side. Remove the salmon fillets and set aside.
4. Sauté the bok choy in the same skillet for 3–4 minutes, return the salmon fillets back to the pan, cover and steam for another 2 minutes. Top with a sprinkle of cashew halves and serve immediately.

everyday paleo

Easy Skillet Scallops and Spinach

Scallops are little jewels from the sea, and I am so happy that we have a local butcher that orders these wild-caught goodies for us valley folks to enjoy. Rowan *loves* these scallops and we have to fight him off to get our share. Well, not really, but it's a funny thought! One tip: do not overcook scallops; they can quickly go from a buttery delicacy right into rubber little discs, so do not walk away from the pan while cooking. Trust me; I have learned the hard way.

◇◇

- 3 tablespoons coconut oil
- 1 small shallot, diced
- 2 garlic cloves, minced
- 6 cups whole spinach leaves
- 1 pound wild-caught sea scallops
- Sea salt and black pepper to taste
- Lemon wedges

Prep Time: **5 minutes**
Cook Time: **6 minutes**
Serves: **3–4**

◇◇

1. In a large skillet, add 2 tablespoons of the coconut oil, along with the shallot and garlic, and sauté for 2 minutes.
2. Add the spinach and cook until wilted.
3. Remove the spinach mixture from the pan, add the remaining coconut oil, season the scallops with salt and pepper, and cook the scallops over medium-high heat for 2 minutes on each side.
4. Serve immediately over the spinach. Garnish with lemon wedges.

Seafood "Enchiladas"

I have been longing to create a good paleo enchilada recipe, but could not figure out what to use as a tortilla replacement. I thought about using egg, but I did not want an omelet, I wanted an enchilada. I continued to ponder and asked myself, "Sarah, what do you love the most about enchiladas?" It's the sauce! My dear friend Laura gave me her enchilada sauce recipe, which I modified only slightly, and I decided to make this dish, sans any sort of tortilla. The end result was the enchilada flavor I long for, but with none of the unnecessary and unhealthy tortilla getting in the way.

- 1 medium onion, minced
- 2 tablespoons coconut oil
- 2 cups tomato puree (make your own—
  about 4 large tomatoes pureed in a food
  processor)
- 4 garlic cloves, minced
- 2 tablespoons chili powder
- ½ teaspoon cumin
- ½ teaspoon dried oregano
- ½ teaspoon sea salt
- 1 pound seafood of choice (wild-caught
  cod pieces, tilapia, shrimp, or crab are all
  great options)

Prep Time: 25 minutes
Cook Time: 10–12 minutes
Serves: 3–4

1. Preheat oven to 375°F.
2. Sauté the onions in the coconut oil until limp.
3. Add the tomato puree, garlic, chili powder, cumin, oregano, and salt. Mix well and let simmer for 20 minutes, stirring often.
4. Pour the sauce into a food processor and process until smooth.
5. Cover the bottom of a glass baking dish with the seafood. Pour the enchilada sauce over the seafood, cover tightly with aluminum foil, and bake for 10–12 minutes or until the seafood is cooked.
6. Serve with sliced avocados, lime wedges, and chopped cilantro.

Shrimp Flying Saucers

I had so much fun coming up with this recipe, mainly because of the help I received from little Rowan! He loves shrimp, or "shrimpies" as we call them, and the first time I made this dish, I literally had to race to complete it before Rowan ate all the shrimp!

- 1 pound medium-sized shrimp, cooked and tails removed
- 2 cups purple cabbage, diced
- 1 small cucumber, peeled, and diced
- ½ small red onion, finely diced
- 4 hard-boiled eggs, peeled and diced
- 1 tablespoon dried dill
- 1 teaspoon garlic powder
- 1 tablespoon spicy brown mustard
- 3 tablespoons extra-virgin olive oil
- 2 tablespoons fresh-squeezed lemon juice
- Sea salt and fresh cracked black pepper to taste
- Pinch of cayenne pepper
- 2 large tomatoes—sliced into rounds ¼ inch thick (Heirlooms are best)
- ¼ cup sliced almonds

Prep Time: 15 minutes
Cook time: 3–6 minutes
Serves: 3–4

1. If needed, remove shell, tail, and vein from shrimp. Cook in boiling water for 3–6 minutes. Shrimp will be done when they float to the top of the water and turn pink and white.
2. Drain the shrimp and let cool in the refrigerator.
3. In a large mixing bowl, combine the cabbage, cucumbers, onion, and egg.
4. Cut the cooked and cooled shrimp into halves or thirds, depending on the size of your shrimp, and add to the bowl.
5. Add the dill, garlic, cayenne mustard, extra-virgin olive oil, lemon juice, salt, and pepper and mix well.
6. Serve huge scoops on top of the thick-sliced tomatoes. Top with a sprinkle of sliced almonds.

everyday paleo

Shrimp Loves Coconut

Shrimp really does love coconut, and so do I. The two together are a match made in heaven. I had to experiment with this recipe a couple of times to get it right, and beating the egg whites is essential to get the coconut flakes to stick properly! I'm glad I got this one right, because it's so, so good. I suggest dipping these guys in guacamole!

- ⅓ cup coconut flour
- ½ teaspoon sea salt
- ¼ teaspoon cayenne pepper
- 3 egg whites
- 2 cups unsweetened coconut flakes
- 1 pound large shrimp (tail on), peeled and deveined

Prep Time: 30 minutes
Cook Time: 12–15
Serves: 4

1. Preheat oven to 400°F.
2. In a mixing bowl, stir together the coconut flour, salt, and cayenne pepper.
3. In a separate bowl, beat the egg whites with a whisk until foamy.
4. In another bowl, pour in the coconut flakes. Taking one shrimp at a time, dredge each shrimp in the coconut flour mixture, dip into the egg whites, and then roll into the coconut flakes.
5. Bake on a lightly greased baking sheet for 12–15 minutes or until the shrimp are pink and the coconut flakes start to brown.

everyday paleo

Shrimp Tacos

I appreciate a meal that includes the meat, veggies, and fat all wrapped up together, and this one takes the paleo cake! Succulent, spicy shrimp, sharing a lettuce leaf with crunchy veggies and a lime wedge, is just darn scrumptious. Every time I make these they take me back to the beach in Mexico. . . . Margarita anyone?

◇◇

- 1 pound large shrimp, shells, tails and veins removed
- 2 tablespoons coconut oil
- ½ red onion, sliced
- 3 garlic cloves, minced
- 1 green bell pepper, sliced
- ½ tablespoon chili powder
- ½ cup jarred salsa verde of your choice
- 10-12 large romaine or butter lettuce leaves
- 2 cups cabbage or spinach leaves, diced
- 6 radishes, halved and sliced
- Lime wedges

Prep Time: 20 minutes
Cook Time: 7 minutes
Serves: 3–4

◇◇

1. Cut the shrimp in half and set aside.
2. In a skillet, heat the coconut oil over medium heat and sauté the onions, garlic, and bell peppers until tender—about 4 minutes.
3. Add the shrimp and sauté until the shrimp are pink—about 3 minutes.
4. Add the chili powder and salsa, mix well, and cook just until simmering.
5. Serve in the lettuce leaves with sliced radishes, shredded cabbage or spinach leaves, and lime wedges.

Salmon Cakes with Ginger Mayo

I am especially proud of this recipe. When I first started eating paleo I felt kind of stuck. Every day for lunch I would eat a salad with a can of wild salmon and some olive oil on top, until one day I thought my head was going to pop off. This recipe was my epiphany, and the beginning of being a bit more adventurous in the kitchen. The comments on my blog about this recipe have been phenomenal—these cakes have been touted as the meal that has converted folks to paleo. They have even been called restaurant quality! I am honored and humbled that my little fishy cakes have been given such high honors, and I love watching my kiddos gobble these guys up.

- 3 cans wild-caught Alaskan salmon
- 3 eggs
- 4 green onions, diced
- 1 tablespoon dried dill
- 1 teaspoon fresh ginger, grated
- ¼ teaspoon dried red pepper flakes
- 3 tablespoons fresh-squeezed lemon juice
- ½ teaspoon finely ground black pepper
- Pinch of sea salt
- ¼ cup coconut oil
- 4 cups green and purple cabbage, shredded

Prep Time: 20 minutes
Cook Time: 6 minutes
Serves: 3–4

1. Drain the water from the canned salmon and dump into a large mixing bowl.
2. Add the eggs, green onions, dill, ginger, red pepper flakes, lemon juice, black pepper, and salt. Mix well.
3. In a large skillet, heat the coconut oil over medium to medium-high heat—make sure there is more than enough to cover the bottom of the pan.
4. Form the salmon mixture one at a time into palm-sized patties or "cakes" and place gently into the oil. Fry for 3 minutes on each side. Important—do not mess with the patties once they are in the pan. Let the cakes cook for the full 3 minutes before you attempt to flip them.
5. Serve the patties over a bed of the shredded green and purple cabbage, with a lemon wedge and the ginger mayo.

Ginger Mayo

- 2 eggs
- 2 tablespoons apple cider vinegar
- 1 teaspoon yellow mustard
- 1 teaspoon sea salt
- ¼ teaspoon pepper
- ¼ teaspoon cayenne pepper
- 1 teaspoon fresh grated ginger
- 2 cups extra-virgin olive oil

1. In a blender or food processor place all ingredients except for the oil. Cover and blend on low while you count to five.

2. Continue to blend while you slowly add the extra-virgin olive oil.

3. Once all of the oil is added, continue to blend while you again count to five. Stop the blender or food processor at this point, and ta-da: homemade ginger mayo for your delicious salmon cakes!

everyday paleo

Avocado Tuna Boats

I love avocados and tuna, and the two are obviously a perfect marriage; therefore, coming up with this recipe was almost effortless. Paleo food can be fun for kids and grown-ups alike, and this meal is all about the fun factor!

◇◇

- 1 egg
- 1½ tablespoons apple cider vinegar
- 1 teaspoon yellow mustard
- Pinch of cayenne pepper
- Pinch of sea salt
- 1 cup extra-virgin olive oil
- 3-4 ripe avocados
- 4 cans tuna packed in water
- 3 celery stalks, diced
- 3 green onions, diced
- 2 tablespoons dried dill
- 1 tablespoon garlic powder
- Fresh ground black pepper to taste
- ½ cup cherry tomatoes, halved

Prep Time: 20 minutes

Serves: 5

◇◇

1. In a food processor, blend the egg, vinegar, mustard, cayenne pepper, and sea salt for five seconds.
2. Continue blending and slowly add the extra-virgin olive oil. Once the olive oil is added, continue blending while you again count to five, turn off the blender or food processor, and the mayo is ready.
3. Cut avocados in half lengthwise and remove the stone—leave the peel on.
4. In a large bowl, mix together the tuna, celery, onions, and spices. Add the homemade mayo mixture to the tuna, mix well, scoop onto halved avocados, and top with tomatoes.

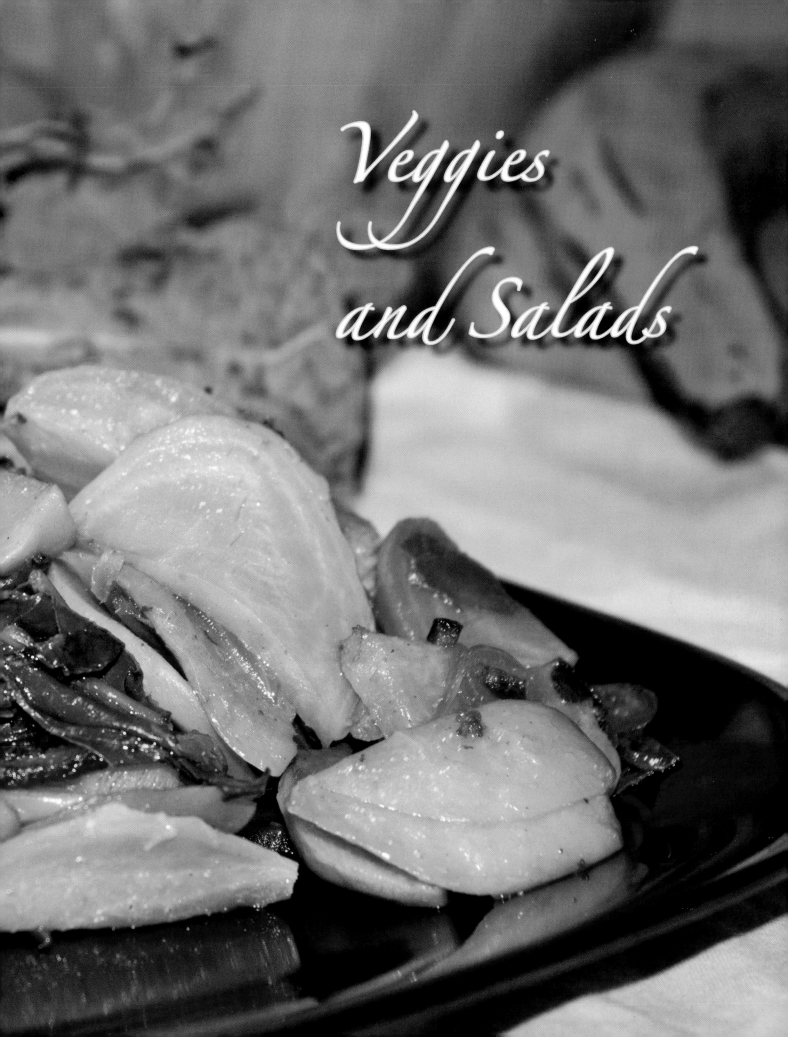

Veggies and Salads

Curried Veggie Hash

The first time I made this hash, I tried to make them into little veggie cakes. To make a long cooking story short, they fell apart and turned into hash, which was really so much easier to begin with and extremely tasty. I love this hash after a workout with whatever leftover protein I have in the fridge, but my favorite way to eat it is with a couple of poached eggs on top.

- 2 sweet potatoes
- 2 zucchini squash
- 2 shallots
- 2 eggs
- ½ teaspoon sea salt (optional)
- 1 tablespoon curry powder
- ½ tablespoon cinnamon
- 5 tablespoons coconut oil

Prep Time: 15 minutes
Cook Time: 10–12 minutes
Serves: 4–5

1. Peel the sweet potatoes and rinse.
2. Using a food processor or a cheese grater, shred the sweet potatoes and the zucchinis.
3. Finely dice the shallots.
4. In a large mixing bowl, combine the shredded potatoes, zucchini, shallots, eggs, and spices.
5. In a large skillet, heat the coconut oil over medium, add the hash, and cook, stirring frequently, until the potatoes are soft and start to crisp up.
6. Serve immediately. This is a great post-workout snack!

Baked Curry Cauliflower

Curry is delicious, and curry and cauliflower are an excellent choice to pair together. Another way to marry these flavors is to steam the cauliflower, mash it, and add the same ingredients that go into this baked curry cauliflower. The mashed version is also amazing. Try serving this curried cauliflower with my "Breaded Baked Chicken" and watch your kiddos eat this stuff like popcorn! (You will too!)

- 4 cups cauliflower florets
- 3 tablespoons coconut oil
- 1 tablespoon curry powder
- 1 teaspoon garlic powder
- ¼ teaspoon turmeric
- Sea salt to taste (optional)

Prep Time: 5 minutes
Cook Time: 40–45 minutes
Serves: 4

1. Preheat oven to 350°F.
2. In a medium-sized mixing bowl toss the cauliflower with the coconut oil until all the florets are coated in the oil.
3. Sprinkle all of the spices over the cauliflower and stir again until all florets are evenly coated.
4. Spread the cauliflower evenly into a glass baking dish and bake for 40–45 minutes, stirring half way through the cooking time.

Ginger Shrimp Salad

I was in the mood for something fresh and different when I made this salad, and that's exactly what I got! The creamy avocado and the bite from the arugula bring this dish together in a way that leaves you wanting more.

◇◇

- 1 pound medium shrimp (tails removed, cooked, and deveined)
- Juice from 1 lemon
- 1 teaspoon fresh ginger, grated
- 2 garlic cloves, minced
- 3 green onions, diced
- 1 teaspoon red pepper flakes
- Pinch of sea salt
- Black pepper to taste
- 4 cups arugula
- 1 avocado, sliced
- Extra-virgin olive oil to taste

Prep Time: 15 minutes

Serves: 3–4

◇◇

1. Remove the shell, tail, and vein from each shrimp and toss into boiling water. Bring the water back to a simmer.
2. Once the shrimp rise to the top, remove them and place in ice water. Then drain and pat dry with paper towels.
3. Toss the cold shrimp with the lemon juice, ginger, garlic, onions, red pepper flakes, and salt.
4. Serve on a bed of arugula garnished with sliced avocado, and top with a drizzle of extra-virgin olive oil.

everyday paleo

Beets, Greens, 'n' Bacon

Beets just might be the perfect root veggie. I'm in love with the beet, and even more in love with beet greens—add some bacon and forget about it. This dish is almost too easy to taste this good, and it goes well with just about any protein that you decide to accompany it with.

⟡⟡

- 4 red or orange beets with beet greens
- 3–4 bacon strips, diced
- ½ red onion, sliced thin
- Black pepper to taste

Prep Time: 15 minutes
Cook Time: 20 minutes
Serves: 4

⟡⟡

1. Cut the greens off of the beets, wash, chop, and set aside (discard the tough end pieces).
2. Wash the beets and cut in half.
3. Cook the beets in a pressure cooker for 20 minutes.
4. Remove the beets from the pressure cooker and let cool for 10 minutes.
5. After the beets are cool, the peels should easily remove from the beets. Remove peels and slice the beets; place them in a mixing bowl and set aside.
6. In a large skillet, cook the diced bacon until brown and crispy.
7. Add the onions and cook for 2 minutes.
8. Add the beet greens to the pan and sauté until the greens become tender, about 3 minutes.
9. Add the cooked greens, bacon, and onion into the bowl of beets, stir well, top with black pepper, and serve.

everyday paleo

Warm Arugula Salad

I did a blog post about my obsession with arugula, and this recipe is what started my love for this awesome ingredient. You can eat arugula raw or cooked, and the smoky, peppery flavor is tantalizing and delicious. After you eat this salad, you might share my obsession.

◇◇

- 7 ounces arugula
- 6 strips bacon, diced
- 2 shallots, finely chopped
- ¼ cup extra-virgin olive oil
- 1 tablespoon balsamic vinegar
- ½ cup walnuts or pecans, chopped
- Ground black pepper to taste

Prep Time: 15 minutes
Serves: 5

◇◇

1. Place the arugula in a large salad bowl and set aside.
2. In a medium-sized skillet brown the diced bacon.
3. Add the shallots and sauté with the bacon until the shallots are translucent.
4. Add the extra-virgin olive oil to the pan and heat just until warm.
5. Pour the oil-bacon-shallot mixture over the arugula, add the balsamic vinegar, and mix well. The heat from the bacon mixture will slightly wilt the arugula—this is what you want!
6. Add some fresh ground black pepper, top with a sprinkle of walnuts or pecans, and serve immediately. You can make this a meal by adding diced cooked chicken breasts.

Carrot and Fennel Salad

I received a bunch of fennel in my CSA box and had no idea what to do with it. Not wanting it to go to waste, I decided to pair it with the bunch of carrots. This fast, fresh, and zingy salad went well with my Perfect Pork Pot Roast recipe.

- 6 carrots, sliced thin lengthwise with a mandoline slicer
- 1 fennel bulb, finely sliced stalks with fronds and stem removed
- ½ red onion, thinly sliced
- 1 orange, cut into segments
- 3 tablespoons extra virgin olive oil
- 2 tablespoons fresh squeezed lemon juice
- 1 teaspoon balsamic vinegar

Prep time: 35 minutes

1. Mix together the carrots, fennel, lemon juice, extra virgin olive oil, and vinegar. Let stand for 20 minutes to soften.
2. Add the onions, orange segments, and black pepper to taste and serve immediately.

everyday paleo

Fancy Pear Salad

The first time I made this salad was for a holiday party at my home. My dad, who is not really particular about food and simply eats what is in front of him without much comment, *raved* about this salad. I was floored. He had prime rib, garlic mashed cauliflower, stuffed mushrooms, and carefully baked asparagus, but what he wanted more of was my easy, yet "fancy," pear salad. I always smile and think of dad when I make this. My dad has always been a source of strength and support, and I'm proud to be his daughter. Thanks dad for loving my salad and for always loving me!

- 5 ounces organic mixed salad greens
- 1 pear, diced
- ½ red onion, thinly sliced
- Extra-virgin olive oil to taste   **Prep Time: 10 minutes**
- 3 tablespoons balsamic vinegar
- ⅓ cup pecans, crushed
- Black pepper to taste

1. Toss the greens, pear, and onion together.
2. Drizzle salad with extra-virgin olive oil, balsamic vinegar, and sprinkle on pecans.
3. Finish with some cracked black pepper.

everyday paleo

Easy Spinach Salad

When in a pinch, you can throw this salad together in minutes, and it's always sure to satisfy. Plus, it has bacon, and I like any excuse to eat bacon.

◇◇

- 6 cups organic spinach
- 4 hard-boiled eggs, diced
- 6 strips cooked bacon, crumbled
- 1 cup cherry tomatoes, halved
- 6 tablespoons extra-virgin olive oil
- Juice from ½ lemon
- Black pepper to taste

Prep Time: 10 minutes

Serves: 2

◇◇

1.   Toss all ingredients together and enjoy!

Wild-Salmon Salad

I mentioned earlier about my boring salmon salad days, but this salmon salad is worth being in this book because boring does not describe how great it tastes. I love roasted red peppers, and adding them in with the salmon really works.

- 4 cups organic mixed salad greens
- 2 cans wild-caught Alaskan salmon
- ⅓ cup roasted red peppers, diced
- 1 avocado, diced
- 4 tablespoons sliced almonds
- 3 tablespoons extra-virgin olive oil
- 1 tablespoon apple cider vinegar
- ½ tablespoon dried dill
- Juice from ½ lemon
- Black pepper to taste

Prep time: 10 minutes
Serves: 2

1. Toss all salad ingredients together, drizzle on oil and vinegar, sprinkle on the dill and pepper, toss together, and serve.

Sun-Dried Tomato Chicken Slaw

This slaw is dedicated to my awesome friend Katie Bug—athlete and trainer extraordinaire at NorCal. She shares my affection for coleslaws, and we both have a dream of collaborating some day on a paleo cookbook that only has coleslaw recipes. I often bring this salad with me to the gym, and I can always count on Katie to share it with me.

- 2 cups cooked chicken breasts, diced
- ½ cup sun-dried tomatoes, julienne-sliced
- ½ apple, diced
- 4 cups green or purple cabbage, shredded
- ¼ cup sliced almonds
- 4 tablespoons extra-virgin olive oil
- 2 tablespoons balsamic vinegar
- 1 tablespoon dried oregano
- Black pepper to taste

Prep Time: 10 minutes

Serves: 2

1. Mix all ingredients together and serve.

Kids Love Cabbage Slaw

My friend America told me about this salad that she makes for her kids and how they can't get enough of it. I added my own twist to her recipe with the mango, and America was right—kids love this cabbage slaw. The first time I made Kids Love Cabbage Slaw, I gave Rowan a bite straight from the mixing bowl, and he looked at me with his big eyes and said, "Can I have the whole thing please?" Enough said. Personally, I love it with lettuce tacos and also with the Pollo Con Salsa Roja.

- 2 cups purple cabbage, diced
- 1 cup cucumber, diced
- 1 shallot, minced
- ½ cup green mango, finely diced
- 1 tablespoon balsamic vinegar
- 2 tablespoons extra-virgin olive oil
- Black pepper to taste

Prep Time: 10 minutes
Serves: 4

1. Combine all ingredients in a medium salad bowl, mix well, and serve!

Yummy Yam Spears

Yams plus coconut oil plus some spices equals Yummy Yam Spears. Eat these with my Dry Rub Burgers!

- 2-3 yams cut into "French Fries" (Trader Joe's carries yam spears already cut in the vegetable section.)
- 3 tablespoons coconut oil
- ½ tablespoon paprika
- ½ tablespoon cinnamon
- ¼ teaspoon cayenne pepper
- Sea salt and black pepper to taste

Prep Time: 15 minutes
Cook Time: 25–30 minutes
Serves: 4

1. Preheat oven to 375°F.
2. In a large bowl, whisk all of the spices together with the oil and then toss the sweet potato spears with the oil mixture until all the spears are coated.
3. Line a cookie sheet with tin foil and evenly spread the potato spears on the foil.
4. Bake for 25–30 minutes, turning the spears over halfway through the cooking time.

Roasted Fennel

After making my carrot and fennel salad, I had these bulbs of fennel and thought, why not roast them? We ended up with a flavor utterly different and delicious. Sweet, buttery, roasted perfection is the only way I can really describe this dish, and served with my Lamb Under Pressure it is terrific!

- 4 fennel bulbs, stalks and fronds removed
- Extra-virgin olive oil
- Sea salt and pepper

Prep Time: 5 minutes
Cook Time: 30 minutes

1. Preheat oven to 400°F.

2. Halve and quarter the fennel bulbs.

3. In a large mixing bowl, toss the fennel with enough extra-virgin olive oil to coat each piece. Season with sea salt and pepper to taste, spread the fennel evenly on a baking sheet and cook for 1 hour, turning over after 30 minutes.

everyday paleo

Southern-Style Greens

I learned from one of my awesome blog readers that in the South, the broth from these greens is called "pot liquor." Better than any liquor experience I've ever had, and no headache or memory loss after eating too much of these yummy greens. We love these collards so much that we'll eat them for breakfast with our eggs!

‹›

- 1 smoked ham hock (1½ pounds), or 1 pound diced bacon
- 1 yellow onion, diced
- 2 tablespoons garlic powder
- 1-2 tablespoons hot sauce
- 2 pounds collard greens

Prep Time: 10 minutes
Cook Time: 1 hour

‹›

1. In a large soup pot add the ham hock, onions, garlic powder, and hot sauce.
2. Wash the collard greens and, using your hands, tear the leaves away from the tough spine of each green.
3. Roughly chop the greens and place in the pot. Add enough water to just cover the greens. Cover and bring to a boil, turn heat down, and simmer, stirring occasionally, for 1 hour.
4. Serve in bowls with bits of ham or bacon and some of the broth.

everyday paleo

Roasted Root Veggies

A beautiful, colorful dish that tastes just as good, if not better, than it looks. Jaden and Rowan like to pick out all the beets—red is Rowan's favorite color, after all.

◇◇◇

- 5 small beets, peeled and quartered
- 2 parsnips, halved and cut into 1-inch pieces
- 2 carrots, cut into 1-inch rounds
- 1 red onion, halved and thickly sliced
- 1 bulb garlic, cloves removed and peeled
- ¼ cup coconut oil
- 1 cup fresh basil, diced
- ½ teaspoon lemon zest (grated lemon peel)
- Sea salt to taste

Prep Time: 15 minutes
Cook Time: 45–50 minutes
Serves: 5

◇◇◇

1. Preheat oven to 400°F.
2. In a large mixing bowl toss all of the vegetables together, including the whole garlic cloves, with the coconut oil, basil, lemon zest, and sea salt.
3. Roast for 45–50 minutes, stirring occasionally during the cooking process.

Stuffed Eggplant

One weekend in late summer, I found myself faced with more eggplant than I knew what to do with. My CSA share included a huge pile of eggplant, and a friend of mine had given me several as well. I decided to stuff an eggplant simply because we all had grown tired of our other eggplant options. We were eating them grilled, in ratatouille and in curry, but I was ready for a change. This dish is what transpired from our overabundance of eggplant!

- 2-3 eggplants
- 5 tablespoons extra-virgin olive oil
- 1 red bell pepper, diced
- 1 small red onion, diced
- 6 garlic cloves, minced
- 1½ cups fresh basil, chopped
- ¾ cup julienned sun-dried tomatoes packed in extra-virgin olive oil
- 2 tablespoons balsamic vinegar
- Sea salt and black pepper to taste

Prep Time: 20 minutes
Cook Time: 40 minutes

1. Preheat oven to 350°F.
2. Remove the green stems from the eggplants and cut in half lengthwise. Using a paring knife, gently cut out the insides of the eggplant and set aside, leaving an eggplant "shell."
3. Drizzle 2 tablespoon of extra-virgin olive oil into the bottom of a 9 x 13 glass baking dish and add the eggplant.
4. Dice the insides of the eggplant that have been removed.
5. In a large skillet, add the five tablespoons of extra-virgin olive oil, diced eggplant, bell peppers, and onions. Sauté over medium heat for 7–10 minutes.
6. Add the minced garlic, basil, sun-dried tomatoes, balsamic vinegar, salt, and pepper. Mix well and cook for another minute.
7. Pile the mixture into the eggplant shells and bake for 30 minutes or until the eggplant shells are tender.

everyday paleo

everyday paleo

Mom's Mashed Yams

Why mom's yams? Because I am the mom, and I make them. If anyone in my house asks for mashed yams, I know they are referring to this specific recipe; therefore, I claim them forever as Mom's Mashed Yams! I like to make extra for post-workout recovery meals, and the kids never get tired of them.

◇◇

- 6 yams
- 4 tablespoons organic butter
- 3 tablespoons cinnamon
- ½ tablespoon nutmeg
- 1 teaspoon ground ginger
- 1 apple, grated

Prep Time: 10 minutes
Cook Time: 12 minutes
Serves: 6–7

◇◇

1. Peel the yams and cut into 2-inch rounds.
2. Cook the yams in a pressure cooker for 12 minutes.
3. Place the cooked yams in a large mixing bowl. Add the butter and spices and mash with a potato masher.
4. Add the grated apple, mix well, and serve with a sprinkle of cinnamon on top.

everyday paleo

Savory Cauliflower Fried Rice

Please use your creativity with this recipe! Switch up the seasoning, and add more veggies or chopped up meat to make it an entire meal. Cauliflower rice is amazingly versatile and really hard to mess up. Try omitting the coconut flour, leaving the cauliflower raw, and chopping it fine before stir-frying. This will create an entirely different flavor and texture to your "rice."

- ½ red onion, minced
- 3 garlic cloves, minced
- 2 tablespoons fresh basil, diced
- 1 head organic cauliflower—stem removed and steamed
- 1 egg
- 2 tablespoons coconut flour
- 1 teaspoon sea salt
- Black pepper to taste
- 3-4 tablespoons coconut oil

Prep Time: 15 minutes
Cook Time: 10 minutes
Serves: 5

1. In a large mixing bowl, add the minced onions, garlic, and basil. Place the steamed cauliflower in the bowl as well, and add the egg, coconut flour, salt, and pepper.
2. Using a potato masher, mash the cauliflower down to the consistency of rice. Mix all of the ingredients well.
3. Heat the coconut oil in a large skillet over medium-high heat. Add the cauliflower rice and sauté for 7–10 minutes or until the onions are tender.

Pureed Turnips

Turnips you ask? Really? Well, I happen to love this unloved root veggie, and somehow pureeing them after they leave the pressure cooker leaves them creamy and as light as air. Who needs mashed potatoes when you can have turnips? I recommend these pureed turnips with a nice steak and a big pile of greens or a salad.

- 4 turnips
- 3 tablespoons organic butter

Prep Time: 5 minutes
Cook Time: 8 minutes
Serves: 3

1. Quarter the turnips and cook in a pressure cooker for 8 minutes.
2. Place the cooked turnips in a food processor along with the butter and puree until smooth and creamy.

everyday paleo

Brussels Sprouts 'n' Bacon

Do not be afraid of the Brussels sprout. Cook them as directed and you will fall in love with the cute little cabbages, I promise! Brussels sprouts have a bad rap because usually they are steamed to oblivion, which makes them very bitter. All they need is a little bit of steam, a friend called bacon, some time spent in the oven, and the Brussels sprout will show you his true and tasty potential.

- 6 bacon strips
- 1 pound Brussels sprouts
- 1 teaspoon garlic powder
- 1 tablespoon dried thyme
- Black pepper to taste

Prep Time: 15 minutes
Cook Time: 30 minutes
Serves: 5

1. Preheat oven to 350°F.
2. Dice bacon and cook in a skillet until crispy.
3. Steam the Brussels sprouts for 4 minutes, cut off stem, and quarter.
4. In a medium-sized mixing bowl, toss the Brussels sprouts with the bacon, bacon grease, garlic powder, thyme, and black pepper. Spread evenly in a glass baking dish and bake at 350°F for 30 minutes. Stir once half way through cooking time.

Soups, Stews,
and Sauces

everyday paleo

Butternut Squash Soup

This is a creamy, easy, and comforting soup. I have always loved butternut squash soup, but adding the coconut milk seemed like a compliment to the lovely winter squash, and indeed it is! Try making it with a touch of curry instead of the nutmeg for an entirely different soup experience!

◇◇

- 1 butternut squash
- 2 garlic cloves
- ½ white onion
- 2 cups gluten-free chicken broth
- 1 cup coconut milk
- ½ teaspoon ground nutmeg
- Black pepper to taste

Prep Time: 20 minutes
Cook Time: 15 minutes
Serves: 5

◇◇

1. Cut butternut squash in half and scoop out seeds. Cook in a pressure cooker for 20 minutes.
2. Scoop the squash out of its skin and into a food processor.
3. Add the garlic and onion into the food processor with the squash and process until completely smooth.
4. Transfer to a large soup pot and add the remaining ingredients. Mix well and bring to a boil over medium-high heat.
5. Turn down to low and let the soup simmer, stirring often for 10–15 minutes.
6. Remove from heat and let sit for 5 minutes before serving.

Seafood "Who Needs Rice" Jambalaya

I like it spicy, and I love seafood, and that is how this recipe came to be. My children devour this recipe every time I make it, and it is one of John's favorites as well. This is another great recipe to get creative with—adding different vegetables or trying it with sausage and chicken instead of seafood are all great options! Find out what your family likes best and make this one of your go-to meals.

- 1 pound wild Alaskan cod fillets (or other wild-caught white fish of your choice)
- 1 pound shrimp, tails and shells removed and deveined
- ¼ cup organic butter
- 4-5 carrots, julienned
- 2 red bell peppers, sliced
- 4 cloves garlic, minced
- 1 leek, diced
- Pinch or two of sea salt
- 1 tablespoon chili powder
- ½ teaspoon paprika
- ½ teaspoon black pepper
- 2 cups chicken broth
- Hot sauce to taste

Prep Time: 25 minutes
Cook Time: 15–20 minutes
Serves: 4

1. Make sure your fish and shrimp are thawed and drained. Pat the fish and shrimp dry with a paper towel; it will have a better texture after cooking if you do this.
2. Cut the fish into bite-size pieces.
3. Melt butter in a large soup pot and sauté carrots for about 4 minutes.
4. Add the bell peppers, leeks, and garlic and cook for another 3–4 minutes.
5. Add all the spices and the chicken broth and bring to a boil.
6. Throw in the fish and shrimp and simmer until the fish begins to flake and the shrimp turn pink and float.
7. Add the hot sauce and stir.
8. Serve in bowls immediately.

recipes

everyday paleo

Thai Shrimp Soup

Our family has a favorite Thai food restaurant that makes the most amazing seafood and coconut milk soup. I knew it would be impossible to duplicate the delicate flavors of my favorite soup, but I wanted to at least get the lemongrass effect! This soup accomplishes that, and although it's not quite as special as the authentic Thai soup from our favorite little spot, it still rocks!

◇◇

- 2 lemongrass stalks
- 2 baby bok choy bundles
- 3 cups broccoli florets
- 2 cans (13.5 ounce) of coconut milk
- Few drops of fish sauce
- 1 pound medium-sized shrimp, shells, tails, and veins removed
- Black pepper to taste

Prep Time: 15 minutes
Cook Time: 9–11 minutes

◇◇

1. To prepare the lemongrass, cut the stalks into 2-inch pieces and bruise the lemongrass by bending it as much as possible (this will help release the lemongrass flavor).
2. Add the veggies and the lemongrass pieces to a large soup pot, pour in the coconut milk, and bring to a simmer.
3. Add the fish sauce and stir. Simmer for 5 minutes.
4. Add the shrimp and cook for about 4–6 more minutes, or until the shrimp flesh turns white.
5. Season with black pepper and serve in bowls.

Bean-Less Chili

Super Bowl Sunday inspired this dish. We used to make a giant plate of chili nachos as our traditional Super Bowl eats. Determined to still get my chili fix, I came up with this meal. It was a crowd pleaser the first paleo Super Bowl Sunday, and it continues to be so on any occasion! I made this chili for Rowan's third birthday along with the Kids Love Cabbage Slaw, and it was a festive, fun, and delicious dinner!

- 7-10 celery stalks, diced
- 1 white onion, diced
- 6 cloves garlic, minced
- 4 tablespoons extra-virgin olive oil
- 2 pounds grass-fed ground beef
- 1 pound spicy Italian pork sausage, casing removed
- 1 teaspoon sea salt
- 2 tablespoons dried oregano
- 2 tablespoons dried basil
- 1 tablespoon cumin
- 3-4 tablespoons chili powder
- 1 teaspoon cayenne pepper (more if you like it spicy)
- 1 (16-ounce) can diced tomatoes with juice
- 16 ounces chicken broth

Prep Time: 15 minutes
Cook Time: 35 minutes
Serves: 7

1. In a large soup pot, sauté the veggies in the extra-virgin olive oil for about 1 minute, add the beef and sausage, and brown.
2. Season the meat mixture with all of the spices.
3. Add the tomatoes and chicken broth and simmer for 35 minutes.
4. Taste and add more seasoning if desired.

Ratatouille

Yes, this meal was totally Disney inspired. After watching the movie *Ratatouille* only 10 million times or so, Jaden was more than inspired to make our own version of the rustic dish. I suggest this as a summertime meal when the tomatoes are at their ripest. We love this ratatouille over grilled hamburgers, chicken, or even pork chops.

- 4 garlic cloves
- 1 large zucchini
- 1 large red onion
- 2 green bell peppers
- 4-5 tomatoes
- 2 Japanese eggplant
- 5-6 tablespoons extra-virgin olive oil
- Sea salt and black pepper to taste
- Pinch of cayenne pepper
- 6 stalks fresh rosemary
- 1 cup fresh basil

Prep Time: 10 minutes
Cook Time: 20 minutes
Serves: 6

1. Peel the garlic cloves, and with the flat side of a chef's knife, press down hard on the garlic to crush the cloves.
2. Cut all other vegetables into large chunks.
3. In a large soup pot heat the extra-virgin olive oil over medium and add the onions and garlic. Sauté until the onions and garlic start to soften, and then add the remaining vegetables except for the tomatoes.
4. Cook the veggies with the onions and garlic for 5 minutes, stirring often.
5. Add the tomatoes, salt, pepper, cayenne, basil, and rosemary; mix well, and bring to a boil. Let the Ratatouille simmer for 15 minutes or until the eggplant is soft and the tomatoes are reduced down to a soup-like consistency.
6. Serve immediately over the meat of your choice.

Albondigas Soup

My sister-in-law Dixie is an amazing cook. I love visiting her house, knowing that we will always eat like kings and queens, and the girl rarely lets me lift a finger! She also has three sons, and long before I started my blog, she had always inspired me. Dixie has a way of taking care of everyone and still smiling, laughing, and giving my husband (her little brother) a hard time—which is why I love her most of all. In early fall, Dixie and I were chatting on the phone about different recipe ideas, and she mentioned Albondigas Soup and how easy it would be to make a paleo version. That's all she needed to say. The very next day, this soup was created. We love it more every time I make it and, honestly, it tastes better the next day!

Albondigas (meatballs):

- 2 pounds ground beef
- 2 cloves garlic, minced
- 2 tablespoons ground cumin
- 2 tablespoons dried oregano
- 1 tablespoon black pepper
- ⅛ teaspoon cayenne pepper
- 1 teaspoon sea salt

Prep Time: 20 minutes
Cook Time: 30 minutes
Serves: 6

Soup:

- 1 shallot, minced
- 3 garlic cloves, minced
- 4 tablespoons extra-virgin olive oil
- 5 carrots, chopped
- 4 cups purple or green cabbage, shredded
- 2½ cups fresh (not canned) diced tomatoes
- 6 cups chicken broth
- 4 cups water
- 1 tablespoon cumin
- 1 tablespoon dried oregano
- 2 teaspoons sea salt
- ½ to 1 full (7-ounce) can El Pato Jalapeño salsa)

1. In a large mixing bowl add all the meatball ingredients. Mix well using your hands and set aside.
2. In a large soup pot, sauté the shallots and garlic in the olive oil until the shallots become translucent.
3. Add the carrots, cabbage, tomatoes, chicken broth, water, cumin, oregano, and sea salt; mix well and bring to a boil.
4. Using your hands, form the meat into golf ball–sized meatballs and gently drop into the boiling soup. Turn the heat down to medium low and simmer for 20–25 minutes, stirring occasionally (stir gently not to break apart the meatballs).
5. Add the El Pato, stir, and simmer for another 5 minutes.

everyday paleo

Garlic Beef Stew with Acorn Squash

The first time I made this stew was February 25, 2010. Why do I remember that so well? I think because it was a month of awakenings for me. I came to the realization that garlic makes everything taste better and, even more importantly, I learned the hard way that eating paleo is not always enough to be healthy. I literally had overtrained and overworked myself to a frazzled mess. That fateful February I remember sitting in my bed, barely able to hold myself upright, eating this delicious stew, and thinking about all that I had been blessed with in life. I was slowly realizing that accomplishing everything at once really wasn't an accomplishment at all. I was too tired, stressed, and fried to realize what the heck I was even working so hard for, so what was the point? This stew symbolizes taking things a little bit slower and focusing on making life a whole lot simpler. Eat good food, get a lot of sleep, work hard, but take each day as it comes rather than taking each day head-on like a freight train.

- 2 pounds stew meat
- 1 yellow onion, finely chopped
- 10-12 garlic cloves, minced
- 1 tablespoon ground marjoram
- Sea salt and black pepper to taste
- ½ cup chicken broth
- 1 acorn squash, halved and seeds removed

Prep Time: 10 minutes
Cook Time: 6–8 hours

1. In a slow cooker, top the stew meat with all ingredients except for the acorn squash and mix well.
2. Cut the acorn squash in half, scoop out the seeds and place directly on top of the stew meat. Cover and cook for 6–8 hours on low.
3. Scoop out the acorn squash from its skin and serve in a bowl with the stew on top of the squash.

everyday paleo

Red Curry Beef Stew

Slow cooker heaven should be the name of this stew. Topping it all with fresh cilantro is a great way to brighten up this meal, and serving it with steamed kale or chard is a way to add more color and a different flavor profile. Thanks to the slow-cooking method, the stew meat in this dish really takes on the Thai red curry, so if you do not like it too spicy, use ½ a tablespoon of the paste rather than the suggested amount. You can find Thai curry paste at most chain grocery stores in the ethnic foods aisle.

- 2 pounds stew meat
- 1 tablespoon Thai red curry paste
- 1 can coconut milk
- ¼ cup chicken stock
- ½ head purple cabbage cut into large chunks
- 3 yams peeled and cut into 1-inch rounds

Prep Time: 5 minutes
Cook Time: 6–8 hours
Serves: 5

1. Place stew meat into a slow cooker and add the red curry paste. Mix well until the stew meat is coated with the paste.
2. Pour in the coconut milk and chicken stock and mix well.
3. Top with the sweet potatoes and cabbage, cover, and cook on low for 6–8 hours or until the stew meat is tender and falling apart and the potatoes are soft.

Béarnaise Sauce

This sauce is yum yum yum over my poached eggs and asparagus in the morning. Oh how it warms my heart to hear Jaden ask me if he can have that asparagus breakfast again. His request should be a commercial—not the sugar-laden cereal commercials blasting obnoxiously about "necessary fiber intake" or a "guaranteed way to start your kids' day off right." Kids *will* eat healthy paleo foods—and they feel like super heroes when fueled with meat, veggies, and good fats. Trust me; sometimes it's as easy as making a great sauce to get the kiddos asking for an "asparagus breakfast."

- 3 egg yolks
- 3 tablespoons extra-virgin olive oil
- 2 tablespoons hot water
- 1 tablespoon lemon juice
- Pinch of sea salt
- Pinch of cayenne pepper

Prep Time: 5 minutes
Cook Time: 30 seconds–1 min

1. In a medium metal mixing bowl, gently whisk the egg yolks. Continue whisking the yolks while adding the hot water, extra-virgin olive oil, lemon juice, salt, and cayenne pepper to the egg yolks.

2. Place the bowl over a pot of boiling water and whisk constantly until the sauce begins to thicken (about 30 seconds–1 minute).

3. Serve immediately over eggs, fish, chicken, or vegetables.

everyday paleo

Baba Ghanoush

I made this to pack in the kids' school lunches as a dip for their veggies. The only problem is that we almost ate it all before we even had a chance to use it for this very purpose. Therefore, I suggest doubling this recipe so that you can eat some of it right when it's done and save the rest for later.

- 1 eggplant
- 3 tablespoons extra-virgin olive oil
- Juice from ½ lemon
- 3 tablespoons parsley
- ½ tablespoon balsamic vinegar
- Pinch of sea salt
- Black pepper to taste

Prep and Cook Time: 50 minutes

1. Preheat oven to 425°F.
2. Prick the eggplant all over with a fork and bake on a foil-lined cookie sheet for 40 minutes.
3. Remove the eggplant from the oven, slit the eggplant open with a knife, and scoop out the insides of the eggplant into a food processor.
4. Add the remaining ingredients to the processor and blend until smooth.
5. Serve with sliced jicama or other veggies to your liking.

recipes

Walnut Red Pepper Dip

My friend and faithful NorCal client Christina e-mailed me this recipe last fall, and, of course, I can never just leave anything alone, so I revised it a bit. This dip is a huge hit at parties and just to have at home for the boys. It offers the same delicious texture and flavors of hummus, but without the legumes!

- 2 cups raw walnuts
- 1 teaspoon ground cumin
- ½ teaspoon salt
- 1 (12-ounce) jar roasted red peppers—drained
- 2 garlic cloves
- 4 tablespoons extra-virgin olive oil
- 2 tablespoons fresh parsley
- 2 teaspoons lemon juice

Prep Time: 5 minutes

1. In a food processor, process the walnuts, cumin, and salt until walnuts are finely ground.

2. Add peppers, garlic, extra-virgin olive oil, parsley, and lemon juice. Whirl until smooth, like the consistency of hummus.

3. Serve with raw vegetables.

Sun-Dried Tomato Salad Dressing or Marinade

I love to use this dressing on organic mixed salad greens with diced chicken and a little bit of diced apple. It's also great to marinate chicken in before it hits the grill! Make a double batch and have it handy in the fridge for whenever you might need it.

- 1 cup sun-dried tomatoes
- 1 cup extra-virgin olive oil
- 1 tablespoon capers
- Juice from ½ lemon
- 2 garlic cloves
- 2 tablespoons fresh rosemary
- Black pepper to taste

Prep Time: 5 minutes

1. Combine all ingredients in a food processor and process until smooth. Use as a salad dressing or meat marinade.

Dixie's Fresh Salsa

This recipe belongs to my sister-in-law Dixie, whom I mentioned earlier in my Albondigas Soup recipe. One of my first trips to visit John's family landed me in Dixie's kitchen, learning how to make this wonderful salsa. I think it was John's ploy to get me to learn Dixie's salsa-making skills, but whatever the reason for the lesson, this is the best darn salsa *ever*, and I'm glad that I know how to make it!

- 6 Roma tomatoes
- 1 jalapeño
- ½ red onion
- 6 garlic cloves
- Juice from 1 lemon
- 1 bunch cilantro
- Sea salt to taste

Prep Time: 15 minutes

1. Place the tomatoes and the jalapeño in a skillet and heat over medium-high heat, turning frequently until the tomato skins start to blacken and begin to peel off.
2. While the tomatoes and the pepper are in the skillet, put the onion, garlic, and cilantro in a food processor or blender and pulse until chopped.
3. Add the lemon juice, blackened tomatoes, pepper, and sea salt, and blend until smooth. I recommend only using about ½ of the jalapeño, but if you like it really hot, toss in the whole thing.

Chimichurri Sauce

Another great way to liven up your protein! It's not a salsa; it's not a dip—it's Chimichurri Sauce!

- ½ red onion
- 4 garlic cloves
- 1½ cups cilantro, chopped
- 1 cup parsley, chopped
- Juice from 1 lime
- ¾ cup extra-virgin olive oil
- 1 teaspoon sea salt
- Black pepper to taste

Prep Time: 5 minutes

1. Place all ingredients in a food processor and process on low until the mixture is almost smooth but still a bit chunky. This is excellent served over grilled flank steak, grilled chicken, or pork.

Walnut Pesto

We all love pesto, and this pesto is held high on a pedestal by my family. Maybe it's the walnuts, or maybe it's the fresh basil, but no one misses the Parmesan that is typically the star ingredient in most pestos. Just make sure to keep your basil fresh. This can be accomplished by putting your bunch of basil in a glass of water and keeping it in your fridge, as it will last much longer this way! We love this pesto spooned over grilled chicken or pork loin, and even over eggs. Jaden and Rowan love to be in charge of squeezing in the lemon juice!

- 1 cup walnut halves and pieces
- 6 garlic cloves
- 1 teaspoon sea salt
- 1 cup extra-virgin olive oil
- 3½ cups fresh basil
- Juice from ½ lemon

Prep Time: 5 minutes

1. In a food processor add the walnuts, garlic, sea salt, and extra-virgin olive oil. Process until smooth.
2. Add the basil and lemon juice, and process again until smooth.

everyday paleo

Super Citrus Salad Dressing

Try this salad dressing on my Carrot Fennel Salad instead of the olive oil and balsamic vinegar! This dressing can also be used as a marinade for chicken or beef, with the citrus acting as a natural tenderizer. I recommend always having fresh ginger, herbs, and lemons or limes on hand. These three ingredients can liven up any dish!

- ½ cup extra-virgin olive oil
- Juice from 1 lemon
- Juice from ½ orange
- 1 teaspoon savory, minced
- ½ teaspoon fresh ginger, grated
- Pinch of salt

Prep Time: 5 minutes

1. Whisk all ingredients together and drizzle over salad greens.

everyday paleo

Avocado Dressing and Dip

It's not really guacamole, but rather a smooth, creamy avocado dip! Jaden helped me come up with this recipe, and he is so proud to have been able to invent a recipe without hardly any help from me! My kids love this dip with carrot sticks, broccoli, and jicama. They even like to dip turkey and chicken pieces! Having this dip on hand is a great addition to school lunches or for a quick after-school snack.

- 2 ripe avocados
- 4 tablespoons extra-virgin olive oil
- 2 garlic cloves
- 1 tablespoon fresh squeezed lemon juice
- ½ teaspoon pepper
- Pinch of cayenne pepper
- 1 cup mild green salsa

Prep Time: 5 minutes

1. Place all ingredients in a food processor and blend on high until smooth. Serve as dip with fresh veggies or as a dressing over organic mixed baby greens.

Egg Dishes

everyday paleo

Egg Houses

I firmly believe that the best place for an egg to live is nestled inside of a juicy tomato and topped with crunchy bacon. Hence, the name "Egg Houses." The amazing thing about this delicious meal is that the egg yolk stays runny, and when you cut into the tomato and the egg together, it creates this beautiful, scrumptious mess, which mixes with the bacon goodness. If you're anything like me, you won't want to eat just one!

⟨⟨⟨⟩

- 4 large tomatoes
- 4 eggs
- 2-3 strips bacon, crumbled
- 1 tablespoon extra-virgin olive oil
- Black pepper to taste
- Diced chives

Prep Time: 10 minutes
Cook Time: 25 minutes
Serves: 4

⟨⟨⟨⟩

1. Preheat oven to 425°F.
2. Cut off just the top of the tomatoes and gently scoop out the insides.
3. Crack one egg in each tomato cup and bake for 25 minutes.
4. While the tomatoes and eggs are baking, cook the bacon.
5. After the egg houses are done baking, crumble the cooked bacon on top. Next, top with chopped chives.

everyday paleo

Huevos Rancheros

You can use this tomatillo salsa for more than just Huevos Rancheros! Although my favorite way to eat this tangy, delicious concoction happens to be over eggs, you can also use the salsa in any of my recipes that call for salsa verde, such as my Avocado Dressing and Dip or for the Chile Rellenos.

- 10-12 tomatillos
- 1 jalapeño
- 3 garlic cloves
- 1 bunch fresh cilantro
- Juice from 1 lime
- Sea salt to taste
- 6 tablespoons organic butter
- 8 eggs
- 2 avocados, sliced

Prep and Cook Time: 15 minutes

Serves: 4

1. Remove the husks from the tomatillos, wash and dry well.
2. Place the tomatillos and the jalapeño in a skillet and cook over medium-high heat, turning often until the skins of the tomatillo and jalapeño begin to blacken (about 10 minutes).
3. Place the tomatillos, jalapeño, cilantro, garlic, lime juice, and salt into a food processor and process until smooth.
4. Melt the butter in a pan and crack in the eggs. Turn the heat down to medium low and cover; do not flip the eggs. Cook until the whites are solid but the yolk still runny.
5. Serve two eggs over sliced avocado topped with the green tomatillo salsa.

everyday paleo

Frittata for All

The frittata can be made in million different ways, so this recipe should never get old! If you explore and experiment with different ingredient options, you will be amazed at how great this meal always turns out! I also love using fresh spinach, sausage, and zucchini squash in my frittatas. Just don't forget to top it with either the Huevos Rancheros sauce or some Dixie Fresh Salsa and sliced avocados!

- 6 bacon strips, diced
- 10 eggs
- 1 bell pepper, finely diced
- 5 green onions, diced
- 1 tablespoon dried oregano
- Black pepper to taste

Prep Time: 15 minutes
Cook Time: 12–18 minutes
Serves: 5

1. In a large skillet, cook the diced bacon until crisp.
2. While the bacon is cooking, whisk the eggs together with the oregano and black pepper and set aside.
3. Add the veggies to the bacon and the bacon grease and sauté another 3–4 minutes or until the veggies are tender.
4. Spread bacon and veggie mixture evenly over the bottom of the pan. Turn up the heat until the layer is sizzling hot and then pour the eggs evenly over the mixture. Turn heat down to low and cook for 3–4 minutes. Make sure the heat is not too high or the bottom will burn.
5. Move the skillet into the oven and under the broiler. Cook on high for another 3–4 minutes or until the eggs are cooked through.
6. Slice like a pie and serve!

everyday paleo

Egg Cupcakes

Be prepared, be prepared, be prepared! I highly recommend doubling this recipe and even freezing the cupcakes for later use. My friend Natalie gave me this recipe, so all credit goes to her. These cupcakes are delicious, portable, and kid friendly for on-the-go families, and when you make a batch on the weekend, all you will have to do in the morning is grab and go! Egg Cupcakes are also great for snacks.

- 10-12 eggs
- 1 green onion
- 2 zucchini squash
- 8 slices bacon
- 1 cup roasted red and yellow peppers
- 4 cups fresh spinach
- Black pepper to taste

Prep Time: 15 minutes
Cook Time: 20–25 minutes
Serves: 6–8

1. Preheat oven to 350°F and grease two muffin pans with coconut oil.
2. Whisk all of your eggs along with your desired amount of black pepper in a big bowl.
3. Put the green onion, zucchini, bacon, and peppers in a food processor and process until finely chopped but not smooth. Add this mixture to your eggs.
4. Next, add the spinach into the processor, finely chop, and then add to the eggs in the bowl.
5. Mix the egg mixture well, and then, using a measuring cup, fill the muffin pans with ¼ cup each (you'll be able to make 18–20 cupcakes).
6. Bake the egg cupcakes for 20–25 minutes or until the eggs are set in the middle.

Breakfast Paleo Pizza

Honestly, who doesn't want pizza for breakfast? Although this is called Breakfast Pizza, you of course can eat this meal any time of day or night. Our family enjoys making this feast on the weekend when we have a little more time to kick back and enjoy our mornings together. The kiddos will love to help you top the pizza, and you will love to watch them gobble up every protein-packed bite!

Crust:

- 8 eggs
- 2 tablespoons extra-virgin olive oil
- 3 garlic cloves, minced
- 1 tablespoon dried basil
- Pinch of sea salt
- Black pepper to taste

Prep Time: 15 minutes
Cook Time: 15 minutes
Serves: 5

Toppings:

- 1 pound ground mild Italian pork sausage
- ½ cup gluten-free organic marinara sauce
- 1-2 sweet bell peppers, diced
- 2 Roma tomatoes, sliced
- 1 cup sliced black, olives
- 3 green onions, diced

1. In a mixing bowl, whisk the eggs together and set aside.
2. In a medium-sized skillet, brown the sausage and set aside.
3. In a large skillet, heat the extra-virgin olive oil over medium-high heat and add the minced garlic. Sauté for 2 minutes.
4. While the garlic is cooking, add the basil, sea salt, and pepper to the scrambled eggs and mix well.
5. Pour the egg mixture over the garlic in the skillet and turn the heat down to medium. Cover and let cook for about 3 minutes, or until the bottom of the eggs is set and firm. Do not stir or disturb the eggs while cooking.

6. Remove the lid and transfer the skillet to the oven and broil for another 3 minutes or until the top of the egg mixture is also firm.

7. Remove from the oven and evenly spread the ½ cup of marinara sauce over the egg "crust."

8. Add the cooked sausage and the rest of the toppings.

9. Place the pizza back in the oven and under the broiler for another 5 minutes.

10. Slice and serve immediately with avocado slices as a garnish!

everyday paleo

Spring Scramble

I love using seasonal ingredients, and this scramble is a perfect example of how you can easily get some veggies in during the morning. By always having fresh veggies on hand, you can have a different scramble every day of the week! Remember, being bored with your food is a choice, and I would personally choose variety and preparedness over boredom any day of the week!

- ½ red onion, sliced
- 1 red bell pepper, sliced
- ¼ cup julienne-cut sun-dried tomatoes
- 2 tablespoons extra-virgin olive oil
- 6-8 stalks asparagus, tough ends removed and chopped
- ½ cup canned artichoke hearts
- 6 eggs

Prep Time: 5 minutes
Cook Time: 5–7 minutes
Serves: 3–4

1. Sauté the onions, peppers, and sun-dried tomatoes in the extra-virgin olive oil for 3 minutes or until the onions become tender.
2. Add the asparagus and artichokes and sauté for another 2 minutes.
3. Add eggs and scramble together.

Meaty Pumpkin Soufflé

Pumpkins are not just for jack-o'-lanterns! Little sugar pumpkins can be eaten like any other squash! Try stuffing them with ground beef, spices, and greens, or making pumpkin soup using the same ingredients as my Butternut Squash Soup! For variations of this recipe, try making just the soufflé without the meat, add in some applesauce to the pumpkin puree before you fold in the egg whites, and you'll have a delicious dessert! You can also use ground lamb in place of the ground beef to add a twist to this recipe.

◇◇

- 1 small sugar pumpkin
- 1 tablespoon coconut oil
- ½ yellow onion, diced
- 1 pound ground beef
- ½ tablespoon garlic powder
- ½ teaspoon sea salt
- ½ teaspoon finely ground black pepper
- 3 cups fresh spinach, finely chopped
- 1 cup fresh basil, finely chopped
- ½ tablespoon ground cinnamon
- ¼ teaspoon ground nutmeg
- ½ teaspoon fresh grated ginger
- 3 egg whites

Prep Time: 25 minutes
Cook Time: 30 minutes
Serves: 4

◇◇

1. Preheat oven to 350°F.
2. Cut the pumpkin in half and remove the seeds (save for roasting later!).
3. Cook the pumpkin in a pressure cooker for 8–10 minutes.
4. While the pumpkin is cooking, heat the coconut oil in a large skillet and cook onion until it begins to soften.

everyday paleo

5. Add the ground beef and cook until browned.

6. Add the garlic, salt, and pepper. Mix well.

7. Add the spinach and basil, stir well, and remove from heat.

8. Spread the meat mixture evenly into an 11 x 7 glass baking dish.

9. Place the cooked pumpkin in a food processor (scoop it out of its skin). Add to the food processor the cinnamon, nutmeg, and ginger. Process until very smooth.

10. In a large mixing bowl, beat the egg whites with a handheld mixer until they are stiff.

11. Fold in the pumpkin puree and spread the pumpkin on top of the meat mixture.

12. Bake uncovered for 30 minutes.

Meaty Pumpkin Soufflé

Pumpkins are not just for jack-o'-lanterns! Little sugar pumpkins can be eaten like any other squash! Try stuffing them with ground beef, spices, and greens, or making pumpkin soup using the same ingredients as my Butternut Squash Soup! For variations of this recipe, try making just the soufflé without the meat, add in some applesauce to the pumpkin puree before you fold in the egg whites, and you'll have a delicious dessert! You can also use ground lamb in place of the ground beef to add a twist to this recipe.

- 1 small sugar pumpkin
- 1 tablespoon coconut oil
- ½ yellow onion, diced
- 1 pound ground beef
- ½ tablespoon garlic powder
- ½ teaspoon sea salt
- ½ teaspoon finely ground black pepper
- 3 cups fresh spinach, finely chopped
- 1 cup fresh basil, finely chopped
- ½ tablespoon ground cinnamon
- ¼ teaspoon ground nutmeg
- ½ teaspoon fresh grated ginger
- 3 egg whites

Prep Time: 25 minutes
Cook Time: 30 minutes
Serves: 4

1. Preheat oven to 350°F.
2. Cut the pumpkin in half and remove the seeds (save for roasting later!).
3. Cook the pumpkin in a pressure cooker for 8–10 minutes.
4. While the pumpkin is cooking, heat the coconut oil in a large skillet and cook onion until it begins to soften.

Spring Scramble

I love using seasonal ingredients, and this scramble is a perfect example of how you can easily get some veggies in during the morning. By always having fresh veggies on hand, you can have a different scramble every day of the week! Remember, being bored with your food is a choice, and I would personally choose variety and preparedness over boredom any day of the week!

- ½ red onion, sliced
- 1 red bell pepper, sliced
- ¼ cup julienne-cut sun-dried tomatoes
- 2 tablespoons extra-virgin olive oil
- 6-8 stalks asparagus, tough ends removed and chopped
- ½ cup canned artichoke hearts
- 6 eggs

Prep Time: 5 minutes
Cook Time: 5–7 minutes
Serves: 3–4

1. Sauté the onions, peppers, and sun-dried tomatoes in the extra-virgin olive oil for 3 minutes or until the onions become tender.
2. Add the asparagus and artichokes and sauté for another 2 minutes.
3. Add eggs and scramble together.

Sunny Deviled Eggs

Try bringing Sunny Deviled Eggs to a party and watch people's reactions as they bite into these babies! The last time I made these for a paleo potluck, they vanished almost before I could set the tray down. These are not your typical deviled eggs by any means. I also make these for school lunches—what a great twist to the standard hard-boiled egg!

- 12 hard-boiled eggs
- ⅔ cup julienne-cut sun-dried tomatoes
- 6 tablespoons extra-virgin olive oil
- 1 teaspoon garlic powder
- Crushed black pepper to taste
- ½ cup fresh basil, diced
- Dried dill for garnish

Prep Time: 30 minutes

1. Place the 12 eggs in a sauce pan and add enough water to cover the eggs. Bring the water to boil and boil rapidly for 8 minutes.
2. As soon as the timer beeps, drain the hot water from the eggs; add cold water and ice to stop the cooking process. The faster you cool off your eggs, the easier it will be to peel them!
3. Leave eggs in the cold water for 5–10 minutes before you peel. Peel eggs, rinse, and cut in half lengthwise. Carefully scoop out all of the yolks into a food processor.
4. Add the remaining ingredients and process until smooth.
5. Fill the egg halves with the mixture and sprinkle with a little a bit of dill if you like.

Snacks, Baked Goods, and Desserts

everyday paleo

BLT with Avocado Spread

When I was pregnant with Jaden, all I wanted was BLTs. I still love the classic BLT, and this option is better than the standard, especially with the added creaminess of the avocado spread. I could eat this meal for breakfast, lunch, or dinner. In fact, I have done just that! Nothing like a big ol' bite of bacon wrapped in crunchy romaine and kissed with fresh, juicy tomatoes and avocado.

BLT:

- 4 bacon strips, cooked
- 2 romaine lettuce leaves
- 4 thick tomato slices

Avocado Spread:

Prep Time: 15 minutes

Serves: 2

- 1 avocado
- 1 tablespoon lemon juice
- ½ tablespoon extra-virgin olive oil
- ½ teaspoon garlic powder
- Black pepper to taste

1. In a small mixing bowl, mash the avocado with a fork.
2. Add the remaining avocado spread ingredients and mix well.
3. Using equal amounts, spread the avocado spread onto each piece of lettuce.
4. Top with the bacon and tomatoes, wrap, and eat.

Sausage-Stuffed Dates

I should have called this recipe "meat candy," because that was the first thought that popped into mind when I took a bite of these little goodies. I love coming up with winners such as this one, and unexpected combinations are sometimes the best combinations. This recipe is exactly what transpired after opening up my fridge to find dates, bacon, and sausage all on the same shelf together. It was fate I suppose, and I am so glad that these three ingredients came together because I could probably live off of this tasty little treat if necessary! Oh, and to watch a three-year-old dig into this snack is about the coolest thing ever. Big eyes, sticky hands, chew, swallow, and "Mom, this is NUM!" That's three-year-old speak for delicious!

- 6 dates
- ½ pound mild Italian sausage
- 6 bacon strips

Prep Time: 20 minutes
Cook Time: 40 minutes
Serves: 3

1. Preheat oven to 375°F.

2. Using a paring knife, cut a slit in the dates lengthwise and remove the seed.

3. Use 2 tablespoons of sausage per date, form into a ball, and wrap the date around the sausage (the date will not be big enough to wrap all the way around). Secure the sausage and date by wrapping a piece of bacon around the date.

4. Bake in a glass baking dish for 35–40 minutes.

5. Optional—serve with organic marinara sauce for dipping.

everyday paleo

Salmon Rolls

This snack is great fun for little hands to help with! I love coming up with snacks that deliver the great nutritional punch this snack offers.

- 1 can wild Alaskan salmon, drained
- 1 tablespoon fresh lemon juice
- 1 tablespoon extra-virgin olive oil
- ½ tablespoon dried dill
- Black pepper to taste
- Pinch of sea salt
- 1 zucchini sliced lengthwise with a mandoline

Prep Time: 10 minutes

Serves: 2–3

1. In a small bowl, mix together the salmon, lemon juice, olive oil, dill, pepper, and salt.
2. Place a small amount of the salmon on the end of one of the zucchini slices and roll like a sushi roll. Continue to roll until the entire salmon filling is gone.
3. Serve with lemon wedges.

recipes

everyday paleo

Portobello Mushroom "Sandwich"

This makes one sandwich, so if you are feeding a crowd, use more mushrooms! Be creative with your sandwich filling—anything goes with this sure-to-please creation. I also suggest using portobellos for burger bun replacements! The first time I made this sandwich, I used leftovers from my Spice Rub Slow-Cooked Chicken recipe, and it was really to die for. Rowan shared that first sandwich with me, and like with the pizza, I laughed days later when he asked me for a sandwich, knowing full well that he was referring to our paleo version!

- 2 portobello mushrooms
- 2 tablespoons coconut oil
- 1 chicken breast, cooked and shredded
- ½ avocado, sliced
- 4 bacon strips, cooked
- 1 slice red onion
- ½ cup raw spinach or arugula

Prep Time: 15 minutes
Cook Time: 10 minutes
Serve: 1–2

1. Scoop out the gills and stem gently from the underside of the mushrooms.
2. Heat the coconut oil in a skillet and cook the mushrooms for 3–5 minutes on each side or until the mushrooms turn golden brown on the top and becomes tender.
3. Remove the mushrooms from the pan. On one mushroom, pile on the chicken, avocado, bacon, onion, and spinach or arugula.
4. Top with the other mushroom, cut in half, and eat!

everyday paleo

Plantain Chips and Guacamole

If you have a craving for some chips and dip, this should be your go-to fix! I sometimes make these chips for my kids without the guacamole and sprinkle them with cinnamon for a tasty sweet treat.

◇◇◇

- 3 ripe plantains (they are ripe when they are almost black)
- ¼ cup coconut oil
- 4 avocados
- Juice from ½ lime
- ½ tablespoon garlic powder
- Black pepper to taste

Prep Time: 15 minutes
Cook Time: 4 minutes
Serves: 5

◇◇◇

1. Leave the peel on the plantain and cut off the ends. Cut thin round slices. Leaving the peel on while slicing will help prevent smashing the plantain.
2. After the plantain is sliced, carefully remove the peel and place the sliced plantains into a skillet of hot coconut oil. Fry for about 2 minutes on each side, using tongs to flip, and being careful not to burn.
3. Mash the avocados with the lime juice, garlic powder, and black pepper, and serve with the plantain chips.

everyday paleo

Turkey Roll-Ups

When I first made these turkey roll-ups, Jaden called them "bugs." How fun for a kid to create his own edible bugs, with little broccoli slaw legs hanging out! Rowan calls these turkey roll-ups "tacos." Whatever *your* family decides to call this snack, I hope you have as much fun as we do eating them!

<><><><><><><><><><><><><><><><><><><><><><><><><><><><><><><><><><><><><><><><>

Step 1: Choose your fillings from options below

- Cherry tomatoes and avocados slices
- Broccoli slaw with balsamic/extra-virgin olive oil drizzle
- Cabbage and apple
- Cucumber and bell pepper
- Artichoke hearts and torn basil leaves
- Pitted kalamata olives and carrots
- 8-10 nitrate-free turkey deli meat slices

Prep Time: 10 minutes

Step 2: Roll and eat!

<><><><><><><><><><><><><><><><><><><><><><><><><><><><><><><><><><><><><><><><>

1. Place your filling option in the middle of the turkey slice, roll up like a tiny burrito, and eat! A delicious snack or lunch box item for kids and grown-ups too! Children love being in charge of their own filling options, and you will be amazed with the creative ideas your little ones will come up with.

Almond-Meal Blueberry Pancakes

I suggest doubling this recipe and either freezing the leftovers or keeping them handy in your fridge for the busy week ahead. Kids will eat them cold right out of the fridge, and having extra can be a real lifesaver.

- 2 cups almond meal
- ½ cup finely shredded unsweetened coconut
- 3 eggs *arrow root, tapioca, flax*
- 1 cup coconut milk
- 2 tablespoons coconut oil
- 1 apple, grated
- 1 cup fresh or frozen organic blueberries
- 3 tablespoons cinnamon

Prep Time: 10 minutes
Cook Time: 8 minutes
Serves: 5

1. Mix all ingredients together.
2. Using ¼-cup scoops, cook the pancakes on a super-hot griddle or in a frying pan greased with coconut oil. Cook for about 4 minutes per side, making sure the pancakes are brown and crisp before flipping.
3. Serve with more blueberries on top and a sprinkle of cinnamon!

Apple Flowers

You can make this apple flower with coconut flakes on top of the almond butter. You can also substitute blackberries or orange or pear slices for the apple, or any other fruit you want to use. My kids love it when I slice a banana in half lengthwise, spread one half with almond butter, sprinkle on finely shredded unsweetened coconut, and then make a banana "sandwich" out of the entire creation. Have fun and get creative!

- 2 tablespoons almond butter
- ½ organic apple, cored and sliced
- 5 blueberries
- 1 raspberry
- Cinnamon to taste

Prep Time: 5 minutes

1. In the middle of a plate, spoon the almond butter into the shape of a circle.
2. Place the sliced apple around the outside of the almond butter and place the blueberries in a circle on top of the almond butter.
3. Place the raspberry in the middle of the blueberries to create the center of the flower.
4. Sprinkle the apple slices with cinnamon and serve.

recipes

Happy Trail Mix

I call this trail mix my emergency mix! I suggest never leaving home without it. You never know when you'll find yourself running late or too busy to make a meal, and having your emergency stash is essential! My kids count on our Happy Trail Mix for road trips, and it has proven to be a great afternoon snack as well.

- 1 cup roasted cashews
- 1½ cups raw almonds
- ½ cup raw pecans
- ⅓ cup unsweetened dried cherries
- ⅓ cup unsweetened dried apples, cut into small pieces
- 3 ounces gluten-free grass-fed beef jerky, cut into small pieces

Prep Time: 5 minutes

1. Mix all ingredients together. Store in an airtight container.

everyday paleo

Baked Apples

These apples are a wonderful holiday dessert, and when you cut them in half, put them in a bowl, and sprinkle cinnamon on top, they look very beautiful. The filling by itself is delicious, but paired with the baked apple, this dessert is something a paleo mom like me dreams about.

◇◇

- 3 Granny Smith apples
- ⅓ cup pecans, chopped
- ¼ cup finely shredded unsweetened coconut
- ¼ cup raisins or dried cranberries
- 1 teaspoon cinnamon
- ¼ teaspoon ground cloves
- ¼ teaspoon ground nutmeg
- 2 tablespoons coconut oil

Prep Time: 10 minutes
Cook time: 40 minutes
Serves: 3–6

◇◇

1. Preheat oven to 350°F.
2. Carefully remove just the core of the apple.
3. Mix all other ingredients together and stuff into the hole in the apple.
4. Bake the apples in a glass baking dish for 40 minutes or until the apples become tender.

Nutty Cookies

What can I say about these cookies except that they have forever changed my relationship with The Cookie. Cookies for me used to mean *a lot* of cookies, followed by guilt, followed by feeling sick, followed by eating more cookies. Not a good relationship to have. My Nutty Cookies, however, make me happy. I can eat one, enjoy it, and move on with my life. I can let my kids have these cookies with breakfast and not freak out. I can say yes every time my kids ask me to make cookies without the added stress of future, "No you can't have another cookie" battles. I hope these cookies improve your cookie relationship as much as they did mine.

- 2 bananas, smashed
- ⅓ cup coconut flour
- ¾ cup almond butter
- ½ teaspoon baking soda
- ⅓ cup raw walnuts, chopped
- 1 apple, finely diced
- ⅓ cup coconut milk
- 1 tablespoon cinnamon

Prep Time: 10 minutes
Cook Time: 25 minutes

1. Preheat oven to 350°F.
2. In a medium sized mixing bowl, use a fork to smash the bananas.
3. Add the coconut flour, almond butter, and baking soda, and mix well. Using a handheld chopper or food processor, chop the walnuts and apples to a very fine dice.
4. Add the walnuts, apples, coconut milk, and cinnamon to the bowl and mix well.
5. Cover two cookie sheets with parchment paper and spoon heaping tablespoons of the cookie mix onto the parchment paper, placing an inch or two apart. Bake for 25 minutes. Makes approximately 20–22 cookies.

Recipe Variation

1. Add ½ cup finely shredded unsweetened coconut and top with a few sprinkles of coconut.

2. Take out 1 banana and add ½ cup of canned organic unsweetened pumpkin

3. Add ½ cup dark chocolate chips.

everyday paleo

Feelin' Peachy

Make this desert at your next dinner party and I guarantee that even your friends who do not eat paleo will beg for more. The last time we made these, they were amazing right out of the oven, and the next day proved just as good cold!

◇◇◇

- 3 tablespoons water
- 4 freestone peaches, halved with stone removed
- ⅓ cup sliced almonds
- 1 cup unsweetened dried apricots
- ½ cup golden raisins
- 2 tablespoons coconut oil
- 1 tablespoon cinnamon
- ½ teaspoon fresh grated ginger

Prep Time: 10 minutes
Cook Time: 25 minutes
Serves: 8

◇◇◇

1. Preheat oven to 400°F.
2. Add the water to the bottom of a glass baking dish and place the peach halves, sliced sides up, into the dish as well.
3. In a food processor, add the remaining ingredients and process until the mixture is finely chopped.
4. Spoon even amounts onto each peach half and bake for 25 minutes.

Paleo Apple Muffins

I woke up early one Saturday morning, rolled over bleary eyed, woke up my husband, and told him, "I really want muffins." John laughed at me and said, "Good luck, babe; that sounds impossible." The challenge was on! I nearly sprinted to the kitchen, gulped down my espresso in order to clear my head, and I made these darn good muffins—just to prove that I could! I dedicate these muffins to my precious, beautiful, amazing little niece Shaela, who was one of the first little people to try and enjoy my Apple Muffins. I love you sweet Shaela!

- 2¼ cups almond meal
- 4 eggs
- 1 organic apple, finely diced *or 1 c blueberries*
- 1 very ripe banana *— or 1 c chopped nuts (pecans*
- ¼ cup coconut oil
- ⅓ cup water
- ½ teaspoon baking soda
- 1 heaping tablespoon cinnamon *+ ¼ c Maple Syrup*

30 minutes

Prep Time: 15 minutes

Cook Time: 20 minutes

1. Preheat oven to 350°F.
2. Using a fork, mash the banana in the bottom of a large mixing bowl.
3. Add all other ingredients and mix by hand. The batter will not be super thick, but more like a cake batter.
4. Using a bit more coconut oil, grease a muffin tin. Fill the tins about ¾ full. Bake for 15–20 minutes. You will know they are done when you can insert a toothpick into the middle of a muffin and it comes out clean.
5. Serve hot out of the oven with some organic butter melted on top, accompanied by eggs over-easy and hot black coffee. Makes approximately 16 muffins.

Berry Good Cobbler

Another crowd pleaser. I have made Berry Good Cobbler many times for paleo and non-paleo eaters alike, always with excellent reviews! Try this same recipe with peaches, apples, or even blueberries.

ⵗⵗⵗⵗⵗⵗⵗⵗⵗⵗⵗⵗⵗⵗⵗⵗⵗⵗⵗⵗⵗⵗⵗⵗⵗⵗⵗⵗⵗⵗⵗⵗⵗ

- 3 cups fresh or frozen blackberries (or other berry of your choice)
- 1 egg
- 1½ cups almond meal
- 2 tablespoons coconut oil
- 2 tablespoons cinnamon
- Drizzle of raw organic honey
- "So Delicious" brand unsweetened coconut milk

Prep Time: 10 minutes
Cook Time: 35 minutes
Serves: 6

ⵗⵗⵗⵗⵗⵗⵗⵗⵗⵗⵗⵗⵗⵗⵗⵗⵗⵗⵗⵗⵗⵗⵗⵗⵗⵗⵗⵗⵗⵗⵗⵗⵗ

1. Preheat oven to 350°F.
2. Pour the blackberries into a pie pan.
3. In a small bowl, mix together the egg, almond meal, and coconut oil, and shake in the cinnamon. Stir well until the mixture starts to crumble. If you wish, drizzle a bit of raw organic honey on top of the blackberries.
4. By hand, evenly crumble the almond meal mixture on top of the blackberries and bake in your preheated oven for 35 minutes.
5. Serve in bowls with cold "So Delicious" brand coconut milk poured over the top.

Great Balls of Dates

These "date candies" are another fun treat for the holidays, and they are easy for little hands to make and eat. Try wrapping these up in little tins, topping with a ribbon, and giving out as gifts!

- 20 medjool dates, seeds removed
- ½ cup almond butter
- ¼ cup coconut flour
- 2 tablespoons unsweetened cocoa powder
- 1 tablespoon cinnamon
- Finely shredded coconut flakes

Prep Time: 20 minutes

1. In a food processor, process together all ingredients except for the coconut flakes. The mixture will be very thick. Make sure it's not chunky—should be as smooth as possible.
2. Using your hands, smash together teaspoon-size portions of the mixture. Roll into small balls, and then roll in the shredded coconut flakes to coat.

Bedtime Blueberries

My boys always want a bedtime snack, and this recipe was first created for them, which is why they are called "Bedtime Blueberries." You of course can eat this yummy treat as early as you like, but if you have them for breakfast, make sure you pair it with some protein!

- 2 cups frozen organic blueberries
- ½ cup unsweetened finely shredded coconut
- ½ cup sliced almonds
- 4 tablespoons freshly squeezed orange juice

Prep Time: 5 minutes
Cook Time: 15 minutes
Serves: 4

1. Preheat oven to 350°F.
2. Layer the blueberries in a pie pan and sprinkle the shredded coconut evenly over the blueberries, followed by the sliced almonds.
3. Drizzle the entire dish with the orange juice and bake for 15 minutes.
4. Finish under the broiler on high for another minute or until the almonds start to brown.

Bugs in a Boat

Prepare to get messy with this fun snack! My little guys insist on making their own Bugs in a Boat, and who wouldn't want to do it "all myself"! I love the look of concentration that Rowan gets when he is making this little snack. It's very serious business to a preschooler!

- 4-5 celery stalks
- Almond butter
- Golden raisins
- Coconut flakes

Prep Time: 10 minutes

1. Cut each celery stalk into 4-inch pieces.
2. Spread the inside of each celery stalk with almond butter.
3. Sprinkle with finely shredded unsweetened coconut flakes and top with golden raisins.

Smoothies

Coconut milk smoothies are a great way to get some good fat into your kiddos in the morning or for a quick after school snack. Pair these smoothies with a good source of protein such as one of my egg cupcakes and your little ones will be raring to go with a happy full belly! All of the smoothies below take five minutes of prep time, and serve four 6-ounce servings.

Blueberry Bonanza Smoothie

- 1 cup fresh blueberries
- 1 cup frozen pineapple chunks
- 1 tablespoon coconut oil
- 1½ cups coconut milk

Add the blueberries, pineapple and coconut oil to a blender. Pour over the coconut milk and blend until smooth.

Tropical Explosion Smoothie

- 1 ripe banana
- ½ cup diced fresh pineapple
- ½ orange
- 1 tablespoon coconut oil
- ½ cup crushed ice
- 1½ cups coconut milk

Place the banana, pineapple, orange, coconut oil and ice into a blender. Pour the coconut milk over the top and blend on high until smooth.

Berry Chocolate Smoothie

- ½ cup frozen cherries
- ½ cup frozen blueberries
- 1 ripe banana
- 2 tablespoons unsweetened cocoa powder
- 2 tablespoons almond butter
- 1½ cups coconut milk

Add the cherries, blueberries, banana, almond butter, and cocoa powder to the blender. Pour over the coconut milk and blend until smooth.

Mango Madness Smoothie

- 1 cup frozen mango chunks
- ½ cup frozen strawberries
- 2 cups coconut milk

Add the mango and strawberries to the blender. Pour the coconut milk over and blend until smooth.

Thirty-Day Family Meal Plan

Day 1

Breakfast: Egg Cupcakes (p. 185)—this recipe makes 18–20 "cupcakes" and a serving size for adults is 2 cupcakes. Plan to double this recipe if needed based on the size of your family so that you can have these ready for the first few days.

Lunch: Wild-Salmon Salad (p. 132)

Snack: Beef Jerky and ½ avocado

Dinner: Spice Rub Slow-Cooked Chicken (p. 45) and Kids Love Cabbage Slaw (p. 134)

Day 2

Breakfast: Leftover Egg Cupcakes

Lunch: Leftover Spice Rub Slow-Cooked Chicken and organic salad greens with Sun-Dried Tomato Salad Dressing (p. 169)

Snack: Bugs in a Boat (p. 220) and turkey slices

Dinner: Easy Steak Skewers (p. 63) and Savory Cauliflower Fried Rice (p. 145)

Day 3

Breakfast: Leftover Egg Cupcakes and blueberries

Lunch: Avocado Tuna Boats (p. 117)

Snack: Leftover Steak Skewers and macadamia nuts

Dinner: Pecan-Crusted Chicken (p. 43) with Fancy Pear Salad (p. 129)

Day 4

Breakfast: Huevos Rancheros (p. 181)

Lunch: Easy Spinach Salad (p. 131)

Snack: Sunny Deviled Eggs (p. 193) and ½ avocado

Dinner: Red Curry Beef Stew (p. 165)

Day 5

Breakfast: Almond Meal Blueberry Pancakes (p. 206) and scrambled eggs

Lunch: Leftover Red Curry Beef Stew

Snack: Jerky and coconut flakes

Dinner: Rockin' Moroccan Chicken (p. 47)

Shopping List Day 1-5

- 4 dozen eggs
- 2lbs bacon
- 2lbs stew meat
- 2 cans wild caught Alaskan salmon
- 1 6lb whole chicken
- 8 boneless skinless chicken breasts
- 2.5lbs of sirloin Steak
- 1 package turkey deli meat
- Beef jerky

- 1 head of broccoli
- 1 bunch of green onions
- 5 zucchinis
- 8 carrots
- 10 tomatillos
- 1 bunch cilantro
- 3 bunches spinach
- 2lbs mixed salad greens
- 1 head celery
- 1 head purple cabbage
- 1 head cauliflower
- 2 red onions
- 1 white onion
- 1 bulb garlic
- 1 carton of cherry tomatoes
- 1 red bell pepper
- 3 yams
- ½ pound of crimini mushrooms
- 8 avocados
- Fresh basil
- Fresh rosemary

- 1 lime
- 3 lemons
- 1 pear
- 4 apples
- Blueberries

- 2 jars roasted red peppers
- 1 jar of pimento stuffed green olives
- 1 box of raisins
- 1 jar of julienned sun dried tomatoes
- 1 jar of Capers
- Thai Red Curry Paste

Day 6	**Breakfast:**	Karina's Sausage Hash (p. 90) and poached eggs
	Lunch:	Shrimp Tacos (p. 113)
	Snack:	Leftover Rockin' Moroccan Chicken
	Dinner:	Hasta La Vista Pasta Lasagna (p. 86)

Day 7	**Breakfast:**	Frittata for All (p. 183)
	Lunch:	Leftover Lasagna
	Snack:	Ham slices and avocado
	Dinner:	Garden Fresh Meatballs (p. 79) and Baked Green Beans

Day 8	**Breakfast:**	Leftover Frittata
	Lunch:	Sun-Dried Tomato Chicken Slaw (p. 133)
	Snack:	Leftover Garden Fresh Meatballs
	Dinner:	Collard-Wrapped Tilapia (p. 99)

Day 9	**Breakfast:**	2 Poached Eggs with Béarnaise Sauce (p. 166) and steamed asparagus
	Lunch:	Leftover Sun-Dried Tomato Chicken Slaw
	Snack:	Salmon Rolls (p. 199)
	Dinner:	Bean-Less Chili (p. 156) and Carrot and Fennel Salad (p. 128)

Day 10	**Breakfast:**	Paleo Apple Muffins (p. 214), eggs over easy, and bacon
	Lunch:	Leftover Bean-Less Chili
	Snack:	Turkey Roll-ups (p. 205)
	Dinner:	Asparagus-Stuffed Chicken Breasts (p. 55) and Roasted Root Veggies (p. 139)

Shopping List Day 6-10

- 3 dozen eggs
- 4lbs ground beef
- 6 chicken breasts
- 1.5lbs ground turkey
- 1lb mild Italian sausage
- 1lb spicy Italian sausage
- 1lb ground pork sausage
- 4 tilapia filets
- 1lb large shrimp
- 1 can wild Alaskan salmon
- 1lb bacon
- 1 ham steak
- 1 package ham deli meat

- 1 bunch of radishes
- 1 head purple cabbage
- 1 head green cabbage
- 1 head romaine lettuce
- 1 head celery
- 1 bunch collard greens
- 1 bunch spinach
- 9 zucchinis
- 1 bunch asparagus
- 1lb green beans
- 8 carrots
- 1 fennel bulb
- 4 avocados
- 1 bag broccoli slaw
- 4 yams
- 2 green bell peppers
- 5 small beets
- 2 parsnips

- 4 red onions
- 1 white onion
- 2 bulbs garlic
- Green onions
- Fresh basil

- 1 lime
- 3 lemons
- 1 orange
- 2 apples
- 1 banana
- Organic grass fed butter (optional)
- 1 jar salsa verde
- 1 16oz box of chicken broth
- 1 16oz can diced tomatoes
- 1 14.5oz can diced tomatoes
- 1 6oz can tomato paste
- 1 jar black olives
- 1 12oz jar roasted red peppers
- 1 jar julienned sun dried tomatoes

Day 11	**Breakfast:**	Egg Houses (p. 179)
	Lunch:	Shrimp Flying Saucers (p. 108)
	Snack:	Leftover Paleo Apple Muffin and a hard-boiled egg
	Dinner:	Grilled Lamb-Burgers (p. 88) with Baked Curry Cauliflower (p. 121)
Day 12	**Breakfast:**	Spring Scramble (p. 189)
	Lunch:	BLT with Avocado Spread (p. 197)
	Snack:	Apple Flowers (p. 207) and jerky
	Dinner:	Everyday Paleo Spaghetti (p. 82) and Baked Apples (p. 209)
Day 13	**Breakfast:**	Breakfast Paleo Pizza (p. 186)
	Lunch:	Leftover Everyday Paleo Spaghetti
	Snack:	Leftover Breakfast Paleo Pizza
	Dinner:	Pollo Con Salsa Roja (p. 54) and green salad with Avocado Dressing and Dip (p. 175)
Day 14	**Breakfast:**	Leftover Pollo Con Salsa Roja
	Lunch:	Ginger Shrimp Salad (p. 123)
	Snack:	Happy Trail Mix (p. 208)
	Dinner:	Skillet Salmon with Baby Bok Choy (p. 103)
Day 15	**Breakfast:**	Poached Eggs over Curried Veggie Hash (p. 120)
	Lunch:	Leftover Ginger Shrimp Salad
	Snack:	Bugs in a Boat (p. 220) and ham slices
	Dinner:	Dry Rub Burgers (p. 69), Yummy Yam Spears (p. 135), and steamed broccoli

Shopping List
Day 11-15

- 4 dozen eggs
- 2lbs boneless skinless chicken thighs
- 4.5lbs ground beef
- 1lb mild Italian pork sausage
- 1lb bacon
- 1 package deli ham slices
- 1lb ground lamb
- 2lbs medium shrimp

- 7 large tomatoes
- 3 heirloom tomatoes
- 2 Roma tomatoes
- 1 head broccoli
- 1 head celery
- 4 carrots
- 2 zucchini
- 1lb organic salad mix
- 1 head purple cabbage
- 1 head romaine lettuce
- 1 bunch asparagus
- 1 cauliflower
- 3 red onions
- 1 yellow onion
- 2 shallots
- 2 bulbs garlic
- 5 yams
- 1 small cucumber
- 3 red bell pepper
- 6 avocados
- 1 spaghetti squash
- 1 bunch cilantro
- 1 bunch arugula
- Green onions
- Fresh rosemary
- Fresh Parsley
- Fresh Mint
- Chives
- Fresh ginger

- 4 lemons
- 1 apple
- 3 granny smith apples
- Blueberries

- 1 can artichoke hearts
- 1 can sliced black olives
- 1 jar marinara sauce
- 1 jar julienned sun dried tomatoes
- 1 jar salsa verde
- 1 28oz can El Pato Salsa Para Enchiladas
- 1 jar raw almond butter

Day 16	*Breakfast:*	Leftover Curried Veggie Hash and Chicken Sausages
	Lunch:	Leftover Dry Rub Burger, Walnut Red Pepper Dip (p. 168), and raw sliced veggies
	Snack:	Hard-boiled egg and macadamia nuts
	Dinner:	Salmon Cakes with Ginger Mayo (p. 114)

Day 17	*Breakfast:*	Egg Cupcakes (p. 185)
	Lunch:	Sliced Chicken Breast, Walnut Red Pepper Dip (p. 168), and raw sliced veggies
	Snack:	Leftover Egg Cupcake
	Dinner:	Everyday Meatloaf (p. 65) and Brussels Sprouts 'n' Bacon (p. 147)

Day 18	*Breakfast:*	Egg Cupcakes (p. 185) and strawberries or blueberries
	Lunch:	Leftover Meatloaf and Brussels Sprouts
	Snack:	Salmon Rolls (p. 199)
	Dinner:	Breaded Baked Chicken (p. 50) and Butternut Squash Soup (p. 151)

Day 19	*Breakfast:*	Leftover Egg Cupcakes
	Lunch:	Ginger Citrus Skillet Chicken (p. 49)
	Snack:	Turkey slices, black olives, and mandarins
	Dinner:	Perfect Pot Roast (p. 92) and Mom's Mashed Yams (p. 143)

Day 20	*Breakfast:*	Leftover Pot Roast
	Lunch:	Grilled Hamburger Patty and Baba Ghanoush (p. 167) with raw veggies
	Snack:	Happy Trail Mix (p. 208)
	Dinner:	Thai Shrimp Soup (p. 155)

Shopping List
Day 16-20

- 4 dozen eggs
- 4lbs boneless skinless chicken thighs
- 2 chicken breasts
- 3lbs ground beef
- 1lb breakfast chicken sausages
- 1 5lb pork loin roast
- 2lbs bacon
- 1lb medium shrimp
- 4 cans wild caught Alaskan salmon
- 1 package turkey deli meat
- Beef jerky

- 1lb brussel sprouts
- 1 large eggplant
- 1 butternut squash
- ½lb crimini mushrooms
- 2 zucchinis
- 6 carrots
- 1 bunch celery
- 2 leeks
- 1 bunch kale
- 1 red bell pepper
- 1 head purple cabbage
- 2 baby bok choy bundles
- 1 head broccoli
- 1 bunch spinach
- 1 red onion
- 1 white onion
- 2 yellow onions
- 2 garlic bulbs
- 2 lemon grass stalks
- 1 jalapeno
- Green onions
- Fresh basil
- Fresh parsley
- Fresh thyme
- Fresh ginger

- 3 lemons
- 1 orange
- Blueberries
- Strawberries
- Mandarins

- 2 12oz jars roasted red peppers
- 2 14oz cans of diced tomatoes
- 1 6oz can tomato paste
- 1 16oz box chicken broth
- 1 can black olives
- Thai fish sauce
- Red wine

Day 21	**Breakfast:**	Scrambled eggs, sliced avocado and Dixie's Fresh Salsa (p. 170)
	Lunch:	Grilled chicken with Chimichurri Sauce (p. 171) and steamed kale
	Snack:	Turkey slices, pecans, and artichoke hearts
	Dinner:	Easy Skillet Scallops and Spinach (p. 105)
Day 22	**Breakfast:**	Eggs over easy, bacon and Bedtime Blueberries (p. 219)
	Lunch:	Leftover Chicken and Chimichurri Sauce and steamed mixed vegetables
	Snack:	Bugs in a Boat (p. 220) and ham slices
	Dinner:	Steak Chile Rellenos (p. 74) and salad with Avocado Dressing and Dip (p. 175)
Day 23	**Breakfast:**	Chicken sausage and sautéed spinach with Béarnaise Sauce (p. 166)
	Lunch:	Portobello Mushroom Sandwich (p. 201) with turkey, avocado, and arugula
	Snack:	Leftover chicken sausage and avocado slices
	Dinner:	Seafood "Who Needs Rice" Jambalaya (p. 152)
Day 24	**Breakfast:**	Frittata for All (p. 183) and blueberries
	Lunch:	Leftover Jambalaya
	Snack:	Leftover Frittata and coconut flakes
	Dinner:	Garlic Beef Stew with Acorn Squash (p. 163) and steamed asparagus
Day 25	**Breakfast:**	Curried Veggie Hash (p. 120) and eggs over easy
	Lunch:	Leftover Garlic Beef Stew
	Snack:	Turkey Roll-Ups (p. 205)
	Dinner:	Better Butter Chicken (p. 56)

Shopping List Day 21-25

- 3 dozen eggs
- 2lbs chicken breasts
- 2.5lbs boneless skinless chicken thighs
- 1lb breakfast chicken sausages
- 1lb of tri tip steak
- 2lbs stew meat
- 1lb wild caught cod filets
- 1lb medium sized shrimp
- 1lb bacon
- 1 package deli ham slices
- 1 package deli turkey slices

- 4 avocados
- 5 carrots
- 2 yams
- 2 zucchinis
- 2 shallots
- 1 leek
- 4 portabella mushrooms
- 1 bunch spinach
- 1 bunch arugula
- 8 Roma tomatoes
- 3 bunches cilantro
- 1lb salad mix
- 1 bunch kale
- 1 bunch asparagus
- 1 head celery
- 1 acorn squash
- 1 bunch red chard
- 3 red bell peppers
- 1 green bell pepper
- 4 red onions
- 1 yellow onion
- 2 bulbs garlic
- 1 jalapeno
- 4 large poblano or Anaheim chili's
- Green onions
- Fresh basil
- Fresh parsley

- 1 lemon
- 1 lime
- Blueberries

- 1 4oz can diced green chili's
- 1 jar salsa verde
- 1 16oz box of chicken broth
- 1 6oz can tomato paste
- Ghee
- Hot sauce

Day 26	**Breakfast:**	Leftover Curried Veggie Hash and poached eggs
	Lunch:	Everyday Paleo Pizza (p. 84)
	Snack:	Leftover Pizza
	Dinner:	Albondigas Soup (p. 160)

Day 27	**Breakfast:**	Almond-Meal Blueberry Pancakes (p. 206) and ham
	Lunch:	Leftover Albondigas Soup
	Snack:	Jerky, macadamia nuts, and blueberries
	Dinner:	Chicken Paleo Piccata (p. 52) and Savory Cauliflower Fried Rice (p. 145)

Day 28	**Breakfast:**	Spring Scramble (p. 189)
	Lunch:	Shrimp Loves Coconut (p. 111) and Kids Love Cabbage Slaw (p. 134)
	Snack:	Turkey slices, Avocado Dressing and Dip (p. 175) and raw veggies
	Dinner:	Spicy Speedy Stuffed Peppers (p. 72)

Day 29	**Breakfast:**	Egg Houses (p. 179)
	Lunch:	Leftover Stuffed Peppers
	Snack:	Salmon Rolls (p. 199)
	Dinner:	Pork Tenderloin w/ Cherry Sauce over Mashed Cauliflower (p. 91) and Roasted Fennel (p. 136)

Day 30	**Breakfast:**	Leftover Pork Tenderloin and poached eggs
	Lunch:	Ginger Citrus Skillet Chicken (p. 49)
	Snack:	Turkey slices, shredded purple cabbage and coconut flakes
	Dinner:	Puerto Rican Beef (p. 61), Plantain Chips and Guacamole (p. 203)

Shopping List Day 26-30

- 3 dozen eggs
- 4 boneless skinless chicken breasts
- 2lbs boneless skinless chicken thighs
- 4lbs ground beef
- 1lb bacon
- 1.5lbs spicy Italian pork sausage
- 1lb mild Italian pork sausage
- 1.5lb pork tenderloin
- 1lb large shrimp
- 1 can wild Alaskan salmon
- 2 packages sliced deli turkey
- Beef jerky
- 3 crookneck yellow squash
- 2 zucchinis
- ½ lb crimini mushrooms
- 1 bunch asparagus
- 2 cucumbers
- 2 small tomatoes
- 8 carrots
- 8 large tomatoes
- 1 head celery
- 1 head purple or green cabbage
- 4 fennel bulbs
- 2 heads cauliflower
- 2 bunches kale
- 8 red bell peppers
- 1 green bell pepper
- 1 yellow bell pepper
- 3 yams
- 2 shallots
- 1 white onion
- 1 yellow onion
- 1 red onion
- 1 bulb garlic
- 1 jalapeno
- 6 avocados
- Chives
- Green onions
- Fresh rosemary
- Fresh basil
- Fresh ginger
- 1 apple
- 1 lemon
- 1 lime
- 1 orange
- 1 green mango
- 3 plantains
- Fresh or frozen blueberries
- Unsweetened dried bing cherries
- 1 jar organic gluten free marinara sauce
- 1 jar roasted red peppers
- 1 jar salsa verde
- 1 jar pimento stuffed green olives
- 1 can black olives
- 1 7oz can El Pato Jalapeno Salsa
- 2 16oz boxes chicken broth
- White Wine
- 1 jar capers
- 1 can artichoke hearts
- 1 jar julienned sun dried tomatoes
- 1 14.5oz can diced tomatoes

Make Sure You Have Stocked The Following list of Dry Spices, Oils, Condiments, and Nuts

- Basil
- Bay leaves
- Cardamom powder
- Cayenne pepper
- Coriander powder
- Cinnamon
- Cumin
- Curry Powder
- Chili Powder
- Dill
- Fenugreek powder
- Garlic powder
- Ground ginger
- Ground cloves
- Ground nutmeg
- Marjoram
- Oregano
- Paprika
- Poultry seasoning
- Red pepper flakes
- Saffron threads
- Thyme
- Turmeric
- White pepper

- Coconut flour
- Canned coconut milk
- Coconut oil
- Unsweetened coconut flakes
- Finely shredded unsweet-
  ened coconut flakes
- Olive oil
- Grass Fed Organic Butter

- Almond Meal
- Raw almonds
- Sliced raw almonds
- Raw pecans
- Macadamia nuts
- Raw walnuts

- Chicken broth
- Yellow mustard
- Spicy brown mustard
- Raw Organic Honey
- Balsamic Vinegar
- Apple cider vinegar
- Baking soda

Two Weeks of School Lunch Ideas

You can find great environmentally friendly and fun lunch boxes at www.planetbox.com

Week 1

Monday: Turkey Roll-Ups (p. 205), mandarin orange, Lärabar

Tuesday: Sunny Deviled Eggs (p. 193), apple slices, carrot sticks

Wednesday: Sun-Dried Tomato Chicken Slaw (p. 133), banana, almonds, or coconut flakes

Thursday: Ham slices, black olives, grapes, and Bugs in a Boat (p. 220)

Friday: Salmon Rolls (p. 199) (if your child does not like salmon, you can also use finely chopped chicken or tuna), dried cherries, cashews, or coconut flakes

Week 2

Monday: 2 Egg Cupcakes (p. 185), kiwi slices, Nutty Cookies (p. 210)

Tuesday: Grilled sliced chicken breasts, carrot sticks, Avocado Dressing and Dip (p. 175), dried apricots

Wednesday: 2 Garden-Fresh Meatballs (p. 79), apple slices, Great Balls of Dates (p. 218)

Thursday: Hard-boiled egg, carrot slices with Baba Ghanoush (p. 167), Paleo Apple Muffin (p. 214)

Friday: Turkey Slices, Bugs in a Boat (p. 220), grapes

Basic Fitness

Now it's time to move that body! Please, no jazzercise, because really, it's just not cool. OK, so I'm kind of kidding. If you really love jazzercise, I'll let it slide, but it is also important to build strength. Being strong *is* cool, and it makes life just so much dang easier. Imagine how great it would be to sling your kids easily out of the car and onto your hip, grab three bags of groceries in your other hand, squat down without dropping anybody or anything to pick up the keys that fell out of your purse, and jog into the house without hurting your back or being out of breath.

Being strong and in shape is sexy. Strong arms, lean legs, and a solid core should be the hottest fashion trend, and if you haven't seen this trend happening in your town, it's time to be the up-and-coming local fashion diva!

Another important note: exercising is for everyone—men, women, and children. If you are not exercising, even if you are eating a clean paleo diet, you are not healthy. Being sedentary is killing people left and right, and when you take a giant step backward and look at our lives, please consider how we are genetically wired. The obvious fact is that we are meant to be extremely active. In order to survive, our hunter/gatherer ancestors had to lift, push, pull, jump, sprint, carry, and climb just to get the basics like food. Our ancestors were athletes, and we are all intended to be the same.

I'm not implying that I expect each of you to train for the Olympic Games, but I do encourage you to get moving.

I strongly believe that working with a personal trainer is the best way to ensure safety and results, so please consider finding a trusted professional to help get you started on your fitness journey. With that being said, I understand that budget, time constraints, and family responsibilities are a factor in being able to work with a personal trainer, so we are back again to making choices. If you choose to work out, you can find a way.

A personal trainer is ideal, but if you want to give this a go on your own, you will need some equipment. Even on a budget, one can acquire a jump rope, used dumbbells, the floor, a wall, or a chair. Furthermore, we all have access to the outdoors, and this is the most essential item necessary for you and your family to use as a place to exercise. If you want to purchase some equipment, I suggest trying used sporting goods stores like Play It Again sports or online communities like Craigslist for the items that I use in the fitness section. I also offer information in the fitness section where specific equipment can be ordered online.

If you are already a gym member, you'll most likely have everything you need at your fingertips, but you'll need to be brave enough to enter the dreaded weight room. The fitness section will also include movements and workouts that you can do with your entire family or your significant other.

Speaking of family, getting the kids to exercise is imperative to their physical and emotional development. Unfortunately, we are raising a generation of sedentary people, which is obviously contributing to the enormous decline in the health of our youth. Not long ago kids played outside after school until sunset, but today, most kids are inside glued to the television or wired on video games, missing out on the precious moments that cannot be recaptured. As a strength coach, I have witnessed children under the age of ten who are not capable of performing basic functional movements like jumping, squatting, and lunging. At this age, children should be able to move in such manners without even thinking about it.

If you know that your kids are not getting enough exercise, the first step in helping them to become more active involves setting boundaries and rules. *You* are the parent, and although there might be some grumbling, your children will thank you later. Set restrictions on TV time and video game time. In our home, we have set the following limits that work well for our family. Take these suggestions as a guideline and adapt a routine that fits into your life.

1. We do not allow *any* video games during the week, and on Saturday we allow only one hour of gaming. The rest of the weekend is reserved for time with family, friends, and playing outside whenever possible. With school, sports, music, books, friends, and family, video games should never be the priority!

2. Second, we do not allow any television after school unless all homework is done, chores are completed, and outside play has happened. We suggest and partake together in other activities with our children and keep busy enough that television is not the first thought that comes to mind. I suggest only allowing 1 hour a day of television, and only if all other obligations (including playing) have been taken care of first.

If rules are set, there can be no arguments. Do not give in or cave in "sometimes" or your children will never take you seriously. Write down on poster board when video games and television are allowed, and post it where all can see. This way there is no question or changing your mind. What's set in stone cannot be undone.

You will find that cutting out the electronics will increase your bond as a family, and regaining this connection is another important step to a healthy paleo lifestyle.

Including your kids into your fitness routine is a great way to start this reconnecting process, and by setting this example, you'll engrain into your children the importance of a healthy lifestyle and the importance of taking care of yourself! Ok, so let's get started!

I will first show you some basic movements that will lay the foundation for gaining strength and endurance. The most important aspect of what I show is that your fitness routine should never become "routine." I take a cross-training approach that focuses on movements that our bodies are intended to do, movements that help us in our real lives, and a realistic approach to working out that works. I will not ask you to exercise three hours a day. Such an approach is unrealistic and simply does not work. I suggest that your workouts are shorter in duration but higher in intensity. Intensity means something different to everyone. If you have already been exercising and have a solid strength base, you may be able to push yourself a little bit harder. On days that you are not following an exercise program, I suggest being active, such as walking, playing with your kids, swimming, playing tennis, or whatever brings you joy!

If you have been sedentary for quite a while, I suggest that you first put the focus on proper technique and adapting to exercise rather than worrying about how intense your workouts actually are. If you are particularly unhealthy, overweight, and out of shape, I suggest that you start by walking and experimenting with a few of the introductory movements. This alone is a wonderful way to begin. However, after the first set of introductory movements, I will offer two weeks' worth of workouts for the beginner. Later in this section, I offer more advanced movements, followed by a more advanced workout routine. It is important to only move on to these routines when you feel ready. Again, working with a personal trainer is your best bet to ensure safety and results.

Squat

In this sequence I demonstrate how to perform an air squat. The squat is a natural movement that we perform countless times throughout the day. Every time we stand up from a chair or get up off the floor after playing with our kids, we are executing a squat-like motion. The key to benefiting from this natural movement is utilizing proper form. When you squat incorrectly, you can injure your back or other parts of your body. However, when you squat correctly, there are a number of benefits. Not only do you strengthen your quadriceps, hamstrings, and glutes, but you also strengthen your core. By performing this exercise regularly, you strengthen your body in such a way that everyday chores become easier, such as picking up children, groceries, and laundry. You also become more aware of how your body is truly designed to move.

MUSCLES USED: Quadriceps, Gluteals, and Hamstrings

1) Start by standing tall with your feet shoulder width apart and your toes angled out slightly. Next, hold your arms straight out in front of you for balance and tighten your tummy, fanny, and leg muscles. When done properly, you should feel tension everywhere.

2) Keeping your tummy tight and your back straight, reach your fanny back and down. Make sure to keep your knees behind your toes and your weight distributed on your heels.

3) Continue to sink your hips lower while still reaching your fanny back. You can allow your chest to come forward, but only as far as necessary to maintain balance. Keep that spine straight, and do not round or arch your back.

4) As your hips lower just below your knees, engage the glutes and push up through your heels until you return to the start position. If you have never squatted before, please look at the next sequence for an easier version of this movement.

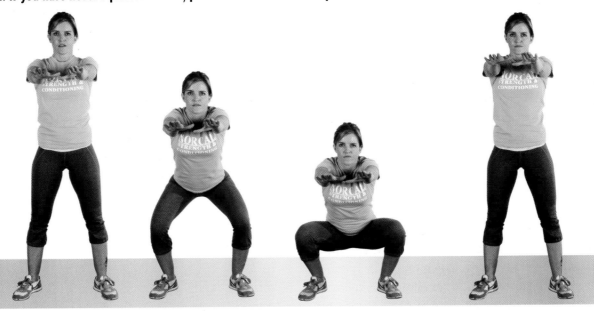

Chair Squat

The chair squat is an easier version of the regular air squat. The exercise is performed the same, but instead of squatting into the open air, you squat down onto a chair. For the best results, make sure the seat of the chair is above knee level. This will prevent you from squatting too deep. Once your fanny reaches the chair, rock forward and push through your heels to return to the start position. As you gain strength, transition to the air squat so you can reach full depth.

MUSCLES USED: Gluteals, Hamstrings, Quadriceps, and Adductors

1) Stand directly in front of a chair with your feet spread shoulder width apart and your toes angled out slightly. Next, hold your arms straight out in front of you for balance and tighten your tummy, fanny, and leg muscles. When done properly, you should feel tension everywhere.

2) Keeping your tummy tight and your back straight, reach your fanny back and down. Make sure to keep your knees behind your toes and your weight distributed on your heels.

3) Continue to sink your hips lower, while still reaching your fanny back. If necessary, your chest can come slightly forward, but keep your spine straight and do not round or arch your back! Once you feel your fanny reach the seat of the chair, continue to keep your back and tummy tight and sit all the way down.

4) Rock forward slightly from the seated position. Make sure to keep your arms out in front for balance and your tummy and back tight. At this point, push up through your heels and return to the standing position.

everyday paleo

Lunge

The walking lunge is another excellent exercise for strengthening the legs, glutes, and core. However, it is important to note that if you are unable to squat to full depth, you may not be ready to safely try this movement. Instead of performing the full lunge, you can modify this movement by simply taking larger than normal steps while walking.

MUSCLES USED: Gluteals, Hamstrings, Quadriceps, and Adductors

1) Start in the same position as the squat, with your feet directly under your shoulders.

2) Looking straight ahead, take a giant step forward. If you start with your left foot, step a little toward eleven o'clock. If you start with your right foot, step a little toward one o'clock. This will help you to maintain balance. As your back knee begins to drop straight down, make sure to keep your chest upright and your tummy tight.

3) Sink your back knee straight down until it is just above the ground. To achieve proper form, make sure the shin of your front leg is vertical and your lead knee is tracking over your heel and not your toes.

4) Pushing up through the heel of your front leg, begin your return to a vertical position. When done properly, you should feel this movement in your fanny as you rise.

5) Return to the start position by stepping your left foot up to your right foot. Keep your feet under your shoulders and your tummy tight.

6) Repeat the movement exactly as described, but this time step forward with the opposite leg. Continue to lunge, alternating legs as you go.

Push-Up

Push-ups can sound very intimidating, I know. I remember the day when doing a push-up seemed impossible. However, there is a starting point for everything in life, and the push-up can be accomplished by anyone with some modifications. In this sequence I demonstrate a classic push-up, but if you aren't ready for this exercise just yet, in the following sequences I offer some options that are a little less advanced. With each variation, it is very important to focus on form. When done correctly, the push-up is not just a chest or arm exercise, but rather a movement that strengthens the entire body.

MUSCLES USED: Pectoralis, Deltoids, and Triceps

1. To achieve the start position, place your tummy, thighs, and chest on the ground, position your hands slightly wider than shoulder width, and keep your neck in a neutral position. Make sure that your tummy, glutes, back, and legs are as tight as possible. The goal is to turn your body into a rock-solid plank!

2. While keeping your body as rigid as possible, begin to push yourself up. Your gaze should be directed down, just a few inches above your hands. Do not let your fanny rise up in the air like a mountain or let your tummy sag down, turning your spine into a valley. Stay tight!

3. Continue to push yourself up until your arms are fully extended.

4. Begin to lower yourself slowly back to the start position by bending at the elbows. Once your chest and thighs are again touching the floor, you may begin the pushup again. Stay tight!

Knee Push-Up

In this sequence I demonstrate the knee push-up, which is easier to perform than the classic push-up because you only have to lift a portion of your body weight. However, the knee push-up can still be too much to tackle for beginners. If you have trouble with this movement, do not give up. Instead, begin the push-up movement by standing a few feet away from a wall, placing your hands on the wall at shoulder height with your elbows bent, and then pushing your body away from the wall until your arms are fully extended. Just like with the classic push-up, tighten everything. This means your tummy, glutes, and legs. Next, bend your elbows and perform another repetition. If this proves too easy, gradually position your feet farther away from the wall each time you perform the movement. Once your strength increases, move on to the chair push-up. The chair push-up can be achieved by placing your hands on the edge of the chair, walking your feet out until your body is straight, and then performing a push-up. However, with chair push-ups it is extremely important to make sure the chair is stabilized against a wall. As you gain more strength, eventually chair push-ups will become too easy, and you will be ready to move on to the knee push-up shown below.

MUSCLES USED: *Pectoralis, Deltoids, and Triceps*

1 The start position for the knee push-up is exactly as the classic push-up, except you place your knees on the ground rather than your toes.

2 While keeping your body as rigid as possible, begin to push yourself up. Your gaze should be directed down, just a few inches above your hands. Do not let your fanny rise up in the air like a mountain or let your tummy sag down. Keep those abdominals tight.

3 Continue to push yourself up until your arms are fully extended. It is important to notice how my fanny is down, and that you could draw a straight line up from my hips to the top of my head.

4 Begin to lower yourself slowly back to the start position by bending at the elbows.

5 Once your chest and thighs are again touching the floor, you may begin the pushup again.

Plank Hold

The plank hold is an excellent movement to help strengthen the core, glutes, and leg muscles. This is one of those sneaky exercises that appears easy enough, but after practicing a few, you become well aware of your abdominal muscles the next morning when you roll out of bed.

MUSCLES USED: *Spinal Erectors, Abdominals, Quadriceps, and Gluteals*

To begin this exercise, place your toes and elbows on the ground. It is important to notice that my elbows are spread roughly shoulder width apart, and my hands are positioned directly beneath my chin. Once you have achieved the proper positioning with your arms and feet, straighten your body into a plank. This will require you to tighten your tummy, fanny muscles, and quads. Hold for 10 to 30 seconds, rest, and then repeat. If this is your first go at the plank hold, you can also modify by supporting your weight on your knees instead of your feet.

Plank Push-Up

The plank push-up incorporates the benefits of both the plank hold and the push-up. This movement can also be modified from the knees or even against a wall! However, make sure you are comfortable with the classic push-up and the plank hold from the toes before you try this movement.

MUSCLES USED:
Spinal Erectors, Abdominals, Quadriceps, Gluteals, Pectoralis, Deltoids, and Triceps

1 As described in the plank hold, begin this movement in the plank position—remember, everything should be tight and strong from head to toe!

2 Shifting your weight onto your left elbow and activating your core to stabilize your body, push up with your right arm until your right hand is on the ground.

3 Push up off of the ground using your left arm until both arms are fully extended. This should place you in the top of the push-up position.

4 Keeping your tummy, glutes, legs, and back tight, slowly lower your right elbow back toward the ground.

5 Slowly lower your left elbow back to the ground. This puts you back into the plank position and you are now ready to repeat the movement.

Body Row

Now that you've had some practice with pushing movements, I'll move on to pulling movements. In this sequence, I demonstrate the body row. Performing this exercise will help increase scapular, core, and arm strength, as well as help you move toward achieving a pull-up. I know full pull-ups might seem like an impossibility, but I have witnessed countless people progress from the body row shown here to eventually being able to perform numerous pull-ups in a row—myself included! To get started, you are going to need a set of rings or TRX strength bands, which can be found online at www.cathletics.com. When the equipment arrives, make sure it is safely and properly secured per the instruction manual before use. I know investing in equipment might seem like a hassle, but this exercise is definitely worth incorporating into your routine.

MUSCLES USED: Biceps, Latissimus Dorsi, Rhomboids, and Trapezius

1) Stand with your feet directly in between the rings, making sure that the rings are evenly adjusted and that the tops of the rings line up with your armpits. Hold tight to the rings.

2) While holding on tightly to the rings, tighten your tummy and legs and slowly begin to lower yourself back. Keep your gaze focused directly up through your hands in order to keep your neck in a neutral position.

3) Continue your controlled decent until your arms are fully extended.

4) Reverse the movement by first squeezing your shoulder blades together and then bending at the elbows to pull yourself back up to the rings, making sure to keep you body tight and straight like a plank. Tighten those tummy muscles and leg muscles! If this is easy for you, walk your feet forward a couple of steps to increase the difficulty. If this is too difficult, walk back a few steps to decrease the difficulty level. As you get stronger, you can attempt this movement with your feet elevated on a box.

Sit-Up

Gone are the days of crunches. In this sequence I demonstrate how to perform a slightly modified sit-up, which when performed correctly will not only work your abdominal muscles, but also your quads, hamstrings, and glutes, providing you with a full-body workout! Be ready to sweat and feel your heart rate go up as you tackle this new way to perform the old-school sit-up.

MUSCLES USED: Abdominals, Gluteals, Quadriceps, and Hamstrings

1) **Lie flat on your back with your knees bent. Your feet should be about 2 feet away from your fanny. For the beginner, have a partner secure your feet or you can tuck your feet underneath a couch or a set of heavy dumbbells for added support. Place your arms overhead and flat on the ground. 2) As you swing your arms forward to generate the momentum needed to sit up, begin to bring your chest toward your knees. 3) Reach your chest upward, avoiding rounding your spine to the point that you are no longer engaging your tummy muscles. Make sure that your chest touches your thighs at the top of the sit-up, and quickly pump your arms back by bending at the elbow. This provides you with the last little bit of momentum needed to completely raise yourself to a seated position. 4) As you begin your return to the floor, quickly pump your arms straight up over your head. This will move your arms back to the overhead position and prepare you for another repetition. 5) Return all the way back down flat to the ground and repeat the movement. Using your arms is not cheating. It allows you to perform more reps at a faster pace, which works more muscle groups, raises your heart rate, and increases the intensity of this movement. If you use support for your feet and your arms to help you sit up, even beginners should be able to perform at least a few repetitions.**

The hollow rock is another fabulous core strengthener. Although the movement varies from the sit-up in that it focuses more on the abdominal muscles, it is still a full-body movement when performed correctly. The key to all of the movements I demonstrate is to maintain a tight body! When you focus on tightening and stabilizing your entire body during these exercises, you train your body to be more aware of how it should move and work, which transfers to real life. If you isolate your muscle use, it inhibits the normal and natural flow of your movements.

MUSCLES USED: Abdominals

Begin on the floor in a "hollow position." Your pelvis should be tilted up and arms positioned overhead. Your legs should be tight, positioned together, and raised about a foot above the ground.

Using your tummy muscles, stay tight and rock by raising your hips off the ground.

Alternate the movement by lifting your shoulders off the ground and letting your hips drop downward. It is important to note that you should rock smoothly. There should be no back and forth thumping of your spine and butt. If you are unable to achieve a smooth rocking motion, modify the position by bending your knees and bringing your arms down to your sides. Use this modification until you are strong enough to perform the hollow rock with straight, outstretched legs and your arms positioned overhead.

Super Woman

This movement can make you feel silly, so I suggest doing it with the kids so that you can all have a good laugh and feel like superheroes together! However, make sure not to laugh too hard because as with all of the previous movements I have demonstrated, you want to maintain muscle tightness, especially with your glutes. When performed correctly, this is a great exercise for strengthening the fanny, hamstrings, quads, and back muscles.

MUSCLES USED: *Spinal Erectors, Gluteals, Deltoids, and Hamstrings*

1) Start lying face down on the ground with your legs together and arms outstretched overhead.

2) Tighten your glutes and raise your legs, chest, and arms off of the floor at the same time. And when I say tighten your glutes, I mean really squeeze your fanny!

3) Return your legs and arms simultaneously to the ground and repeat.

Jumping Squat

The jumping squat is an advanced movement and should only be performed if you are strong enough to achieve a full-depth squat and you have been working out using a cross-training method for longer than six months. Furthermore, you should not attempt this movement if you have any injuries or orthopedic issues with your knees, hips, or spine. If you fall into the category of being able to try this movement, hold on, because these get really fun really fast! Not only does this movement strengthen the same muscle groups as the regular squat, but the jumping squat is a very explosive movement that will get your heart rate up quickly and your legs burning—in a good way, of course!

MUSCLES USED: Gluteals, Hamstrings, and Quadriceps

1) Start in a squat stance with your feet under your shoulders and arms outstretched in front of you for balance. **2)** Reach your hips back and down, keeping your chest upright and the weight in your heels. **3)** Continue to squat down to full depth, making sure that your hips are lower than your knees. **4)** Without resting at the bottom of your squat position, push up quickly through your heels, using your arms to give you more momentum. **5)** Bring your arms down quickly by your side as you jump into the air. **6)** Land with bent knees onto your forefoot and then transfer your weight back to your heels. Do not land on your toes and avoid letting your knees track forward. As you land, go immediately back into a squat and jump again. Repeat a few times and notice how quickly this movement starts to turn up the intensity!

Workouts
for Beginners

Week One

Day 1: Warm up with a 5-minute walk (around the block will work just fine). Rest for a minute and then perform 10 air squats or chair squats. Rest for a minute and then perform 10 push-ups. Rest for another minute and then perform 10 sit-ups. Finish with another 5-minute walk. Assess how you feel? If at any time during your workout you begin to feel light-headed or dizzy, slow down, rest longer, or cut the reps in half.

Day 2: Do something active that you enjoy. Take a brisk walk. Walk fast for a minute or two and then slow down and saunter along at a slower pace for a minute or two. Plan to be active for at least 30 minutes. Play a game of soccer, catch, or tag with your kids, and make sure you alternate between moving quickly and moving slowly. If you start to feel light-headed or dizzy, stop and rest for a few minutes.

Day 3: Repeat day 1 but instead of sit-ups, do body rows.

Day 4: Rest today but stay active. Do some stretching, yoga, or simply take a slow leisurely walk with the family.

Day 5: This should be another active day. Swim, ride bikes with the kids, or take another brisk walk. Discover a new hobby that you might enjoy. Take a tennis class with your spouse or your children, try shooting the basketball, or take a trip to the batting cages. When you are exercising again, try to work hard for a few minutes, and then go at a slower pace. Alternate back and forth and make sure you get in at least 30 minutes of activity.

Day 6 & 7: Maintain an active lifestyle but focus more on relaxation, meal planning and preparation, and spending time with family.

Day 1: Walk or jog slowly for 5 minutes to warm up. Perform 10 squats, hold for an accumulative total of 30 seconds in a plank hold, and execute 10 push-ups. Rest for 1 minute and then repeat the squats, plank hold, and push-ups. Rest for another minute and then again repeat the squats, plank hold, and push-ups. Walk or jog slowly for 5 minutes. Again, if you are feeling light-headed or dizzy, slow down or cut the down the number of reps. If you are feeling great and up for more of a challenge, try to move a bit quicker through the workout in order to raise the level of intensity. Listen to your body!

Day 2: Be active for at least 30 minutes today. Try alternating between walking and jogging. Play with the kids—this is always a sure way to get in at least 30 minutes of activity! Go to the park and run around with your children. Do everything that they do and you'll be amazed by the energy that is required to simply act like a kid!

Day 3: Repeat day 1 except do 15 reps of the super woman movement instead of the plank hold.

Day 4: Rest today but stay active with stretching, yoga, walking, and playing with the kids.

Day 5: This should be another day of fun activity! Play tag with the kids, a great way to have a burst of activity followed by a period of rest.

Day 6 & 7: Rest, recuperate, meal plan, and play!

Increasing Workout Intensity

As you begin to feel better and get healthier and your workouts become easier, start thinking about increasing the reps for these workouts and adding in some of the other movements that I have demonstrated in the above section. Try completing more rounds of each suggested workout and try adding in a sprint at the end, middle, and beginning of the workout rather than just a jog or a walk.

Following are a few more workouts for you to include in your weekly routine once you are able to squat to full depth and feel healthy and strong enough to increase the intensity of your workouts. You should continue to follow the same model as described in the two-week workout plan. On days 1 and 3, do one of my suggested workouts below. With the other days, either do activities such as sprinting, walking, swimming, biking, or playing, or spend your time resting, relaxing, stretching, and playing with the kiddos.

Workout 1: Run or walk for 5 minutes. Perform 15 body rows followed by 10 lunges on each leg (20 total). Rest for 1 minute and then repeat the 15 body rows followed by the 10 lunges on each leg. Rest again for 1 minute and then repeat the 15 body rows and 10 lunges each leg.

Workout 2: Repeat as many times as possible within a 7–10 minute time period: 20 squats, 20 hollow rocks, 10 sit-ups, and 10 push-ups.

fitness

Workout 3: Perform 3 rounds of: 5 plank push-ups, 10 body rows, and 15 jumping squats

Workout 4: Sprint 100 meters, or about 6 car lengths, walk back, and then perform 30 seconds of hollow rocks followed by 30 seconds of the super woman movement. Rest for 1 minute and then repeat the entire sequence 3–4 times.

Workout 5: Warm up with a 5-minute jog. Perform 30 squats and 15 push-ups followed by 20 squats and 10 push-ups, followed by 10 squats and 5 push-ups.

everyday paleo

Dumbbells!

Time to move on to the weights. Please ladies, understand that lifting weights does not give you humongous or unsightly muscles. By incorporating weight training into your fitness plan, you will gain the strength and ability to make it through your day, add bone density, and decrease the signs and symptoms of aging. Another bonus of weight lifting, just like with the introductory movements, is that it transfers over to what we do every day in real life. You will learn how to safely lift, push, and carry heavy objects without injuring yourself, all the while working toward a healthier,

more fit you. Most importantly, I want you to have fun! Exercising should make us feel better and should not be a dreaded experience. It should give you confidence and add joy to your day. Finding a friend to join you, getting the kids involved, and having your spouse be your workout partner are all ways to make exercise more fun and rewarding.

Dumbbell Press

Although the dumbbell press is a very straightforward movement, when you first begin using this technique, I suggest starting with a lighter weight. Only after you are extremely comfortable with the movement should you start lifting more. This is true for all movements that involve weights. Start out light, get used to moving with proper form, and then think about gradually increasing the load.

MUSCLES USED: Deltoids, Triceps

1) Bring the dumbbells up to your shoulders and position your elbows under the weights. It is important to notice how the weight plates are facing forward rather than to the sides. Your feet should be placed between hip and shoulder width, with your toes turned out just a bit for support. **2)** Tighten your tummy, fanny, and leg muscles. Take a small breath and hold it as you begin to press the dumbbells straight overhead, engaging the muscles in your shoulders and arms. **3)** At the top of this movement, your arms should be fully extended to the point that you feel as if your shoulders are up around your ears. Pretend you are holding up the sky—if your shoulders are relaxed, you will not be strong enough to do so! The dumbbells should be directly over your shoulders and lined up directly over your hips and heels. **4)** Begin to return the dumbbells back to your shoulders. You can let gravity help, but you must also control the weights on the way down. Dumbbells crashing onto your shoulders does not feel good; trust me, I know from experience. **5)** Finish with the dumbbells resting back on your shoulders, with your elbows under the weights and facing forward. Take a few breaths of air, get tight, hold that little breath again with a tight tummy, glutes, and legs, and repeat.

Push Press

Although the push press looks similar to the press, there are some key differences, the most prominent one being that the push press is a dynamic movement. The push press incorporates power generated from the legs in order to move the dumbbells overhead, adding a metabolic component to this movement that is sure to get your heart racing a bit faster than the standard dumbbell press does.

MUSCLES USED: Deltoids, Triceps, Gluteals, and Quadriceps

1) Start in the same position as the press—holding the weights up on your shoulders, with your feet placed between hip and shoulder width and your toes turned out just a bit for support.

2) Take in a small breath and hold it, making sure your tummy is super tight. Next, keeping your gaze forward and your torso straight up and down, bend your knees slightly.

3) As if you were jumping, use a quick upward movement, letting the power generated from your legs help press the dumbbells overhead. This should be a fast and explosive movement. However, you must make sure to keep your torso upright!

4) As with the press, finish this movement with your arms fully extended and let your breath out.

5) Begin to return the dumbbells back to your shoulders as your knees bend again slightly.

6) Once the dumbbells reach your shoulders, your knees should again be bent so that you are ready to repeat the movement and explode the dumbbells back up and overhead. Find a rhythmic breathing pattern during this exercise so that you are not holding your breath through the entire movement.

7) Finish in an upright position.

everyday paleo

Dumbbell Dead Lift

Unlike the squat, the dumbbell dead lift predominately works the glutes and the hamstrings rather than the quadriceps. We all pick stuff up, but most of us tend to do this everyday movement incorrectly. Some health professionals have warned that the dead lift can cause back injury. Can you hurt your back dead lifting? Of course, but you can also hurt your back just as badly or worse by incorrectly lifting a kitten; therefore, learning how to dead lift with proper technique transfers over to real life quite nicely, and you will actually be strengthening and training your body in order to prevent injury. Again, working with a trained fitness professional is always the best option!

MUSCLES USED: Erector Spinae, Gluteals, and Hamstrings

1) Your feet should be positioned directly under your hips with your toes angled out slightly. The dumbbells should be on the floor, just outside of your feet and directly under your arms. Before you reach down to grab the dumbbells, take in a little breath of air and hold it, bend forward at the waist, reach your fanny back, and bend your knees. It is important to note that you want your knees tracking over your heels, not your toes. Next, grip the dumbbells tight. Your back should be flat, straight, and flexed, and your shoulders should be just in front of the dumbbells. 2) Pushing through your heels and holding the dumbbells close to your legs, begin to stand upright while looking slightly down and straight in front of you. Make sure that your hips and knees rise in unison. 3) Continue to rise until you are standing upright, keeping the weights in close to your body and not letting them drift out in front of you. 4) To return the dumbbells back to the floor, take in another few breaths and hold a little bit of it to help your body stay tight. Again, reach your fanny back as your chest comes forward. Your knees should bend, but do not allow them to track forward over your toes. 5) Keep reaching your fanny back. As your chest comes forward, maintain a tight back and tummy until the heads of the dumbbells touch the floor. From there, take a few breaths, hold in a little bit of air, and repeat the movement.

Special note: if you still are unable to perform a full-depth squat, you may not yet be ready to dead lift. Furthermore, if you have extremely tight hamstrings or hips, this movement might prove to be too challenging.

Dumbbell Squat

The dumbbell squat adds more resistance to the already beneficial movement of the squat. This movement should only be performed if you can properly execute a full-depth squat. Again, I'll remind you to use a lighter weight when you are first learning these dumbbell techniques.

MUSCLES USED: *Quadriceps, Gluteals, and Hamstrings*

1) Raise the dumbbells to your shoulders so that your elbows are high and pointing directly in front of you. Your feet should be positioned directly under your shoulders, just as with the regular air squat. Make sure you stabilize your midsection by tightening your tummy muscles before you start this movement.

2) Begin to reach your fanny back, keeping your tummy tight, elbows high, and chest upright.

3) Perform a full depth squat while maintaining a tight tummy, high elbows, and upright chest.

4) Keep your chest upright, push through your heels and return to the standing position. As you do this, it is important not to let the weights drag you forward.

5) Finish the movement by standing all the way upright. Leave the dumbbells on your shoulders and repeat.

everyday paleo

Thrusters

This movement is a dynamic combination of the dumbbell squat and the dumbbell press. As with some of the previous exercises, it's a more advanced movement and should only be attempted once you are comfortable with a dumbbell squat. With the added weight of a set of dumbbells, you must not only move from a squat position to a standing position, but you must also simultaneously move the dumbbells overhead. Although this movement might sound easy enough, thrusters are sure to give you a wake-up call in the intensity department!

MUSCLES USED: *Quadriceps, Gluteals, Hamstrings, Deltoids, and Triceps*

1) Bring the dumbbells up to your shoulders. You want to assume the start position for a dumbbell squat, meaning your elbows are high, your feet are under your shoulders, and your tummy is tight. **2)** To begin the dumbbell squat, reach your fanny back and bend at the knees. Remember to stay tight, keep those elbows high, and keep your chest up. **3)** Make sure to reach full depth in the squat. **4)** At the bottom of your squat, push quickly and powerfully up through your heels, as if you are jumping. As you drive up through your heels, let the power that you generate from your legs and fanny help you explode the dumbbells straight overhead. The squat and press should not be two separate movements, but rather one fluid movement. The dumbbells should start to push overhead before you are completely back to a standing position. **5)** Once you are standing, finish with your arms fully extended and the dumbbells lined up over your shoulders, hips, and heels, just as with the dumbbell press. **6)** As you lower the dumbbells back to your shoulders, begin to drop back into another squat. **7)** Finish back in the full-depth squat position and repeat the movement. It is important to find a rhythmic breathing pattern during this movement. You want to keep your midsection stabilized and strong, but because this is a high-intensity movement, you are still going to need your breath.

Weighted Walking Lunge

Once you have mastered a full-depth squat and feel comfortable with walking lunges, you are ready to try the weighted walking lunge. With a dumbbell in each hand, it adds resistance and intensity to this awesome fanny burning movement.

MUSCLES USED: Gluteals, Hamstrings, Quadriceps, and Adductors

1) Start in the same position as a squat, with your feet under your shoulders and holding the dumbbells down at your sides. Do not allow the dumbbells to pull your shoulders forward. Instead, squeeze your shoulder blades together and keep your chest up.
2) Keeping your torso upright, your gaze forward, and the dumbbells held close to your body, take a giant step forward with your right foot. If you look at the photo, you'll notice I move my foot a little toward one o'clock. This will help you to maintain balance.
3) Making sure to keep your chest upright and your tummy tight, lower your left knee straight down. The shin of your front leg should stay vertical with your knee and track over your heel, not your toes. Your back knee should continue to sink down until it's just above the ground. **4)** Pushing up through the heel of your front leg, begin your return to a vertical position. You should feel this movement in your fanny as you rise. **5)** Return to the start position by stepping your left foot up to your right foot. Your feet should be positioned under your shoulders and your tummy should remain tight. **6)** Repeat the movement exactly as described, but this time step forward with the opposite leg. Continue to lunge, alternating legs as you go.

Overhead Dumbbell Lunge

The overhead dumbbell lunge is similar to the walking weighted lunge, but instead of holding two dumbbells at your sides, you hold a single dumbbell over your head. As a result, the movement works the shoulders and arm muscles, as well as the glutes, quads, hamstrings, and core. It is important to note that the movement requires torso stability and balance, so if the walking lunge still proves to be challenging, hold off on this movement until you can perform the basic walking lunge as well as the weighted walking lunge with ease. In addition, make sure to use lighter weight when first starting out with this advanced movement.

MUSCLES USED: Gluteals, Hamstrings, Quadriceps, Adductors, Deltoids, Trapezius, and Core

1) Begin the movement with the right dumbbell extended directly overhead and your left arm held straight out in front of you for balance. **2)** Keeping the dumbbell extended straight overhead, your torso tight, your gaze directed forward, and your left arm extended out in front of you for balance, take a giant step forward with your right foot. If you look at the photos, you'll notice I step toward one o'clock. This will help you to maintain balance. Since added weight is involved in this movement, it is important to start slowly at first in order to maintain balance and allow yourself to get used to the feel of lunging while holding something overhead. **3)** Slowly lower your left knee toward the ground. The shin of your front leg should stay vertical with your knee and track over your heel, not your toe. The back knee should continue to sink down until it's just above the ground. **4)** Pushing up through the heel of your front leg, begin your return to a vertical position. You should feel this movement in your fanny as you rise. **5)** Step your left foot up to your right foot, returning to the start position. Your feet should be under your shoulders and your tummy should remain tight. **6)** Repeat the movement exactly as described, but this time step forward with your opposite leg. Continue to lunge, alternating legs as you go. Make sure that you switch arms after performing a predetermined amount of lunges. For example, if the workout calls for 20 overhead walking lunges, perform 10 with one arm holding the dumbbell overhead, switch arms, and perform the final 10 with the opposite arm holding the dumbbell overhead.

Dumbbell Swing

The dumbbell swing is a dynamic movement that is great for building up the muscles in the glutes, legs, and core. And when performing several reps, it will dramatically raise the intensity level of your workout. As always, make sure you start out with a lighter weight in order to learn the technique before you load yourself with a more challenging weight.

MUSCLES USED: *Gluteals, Hamstrings, Erector Spinae, and Deltoids*

1) Begin with your feet approximately shoulder width apart and grip the handle of the dumbbell with both hands. If gripping the dumbbell in this manner proves difficult, you can also hold the head of the dumbbell. Next, push your bottom back, keep your chest up, and make your back strong and straight. It is important to note that during the entirety of this movement, you want your weight in your heels and your gaze directed forward. **2)** To generate the power needed to swing the dumbbell upward, quickly move your hips forward. You do not want to move the weight with your arm muscles, but rather with the force generated by your fanny and leg muscles. **3)** Swing the dumbbell up to chest level. **4)** As gravity brings the dumbbell back down, drop your hips back. This allows you to "catch" the dumbbell as it falls. Once accomplished, repeat the movement and get ready to feel your fanny get put to work!

Advanced Body Weight
and Bar Movements

I will now demonstrate for you a few body weight movements that are appropriate for the advanced beginner and for those with a higher level of fitness. These movements can be incorporated into your workouts if you are already in good health or you have been following the beginner's workouts for at least thirty days and feel healthy and strong. However, if you are unable to squat to full depth or lack the ability to perform modified knee push-ups off the floor, it's best to continue with the beginner's workout for a while. As long as you stick with it, your core strength will improve, and soon you will be astonished by what your body can achieve. And when you are finally ready to add some of the upcoming workouts to your regimen, you will only advance your already improved strength. At the end of this section, I will offer several more workout options that include all of the movements that you have learned thus far.

L-Sit Progression

The L-sit is an excellent core strengthener. In addition to focusing on the abdominal muscles, it works the arms and legs as well. Achieving an actual L-sit is quite challenging, but it is certainly worth the effort. Personally, I thought I would never get there when I first started practicing, but each training session I progressed a little more, until the movement was easily attainable. If you look at the photos below, you'll notice that I perform the movement on a pair of "parallettes" constructed out of PVC pipe. Instructions on how to build a set of parallettes can be found at www.parallettestraining.com.

MUSCLES USED: *Abdominals, Iliopsoas, Quadriceps, and Triceps*

1) Before beginning this movement, it is important to set the parallettes the proper distance apart. The distance between the two should be the same as the distance between your elbow and fingertips. Once properly set, position yourself between the parallettes, knees down, and place your hands near the back or middle of the bars. Make sure your body is not leaning forward or backward—you want your hands positioned directly under your shoulders. 2) Press down on the parallettes, moving your body away from the ground. Your shoulders should not be shrugged up, but rather strong and flat. Keep your tummy tight, arms strong, and rest your toes on the ground for support. If you are a beginner, this might be a good place for you to start. Try holding yourself here for 10-second increments, using your toes on the ground as support. 3) If the first movement feels easy, try lifting your feet off the ground and holding a tuck position. Make sure not to rock forward or back—keep your center of gravity in between your hands. Try holding this position for 10- to 30-second time increments. 4) If you feel ready, try the actual L-sit. From the tuck position, slowly straighten your legs out in front of you. Try not to bend at the knees and keep your legs above the height of the parallettes. If you have limited hamstring flexibility or tight hips, this advanced movement might take a while to achieve, but that is OK—remember, anything worth achieving is always hard work! Another variation is to balance in the tuck position, place one foot on the ground for some support, and straighten the other leg and hold for 10- to 30-second increments. Switch legs and repeat. 5) After achieving the L-sit or after performing the tuck position, place your feet back on the ground underneath your body to support your weight and relax your arms. Rest and repeat.

Jump Rope

Do you remember jumping rope as a child? Maybe it wasn't your thing, but I remember jumping rope for what seemed like hours when I was a kid, and I do not remember it being challenging, only fun! Wow, it's a heck of a lot different as an adult, and every time I jump rope I wonder why it was so easy as a child. The good news is that jumping rope, especially with your kids, can still be a lot of fun! Oh, and be ready to be reintroduced to your calf muscles after your first jump rope experience. A jump rope is about the least expensive, easiest to store, and most portable workout tool one can have. However, it is important to purchase a jump rope where the rope rotates within the handle. This makes the rope turn easier and faster, resulting in less mishaps when performing the movement. Most fitness stores have a variety of jump ropes available, but you can also find them online at www.roguefitness.com.

MUSCLES USED: Full body exercise with emphasis on calves

1) This movement can be a nightmare if your rope is not the correct length. When purchasing a jump rope, hold both handles at the top of your armpits. If the rope just touches the ground, you are good to go. **2)** Start with the jump rope behind you. Next, rotate your wrists so that the rope moves over your head in a fluid arc. At the same time, bend your knees in preparation for your first jump. **3)** As the rope swings toward the front of your body, leap off the ground so that the rope can move underneath of your feet. The goal is to jump just high enough to allow the rope to move underneath you, but this requires timing. When first starting out, it might take a rather high jump in order to accomplish this goal. Just remember to take things slow to find your rhythm, look straight ahead, and keep your torso tight. **4)** Allow the rope to pass underneath your feet while you are in the air. Make sure you are jumping on your toes, and make sure not to "donkey kick" your legs behind you. Remember, straight up and down, keeping your body tight. As you begin to get the hang of this movement, you can try what is known as the "double-under." This is when you quickly spin the rope, allowing it to move twice underneath your feet with each jump. Jumping rope is an excellent exercise for getting your heart rate up, as well as for working a few of those undiscovered muscles. Have the tops of your feet and ankles ever been sore? They will be after a good session of jumping rope!

Broad Jump

The broad jump is a dynamic movement that should only be performed if you do not have any orthopedic knee or spine issues. This movement is powerful, explosive, and something your kids will most likely love! You can turn broad jumps into a fun game with your family, while at the same time strengthening your legs and fanny.

MUSCLES USED: *Abdominals, Gluteals, Quadriceps, Hamstrings, and Calves*

1) Start with your feet positioned under your hips in the "jump position." **2)** Reach your hips and arms back behind you, keeping your chest up, back straight, and gaze straight ahead. **3)** Jump up and forward, using the power generated from your legs and fanny. At the same time, propel your arms forward to give you more momentum. **4)** Land with bent knees. Your weight should be in your heels and your arms out in front for balance. Try to land gently, and not on your toes. In order to keep your spine and knees safe, let your fanny absorb the impact of your landing. **5)** Return back to a standing position and be ready to again reach your hips back and repeat the move.

Box Step-Up

Do you have an old aerobics step-up that you purchased along with that Jane Fonda workout video years ago? Well, you can toss the video if you like, but keep the step-up. By using this piece of equipment in conjunction with a few of the movements from this section, you can add an interesting piece of intensity to your routine. We'll start with the box step-up, which is great for working the quads, glutes, and hamstrings.

MUSCLES USED: Gluteals, Hamstrings, and Quadriceps

1) **Stand directly in front of the box or step-up. Your feet should only be a couple of inches away from the box.**

2) **Step your right foot on top of the box.**

3) **Push off your left leg and then place your left foot next to your right foot on top of the box. Make sure your posture is straight and your body is tight.**

4) **Step your left foot back to the ground.**

5) **Step your right foot off the box and return to the start position. From here, alternate legs by stepping your left foot up to the box first. If you are a beginner, it is important to start out slowly. Once you begin to feel balanced and safe with this movement, you can increase repetitions and speed.**

Box Jump

The box jump is the dynamic cousin to the box step-up and adds a new level of intensity. It works a number of muscles, including your calves, glutes, quads, and hamstrings. When performed in repetition, expect hard breathing and some sweating. However, you only want to utilize this movement if you can easily step up and down onto a small box, squat to full depth, and if you do not have any orthopedic problems with your knees or spine. I recommend starting with a 12-inch box, and slowly progressing higher as your strength and agility improves.

MUSCLES USED: Abdominals, Quadriceps, Hamstrings, Gluteals, and Calves

1) Stand in front of the box as described in the box step-up.

2) Reach your fanny and arms back slightly, bending at the knees and keeping your chest up and your gaze forward.

3) Swing both arms forward as you jump up and onto the box, using the power from your fanny and your legs to propel yourself up. Explode up off of the ground and do not be timid!

4) Land with bent knees and with both feet on the box. Your weight should be in your heels and both of your arms out in front of your body for balance. Try to land gently by letting your fanny absorb the impact of the jump rather than your knees.

5) Once on the box, stand completely upright.

6) Carefully step one foot back down to the ground.

7) Return the opposite leg to the ground and get ready to repeat the movement. At some point, you might feel confident enough to jump back down from the box, allowing you to quickly repeat this movement, but do not attempt this option until you feel extremely confident with stepping down and repeating the jump several times in a row.

Jumping Pull-Up

The jumping pull-up can be performed in your gym or at your local playground, or you can install a pull-up bar in your garage by purchasing one online at www.studpullupbar.com. In addition to strengthening your upper body, this movement is great for the fanny, calf muscles, and quads. However, the jumping pull-up is an incredibly dynamic movement, so I recommend only trying a few at a time during your first attempt.

MUSCLES USED:
Latissimus Dorsi, Trapezius, Deltoids, Hamstrings, Gluteals, Quadriceps, and Calves

1) Stand directly under the bar, reach your arms up, and grab the bar slightly wider than shoulder width. For this particular movement, you want your palms facing away from your body.

2) Bend your knees and reach your fanny back, putting you into the squat position. If the bar is too high, you may need to stand on a box in order to achieve the correct position. If the box still does not give you adequate height, you can always place a single rubber weight plate on top of the box as I do in the photos above—just make sure both the box and the plate are secure.

3) Keeping your chin tucked and your gaze straight in front of you, jump up, making sure that your chin makes it over the bar. You should not be pulling yourself up as much as you should be using the power from your legs to help jump your chin over the bar.

4) After your chin passes the bar, let gravity quickly pull you back down. Do not slowly lower your body back to the start position. Instead, continue to hold the bar and allow gravity to quickly pull your feet downward. You want to land on your heels in the squat position, which allows your fanny to absorb the impact rather than your arms. Repeat immediately. Try a set of 5 and see how you feel. I guarantee your heart will be pounding and you will be breathing hard! Start out with a low rep count with this exercise.

Working
Toward That Pull-Up

The pull-up can be achieved! I remember clearly when I first started working out at NorCal Strength and Conditioning and thinking, "There is no way this body of mine will ever be able to do a pull-up." Fast-forward a few hardworking months later and there I was, stringing multiple pull-ups together! As I have mentioned before, I highly recommend working with a trainer in order to achieve your maximum potential and to make sure you are performing these movement correctly. However, if finding a trainer simply is not a possibility, here is a guideline to go by to know if you are ready to begin doing the exercises that will eventually lead to a full pull-up: Grab your set of hanging rings, walk your feet all the way forward, and then try to perform the body row demonstrated earlier. Walking your feet all the way forward increases the difficulty of the body row to the highest degree. If you can easily and safely pull your own body weight this way, you are ready to move on to working for the pull-up.

The first pull-up we'll focus on is the negative pull-up, which starts much like the jumping pull-up. However, once you get your chin above the bar, instead of immediately dropping down, you hold the position for five seconds. After those five seconds are complete, you slowly lower yourself back down to a full arm extension. When starting out, I recommend doing just one or two reps of this movement, as they can make you very soar. I also recommend alternating your grip. First do it with your palms facing away from you (pronated), and then practicing it with your palms facing toward you (supinated). Both versions are demonstrated in this section. Continue incorporating repetitions of the negative pull-up, both pronated and supinated, into your workouts at least two times a week. Start with only two repetitions at a time for the

first two weeks, and then start performing three sets of two repetitions for the third and fourth weeks. If these workouts prove easy, increase to three sets of three repetitions. When done in this progressive manner, you'll soon discover that you can hold your chin over the bar for a much longer time than the five-second duration, and you will be able to lower yourself down to full extension slowly and without losing tension. Once you get to this level, you might be ready to attempt that first pull-up! There is no way to know for sure until you grab the bar and pull, so just go for it when you feel ready. You might surprise yourself with how easy you accomplish your first pull-up. Even if you can only get halfway there, you'll still be able to tell that your hard work is paying off and soon you will be strong enough.

Pull-Up (Pronated)

In this sequence I demonstrate how to do a pull-up with your hands facing away from you, which is known as a pronated grip. Doing a pull-up in this fashion focuses more on the muscles in your back and chest. In the next sequence, I demonstrate how to do a pull-up with your hands facing toward you.

MUSCLES USED: *Latissimus Dorsi, Trapezius, Deltoids, and Rhomboids*

1) **Stand directly under the bar, reach your arms up, and grab the bar slightly wider than shoulder width. For this particular movement, you want your palms facing away from your body.**

2) **As you pull your elbows down and back, reach your chest up toward the bar.**

3) **Keep your chin tucked down until it passes the bar.**

4) **Lower yourself down to the start position. Your descent shouldn't be as slow as when performing a negative pull-up, but it should be slower than when performing a jumping pull-up. With this movement, it is very important that your descent is controlled. Once you are back to the start position, rest if necessary and repeat.**

Chin-Up (Supinated)

In this sequence I demonstrate how to perform a pull-up with your hands facing toward you, which is known as a supinated grip. Assuming this grip places a greater emphasis on your biceps muscles. To get the most well-rounded pull-up workout, I recommend performing pull-ups with both a pronated and supinated grip.

MUSCLES USED: Latissimus Dorsi, Trapezius, Deltoids, Rhomboids, and Biceps

1   2   3   4   5

1) Stand underneath the bar with your palms facing toward your body.

2) Reach your arms up and grab the bar slightly narrower than shoulder width. For this particular movement, you want your palms facing toward your body.

3) As you pull your elbows down and back, reach your chest up toward the bar.

4) Keep your chin tucked down until your chin passes the bar.

5) Lower yourself down to the start position. Your descent shouldn't be as slow as when performing a negative pull-up, but it should be slower than when performing a jumping pull-up. With this movement, it is very important that your descent is controlled. Once you are back to the start position, rest if necessary and repeat.

Knee-to-Elbow

The knee-to-elbow movement can be done in the gym, at the playground, or in your home with the stud pull-up bar previously mentioned. In addition to being an excellent movement to work your abdominal muscles, it's also a great workout for your lats and pectoral muscles. One of the best things about this movement is that it is suitable for most people—as long as you feel comfortable holding your own body weight while hanging from a bar, you should be able to perform some variant of this movement.

MUSCLES USED: Abdominals, Iliopsoas, Latissimus Dorsi, and Pectoralis

1 *2* *3* *4* *5*

1) Stand directly under the bar, reach your arms up, and grab the bar slightly wider than shoulder width. For this particular movement, you want your palms facing away from your body.

2) Keeping your chin down, raise your knees up slightly toward your waist. If you feel like this is as far as you can go, stop here, lower your legs back to the floor, and repeat.

3) If you feel like you can raise your knees farther, continue bringing your knees up higher toward your chest using those tummy muscles!

4) If you are able to bring your knees all the way up to touch your elbows, do so by pushing away from the bar using your lats and squeezing those knees up as high as possible using your abdominals.

5) Return to the start position and repeat.

Intermediate Workouts

Following are workouts that incorporate all the movements that we have learned thus far! Follow the same guidelines as outlined in the two-week beginner's workout program by simply replacing day 1 and day 3 with one of the workout options listed below. The key is to keep your workouts as varied as possible. Remember, the majority of these movements are full-body movements that focus on core strength and overall fitness, strength, and agility, and keeping it varied will give you the most optimal results in the shortest amount of time. Please feel free to create your own workouts, and remember, often less is more. The goal is to not overwork your body, but rather to find a good balance of intensity, rest, and normal activity.

Workout 1

Workout 1: Warm up with a 5-minute jog. For your workout complete as many rounds as possible of the following movements within 7 minutes: 20 walking lunges (10 each leg), 20 sit-ups, 10 jumping pull-ups.

Workout 2

Workout 2: Warm up with 30 jumping jacks, rest for 1 minute, and then repeat 2 more times. For your workout, perform 3 rounds of 5 knee-to-elbows, 10 push-ups, 25 jump rope skips

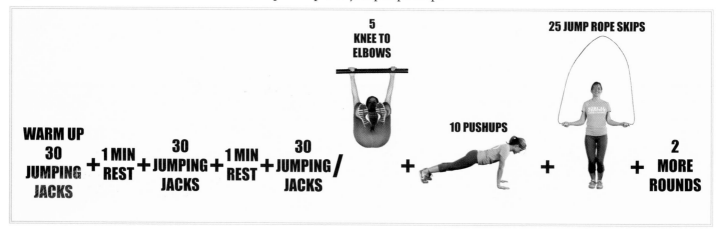

Workout 3: Warm up with 100 jump rope skips. For your workout perform: an accumulative total of 30 seconds in the plank hold, 20 weighted walking lunges (10 on each leg), 5 shoulder presses, a sprint of 6 car lengths and then walk back, and 30 step-ups or 15 box jumps. Continue back through the above list for 20 minutes. Pace yourself; this workout should focus on technique rather than on how fast you can move through each movement.

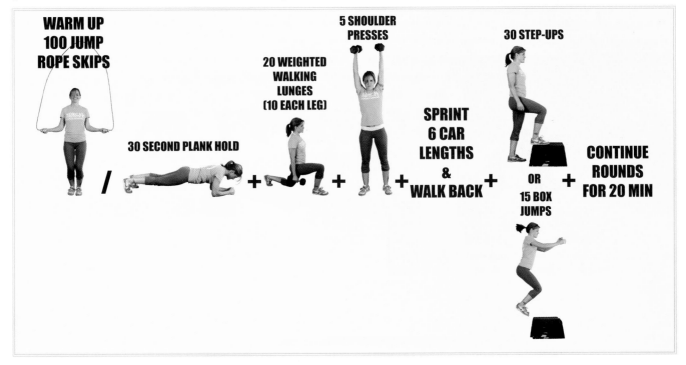

WARM UP 100 JUMP ROPE SKIPS / **30 SECOND PLANK HOLD** + **20 WEIGHTED WALKING LUNGES (10 EACH LEG)** + **5 SHOULDER PRESSES** + **SPRINT 6 CAR LENGTHS & WALK BACK** + **30 STEP-UPS** OR **15 BOX JUMPS** + **CONTINUE ROUNDS FOR 20 MIN**

Workout 4: Warm up with a 5-minute jog. For your workout perform: 5 dumbbell dead lifts, 10 body rows, and 15 squats. Rest for 1 minute, and then repeat 3 times. While still maintaining proper form, try to move quickly through this workout, using the 1 minute of rest to catch your breath, recover, and be ready for the next round. Time yourself and see if you can complete each round a little bit faster than the last. At the very least, you want to maintain the same time.

WARM UP 5 MIN JOG / **5 DUMBBELL DEAD LIFTS** + **10 BODY ROWS** + **15 AIR SQUATS** + **1 MIN REST** + **3 MORE ROUNDS**

Workout 5

Workout 5: Warm up with 100 jump rope skips. For your workout perform 4 rounds of the following: 5 thrusters, 30 seconds of hollow rocks, 30 seconds of the super woman movement, and 50 jump rope skips

WARM UP 100 JUMP ROPE SKIPS / **5 THRUSTERS** + **30 SECONDS OF HOLLOW ROCKS** + **30 SECONDS OF SUPER WOMAN** + **50 JUMP ROPE SKIPS** + **3 MORE ROUNDS**

Workout 6

Workout 6: Warm up with a 5-minute jog. For your workout perform 4 rounds of 10 dumbbell squats, hold the L-sit or a modification of the L-sit for an accumulative total of 30 seconds, and 5 broad jumps.

WARM UP 5 MIN JOG / **10 DUMBBELL SQUATS** + **30 SECONDS OF L-SIT** + **5 BROAD JUMPS** + **3 MORE ROUNDS**

Workout 7: Warm up with 200 jump rope skips. For your workout perform 3 rounds of 15 dumbbell swings, 20 overhead dumbbell walking lunges (10 on each leg), and 15 push-ups

WARM UP 200 JUMP ROPE SKIPS

15 DUMBBELL SWINGS

20 OVERHEAD DUMBBELL WALKING LUNGS (10 EACH LEG)

15 PUSH UPS

2 MORE ROUNDS

Workout 8

Workout 8: Warm up with a 5-minute jog. For your workout perform 10 push presses, 10 knee-to-elbows, 9 push presses, 9 knee-to-elbows, 8 push presses, 8 knee-to-elbows, etc. Keep going until you finish with 1 push press and 1 knee-to-elbow.

10 PUSH PRESS

10 KNEE TO ELBOWS

9 PUSH PRESS

9 KNEE TO ELBOWS

WARM UP 5 MIN JOG

KEEP DROPPING NUMBER OF REPS UNTIL YOU FINISH WITH 1 PUSH PRESS & 1 KNEE TO ELBOW

Workout 9 Warm up with 50 jumping jacks followed by 30 squats. For your workout perform 3 rounds of: 15 jumping pull-ups, 10 dumbbell dead lifts, and 100 jump rope skips. Rest 1 minute in between each round.

Workout 10: Warm up with 100 jump rope skips followed by 30 jumping jacks. For your workout: run 400 meters (around the block), perform 20 push-ups, 15 dumbbell squats, 40 box step-ups or 20 box jumps, and finish with an 800-meter run (twice around the block).

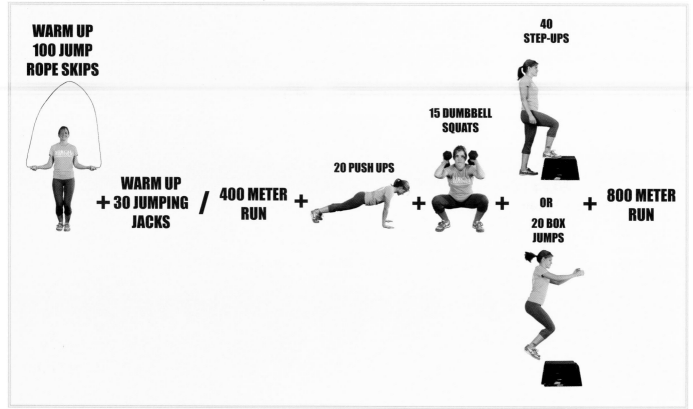

Workout 11: Warm up with a 10-minute walk/jog. For your workout perform 6 rounds of: a 100-meter sprint and walk back (sprint to the end of the block and walk back), followed by 10 thrusters.

10 THRUSTERS

WARM UP 10 MIN WALK OR JOG / **SPRINT 100 METERS WALK BACK** + **5 MORE ROUNDS**

Workout 12

Workout 12: Warm up with partner ball-toss drills (see the Partner Movements section below) or throw the ball against a wall solo, performing ten repetitions of either drill. For your workout, perform 3 rounds of 8 dumbbell push presses, 40 walking lunges (20 each leg), and 200 jump rope skips.

200 JUMP ROPE SKIPS

8 DUMBBELL PUSH PRESS

WARM UP 10 PARTNER BALL TOSSES

20 LUNGES EACH LEG

/ + + **2 MORE ROUNDS**

Workout 13: Warm up with a 5-minute jog followed by 20 squats. For your workout perform 4 rounds of: 7 dumbbell squats, 7 jumping pull-ups, and 7 push-ups.

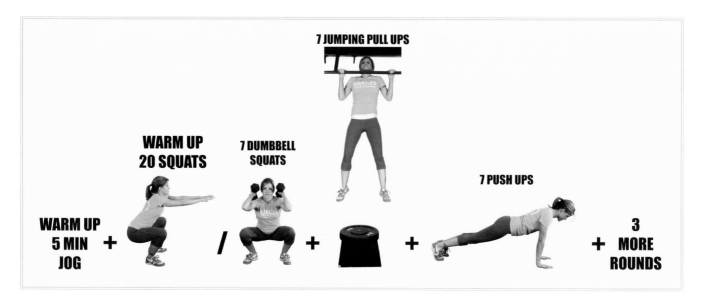

WARM UP 5 MIN JOG + **WARM UP 20 SQUATS** / **7 DUMBBELL SQUATS** + **7 JUMPING PULL UPS** + **7 PUSH UPS** + **3 MORE ROUNDS**

Workout 14: Warm up with a 10-minute walk/jog. For your workout perform: 20 dumbbell dead lifts, 30 dumbbell push presses, 40 dumbbell swings, and 50 squats. Remember to stop and rest for a few seconds in the middle of your reps if you need to.

WARM UP 10 MIN WALK OR JOG / **20 DUMBBELL DEAD LIFTS** + **30 PUSH PRESS** + **40 DUMBBELL SWINGS** + **50 SQUATS**

Workout 15

Workout 15: Warm up with a 5-minute jog followed by 100 jump rope skips. For your workout perform 5 rounds of: 5 dumbbell dead lifts, 5 dumbbell push presses, and 5 dumbbell swings. After you finish 5 rounds of the preceding movements, finish your workout with a 400-meter run (or around the block).

Workout 16

Workout 16: Warm up with a 10-minute walk/jog. For your workout, in 10 minutes perform as many rounds as possible of the following: 10 body rows, 10 dumbbell squats, and 10 broad jumps.

Workout 17

Workout 17: Warm up with 300 jump rope skips. For your workout perform 5 rounds of: 20 walking lunges (10 on each leg), 10 sit-ups, and 10 box step-ups or jumps.

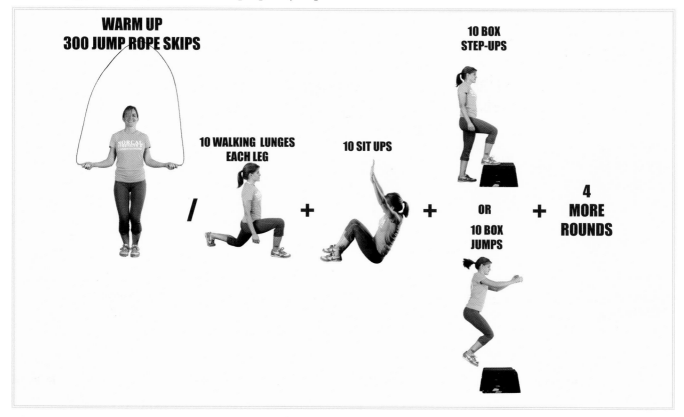

**WARM UP
300 JUMP ROPE SKIPS**

**10 BOX
STEP-UPS**

**10 WALKING LUNGES
EACH LEG**

10 SIT UPS

OR

**10 BOX
JUMPS**

**4
MORE
ROUNDS**

Workout 18

Workout 18: Warm up with a 5-minute run. For your workout perform 4 rounds of: 15 plank push-ups, 30 hollow rocks, and 10 jumping squats.

**10 JUMPING
SQUATS**

30 HOLLOW ROCKS

15 PLANK PUSHUPS

**WARM UP
5 MIN
JOG**

**3
MORE
ROUNDS**

Workout 19

Workout 19: Warm up with 50 jumping jacks followed by 10 push-ups and 10 squats. For your workout perform: 100 jump rope skips and 50 sit-ups, 75 jump rope skips and 40 sit-ups, 50 jump rope skips and 30-sit-ups, and 25 jump rope skips and 15 sit-ups.

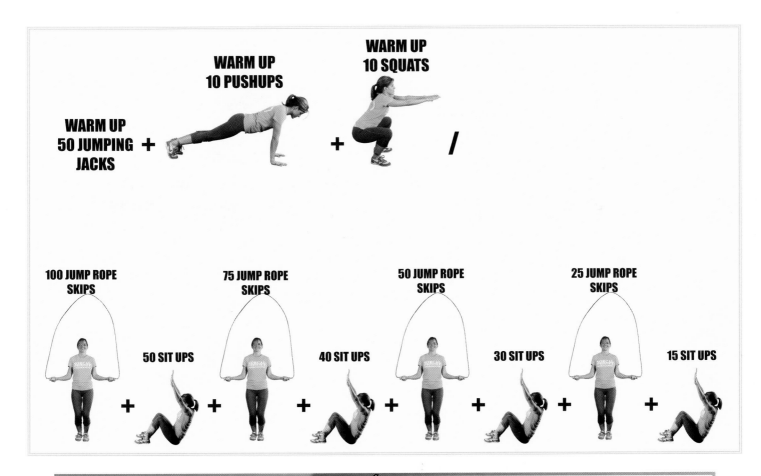

Workout 20

Workout 20: Warm up with a 10-minute walk/run. For your workout perform 4 rounds of: a 400-meter run, 10 thrusters, and 10 push-ups.

Kids' Fitness

As I mentioned during the introduction to the fitness section, kids today are way more sedentary than they should be. Getting your kids to exercise should be approached with a focus on fun rather than treated as a chore, a threat, or something that they have to do. The best way to convince children to do something is to model the behavior that you want them to follow. What does this mean? Get moving together! Kids are capable, if not more capable, of tackling the movements shown in this book. With that being said, it is also important to note that as adults we know how to push ourselves to the limit in and outside of the gym, but we should not push our kids outside of their limits when exercising, ever! Even if your child is seriously out of shape and/or overweight, pushing him or her too hard will result in your child rebelling from the idea of fitness or, even worse, getting injured during training.

If you watch children play naturally, they will run, walk, jump skip, throw a ball, wiggle, sit down for a while, roll around for a bit, take a drink of water, rest a bit more, look around, get back up, and run some more. Kids know how far to push themselves and will naturally stop and rest when they need to. Be respectful of your child's innate ability to monitor his or her capability level. If you make exercise fun, kids will participate. If they need to stop and rest, then by all means let them! Have plenty of water available, and make use of the rest time to chat with your child about whatever he or she wants to chat about. When children exercise in a safe and supportive environment, they gain a sense of well-being and confidence that all kids should innately have. Furthermore, working out together is a wonderful way to reconnect, share, and discover the path back to health as a family.

In the upcoming section, we will look at Jaden showing us examples of how a kid can perform some of the same movements as adults, and below I give a few tips and some fun ways for kids to incorporate these movements into kid- and family-friendly workouts.

The Prepping Process

When you first start introducing exercise to your children, I suggest starting out by simply being more active together as a family. If your children have been extremely sedentary and you know that exercising is going to prove challenging, start the shift by simply taking walks together rather than turning on the TV or the games. Begin visiting parks and playgrounds and just have fun! If you tell your kids that they are going to follow an exercise plan, you will most certainly be met with resistance. Remember, exercise is supposed to be focused on fun, and I suggest approaching fitness with your family the same way you would if you were going to play a game together. Make it exciting, new, and intriguing! To introduce the movements to your children, let them know that you are going to teach them a new game! Teach them a few basic movements such as the squat and the push-up and incorporate those movements into a game of Simon Says. This game alone is fun for the whole family and gets everyone moving. Make sure each child gets a turn being "Simon" and see how fast your heart is racing!

My kids love to play Red Light Green Light, but instead of just running, we will also bear crawl, crab walk, broad jump, or leap like frogs! Kids love to play games like freeze tag, hide and seek, soccer, and catch—all of which are exercises hidden in a fun game being played outdoors. Many of these games can also be played inside! Move the furniture aside and have bear crawl races in the living room or simply turn on the radio and have each child make up his or her own dance routine to perform!

After your kids learn a few basic movements such as the squat, push-up, lunge, and sit-up, have them create a workout that you both can do! Jaden loves to make up workouts for us to do together as a family. He is so proud to be able to design something that we all can do as a group! Most importantly, praise your children. Do not make them feel bad if they are unable to do a complete movement. Just having your kids move at all is a step in the right direction. Kids will exercise without being told to if they're simply given the opportunity.

Last but not least, find ways to get your children involved in the community. There are many organized sports available for kids to be a part of, and if they do not enjoy the competitive aspect of some youth organized sports, there are other options that are less aggressive, such as swimming, tennis, and golf. The martial arts are another wonderful sport to look into. Most martial arts programs do not focus only on competition, but also on learning the techniques, being respectful, and on general fitness. My two oldest boys both have taken martial arts classes, and we have had wonderful experiences with the programs. Jaden continues to train in Kenpo Karate and it has been amazing to see his self-confidence, self-control, and positive demeanor improve.

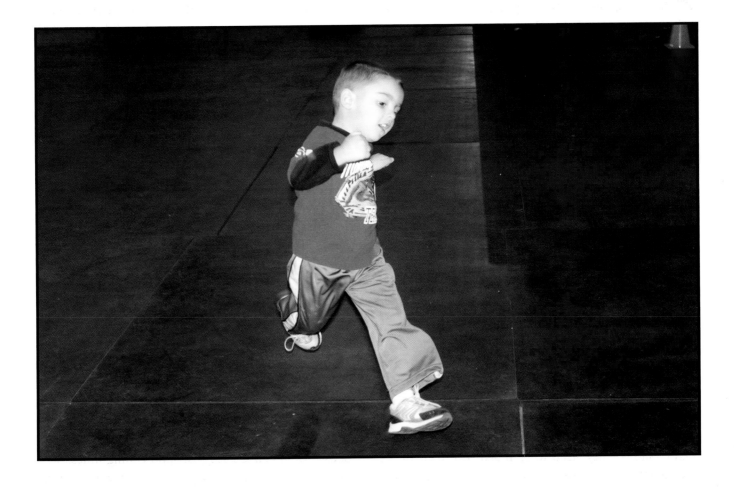

fitness

Squat

As described in the first part of the fitness section, the squat is a natural movement that we perform several times a day. However, children these days spend a great deal of time indoors playing video games and watching television rather than engaging in normal everyday movements like the squat, which leads to less development in their primary muscles. By performing squats on a regular basis, children not only become more fit, but they also learn how to correctly bend to pick up objects, which will help them later on in life.

MUSCLES USED: Quadriceps, Gluteals, and Hamstrings

1) To begin the movement, Jaden stands with his feet spread roughly shoulder width apart, his back is straight, and his arms positioned straight out in front of him for balance.

2) Jaden performs a squat exactly as outlined in the previous squat sequence that I demonstrated.

3) Still keeping his back perfectly straight, Jaden pushes through his heels and returns to the standing position. The same rules for modification apply to children. If your child is not capable of squatting to full depth, let him or her practice by squatting to a beanbag or a size-appropriate chair.

Rocket Jump

The rocket jump is very similar to the squat jump that I demonstrated earlier in the fitness section, but when kids perform the rocket jump, they should definitely make rocket noises! If your kids cannot squat down to full depth, have them simply bend down as much as possible by reaching their fanny back and bending at the knees, and they can still jump into the air . . . and have fun being a rocket!

MUSCLES USED: Abdominals, Gluteals, Quadriceps, Hamstrings, and Calves

1) Jaden stands in the squat stance.

2) As Jaden reaches his fanny back and bends at the knees, he keeps his back straight and his chest up as much as possible. His eyes are looking straight ahead and his fingertips are on the ground.

3) Pushing through his heels, Jaden jumps straight up out of the squat position with arms outstretched overhead.

4) Jaden lands with bent knees on his forefoot and then transfers his weight to his heels. From here, he will immediately jump again.

Lunge

When kids perform walking lunges, it builds up their gluteal and inner-thigh muscles. In addition to helping improve their overall athleticism, it also increases their strength and self-confidence. As with the squat, if they are unable to perform a lunge at the correct depth, just have them walk with giant steps. They will still be using those important muscles and working toward the full movement.

MUSCLES USED: Gluteals, Hamstrings, Quadriceps, and Adductors

1) Jaden stands with his feet positioned together.

2) Jaden performs the same lunge described earlier in the book. Make sure your child starts out slow and maintains his balance by stepping a little to the right or to the left, depending on which foot he is using.

3) Jaden pushes up through his heel and is ready to repeat the movement with his opposite leg. Notice that Jaden keeps his chest upright and his gaze forward.

Push-Up

When it comes to push-ups, I recommend starting your child with the easiest version possible, which is with his or her hands against a wall. Push-ups can be just as difficult for children as they are for adults, and if they start with a version too difficult, they can quickly get discouraged. Once your child has an easy time with the wall variation, increase the difficulty by moving on to chair push-ups. And once chair push-ups are a cinch, progress to the modified knee push-up demonstrated earlier. As long as you progress slowly in this fashion, your child will eventually be able to execute the full movement Jaden demonstrates below.

MUSCLES USED: Pectoralis, Deltoids, and Triceps

1) Jaden starts with his arms fully extended. His tummy is tight and he is squeezing his fanny and leg muscles.

2) Jaden slowly lowers himself down to the ground, staying as tight as possible from head to toe!

3) Jaden pushes back up to the start position, making sure that his arms are fully extended before he begins another repetition.

Plank Push-Up

In this sequence Jaden demonstrates a plank push-up. If this proves too difficult for your child, have him or her switch to the knee variation, which lessens the load. Just remember to cue your child to tighten his or her tummy and legs during the movement.

MUSCLES USED: Abdominals, Quadriceps, Gluteals, Pectoralis, Deltoids, and Triceps

1) **Jaden starts in the same position as the push-up.**

2) **Keeping his back straight and tummy tight, Jaden lowers down to his right elbow.**

3) **Jaden lowers down to both elbows, achieving the plank position. He keeps his body tight and strong from head to toe.**

4) **Jaden comes back up onto his right hand.**

5) **Jaden comes up to his left hand. He finishes with his arms fully extended and his body tight.**

Bear Crawl

Most children love crawling around on their hands and feet, acting like a bear. In addition to being an extremely fun movement, it also develops shoulder strength. There is really not a right or wrong way to perform this movement. By simply moving around on your hands and feet, you get your heart rate up, strengthen your body, and get a good sweat going. For this reason, it is one of the most popular movements at NorCal Strength and Conditioning—both with children and adults! That's right, I said adults. If you decide not to partake in this movement with your child, you will be missing out.

MUSCLES USED: Overall body movement

1) **Jaden starts with his feet and hands on the ground. He is looking down and slightly in front of his hands.**
2) **Jaden first moves his left hand and right foot forward together.**
3) **Jaden then moves his right hand and left foot forward together.**
4) **Crawling along like a bear, Jaden continues to move forward by walking on his hands and feet. Have your child start out slowly, but I guarantee you will have some pretty speedy bears crawling around once your child gets the hang of it! Bear crawl races in the living room anyone?**

everyday paleo

Crab Walk

The crab walk is another fun movement that you and your child can do together! First a bear and now a crab—see if you and your child can come up with other silly ways to move your body from one place to another! Rowan's favorite is leaping around like a frog! Of course he makes us all join him for frog races! Other family favorites are skipping and galloping, both great movements that help with large motor skill development and coordination.

MUSCLES USED: Another great full body exercise

Jaden pushes up on his hands, tummy facing up, and he supports his legs with his feet flat on the ground. He keeps his tummy and back muscles tight, and he uses his thigh muscles as well as his fanny to keep his back up off the ground.

Jaden moves his left foot and right hand forward at the same time.

Jaden moves his right foot and left hand forward.

Jaden repeats this movement as he scuttles around like a crab.

Jumping Pull-Up

By simply turning off the TV and video games and making routine visits to the nearest park, you and your child can find a fun and relaxing way to unwind and exercise together! You can both use the playground equipment to simply play, which is the best form of exercise for all children, and you can also take the opportunity to show your kids some of the movements you have learned earlier in the fitness section. The jumping pull-up is great for kids. It helps them build their leg muscles, which is important for the growing and changing body of a child, as well as for supporting strong skeletal growth and development.

MUSCLES USED: Latissimus Dorsi, Trapezius, Deltoids, Hamstrings, Gluteals, Quadriceps, and Calves

1) Standing directly underneath the bar, Jaden grabs the bar at slightly wider than shoulder width with his hands facing away from his body.
2) Jaden reaches his fanny back and bends at the knees like he would if he were performing a squat. He drops down until his arms are fully extended.
3) Jaden jumps quickly off the ground and raises his chin over the bar.
4) Jaden lets gravity take him back down to the ground, landing with bent knees and his weight in his heels.

Knee-to-Elbow

Most kids will naturally swing, twist, and turn their bodies while playing on monkey bars, and the knee-to-elbow is a natural movement that most little kids will do without even being shown how. I remember when Rowan was barely walking, I would let him hang from the rings at the gym and the first thing he would do would be to kick his toes all the way up to his hands, laughing like crazy! Showing your child how to do a knee-to-elbow will help strengthen his or her abdominal muscles while reminding your kid how fun it is to just be a kid!

MUSCLES USED: Abdominals, Iliopsoas, Latissimus Dorsi, and Pectoralis

1) Jaden starts in the same position as the jumping pull-up.
2) Squeezing his tummy muscles, Jaden lifts his knees up toward his chest.
3) Jaden continues to use his tummy muscles to touch his knees to his elbows. Have your child simply raise his or her knees up as much as he or she can. If that means only raising his or her knees up a few inches, that is just fine. We all have to start somewhere!
4) Jaden drops his feet to the floor, returning to the start position.

Family Fitness

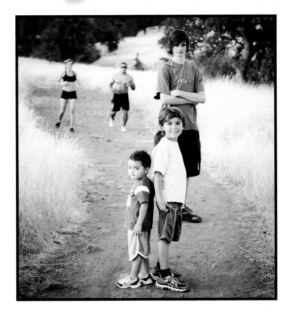

This section focuses on movements that you can do with either a baby or toddler. After learning these movements, feel free to use them to replace the movements in the beginner workouts or advanced beginner workouts laid out earlier in the book. I know how hard it can be to find the time to exercise when you have a baby or a toddler, but the truth is that when you set aside even a few minutes during the day, or a couple of hours a week, especially if using a cross-training method, it will garner you results! And when you add a Paleo diet to this regimen, you will not only see visible improvement, but your overall physical and mental health will benefit almost immediately.

I know from experience how cooped up one can feel with a baby or toddler at home, but feeling trapped is another choice that we often end up making. We end up feeling bogged down and unable to do anything other than the endless laundry, dishes, diapers, feeding, and meal planning. Unless we take time out to exercise, we will continue to come up with a million excuses not to. The truth is, before you can say, "I hate being out of shape," your little baby will be fifteen years old and you will wonder why you worried so much about having clean sheets and a spotless sink. So my advice is, let go a little bit, grab your baby or toddler, strap him or her into the stroller, and take a walk!

While you are walking, look around you—take a few deep breaths of air, let it out, and feel your shoulders relax. Let go of all the silly stuff that made you so tense in the first place. Smile at people as you walk by them, notice detail—how the leaves look on the trees, if birds are singing, and what the rhythm of your footsteps sound like. In other words, just be.

Another great way to exercise with your baby is to wear your baby! Purchase a Moby Wrap (www.mobywrap.com) or another form of a sling or baby carrier and strap the little guy or girl close to you. You'll enjoy the up-close and personal time with your little one, you'll be able to get more done around the house and with your other kids, and you'll be getting a workout in without even thinking about it. Rowan lived in a Moby Wrap for the first year of his life happily snuggled up to me, watching everything we were doing together or snoozing away in his little nest on Mommy. I even figured out how to nurse him while he was in there. He was happy and content most of the time, and I was more productive and able to spend more time with the older boys.

Some of the movements that I show you in this section incorporate holding a toddler, but if you feel stable and strong enough, you can do these movements while wearing a baby in a wrap or sling as well! So, let's get started with a few of the basic movements that you can easily do while baby is in the stroller.

The squat is one of the best exercises that you can do to help strengthen the legs, glutes, hamstrings, and core. Especially after having children, women often struggle with core strength. By incorporating this movement into your workout routine, you can quickly regain any lost strength and get back to pre-baby shape or even better—especially when eating a healthy Paleo diet!

MUSCLES USED: *Quadriceps, Gluteals, and Hamstrings*

1

Stand directly behind your stroller, grab the handles tight for balance and support. Just as when performing the traditional squat, you want your feet under your shoulders, your tummy and legs tight, and your back straight.

2

As you push your fanny back, push the stroller out in front of you until your arms are fully extended

3

Sink your fanny back and down while maintaining a tight hold on the stroller handle. Maintain that tight tummy and straight back. The goal is to lower your hips below your knees, but if that does not feel safe or comfortable, just go as far as you can. Make sure to always keep the weight in your heels and do not let your knees track forward over your toes.

4

Push through your heels as you begin to rise back up to a standing position. Keep your arms extended and holding on to the stroller for balance.

5

Return to a full upright position.

Stroller Sit-Up

Instead of using your baby or toddler as an excuse not to exercise, I challenge you to consider your little person a perfect excuse *to* exercise. Your little guy or girl loves to be with you, loves to see you happy and energized, and really doesn't care what the heck you are doing, as long as you are doing something together. Every baby loves a game of peekaboo, and the stroller sit-up can be just that. If you are not at home, you can easily stash a yoga mat or towel in your stroller and while at the park, pull off to the side, and add some sit-ups to your stroller routine!

MUSCLES USED: Abdominals, Gluteals, Quadriceps, and Hamstrings

Lay down directly in front of your stroller with your knees bent and your feet next to the front wheels; make sure you set the brakes on your stroller! Raise your arms overhead and then place them flat on the ground above you.

Swing your arms forward to generate the momentum needed to sit up. Instead of trying to crunch your head toward your knees, move your chest toward your knees.

Reach your chest upward, avoiding rounding your spine to the point that you are no longer engaging your tummy muscles. As your chest touches your thighs at the top of the sit-up, quickly pump your arms back by bending at the elbow. This will give you the last little bit of momentum you need to completely raise yourself to a seated position. When in the seated position, say peekaboo to the baby, or give him or her a little tummy tickle.

As you begin your return to the floor, quickly pump your arms straight up over your head. This will ensure that you are ready to use your arms again to help raise you back up to the seated position.

Return all the way back down flat to the ground and repeat the movement.

fitness

Stroller Push-Up

The idea of the stroller push-up is the same as the stroller sit-up. Getting in some exercise while interacting and modeling good health to your little one! Get out there, get active, and make it fun. Your mood and the mood of your baby or toddler will improve every time you make the effort to be active and healthy as a family!

MUSCLES USED: Pectoralis, Deltoids, and Triceps

1) Set the brakes on your stroller and position yourself in front of baby in the push-up position with your head facing your little one. Modify from your knees if necessary.

2) Perform a push-up exactly as described in the previous push-up sequence and remember to keep those tummy, fanny, and leg muscles tight!

3) Every time you push up to full arm extension, say hello or peekaboo to your little one!

everyday paleo

Toddler Squat Lift

Whoever said that exercise is not fun obviously did not have children! Having kids is really an excuse to behave like one (at least now and then), and simply playing with your kids can often be one of your more enjoyable workouts. Take time every day to just play. Forget about the clutter around you, because your children couldn't care less if the laundry is not folded. However, they do care if you get down to their level and play, and I do not mean in a half-hearted, distracted sort of way, but really playing! My little boys love nothing more than a good wrestling match with mom, and we all end up tired, laughing, and gasping for air on the floor. None of us even thinks about the fact that we are exercising but, in reality, we are. Even more importantly, we are creating special memories and are bonding and connecting with each other. At the very least, for a few minutes I am not worried about anything else. In the sequence below, I demonstrate the toddle squat lift. It's the same movement as the traditional squat, but I am turning this wonderful movement into a fun game with my little guy.

MUSCLES USED: Quadriceps, Gluteals, Hamstrings, Trapezius, Biceps, and Deltoids

1) **Stand directly in front of your toddler with about a foot of space in between you both.**

2) **Squat down as described in the squat sequence and hold on to your child under his arms.**

3) **Pushing through your heels, explode up off of the ground, lifting your little one with you. As you bring your child up, quickly, shrug your shoulders to engage your traps.**

4) **Instruct your little guy or gal to tuck or bend his or her knees. This will allow you to catch your toddler on your chest as you stand up completely.**

5) **As you return to the squat position, return your child to the ground. Once accomplished, repeat the movement.**

*Special note: If you are unable to reach a full-depth squat or if you have any knee or spine injuries, I do not recommend this movement. This movement should only be performed if you are strong enough to easily lift your child and easily squat to full depth.

Baby Bridge

This movement helps to strengthen the fanny and hamstring muscles, and again incorporates your baby or toddler into your workout routine. Children make great weights when you can't make it to the gym!

MUSCLES USED: Gluteals, Hamstrings, Erector Spinae, and Abdominals

1. Lie down flat on your back with your knees bent. Your heels should be about 6 inches away from your fanny. Place your baby on your chest or have your toddler sit on your stomach and give you a hug.

2. Tightening your tummy muscles, squeeze your glutes as hard as you can, keep your back as straight as possible, and push through your heels to elevate your hips up off the floor.

3. Still squeezing your fanny and tightening your tummy, continue to push through your heels and raise your hips. When you reach the top of the movement, you should be able to draw a straight line from the backs of your knees down to your shoulders. When in this position, it is important to support your weight with your feet and shoulders, not your neck. Hold this position for 10- to 30-second increments.

4. Slowly lower yourself back down to the floor, holding tight to baby. Do not crash back down—this should be a controlled decent.

288

everyday paleo

Baby Bridge with Press

This movement has the same benefits as the baby bridge, but due to the added press, you also build strength in the chest and shoulders. As a side note, be sure to make airplane noises for your little one and enjoy the giggles!

MUSCLES USED:
Gluteals, Hamstrings, Erector Spinae, Abdominals, Pectoralis, Deltoids, and Triceps

Start in the same position as the baby bridge, but this time hold your child under his arms and around his chest.

As you raise your hips into the bridge position, press your child directly above your chest. Your hands should be lined up with your shoulders in the finished positioned, arms fully extended. With your baby held up, maintain the bridge position for 10–30 seconds.

Slowly lower your hips back to the ground and your baby back to your chest. Once accomplished, repeat the movement.

Baby Squat

Again, toddlers and babies make excellent weights and offer a wonderful excuse to exercise! This movement is the same as the traditional squat, but with a little added resistance. If your baby is small enough to still fit in a baby wrap or front carrier, you can also wear your little one while you perform this movement. However, do not try this movement unless you are strong enough to squat to full depth on your own!

MUSCLES USED: Quadriceps, Gluteals, and Hamstrings

1) Hold your child in front of you, wrapping your arms around him or her tightly. If you have a toddler, instruct him to wrap his legs around your middle. Stand with your feet shoulder width apart.

2) Keeping your weight in your heels, begin to reach your hips back and down. Make sure to keep your weight in your heels, hold your baby tight, and keep your chest upright.

3) Continue to lower yourself down until you reach a full-depth squat position.

4) Push up through your heels and begin to return to the standing position.

5) Once you return to a full upright position, you are ready to repeat the movement. Remember to keep your tummy and leg muscles tight, and when you begin to feel fatigued, put baby down and rest or finish your reps without holding your little one.

Baby Lunge

What is great about performing baby lunges with your little one is that you do not need a whole lot of room. While walking lunges demand a great amount of space, baby lunges can be performed indoors. All you have to do is clear a space in your living room or bedroom! Again, no excuses not to get moving! This movement works the glutes and inner-thigh muscles while also helping to strengthen your core.

MUSCLES USED: Gluteals, Hamstrings, Quadriceps, and Adductors

1) Hold baby as instructed in the previous baby squat sequence and position your feet directly under your shoulders. You can also wear baby in a wrap or front carrier for this movement.

2) Looking straight ahead and holding baby tightly to your chest, take a giant step forward with your right foot. Since you are beginning with your right leg, you want to step slightly toward one o'clock. This will help you to maintain balance.

3) Drop your left knee toward the ground, making sure to keep your chest upright and your tummy tight. The shin of your front leg should stay vertical with your knee and track over your heel, not your toes. Continue to sink your left knee down until it is just above the ground.

4) Pushing up through the heel of your front leg, begin your return to a vertical position. You should feel this movement in your fanny as you rise.

5) As you return to the start position, make sure that your shoulders and tummy are tight. Once accomplished, repeat the movement exactly as described, but this time step forward with your left leg. Continue to lunge, alternating legs as you go.

Partner
Movements

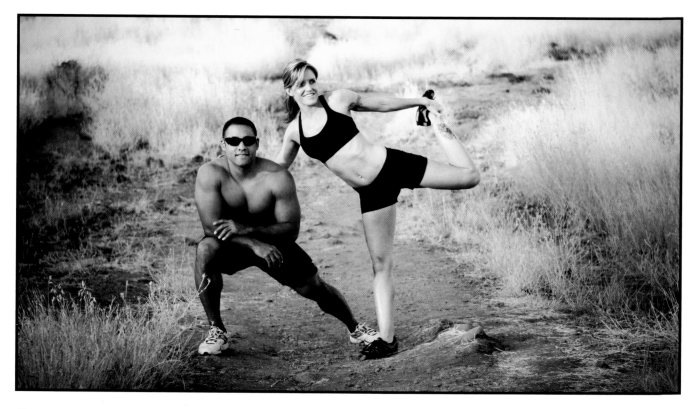

Last but not least, we will look at some fun movements that you can try with your significant other or with a friend. Working out together as a couple is a great way to reconnect after a long day and can truly enhance a relationship as you both work toward the goal of optimal health. A few of the following movements might be a bit more advanced, but I will offer either modifications or other options. The main point of this section is to focus on having fun with your partner while working out. Make sure to be encouraging and supportive of one another. Part of exercising together should be about building one another up instead of focusing on one another's weaknesses. Working together toward a common goal can strengthen relationships, open lines of communication, build trust, and lend insight to different things about one another that you might not have noticed before. One of my first dates with John was at a gym. Yes, we were that couple, flirt-

ing with each other on the treadmill, making you want to scream because obviously we were not getting a whole lot of working out actually accomplished. Fast-forward twelve years later and we still enjoy working out together, although our lives are completely different and so are our health and fitness goals. John likes the competitive side of being athletic, and I simply enjoy being strong, fit, and healthy enough to keep up with my boys. With that being said, we have found a wonderful balance. John pushes me to work harder in the gym, but always with love and respect because he knows when I am just being lazy and can step it up a bit. I keep John focused and remind him that over-training is just as bad as not training enough, and I never let him get away with anything other than solid technique. Together, we make a pretty good team, and we have learned how to be good partners in and outside of the gym.

Wheelbarrow

The wheelbarrow is about the fun and balance that a couple should have when exercising together. Balance refers to understanding when to encourage your partner and when just to be there. And the fun aspect refers to never taking yourself or each other too seriously.

MUSCLES USED: All of them, a great full body exercise!

Start in the push-up position, and then have your partner grab your ankles and lift your lower body off the floor. It is very important to make sure that your tummy and back are tight, as well as your glutes and legs.

As you step your left hand forward, your partner steps his left foot forward.

As you step your right hand forward, your partner steps his right foot forward.

Going at your own pace, walk your hands forward as your partner walks behind you supporting your legs. It is important for your partner to match your pace rather than the other way around. Walk this way for a predetermined distance (start out going just a few feet to see how you feel.) Make sure your partner lets you down gently; trade places and repeat!

Partner Push-up

The partner push-up provides great exercise for both parties involved! The person on bottom works his or her core while the person on top works his or her chest and shoulders. The optimal goal is to switch positions at some point in your workout, but if there is a great weight difference between you and your partner, I recommend starting out with the heavier partner holding the plank position on the ground and the lighter partner perform the push-ups in the top position. Once the lighter partner develops the strength needed to safely hold the weight of the other, you can begin switching positions.

MUSCLES USED: *Plank Position—Erector Spinae, Abdominals, Quadriceps, and Gluteals.*
Push-Ups—Pectoralis, Deltoids, and Triceps

1) Have the heavier/stronger partner hold the plank position. The lighter partner should position herself with one palm on the upper back and one palm on the lower back of the partner holding the plank. If you are on top, walk your feet out until your spine and legs are one straight line. Make sure to look down in front of you and keep your neck in a neutral position.

2) Perform a push-up, lowering your chest all the way to your partner's back.

3) Push all the way back up until your arms are fully extended. See how many push-ups your can perform in 10- to 30-second time increments or until your plank partner needs a break. Rest for a minute, and then switch positions. Just make sure you can safely hold the weight of your partner in the plank position.

everyday paleo

Although this movement does not add to the difficulty level of the push-ups described earlier in the book, it adds an element of fun. Personally, I like to match my partner's pace so that we can high-five every time we perform a sit-up. If you hadn't guessed it, this is a great movement to have the kids be involved in as well.

MUSCLES USED: Abdominals, Gluteals, Hamstrings

To begin this movement, both you and your partner should lie flat on the floor with your knees bent and your feet interlocked. Your feet should be about two feet away from your fanny, and your arms should be lying flat on the ground above you.

At the same time, both you and your partner should swing your arms forward to generate the momentum needed to sit up. When done correctly, both of you should elevate your chest toward your knees at the same pace.

As your chest touches your thighs at the top of the sit-up, touch hands or high-five with your partner.

As you slowly lower your back toward the ground, keep your arms positioned straight overhead. This will ensure that you are ready to use your arms to help with another repetition.

After you return to the start position, repeat the movement.

Partner Leg Raises

In addition to being a great movement for working the tummy muscles, this exercise is also a fun way to work together with your partner. Just make sure to take turns.

MUSCLES USED: *Abdominals, Iliopsoas*

1

With your partner laying flat on his back, position your feet to either side of his head so he can grab your ankles for support.

2

As your partner tightens his tummy and leg muscles and swings his legs upward, position your hands out in front of your body to catch his feet. It is important to keep your arms bent in order to absorb the upward momentum of your partner's legs.

3

As your partner's feet touch your hands, absorb the impact by moving your arms toward your body, increasing the resistance the closer his feet get to your stomach. The goal here is to gradually stop the upward momentum of his legs.

everyday paleo

4

Move your arms forward and push your partner's legs back toward the ground. His job is to resist the push, allowing him to reverse the momentum of his legs before they touch the ground. To ensure that he is able to make a tight and controlled decent, do not push his legs too hard.

5

Having not been pushed too hard, your partner should be able to stop the decent of his legs so that they come to rest just a few inches off the ground.

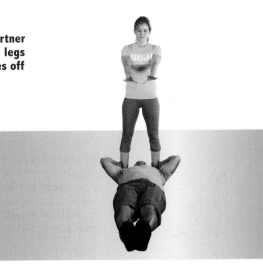

6

Once again, your partner raises his straight legs upward and you catch his feet in your hands. After doing several repetitions, trade places.

A medicine ball is a great exercise tool to have around. If you don't already have one, they can be purchased at most sporting goods stores or online at www.cathletics.com. I recommend the Rage brand, and starting with a four- or six-pound ball. As you will discover, there are many ways to put this simple piece of equipment to use. In the sequence below, I demonstrate a simple ball drill that is excellent for warming up your body prior to a workout. It's another movement that kids love. However, if your child is still small, you'll want to use a soccer ball or basketball instead of a heavy medicine ball.

MUSCLES USED: Quadriceps, Gluteals, Hamstrings, Biceps, and Deltoids

To begin this movement, stand about 10 feet apart from your partner and face one another. In this sequence, my partner begins with the ball, so he pushes his fanny back and squats down, keeping his torso upright and his tummy and back tight. Notice how he grips both sides of the ball, and how it is positioned between his legs and directly under his shoulders.

As your partner swings his hips forward, he uses the power generated by his fanny and legs to propel the ball forward into the air. To prepare to catch the ball, outstretch your arms.

With your weight in your heels, bend your knees and catch the ball in your outstretched arms.

Once you've caught the ball, push your fanny back, bend at the knees, and allow the ball to move between your legs. Before throwing the ball, make sure your torso is upright and the ball is positioned directly underneath your shoulders.

Swing your hips forward and use the power generated by your fanny and legs to propel the ball forward into the air. When doing this movement correctly, you should feel it in your fanny and legs, not your arms.

Partner Ball Toss (Overhead)

The partner ball toss is another excellent movement to warm up for a workout or get the kids exercising and having fun. In addition to being an excellent movement to train your arms and shoulders, it is also a great core strengthener.

MUSCLES USED: *Abdominals, and Latissimus Dorsi*

To begin this movement, stand about 10 feet away from your partner and face one another. If you are starting the movement, raise the ball directly over your head and have your partner step one foot slightly forward. If he stands with feet together, it increases the chance that he will get knocked off balance as he catches the ball.

Step forward with your left foot, hinge slightly at the hips, tighten your tummy muscles, and throw the ball forward from the overhead position. It is important not to throw the ball directly at your opponent, but rather slightly upward. This will make it easier for your partner to make a successful catch.

Your partner should catch the ball at chest level using both of his hands.

Your partner should raise the ball over his head.

As your partner returns the ball back to you, raise your arms to catch the ball. Once you catch the ball, you want to complete another repetition, but this time step forward with your opposite foot as you throw the ball.

Ingredient Index

crab, 106, 277, 281

cracked black pepper, 63, 79, 108, 129, 63, 79, 108, 129

cranberries, 209

cremini mushrooms, 49, 63, 49, 63

crushed black pepper, 92, 129, 193, 92, 129, 193

crushed ice, 221

cucumber, 108, 134, 205, 108, 134, 205, 224

cumin, 47, 61, 69, 74, 88, 100, 106, 156, 160-161, 168, 47, 61, 69, 74, 88, 100, 106, 156, 160-161, 168, 228

curry powder, 120-121, 120-121, 228

dates, 198, 218, 198, 218, 228, 292

diced bacon, 125, 127, 137, 183, 125, 127, 137, 183

diced fresh pineapple, 221

diced organic salt-free tomatoes, 92

Dijon mustard, 71

dried basil, 49, 63, 66, 76, 82, 156, 186, 49, 63, 66, 76, 82, 156, 186

dried cranberries, 209

dried dill, 108, 114, 117, 132, 193, 199, 108, 114, 117, 132, 193, 199

dried ground ginger, 47

dried oregano, 61, 63, 66, 72, 74, 80, 86, 89, 106, 133, 156, 160, 183, 61, 63, 66, 72, 74, 80, 86, 89, 106, 133, 156, 160, 183

dried tarragon, 76

dried thyme, 71, 147, 71, 147

egg, 50, 76-77, 88, 106, 108, 111, 117, 145, 166, 177, 179, 185-187, 190-191, 193, 216, 221, 50, 76-77, 88, 106, 108, 111, 117, 145, 166, 177, 179, 185-187, 190-191, 193, 216, 221-222, 224-225, 227-228

egg whites, 111, 190-191, 111, 190-191

egg yolks, 166

eggplant, 140, 158, 167, 140, 158, 167, 225

El Pato Salsa Para Enchiladas, 54, 224

extra-virgin olive oil, 52, 55, 61, 63, 66, 72-73, 76-77, 84, 86-87, 89, 91, 100, 108, 115, 117, 123, 127, 129, 131-134, 136, 140, 156, 158, 160, 166-169, 171-173, 175, 179, 186, 189, 193, 197, 199, 205, 52, 55, 61, 63, 66, 72-73, 76-77, 84, 86-87, 89, 91, 100, 108, 115, 117, 123, 127, 129, 131-134, 136, 140, 156, 158, 160, 166-169, 171-173, 175, 179, 186, 189, 193, 197, 199, 205

fennel bulb, 128, 223

fenugreek powder, 56, 228

finely ground black pepper, 45, 65, 114, 190, 45, 65, 114, 190

fish, 99, 103, 152, 155, 166, 99, 103, 152, 155, 166, 225

fish sauce, 103, 155, 103, 155, 225

free-range chicken broth, 49, 92, 49, 92

free-range organic chicken, 45

freestone peaches, 213

fresh basil, 65, 72, 80, 84, 86, 139-140, 145, 158, 172, 190, 193, 65, 72, 80, 84, 86, 139-140, 145, 158, 172, 190, 193, 222-223, 225-227

fresh ginger, 49, 100, 114, 123, 173, 49, 100, 114, 123, 173, 224-225, 227

frozen blackberries, 216

frozen blueberries, 221, 227

frozen cherries, 221

frozen mango chunks, 221

frozen pineapple chunks, 221

frozen strawberries, 221

garlic cloves, 52, 56, 65, 71, 74, 76, 80, 82, 88-89, 92-93, 100, 105-106, 113, 123, 139-140, 145, 151, 158, 160, 163, 168-172, 175, 181, 186, 52, 56, 65, 71, 74, 76, 80, 82, 88-89, 92-93, 100, 105-106, 113, 123, 139-140, 145, 151, 158, 160, 163, 168-172, 175, 181, 186

garlic powder, 45, 50, 63, 72, 80, 82, 84, 89, 108, 117, 121, 137, 147, 190, 193, 197, 203, 45, 50, 63, 72, 80, 82, 84, 89, 108, 117, 121, 137, 147, 190, 193, 197, 203, 228

ghee, 52, 56, 52, 56, 226

giant Portobello mushrooms, 76

ginger, 47, 49, 100, 114-115, 123, 143, 173, 190-191, 213, 47, 49, 100, 114-115, 123, 143, 173, 190-191, 213, 224-225, 227-228

gluten-free chicken broth, 151

gluten-free grass-fed beef jerky, 208

Golden raisins, 213, 220, 213, 220

Granny Smith apples, 209, 224

grass-fed organic butter, 55

green bell pepper, 76, 113, 76, 113, 226-227

green bell peppers, 158, 223

green chilies, 74

green mango, 134, 227

green onion, 185

ground beef, 61, 65, 69, 72-73, 76-77, 79-80, 82, 86-87, 156, 160, 190-191, 61, 65, 69, 72-73, 76-77, 79-80, 82, 86-87, 156, 160, 190-191, 223-225, 227

ground black pepper, 45, 65-66, 100, 114, 117, 127, 190, 45, 65-66, 100, 114, 117, 127, 190

ground cloves, 209, 228

ground coriander, 61

ground cumin, 47, 61, 69, 74, 88, 160, 168, 47, 61, 69, 74, 88, 160, 168

ground ginger, 47, 143, 47, 143, 228

ground lamb, 88, 190, 88, 190, 224

ground marjoram, 163

ground nutmeg, 151, 190, 209, 151, 190, 209, 228

ground pork sausage, 90, 223

ground turkey, 79, 223

ham steak, 55, 223

hard-boiled eggs, 108, 131, 193, 108, 131, 193

hot sauce, 72-73, 137, 152, 72-73, 137, 152, 226

Italian parsley, 82

Italian pork sausage, 72, 76, 84, 156, 186, 72, 76, 84, 156, 186, 224, 227

Italian sausage, 86, 198, 86, 198, 223

jalapeño, 49, 160, 170, 181, 49, 160, 170, 181

jalapeño minced, 49

jalapeño salsa, 160

Japanese eggplant, 158

jar roasted red peppers, 79, 168, 79, 168, 223, 227

jarred roasted red peppers, 84

julienned sun-dried tomatoes, 140

kale, 49, 61, 71, 74, 165, 49, 61, 71, 74, 165, 225-227

lamb, 59, 88-89, 136, 190, 59, 88-89, 136, 190, 224

large poblano, 74, 226

large romaine, 113

large tomatoes, 106, 108, 179, 106, 108, 179, 224, 227

leek, 152, 226

lemon, 52, 54, 66, 89, 99-100, 105, 108, 114, 123, 128, 131-132, 139, 166-170, 172-173, 175, 197, 199, 52, 54, 66, 89, 99-100, 105, 108, 114, 123, 128, 131-132, 139, 166-170, 172-173, 175, 197, 199, 225-227

lemon juice, 52, 54, 89, 108, 114, 123, 128, 166, 168, 170, 172-173, 175, 197, 199, 52, 54, 89, 108, 114, 123, 128, 166, 168, 170, 172-173, 175, 197, 199

lemon wedges, 100, 105, 199, 100, 105, 199

lemon zest, 139

lemongrass stalks, 155

lettuce, 45, 69, 113, 134, 197, 45, 69, 113, 134, 197, 223-224

lime, 106, 113, 171, 181, 203, 106, 113, 171, 181, 203, 222-223, 226-227

marinara sauce, 84-85, 186-187, 198, 84-85, 186-187, 198, 224, 227

marjoram, 65, 163, 65, 163, 228

medium onion, 106

medjool dates, 218

Meyer lemon, 66

mild green salsa, 175

mild Italian pork sausage, 84, 186, 84, 186, 224, 227

mint, 88, 224

mixed salad greens, 129, 132, 169, 129, 132, 169, 222

mustard, 43, 71, 108, 115, 117, 43, 71, 108, 115, 117, 228

nitrate-free turkey deli meat slices, 205

nutmeg, 143, 151, 190-191, 209, 143, 151, 190-191, 209, 228

olive oil, 52, 55, 61, 63, 66, 72-73, 76-77, 84, 86-87, 89, 91, 100, 108, 114-115, 117, 123, 127-129, 131-134, 136, 140,